This work is dedicated to our two sons:
Kazimierz (Kenneth) and Marian (Mark).

CONTENTS

INTRODUCTION

At the outset I would like to describe the circumstances which led to the writing of this book. In 1943, after being driven from one place to another on the "Aryan" side of Warsaw, we finally found shelter in a tinsmith's shop located on 27 Belwederska Street. It belonged to Antoni Michalski, the father of our protector. This was a time of relative peace and quiet for us. We had seemingly been able to cover our tracks from those who had been in pursuit of us, for the blackmail and denunciations to the police finally stopped.

The little factory which we had set up on the Aryan side was operating at a good profit. My husband spent most of the day preparing material for our workers, leaving me with nothing to do.

One day my husband suggested to me that I write down all that had happened to us since the time of the destruction of the Warsaw ghetto, beginning on July 22, 1942. These events had been burned into my memory in vivid and lasting detail. We realized full well that our chances for survival were minimal. Our main idea was to leave our child a description of Hitler's horrible crimes, of the grisly and sordid extermination of the Jews.

We presented this idea to our benefactor, Henryk Michalski, who took up the idea with enthusiasm. Next day he brought me several notebooks. Our good friend Zygmunt Dobosz, as always, was of the greatest help. He hammered together a makeshift table and dug up a chair for me somewhere.

In this way I set out to describe the terrible experiences we had lived through. Every morning my husband and I would go over in sequence the events leading up to the destruction of the ghetto, as well as subsequent events in the Karl George Schultz Shop (a prewar hosiery and undergarment factory within the so-called BRO-RO (Braun & Rowiński) firm. It was located on 78 Leszno Street. My husband had worked in this shop while the ghetto was being liquidated.

As time went on I warmed to the task and derived a great deal of satisfaction from describing these events and incidents and from knowing that we, living witnesses of what had happened, were leaving to the world and to future generations a description of the heinous crimes of the Nazis as they applied their "infernal machine" to the destruction of the ghetto.

The Germans, with characteristic overweening pride, had always called themselves the "master race" and a "nation of poets and thinkers," and pretended to have attained a lofty level of culture and civilization. Now they had shown a horrible face that I could never have imagined before the war, but the world was silent and allowed them to perpetrate their terrible crimes without protest. With each new day more innocent and defenseless blood was shed, and no one seemed to care.

My husband was a great help to me and always encouraged me to write. Henryk Michalski also contributed a great deal. Each day he brought us the daily papers and the illegal newspapers published by the underground resistance. For my part, I tried to describe all events, both in the ghetto and on the Aryan side, as exactly and as objectively as possible, selecting as my model simply the course of everyday events. I am not a professional writer and I harbor no pretentions as to my skill in this area.

I would like to mention that all names of people, whether from the ghetto or from the Aryan side, are real. I tried to present everyone as neutrally as possible on the basis of my personal observations and experiences.

Time slowly passed, and before long I had filled three thick note-books. The uprising which broke out on the Aryan side on August 1, 1944 forced me to interrupt my work. My husband and Zygmunt, who was living in the same building, carefully enclosed our notes in a tin box and buried it deep in the ground beneath the workshop's rubbish room.

After the liberation in January 1945, Zygmunt was the first to return to Warsaw, which had been almost completely burned and destroyed. The building on 27 Belwederska Street shared the same fate as the others: only burned ashes remained. Everything we owned had perished in the conflagration. The only thing that was saved was our diary, which Zygmunt uncovered and handed to my husband at their first meeting. We had also buried a large collection of papers from the underground press which my husband had carefully collected. Zygmunt, fearing that they might fall into the hands of the Soviets, who were hostile to the AK (the underground Home Army),[1] and that this might result in unpleasant consequences, burned them all. The only paper to be saved was a communication from the NSZ (National Armed Forces) describing the fighting during the ghetto uprising in April 1943. After the war, my husband guarded these notes like the apple of his eye.

When we left Poland in 1946, legally, as tourists headed for Paris through Prague, we were afraid that customs officials on the Czech-Polish border would try to confiscate them. Fortunately, none of our baggage was opened.

After a year's stay in Paris we emigrated to Venezuela, in search of a quiet little corner of the world. It seemed we were always starting life over again from scratch. Finally, in 1962, after a long and wearisome journey, we came to the United States which, as a loving mother, gathered us to its bosom and granted peace and consolation to our aching hearts. Our first years in this country were not easy. We were particularly troubled by our not knowing the English language. However, in time we overcame even this difficulty. In 1966, we settled permanently in Phoenix, Arizona, and my husband began encouraging me to finish my diary.

The events beginning with the Warsaw Uprising on August 1, 1944 until our liberation in January 1945 have been described from memory. My husband and I would sit and recall to one another all the facts, details, and events we had been through.

My husband typed the entire manuscript on an English typewriter, which was not very successful due to the lack of Polish diacritical marks. Then we bought a Polish typewriter especially for this purpose and retyped the entire book. All of this work together took more than two years. My husband subsequently retyped the entire English translation onto clean paper, which took more than a year.

At this point I would like to extend our thanks and appreciation to Dr. Oscar Swan, Professor of Slavic Languages, formerly of the University of California, Berkeley, and now of the University of Pittsburgh in Pittsburgh, Pennsylvania, for translating this book into English. We greatly value the time and immense outlay of effort that went into the translation.

1. **Home Army** (*Armia Krajowa*, AK). The Home Army was the main Polish resistance force in occupied Poland during World War II. By 1944 it had incorporated most other resistance movements and is estimated to have numbered around 400,000 members, making it one of the largest resistance movements in Europe. It had allegiance to the Polish Government in Exile in London, and was disbanded in 1945 after the Soviet takeover of Poland.

HISTORY OF THE TRANSLATION

Sometime in 1972 my wife and I were visited in our apartment in Oakland, California by Leokadia and Józef Schmidt of Phoenix, Arizona, friends of the parents of a colleague of ours in graduate school at the University of California, Berkeley, where I had just received a doctorate in Slavic languages. Mrs. Schmidt wanted me to translate from Polish her wartime manuscript, part memoir and part diary, which she had entitled *Cudem przeżyliśmy czas zagłady* (Miraculously we survived the Holocaust). Since at the time I was looking for gainful employment, I readily agreed to undertake the translation, in the process learning a good deal about the tragic experiences of the Jews in Nazi-occupied Poland, a subject with which I previously had not been especially familiar. Over the course of the next forty-five years I did not give the manuscript much thought. Then, in late 2017, I was contacted by the younger of the Schmidts' two sons, Marian, who proposed to help me publish my translation of his mother's extraordinary diary.

Unfortunately, Marian Schmidt died unexpectedly in March 2018, without my having had the opportunity to meet him. He is survived by his wife Marta and son Arthur, whom I have visited in Warsaw, and with whom I consulted regarding various details mentioned in the diary. Later I had the opportunity to meet Marian's older brother Kazimierz (now Kenneth), who lives with his wife Shelley in Cherry Hill, New Jersey, and who filled in additional blanks regarding his family's history. The revision of my original translation and the providing of historical notes took the better part of a year.

For its extraordinary, almost unbelievable drama and its unique documentary value, Leokadia Schmidt's wartime diary and memoir deserves the broadest possible dissemination, and I am glad to have played a role in its appearance in English.
- Oscar E. Swan, University of Pittsburgh

I

THE DESTRUCTION OF THE WARSAW GHETTO

1

THE COMING EVENT

On July 22, 1942, in the Warsaw ghetto where some 500,000 inhabitants were concentrated, anxiety had been spreading since early morning. We heard rumors that the walls surrounding the ghetto were lined on the outside every ten paces with Lithuanian, Latvian, Ukrainian, and SS troops, and by the Polish Blue Police.[1] Our concern increased with each passing hour. People gathered in apartment house courtyards and on the streets in order to assess the new situation and to make various suggestions as to what was happening.

The day was cloudy, the sky leaden. It had been drizzling all day. The weather itself added to the atmosphere of gloom and covered our hearts with a shroud of doom, as if nature, or even God himself, was lamenting our situation.

Several months earlier rumors had circulated among the people concerning some sort of "event" that was supposed to take place in the ghetto, but human fantasy, even for those who had a good imagination, could never have reached so far. At night, even while asleep, people remained vigilant. When the noise of an automobile was heard on the streets, terror would grip their hearts. We knew that the Germans were about to break into several apartments, take out the men and shoot them, either out on the street or on the "Aryan" side outside the walls of the ghetto, and throw their corpses back into the ghetto. The Gestapo did the same even with the Poles.

A large number of Jewish Gestapo officers from the so-called "Thirteenth Brigade," who were collaborating with the Germans, had escaped several weeks earlier.[2] Rumor had it that they had escaped to Switzerland, but only the "big" ones. The rest had been killed on the Aryan side and their bodies thrown back into the ghetto. Passers-by returning from other streets were besieged with questions: what was going on? They replied that all openings in the ghetto walls were under guard by Polish and German police, the Gestapo, and others. The Jewish Police had been removed from their positions at the ghetto exits. No one was being allowed either into or out of the ghetto. Even Jews who had jobs in German establishments outside the ghetto were not being sent to work. No one knew anything definite, but everyone was worried.

Earlier that morning the Jewish Police had been called to command headquarters and had stayed there for several hours. After receiving a briefing, they immediately moved to their locations, that is, to the shelters harboring Jews evacuated from the smaller towns and to the Jewish prison located on Gęsia Street in the former Main Post Office building. For the most part the prison housed people caught on the Aryan side who were awaiting death for having crossed ghetto lines.

In this same prison the first seventeen people had been shot, including a pregnant woman near delivery and a fourteen-year-old girl.[3] These were the poorest sort of people who, not having any means of supporting themselves in the ghetto, would go over to the Aryan side and beg on the streets without paying any heed to the posters announcing that any Jew caught outside the ghetto would be shot. These people, who faced death from starvation, risked everything in their search for food for themselves and their families. They had no other choice.

These seventeen people had been shot by a platoon of Polish Blue Police composed of two policemen selected from each precinct. The sentence was carried out in the presence of German officials and the "authorities" of the *Judenrat* (Jewish Council).[4] Before the execution hearses had driven up in front of the prison in view of the condemned.

The first day they took away the poorest inhabitants of the ghetto as well as people from the so-called "centers". Those living in these centers had been resettled from the provinces. They were extremely poor, because the Germans had driven them out suddenly and without allowing them to take any of their belongings. The Jewish Council had quartered them in synagogues, schools, and other public buildings. Things were incredibly filthy there, full of lice and other vermin. The House Committee (each apartment building organized a housing committee which administered food and other necessities for the poorer occupants) did what it could, but had enough trouble easing the misfortune of those already under their official administration.

In the early hours of the evening, the Germans posted placards all over the ghetto containing the following information:

Beginning on the 22nd of July, all Jews will be resettled to the "East." Each person may take with him 15 kilograms of baggage, in addition to whatever gold, jewelry, and money was not confiscated. Food for three days.

The following were said to be exempt from "resettlement":

1. Workers in shops and factories under contract to the Germans.
2. Workers traveling to work outside the ghetto.
3. Council members (members of the *Judenrat*, or Jewish Council).
4. Workers in non-profit organizations such as ZTSS, Centos, Toz (Medical Societies and a Children's Agency), and similar organizations.
5. The Jewish Police.
6. Hospital personnel.
7. Members of the Union of Artisans.

Each working man was allowed to keep with him his wife and children up to the age of fourteen. Men fit for work were to be quartered in buildings next to their place of work.

The contents of the placards caused unimaginable panic among the population not employed by the Germans. Speaking for myself, no one slept a wink that night. Everyone was thinking about how to become a shop member or to find a job outside the ghetto so as not to be subject to resettlement.

Judging from the placards—in any case this was what we made out of it—some kind of structural change was being instituted concerning the Jewish population in the ghetto. Similar changes had already occurred in several other ghettos, in Łódź, Kraków, and elsewhere. No one dreamed that this was the beginning of the complete destruction of the Warsaw ghetto or the extermination of the Jews living there. Would Germany, a people of such strong cultural traditions, be capable of doing something like that? Unfortunately, we were all much too naive then.

In the ghettos mentioned above all private enterprise had been eliminated. All that was left were the shops set up and run by the

Jewish Council. There was no other means of subsistence. We all became reconciled to the idea that the same system was going to be implemented here. Everyone began running around trying to get into a shop. There were no openings at all in any of the official shops, that is, the ones run by the Germans. They accepted only qualified professionals, and then only the very best and only the ones with influence.

People were in a panic to start their own shops. Everyone was trying to get a permit and find people to go in with them. But such matters could not be arranged overnight, and time was of the essence. In the meantime, it became illegal to be found on the streets without a worker's identification card showing that you were employed or had been accepted for work, because roundups had already begun in the town and on the streets of the ghetto. Every policeman was supposed to "provide" five persons a day, and there were 5000 of them. Anyone walking around town without a work permit left himself open to the utmost danger.

People began buying and selling work permits. Older shop workers who had influence with those higher up struck deals and began signing up new workers—for a lavish price, of course. At the same time, a whole crop of small shops sprang up, none of which as of yet had official sanction. Still they would hire workers in the hope that somehow things would work out. Anyone who could contribute some kind of machine to a shop could become a worker there. People would bring in their machinery, but no receipts were given. In order to receive a shop permit, it was necessary to demonstrate to the German authorities that you had a place of work, the requisite machine inventory, and a list of workers. The permit had to be issued by the *Arbeitsamt* (employment office). In short, from dawn to dusk people thought about little else other than how to set up shops.

In the meantime the Jewish Police would set out early in the morning with a list of streets where blockades were to be set up. The exits from given streets were blocked, and the inhabitants of the buildings were taken away. During the first days only the poorest inhabitants were blockaded and taken away on horse-drawn freight wagons to the *Umschlagplatz.*[5]

The blockades set up by the Jewish Police in those first days began at about eight o'clock in the morning and lasted until around four or five o'clock in the afternoon. During this time traffic on the streets came to a standstill. Only people who had work permits would dare show their face on the streets. Stores had been closed since the very first day the destruction of the ghetto had begun. Since the ghetto was completely surrounded by police, the smuggling network came to a halt and food shortages began to make themselves felt. All kinds of provisions were in very short supply.

Bakers came out better than anyone else during this time. Instead of providing their bread rations on time to the food stores, they would sell them for much higher prices on the black market. They took gold and jewelry in exchange for bread, and even when they did bring bread to the food stores, the stores would sell it in turn at much higher prices, explaining that the bakers had not fulfilled their quota. In the evenings, the doors of the stores would be wide open and whatever was left was sold at black-market prices. People returning from work on the Aryan side also smuggled whatever they could get across and sell. Prices increased by the hour, while people's spirits dropped lower and lower. As if to fill our cup to overflowing, it rained steadily through the entire first week.

---

1. **Blue, or Navy-Blue Police.** The common name for the Polish police under German administration in occupied Poland. The Blue Police were recruited from among members of the former Polish State Police. Their primary responsibility was routine police work, such as combatting banditry and smuggling. They were not so much used in the ghetto after it was closed, for they were considered by the Germans to be too unreliable. As becomes abundantly clear from Mrs. Schmidt's diary, their main interest in the Jews was as a source of money in return for not turning them over to the Gestapo.
2. **Thirteenth Brigade.** A Jewish collaborationist organization in the Warsaw ghetto . Also known as the Jewish Gestapo, the brigade reported directly to the German Gestapo. It took its informal name from the address of its main office at 13 Leszno Street.
3. **First execution of seventeen people.** Already on November 17, 1941, i.e., before the period encompassed by Mrs. Schmidt's diary, the Blue Police had executed six women and two men who had been condemned to death by a German Sondergericht (Special Court) for "leaving the Jewish quarter without permission."
4. **Judenrat** (Jewish Council). The German authorities required that every Jewish community in territories occupied by them form a Judenrat, to which the Germans paid successively less attention as the extermination campaign proceeded. Upon hearing of the Nazi plans to deport the entire population of the Warsaw ghetto "to the east," its Judenrat chairman, Adam Czerniaków, committed suicide on July 22, 1942.
5. **Umschlagplatz** (Transfer Depot). In Warsaw, a holding area on Stawki Street set up next to a railway station, where Jews in the ghetto were assembled for deportation to death camps—in the case of Warsaw, primarily to Treblinka.

2

SHOP FRENZY

The day after the posters appeared everyone was in despair. Up until that time we had had a private shop manufacturing luxury ladies' footwear, which we operated with the permission of the German authorities. Considering the general situation, we were prospering. We continued to do business with our pre-war customers, in particular with the Mrs. Józefa Hebda firm on Marszałkowska Street. Mrs. Hebda would send a smuggler around to take whatever we produced out of the ghetto. In this way we were able to make a living and not die of starvation.

I had only the vaguest idea as to what the shops were all about. Our friends who were "fortunate" enough to be working for the shops were slowly dying of hunger. They were making from four to six zlotys[1] per day, depending on their qualifications, and three-quarters of a liter of watery soup. At that time, however, belonging to a shop became my sole ambition in life. I never stopped thinking for a moment about how to get my husband into a shop so as to save myself and my son from evacuation. Our son was three and a half months old at this time.

My husband became possessed of the unrealistic ambition of starting his own shop together with some of his friends in his profession. They would go from one place to another from five o'clock in the morning until nine o'clock at night trying to get their shop started. Two days passed, and our friends had already been able to buy work permits for themselves with huge sums of money, whereas our shop was still in the planning stages. We found someone who could get a shop permit for us in a couple of hours if we could get 50,000 zlotys together (there were plenty of swindlers left even in those days; the Germans themselves would lie in wait for suckers and try to cheat them out of their money).

We began looking for people willing to buy into our shop, going to our richest friends and offering shares at 10,000 zlotys per person. Finally we found someone willing to go in with us, provided he could bring several of his friends into the shop along with him. When at last my husband arrived home, starved and soaked to the skin, it turned out that the permit had already been given to someone else. (Later it turned out that all these permits were fictitious anyway; these new shops were the first to go when the destruction of the ghetto got fully underway.)

Next morning people showed up with three more shops. One already had a permit and the others had enough people, so once more my husband set out to start his own shop. Because we still didn't have a work permit, and the blockades set up by the Jewish police were coming closer and closer —although so far they had taken away only the poorest inhabitants—I started to get ready to leave. There were three adults in our house: myself, my husband, and a registered nurse, evacuated from Germany, who took care of our baby. We could take fifteen kilograms of baggage per person, which made forty-five kilograms in all. I packed three suitcases with our best clothes, table linen, and bedding. Besides that, I packed a basket of food and got our winter coats out, even though July in Poland is the hottest month of the year. Our neighbors did the same, sewing themselves large knapsacks to carry the allotted baggage.

The doors of all the apartments stood open all day long. The women would stand in the doorways and gossip, for the most part about who had made it into a shop, and for how much.

On the third day I finally told my husband once and for all to get himself a place in a shop, but above all a large one that had been in existence for a long time, for I had no faith in the newly-created ones. I knew from experience that my husband would never be satisfied until he had established his own shop, so I begged him to buy himself a place in a shop first and worry about creating his own shop later.

As I was standing on the balcony of our apartment full of such worries and cares, I noticed our neighbor Mr. Rosenberg in the next window, and I immediately recalled that his wife had been working for the past fifteen years in the Bro-Ro (Braun and Rowiński) factory[2] on Leszno Street, which at that moment was engaged in the manufacture and supply of clothing for the German army. Without the slightest bit of hope, I asked him if he thought he might be able to arrange something for my husband. To my surprise, he said that he could probably arrange a certificate of employment for him, including the names of his wife and child, that very day. All it would take would be 1000 zlotys.

I wrote down all the information he needed and asked him to hurry. In an hour Rosenberg had returned with a form to be presented to the personnel office in order to obtain work. When my husband arrived home, he was pleasantly surprised. He had asked for work at the so-called "Big Schultz" shop on Nowolipie Street. (This was a large shop located on the grounds of the Blunk tannery; a number of shops located there were engaged in work for the Germans.) Without a moment's hesitation I advised him to withdraw his application. Just how significant the results of this impulsive action on my part were, thanks to which we were able to avoid certain death, will come out later.

We submitted our application to the Karl George Schultz shop, formerly the Bro-Ro firm, on 78 Leszno Street. This firm had nothing to do with the "Big Schultz" shop.

Next day, the fourth day after the destruction of the ghetto had begun, in spite of an enormous round-up taking place in the city, our neighbor Mr. Rosenberg, without regard for his own personal safety, brought my husband an official identification card with his photograph. It stated that my husband was a newly-employed garment cutter and named me and our son as family. We breathed a sigh of relief; for 1000 zlotys we had purchased momentary peace and quiet. This was a quite modest price compared to what other shops were charging. One of our neighbors, a veterinarian, had bought a work certificate for himself and his family for 21,000 zlotys, and it later turned out that no such shop existed.

Our son's nurse had also been trying everything she could to avoid resettlement. She had a friend employed at Hejman's, a company engaged in removing garbage from the ghetto. According to the notices, the friend should have been safe from being resettled, so we tried to talk him into marrying our nurse. However, this turned out to be harder than anticipated, since he and his younger brother, also employed at Hejman's, had two sisters subject to resettlement, and they had agreed to marry them, at least on paper. The younger brother got married the next day to some girl for several thousand zlotys, and they used the money to buy the sisters places in the Toebbens shop.[3] The following day at six o'clock our nurse and her friend went to the rabbi. My husband was their only witness. The rabbi took six times the normal fee

16

for performing the marriage. This was not the only such wedding; a large group of other "engaged couples" was waiting in line, all overcome by the same marriage psychosis.

Everyone tried to save himself as best he could. The better and more secure a man's job, or the longer he had been employed in a shop, the higher a price he charged for such a marriage on paper. It was impossible to obtain a proper marriage certificate, so we had to be satisfied with a little card, signed by the rabbi, attesting that the marriage had taken place. Still, everyone hoped for the best. How naive we all were then, thinking that everything would return to normal as soon as these formalities were taken care of.

I learned that one of my sisters had managed to make it over to the Aryan side by going through the courthouse located on Leszno Street the day after the placards appeared. She had a christening certificate belonging to a Catholic friend of hers who had died. My second sister's husband had been accepted at the "Big Schultz" shop on 44 Nowolipie Street, and my third sister was safe as the mother of a policeman. Her husband's son from his first marriage belonged to the police force and had listed my sister as his mother. Almost all of our friends had managed to find some way of protecting themselves from evacuation. At least that was what we thought.

---

1. **zloty.** The Polish currency before, during, and after the war. During the war, the zloty ranged from 5.3 to 6 to the dollar. 1,000 zlotys would have been worth around $175.
2. **Bro-Ro** (Braun & Rowiński) factory. A pre-war knitted-goods factory on 78 Leszno Street, taken over during the war by Karl Georg Schultz. The K. G. Schulz factory was one of the largest of the ghetto's "shops."
3. **Toebbens & Schultz.** A German-run textile manufacturing conglomerate in the Warsaw ghetto operating with slave labor, making uniforms, socks and garments for the German war effort. It was owned and operated by two infamous war profiteers: Fritz Emil Schultz and Walther Caspar Toebbens.

3

THE NOOSE DRAWS TIGHTER

All night long we heard the continuous sound of rifle and machine-gun fire, making a ghastly impression on everyone. Too much was happening all at once; everyone was numb with fear. I was exhausted. The shots, people said, were the sounds of the infirm and cripples being executed at the cemetery, where they had been taken from the Umschlagplatz located on Stawki Street. It was to this point that the Germans shipped raw materials for the factories and shops working for them, and where they picked up finished goods and loaded them on freight trains. During the destruction of the Warsaw ghetto the Germans adapted it for use as a holding point. Instead of goods or raw materials, they would load Jews onto the cars and ship them to the gas chambers. Of course, we were still too naive to have any idea as to what the *Herrenvolk* were doing with the people being "resettled to the East."

With the beginning of the blockades, the Germans, assisted by the Jewish Police, would take the captured Jews to the Umschlagplatz. The elderly and crippled were shot and the others were sent to labor and farm camps. The first letters had already arrived from people who had been evacuated to Białystok. According to these letters, the Jewish community had been very hospitable and provided them with food, after which they had been assigned to various villages for work. All those marvelous letters had been fabricated by the Germans.

A new edict appeared, according to which every policeman had to furnish ten persons per day to the Umschlagplatz.

Several days later, around dusk and after the apartment house gate had been closed, the superintendent of our house, in which more than seventy families lived, handed a letter to my husband, who was at that time president of our House Committee. He said it was from the Jewish Council. Since it was too dark to read out in the courtyard, my husband invited the members of the committee to our apartment so that they could learn its contents. It turned out not to be from the Jewish Council at all. Rather, it was an anonymous appeal to the Jewish population, explaining that the resettlement was nothing less than murder aimed at the complete extermination of the Jewish population in Poland. The unknown author went on to call the people to come to their own defense and to put up a resistance rather than allow themselves to be led like lambs to the slaughter. If we must perish, then let it be with honor. The members of the House Committee merely shrugged their shoulders, thinking it must be some kind of German provocation.

After my husband had begun working in the Karl George Schultz factory, he told me how he had met a worker by the name of Stefan Grajek.[1] As it turned out, he was an important and active Zionist. He belonged to the *Hechalutz* (pioneers)[2] and was director of the *Hachshara* in Grochów outside Warsaw (Hachshara means preparation for agricultural work.) They became close friends; together they would distribute soup among the workers.When my husband told him about the anonymous appeal, Grajek explained that it had been issued and distributed throughout the ghetto by his own Zionist organization. Unfortunately, the appeal had awakened no response at all. This was not surprising; everyone was absorbed in himself and his own family and did not care about anything else. They had turned to all organizations, both right- and left-wing, for help in organizing a mutual defense, but were unable to come to an understanding with any of them.

On the fourth day of the resettlement I personally witnessed one of the Jewish Police blockades for the first time. It took place two buildings down from our apartment house. It was raining. The police surrounded the building and locked the gate. Into the horse-drawn wagons that had arrived poured a stream of human skeletons, dressed in rags and carrying a miserable assortment of bundles. The thin, half-starved bodies of the children made a particularly pitiable sight as they clung to their mother's skirts. The men stood in gloomy silence, while the women sobbed hysterically. The wagons slowly pulled away, while those fortunate relatives and friends who had work certificates walked behind and accompanied them part of the way. They took leave of one another with a desperate finality, as though sensing that it was for the last time. I stood on our balcony, for the moment still a spectator. My eyes were blinded with tears, and an evil premonition gripped my heart. Involuntarily, my lips moved in a prayer to the Almighty, beseeching him to keep watch over these destitute creatures and let them live to see happier days.

Next morning we had the first blockade in our own building. They locked the gate and posted a guard beside each stairwell entry, of which there were seven. Going from apartment to apartment, they ordered the tenants to assemble in the courtyard and to leave all doors open. My husband was not at home, but I was not worried about myself and my child, because I had an identification card. But I was troubled by something else. Our workshop was located on the ground floor in the same stairwell as our apartment, and two of our workers with their wives and children were hidden in it. They had no identification of their own; this was one of the reasons my husband had tried so hard to set up his own shop, so that he would be able to employ them and assure their safety. We were tied to them by the sincerest bonds of friendship. They had worked in the shop ever since my husband had first established it in the days before we were married.

We kept the doors padlocked and the shutters closed at all times, so as to create the impression that the workshop was uninhabited. We were also hiding several of our neighbors who hadn't been able to get work permits yet. The rest of our workers had gone to Russia immediately after the outbreak of the war.

Other people in our building were hiding in the cellars or wherever else they could. For example, in the apartment at 63 Nowolipki Street (we lived at number 57) there was an air raid shelter with an entrance from the courtyard, looking as if it led to the sewers. There they set up a hiding place where one had to pay for entrance. The house superintendent collected the admission fee. After it was full, the lid was shut and covered with sand. In this and other ways, people were hiding wherever they could find a place. The ones who had work permits assembled in the courtyard and, after being checked by the police, returned to their apartments. Because of my small son and the rain, I was allowed to remain indoors. No one was taken from our building, and the wagons moved on without accepting any more "passengers." It was still early in the game of "resettlement."

---

1. **Grajek, Stefan** (1916-2008). One of the founders of the Jewish Combat Organization, Grajek was hidden on the Aryan side by a Jan Sitarski and his two sons, who also helped other Jews flee the ghetto and hide (the Sitarskis were recognized

in 1984 as Righteous Among Nations by Yad Vashem). Grajek took part in the Warsaw Uprising of 1944 and emigrated to Israel in 1950, where for many years he was leader of the World Federation of Jewish Combatants.

2. **Hechalutz** (pioneers). A Jewish youth movement that trained young people for agricultural settlement in the historical lands of Israel.

4

ROUNDUPS IN FULL SWING

Stores were completely empty. The only salespeople left were the wives of policemen. The Jewish police really flourished during this time. Having nothing to fear from the roundups, they would begin by taking as much food from the wholesalers as they could carry and then, since they had to get it home somehow, they would commandeer a passing rickshaw driver on the street and force him to carry the food for nothing. If the driver put up any resistance, he would be beaten without mercy. Since the closing of the ghetto, rickshaws were the only means of transportation. They performed great services for us all, and the drivers were making a good living, since circumstances forced people to constantly move from one apartment to another.

As time went on, more and more blockades occurred, and the excesses and ruthlessness of the Jewish Police increased. Their audacity and bestiality knew no limits.

My husband told the story of how he had seen a poor woman apprehended on Nowolipie Street not far from the corner of Karmelicka. In her hand she was carrying a small bottle of milk, doubtless purchased at no little cost in those days. Two policemen fell on her and began trying to shove her onto a wagon. The woman began to put up a pathetic resistance, all the while holding the bottle of milk. She begged them to let her go, saying that her little baby at home was starving, and that she was taking him this little bit of milk, which she had managed to obtain with great difficulty. She begged them at least to let her take her child with her. One of the policemen tore the bottle from her grasp and threw it on the ground. The woman fell onto the pavement screaming and trying to protect herself, but the two ruffians grabbed her by the hair, dragged her across the ground and threw her onto the wagon. Similar incidents were an everyday occurrence. The Germans knew how to divide the Jewish population, setting one against the other in order to achieve their aims.

After approximately six days of street roundups, the first blockade with the participation of the Germans was held on Muranowska Street. Latvian, Lithuanian, and Ukrainian soldiers took part in it. These people were more like beasts than men. They had been specially trained by the Germans in the so-called Ausrottungsbattalion (extirpation corps), which was composed of a ragged assortment of the worst castoffs of society: instinctual brutes and criminals. They reveled at the sight of human blood, especially Jewish blood. They had no scruples whatsoever. The murder and torture of the Jews provided their daily nourishment. They had been brought in at the beginning of the resettlement campaign. The headquarters of these beasts was located at 103 Żelazna Street, where the former tenants had been given fifteen minutes' notice to evacuate.

During the blockade on Muranowska Street, no work certificates were honored at all. All of the inhabitants of the building were taken straight to the Umschlagplatz. Among them were people who had been working in the shops for more than a year. My cousin managed to escape by jumping out of a second-story window with her three-year-old son. The windows of her apartment looked out on property along Niska Street. Seeing no other way out, she threw her son into the arms of some people on the street below before jumping out herself.

We couldn't understand why the Germans were no longer honoring work permits. After all, it was their own ordinance that said that whoever was working for them would not be removed from the ghetto.

That same evening our son's nurse, while on her way home to her apartment on Ceglana Street in the so-called Little Ghetto, was forced to turn back. She was very frightened. She said that Nowolipie Street from the corner of Smocza to Karmelicka was surrounded by a cordon of German and Jewish Police. As I later learned from my sister, who lived on that street, this had been a large-scale blockade lasting from six o'clock in the morning until nine o'clock at night. All the inhabitants of the block were ordered to assemble in the yard. They said that anyone left in their apartment would be shot on the spot. My sister had been one of those who stayed in her apartment in spite of everything and because of that she had been saved for the moment. Several thousand people were taken in that blockade. I saw them being led along Smocza Street. That night we slept not a wink.

In our entryway, besides ourselves and Mrs. Hekselman, none of our former neighbors were left. One of our neighbors, an old bachelor named Weksler, found work in a shop mending clothes and entered his sister, also unmarried, as his wife, hoping in this way to assure her safety. Still fearing that this would be discovered during one of the blockades, his sister would go over to her nephew's house every day at five o'clock in the morning. Her nephew was a policeman, and she believed that no one would dare bother her there. Unfortunately, we soon heard that Miss Weksler would no longer be returning home, because during a blockade in her nephew's building, she had been taken to the Umschlagplatz. Her own nephew had to load her onto the wagon and was unable to offer any help. This piece of news had a thoroughly demoralizing effect on all of us.

During this same time a blockade occurred in the buildings located at 27, 29, and 31 Ogrodowa Street, during which everyone was taken without exception. The niece of one of our neighbors, whose husband worked at the Ursus factory (which produced trucks for the Germans), was taken along with her two-month-old child. She was certain that when she showed that she was the wife of an Ursus worker she would be set free. But they did not listen to her. She wasn't even allowed to go back to her apartment for diapers.

The atmosphere in the town became increasingly tense. People moved out of their apartments leaving everything they owned behind. They set up hiding places wherever they could. Cellars became apartments. Doors were padlocked from the outside to create the impression that no one was inside. Hiding places were set up in private shops and factories. Anyone who had a friend with a place to hide was leaving his own apartment and going into hiding.

While all of this was happening the news spread throughout the ghetto that the present campaign was only going to last for two weeks. Whoever managed to hide that long would be saved, because supposedly only 70,000 people were going to be evacuated. Since the police learned at each morning's briefing how many people were needed that day (some five to ten thousand), it was estimated that in two weeks' time life would return to normal.

We ourselves were faced with a new problem. On Nowolipki Street, next to the building in which we lived, a furniture shop was located belonging to a German named Hallman. My husband, as president of the House Committee, along with the presidents of several other neighboring buildings, was summoned by this man. He told them that he would prefer to settle the question of housing for people employed in his factory amicably and not use force, as had been done in other shops. Each shop housed its workers in buildings near the place of work, and toward this end the Germans would blockade the buildings and send all the tenants to the Umschlagplatz. In order to avoid this, Hallman asked the presidents to yield him twenty apartments in each building. An emergency meeting was convened, at which it was decided that smaller families were to move in with families occupying two- and three-room apartments. In this way the necessary number of apartments was produced in the course of a single day.

5

GOODBYE TO OUR APARTMENT

In the meantime another blockade had been set up around our building by the Jewish Police. The blockade proceeded in the same way as the first, except that this time the attics had to be opened, and all owners of cellars or basements had to open them up for inspection before the house superintendent and the police.

Many people were taken, primarily those hidden in the attics and cellars and those without work certificates. The police did not honor all work permits, only those from the larger and better-known shops that had been in existence for a long time. The women were crying inconsolably; one of them, even though she had identification papers, because she didn't want to go of her own accord, was carried away by force while still sitting in her chair and thrown that way onto the wagon.

Among other people they took the secretary of our House Committee, Mr. Rosenpick. As president of the committee my husband did everything he could to have him freed. His efforts were about to be rewarded when unexpectedly Colonel Szeryński came up to see what was going on. He was commandant of the Jewish Police and well known throughout the ghetto.[1]

Colonel Szeryński, a converted Jew and anti-Semite, had held the position of commandant of the Jewish police force even before the destruction of the ghetto, but for some minor crime he had been arrested by the Germans and sentenced to prison. After him the position was held, among others, by a certain Marian Haendel, who escaped to the Aryan side just before the destruction campaign got underway, leaving behind no trace.

As chance would have it, after the war when we were living in Caracas, Venezuela we found ourselves doing business with a certain Mr. Klinowski. After a while someone recognized him as Marian Haendel and informed on him to the Jewish Council there. He was about to be tried for collaborating with the Germans when, seeing the ground crumbling beneath his feet, he disappeared completely from view one day, leaving behind a wife and son.

As the destruction of the ghetto was getting underway, the Germans set Szeryński loose from prison and once more appointed him commandant of the Jewish Police. As the saying goes, if you need a murderer, take him even from the gallows.

When Colonel Szeryński poked his nose into the affair, the fate of our secretary was a foregone conclusion. He was loaded together with the others into the wagon to the accompaniment of crying children and wailing women. Those who had been passed over, among whom we belonged, returned to their apartments.

We were very sorry for Mr. Rosenpick, a very wise and cultured gentleman. He would always tell my husband, "We European Jews are condemned to extinction, but a new Jewish nation will arise in Palestine out of those who are saved and from the Jews of North and South America."

We now felt the specter of doom hanging over us and were unable to rest for a moment. Everywhere the bloody, nightmarish phantom called Germany was reaching out its tentacles to crush us. Where could we turn?

After talking it over with our neighbor Mr. Hekselman we all decided to go and ask another neighbor of ours, Mr. Flantzman, who had a lace factory at 10 Sochachew Street in the industrial district to let us hide in it. That same day his son, who worked on the Jewish Council and who was therefore temporarily safe from evacuation, brought us an affirmative reply from his parents. They themselves were already hiding in their factory.

My husband went to ask the advice of Jadzia, who was something of a protectress for him. She advised him to get to the factory as soon as possible and ask to be assigned to the cutting division, for company workers were being assigned apartments in the building left vacant as the result of German blockades on 27 and 29 Ogrodowa Street. We decided to take out an apartment together with Jadzia. My husband applied to the factory for a work assignment, paying the person in charge generously. The man assigned him to the cutting department where he began work; Jadzia was immeasurably surprised and at the same time delighted. A very small percentage of those applying for new assignments received them. Sometimes even money didn't make a difference. Since there was no longer enough room in the old factory, new branches were created to accommodate the newly accepted workers. Officially only eight hundred persons were supposed to be employed, but 2800 had been accepted for work, my husband being among the lucky ones.

When he returned from work I told my husband that I had decided to leave our apartment that very day, for I was afraid that during his absence I would be taken along with the child by a German blockade. My husband agreed with my plan. We asked one of our neighbors who was a policeman and had a rickshaw if he would move us to Sochaczew Street. He first took our neighbor Mrs. Hekselman and her children, and then us. I packed only the most essential things for the child and a modest supply of food. I still had three kilograms of cube sugar, two cans of condensed milk, and a box of Nestle's chocolate. All of this together constituted something of a treasure at the time in the ghetto. Our son had been fed up until then exclusively from the breast, but I was beginning to dry up due to all the tension and sleepless nights, and the insufficient nourishment.

For the first few days of the evacuation it was still possible to obtain milk. There were a great many dairies in the ghetto, and my husband would steal out of the house without my knowing and go to them. At the time he still didn't have a work permit and could have been seized at any time. Then placards appeared announcing that anyone who owned a cow would be accepted into a shop, together with their livestock, so people began signing up and giving their cows away. Soon the barns were empty, and it was no longer possible to get hold of milk.

We comforted ourselves by thinking that all this confusion would soon be over and peace and harmony would return. After all, my husband belonged to a shop, and for such a small child we would receive a milk allotment. The main thing was to put up with things for a while. After all, they said that this was only going to last for two weeks, and there were only six days remaining.

And so we left our apartment, full of hope and trust in the future. We had no idea that we would never see our little home again. In it we left behind our happiness and peaceful normal life of the past. From that moment on we were without a home and condemned to wander from place to place.

As we left our apartment, we gave the keys to our son's nurse, for it was becoming increasingly difficult for her to get to the Little Ghetto where she lived. The two ghettos were divided by Chłodna Street. In order to pass from the main ghetto into the little one, it was necessary to cross a bridge that had been specially constructed for the purpose, because along Chłodna Street ran the Germans' main rail artery. A guardhouse manned by German soldiers and Jewish police was located on the corner of Chłodna and Żelazna Streets. From time to time they would allow rail traffic into one ghetto or the other, but pedestrians always had to go by the bridge.

---

1. **Szeryński, Józef Andrzej**, born Josef Szynkman (1893-1943), commander of the Jewish Ghetto Police. He was arrested and briefly jailed by the Gestapo for smuggling furs out of the ghetto, and then released on the condition that he lead the deportation action to Treblinka. The target of several unsuccessful assassination attempts, he committed suicide after the deportation action was over.

6

TEMPORARILY AT FLANTZMAN'S

Terrible things were taking place in the Little Ghetto. It was said that it was earmarked for total destruction. All that was to remain was the main building of the Toebbens shop on Prosta Street and neighboring buildings allocated to the workers as living quarters. In the face of such rumors people began to move out of the Little Ghetto into the main one as fast as they could. From five o'clock in the morning (it was illegal to be out between nine o'clock at night and five in the morning) the streets would be filled with streams of horse-carts, handcarts, rickshaws, and other contrivances loaded down with furniture, bundles, bedding, and valises. Bending under the weight of their possessions, people were hurrying to their relatives and friends in the Big Ghetto to hide and salvage whatever they could.

As we looked at all this we were reminded of the year 1939, when Warsaw suffered its first bombing and fires were breaking out everywhere. Everyone fled from their own home, certain that it was going to be safer "someplace else." The same frantic flight was being reenacted, but this time under different circumstances.

At seven o'clock in the morning, at which time the blockades would begin, all movement and life on the streets would come to an end. People hid like hunted animals in their burrows. Throughout the day long columns of people were led out of the Little Ghetto to the Umschlagplatz. There were several thousand of them. The procession of bundles, bags, and crying children presented a most pitiable sight.

Involuntarily I felt my lips repeating the words "Jew, the eternal wanderer," but this time they were wandering to their utter destruction. We Jews, with no country of our own, scattered over the face of the earth, pointed out contemptuously at every turn with the cry: Jew! Murdered, beaten, and humiliated for three years by the Germans, branded with their stripes (for each Jew over the age of twelve had to wear a white band with the yellow Star of David on the right sleeve), cast out of our homes, deprived of our personal property, we asked ourselves: Why? Why are we beyond the pale of normal life and law? Where are we being taken? What do they want from us? What crimes have we committed?

That same day, in the early hours of the evening, after the blockades had been lifted, we moved out of our apartment. The streets were once again filled with throngs of people, noise, and activity. As we were locking the door behind us, my husband said to me: "Remember this place! We'll never be back."

Downstairs a small group of friends and neighbors was waiting to say goodbye. We shook hands with them warmly and sincerely. We were still hoping that everything would turn out all right. Our neighbor the policeman pushed the carriage with our child in it. As we walked along we gazed into the troubled faces of passers-by, picking out among them many of our friends.

We arrived safely in Sochaczew Street. This was a small, thinly populated side street, occupied for the most part by factory buildings. We were told that so far there had been no blockades on this street, even by the Jewish Police. The shop belonging to our neighbor, Mr. Flantzman, was a large one, occupying all of a two-story building. We were to be placed on the upper floor in a huge room with thirteen large windows. The room was full of lace manufacturing equipment. There was water, a sink, and electricity. We were able to cook on two hotplates. We set up the field cots we had brought with us in the space between the machines, and the baby carriage in the space left between one machine and a window. The windows were barred. For safety we left them closed, opening only the transom so that the baby could get a little fresh air. The room had double doors made of wood, reinforced with iron. We all decided, and there were fourteen of us, that in case of a German blockade we would hide behind the machinery and not answer any calls from the yard below. Even if it meant death we were not going to respond to any commands. We counted on the doors not giving way. After evaluating all the positive aspects of our hiding place we were quite satisfied with it.

When the evacuation began all we had by way of money was a

hundred zlotys in cash. One of our customers from before the war, Mrs. Józefa Hebda, whose store was located on 77 Marszałkowska Street, continued to do business with us even after the ghetto was closed in the fall of 1940. A Mr. Henryk Michalski would run errands for her up until the ghetto began to be destroyed. He worked at the post office on the corner of Zamenhof and Gęsia Streets, and for this reason he had a pass which enabled him to come and go in the ghetto. He would come to us almost every day and take away practically everything we made. When Poles were no longer allowed into the ghetto, and the post office had been shut down and turned into a Jewish prison, he would smuggle goods through the walls surrounding the Warsaw ghetto. By the time the evacuation began, Mrs. Hebda owed us a large sum of money, but there was no way for us to communicate with her. Eventually, however, an opportunity presented itself.

One of our neighbors was Mr. Morawski, who before the war worked in the Third Precinct of the Polish Police (the so-called "Blue" or "Navy Blue Police") on 53 Nowolipki Street. We had been friends with him since before the war, and would secretly listen together to the Allied radio broadcasts. The Germans had confiscated all radios, and it was against the law to listen to the radio under penalty of death. Mr. Morawski had picked out the best one from among those that had been confiscated and brought it home. He and my husband found a good hiding place for it in the attic, and at night we would listen to the radio broadcasts from London.

After the ghetto was closed, the Morawskis moved away, but in the early stages of the evacuation the Polish police stations continued to operate throughout the ghetto.

Thus it was that one day my husband met Mr. Morawski on the street and asked him to find out from Michalski about our getting paid. He agreed, and to our surprise and happiness, Michalski sent us 1500 zlotys. This money sufficed for our most essential immediate needs. We still had a small stock of goods from our factory, and because there was a so-called commuter living in our building (he was allowed to work outside the ghetto), we were able to give him a few things each day which he would carry stuffed inside his pants. He would sell these things to Poles he knew and when he returned from work he would bring us either money or food. In this way, by the time we moved into the Flantzman factory, our material circumstances were much more tolerable. However, we were full of worry and under constant emotional stress; yet this was only the beginning.

7

DYSENTERY

At this time a new burden came upon us. My husband had drunk some pickle juice out of a large jar in our old apartment, and afterwards he had a drink of water. The result was easy to foresee: dysentery! This new blow of fate crushed me completely. Even under normal circumstances this is a serious disease which requires an enormous amount of attention and a proper diet. But what was one to do? He had to go to work, because one could be dismissed from work for two days' absence, and that would have meant death for all three of us. The drugstores were all shut and no doctors were living at their old addresses. At the factory where, in general, chaos and hopeless disorganization was the rule, medical aid was unavailable. For the moment the disease, as is usually the case in the beginning, was not too bad. Fortunately I still had a little rice, so I fixed him nothing but rice pap and hoped that his body would be able to carry him through the illness.

On the third day of our stay in this hiding place, my husband returned from work with good news. He related how Schultz had driven up ostentatiously and taken out a sign for all of them to see. The sign said that his factory was working for the army. The next morning the workers' identification cards were stamped with a new mark that the men called "birds", in other words, swastikas. Identification cards with swastikas were always honored by the Jewish Police during roundups, because only factories operating legitimately were able to issue them.

Apartments began to be allocated. 27 and 29 Ogrodowa Street

were already completely filled with workers from our Schultz's shop. Since the above-mentioned buildings were not large enough to accommodate all the workers and their families, the buildings next to the factory on Leszno Street began to be vacated. It was in this building, thanks to the enormous efforts and influence of our protectress, Jadzia, that we received an assignment to a two-room apartment. Unfortunately, it was still not possible to move in, because the previous tenants had not yet received their assignment to an apartment near their own shop.

Notices were placed around town stating that by September 22 all shop workers and their families had to be quartered in buildings assigned to their shops. The notices also listed buildings that were to be vacated by their tenants by five o'clock in the morning on that date. Those buildings were eventually joined to the Aryan quarter.

People began moving their belongings and it was impossible to get a horse-cart. The cost of hiring a horse-cart from one street of the ghetto to another started at five hundred zlotys and went up from there. People would pack their things feverishly by night and set out at daybreak for their newly assigned apartments. How we envied those who were already living in their assigned housing! How lucky they were, we thought. They are under the protection of their factory. They have nothing to fear from blockades. How naive, stupid, and blind we all were then! We hadn't yet figured out that the Nazis were concentrating the people in order to take them away to the Umschlagplatz all the more easily.

We too were ready to move into our own sanctuary, but still the apartment assigned to us and Jadzia had not been vacated. In an effort to make things easier for us, Jadzia asked one of her co-workers to take me and my baby into her home for a few days. Because Jadzia had been employed in that factory for fifteen years, she knew a great many people, both in factory management and among the workers. One of the women who did piecework for the factory and who brought her work to Jadzia understood the situation and agreed to take in me and the baby. They were wonderful people.

After our six days in hiding at the Flantzmans we packed our chattel and, in the early evening, bade farewell to our neighbors. Little did we know that we would never see them again. We loaded our things onto a rickshaw and set out on our way. My husband walked out in the street, and I pushed the baby carriage on the sidewalk. After our stay in that stifling factory I was breathing as deeply as I could. The movement of traffic was frenzied, as crowds were surging in all directions. The sidewalks and streets were full to overflowing with people. The traffic and the noise from the street literally left me speechless. For several days I had grown used to a silence as still as the grave, to constantly walking on tiptoes and to talking in whispers. Now that I found myself once again among a crowd, it was difficult for me to realize at first that I could speak out loud again.

I was most frightened as I walked past the guardhouse, which was impossible to avoid if one went along Ogrodowa Street. As we passed the guardhouse at the corner of Żelazna and Leszno Streets, I did not glance in the direction of those hated German faces, those beasts in uniform standing there so proudly. They were so strong and so cock-sure of themselves, lords and masters over our existence. But I, miserable speck of dust that I was, whose chances for continued survival were almost nil, raised a fervent prayer to God that He let us see the day when those proud heads would be bent in utter submission. Then at last I could die in peace.

We arrived at our destination without incident. In the courtyard clouds of smoke were rising. The ground was strewn with books in beautiful bindings, bedding, pillows, feather beds, quilts, crystal, porcelain, tableware, and other items. The entire courtyard was stacked high with various sorts of furniture: elegant armchairs, beds, bureaus, and an immense amount of pots, pans, and clothes-wringers.

The previous tenants, victims of the first Nazi blockades, had been taken away suddenly and had left behind everything they possessed. When people came to take over these apartments, they had no place to put their own belongings and left everything they owned out in the courtyard. These things were piled up and set on fire, and the smoke and stench filled the air. The heat was unbearable; it was difficult even to breathe.

The apartment where I was to stay consisted of a single room with kitchen. In it two families were living. A kitchen had been set up in the anteroom, and the real kitchen had been made into a bedroom, in which a newly married couple was residing. The woman was in her seventh month of pregnancy. The other room, which was very small and narrow, was occupied by another couple, including the sister of the pregnant woman. They received me very politely and showed me the greatest sympathy. I stayed with them for six days. I will always remember them with fondness. The belief that there would be no blockades in this building because it housed quartered workers gave me temporary peace of mind. However, the people lived in utter poverty. Their child would beg for a crumb of black bread, but they were not always able to give him anything. Still they did not want to accept payment from me.

My husband, who worked from dawn to dusk without having a bite of cooked food to eat, was growing weaker and weaker. It was impossible for me to look after him properly. He wasn't even able to sleep with us, for there was barely enough room for me and the baby. The dysentery was making rapid progress, and he was hardly able to stand on his feet. Fortunately, the apartment assigned to us on 76 Leszno Street was soon vacated by the previous occupants. My husband came for me that day, which was Saturday, and proposed that I and the child move into the new apartment.

He said that he and Jadzia would move the rest of our things over on the following day, and I readily agreed. I dressed quickly, and soon I was ready to leave with the baby. At that moment Jadzia came in and asked me in surprise where I was going. She immediately began to dissuade us from going until all our things had been moved and we could all go together. I listened to her advice and in this way I saved my own life and that of the baby. As it turned out, an hour later a German blockade took place on 76 Leszno Street under the pretext that the building had to be vacated for the workers of the Karl George Schultz factory. Everyone was taken without exception, including the families belonging to our shop that had already moved in. If Jadzia had not come at that moment we would have been lost.

Next morning my husband took our things from our apartment on 57 Nowolipki Street. We left our furniture, because there would have been no place to put it in our new quarters. All through the night my poor sick and exhausted husband was busy packing. The next day he was unable to get out of bed. When I learned how serious my husband's condition was, I decided to move into our new apartment immediately, danger or not.

I left almost all my things behind and just took the baby in my arms and left. We decided to go by a circuitous route through a double-exit building on Ogrodowa Street in order to avoid passing the guardhouse on the corner of Leszno and Żelazna Streets. No one stopped us, and we arrived safely. I found my husband in a pitiful state. My only thought at that moment was to help him recover, because without a husband we were all lost. I learned that a Dr. Knaster had already moved into our shop, and so I went to him and asked him to examine my husband.

In the initial stages of his illness my husband had been to see our house doctor, and he had actually been able to get some medicine in a pharmacy that was still operating. When my husband returned to this doctor a second time he was no longer living at his old address. Now Dr. Knaster confirmed that the illness was a serious one and prescribed some medicine. Since no pharmacies were open in the ghetto, the doctor wrote the prescription as illegibly as possible so that we might be able to buy the medicine on the Aryan side. We were able to get it through one of Jadzia's co-workers named Janina, and now could devote all our energies to getting my husband cured.

8

OUR NEW APARTMENT

The apartment to which we were assigned was a total mess. It turned out that this one room with kitchen to which we had been assigned was supposed to be occupied by nine people. Since there were only five of us, Jadzia's mother and her sister's fiancé moved in with us. Each person brought with him an enormous amount of bags, bundles, bedding, and various other items necessary for running a household. It was impossible to walk a step without knocking into something. Besides that, bedbugs and fleas were running rampant in such numbers that in the morning we would wake up covered from head to foot with bites. On the other hand, the enormous amount of odds and ends which cluttered our apartment had its positive side, because we were able to sell these objects or exchange them for food with the Poles.

A number of Poles worked in our factory. They would bring food with them and exchange it for goods. A loaf of bread weighing a kilogram would cost twelve zlotys over on the Aryan side but seventy-five in the ghetto. A roll would cost 1.80 on the Aryan side and eight to nine zlotys in the ghetto. There wasn't anything that could not be bought for money. One other advantage to our factory was that it had a branch over on the Aryan side on 51 Ogrodowa Street with several Jews working in it. Every morning a group of them, led by a so-called group leader and several policemen, would assemble. Each person was entitled to take past the guard on his way home five kilograms of vegetables and a loaf of bread. Needless to say, smuggling was going full steam. They were even taking bacon across, for which, if caught, you were shot on the spot. But people would take the risk anyway. It was possible to buy food from people returning from these work groups, but at truly astronomical prices.

In other shops the food situation was very bad. For example, the Big Schultz shop on Nowolipie Street where twelve thousand people were originally employed had no branches on the outside, and no one beside Jews were employed there. Each day at noon the workers would receive three-quarters of a liter of watery soup in which some pieces of potato or other vegetables were floating. According to regulations each worker was supposed to receive one-eighth of a loaf of bread, but in actuality no one ever saw it.

Returning to the first days of our stay in our new apartment, I finally had my own private corner near the window in which I was able to set up my baby's bed. Even more importantly, after three weeks of wandering from place to place I was finally able to bathe my child and wash out his diapers. It is easy to imagine my happiness as I saw the color beginning to return to his face under the influence of clean water and fresh air. Another problem which had been troubling me also disappeared, and that was the matter of the baby's food. Here at last I was able to obtain kasha, butter, oatmeal, and other food items and, besides that, Jadzia asked her Aryan friends to bring various sorts of food preparations for him. One of them brought a box of malted milk (Klawe's Malton, a powder preparation for babies). My husband's health slowly began to improve. After two days of bed rest, he had to go back to work, pale and unsteady on his feet as he was. We were afraid that his absence would serve as a pretext for removing him from the list of workers.

In the meantime, however, a new worry appeared in the form of my sister. Her story was a short one. She was her husband's second wife, and one of his married children, who was a policeman, had obtained identification papers for her and his father and mother. Eventually the police were assigned to their own section of town, to which they were allowed to take only their wives and children. So the parents were left without a roof over their heads, and their identification papers ceased to be honored. My sister had to move out of their apartment. Her husband was able to move in with his sister, but my sister was left out on the street. After talking things over, we decided that for the time being she could stay with us.

After several days of relative quiet, we were taken unawares by a new turn of events. A German blockade was set up in the building next to ours, in the Toebbens shop on 72 Leszno Street, and all women and children were removed from the worker's quarters. Once more we were seized with terror. How can this be?, we wondered. The notices clearly stated that a husband working in a shop could keep with him his wife and children up to the age of fourteen, so how is it that now they are taking them away?

At the same time rumors began circulating to the effect that only people who were actually working would be allowed to stay in the worker's quarters. In other words, no one was protected. Only a working husband and wife would be allowed to keep their children.

My husband began trying to get himself entered on the list of workers and to obtain identification papers for me. Toward this end he went to the same director who had accepted him for work, offering him a brand new typewriter and fifteen hundred zlotys cash for the favor. The director said that I would be employed, but it would be necessary to wait for an opening, and pay for it separately.

When people had first been quartered in the buildings adjacent to the shops, wooden barriers had been constructed along the sidewalks so as to prevent immediate contact with the street. Exits were guarded by detachments of Jewish Police who saw to it that no one went into the area without a pass.

Beginning on August 22 it was no longer possible to be on the streets without a pass under penalty of death. Workers were confined to the grounds of the factory in which they were employed. However, at first there was such chaos and confusion that people did not keep to these regulations. For example, our building had an opening leading from the third courtyard onto 67 Nowolipie Street. The Big Schultz shop on Nowolipie had a passage leading to the bazaar on Leszno next to the Toebbens shop. Food would be smuggled along this route from our shop to the others, but after having passed through the third set of hands the price would have increased enormously.

In our shop trade was flourishing. The Poles working in our shop would buy anything, and our people would sell everything they owned —clothing, bedding, shoes, and anything else. Whatever they could find a buyer for, they sold. People were setting up machines in the corners of their apartments and making socks, stockings, gloves, and so on. If we had just been left in peace to make out as best as we could, life for us would have been tolerable. But the Nazis had other plans.

9

"RESETTLEMENT TO THE EAST"

A sense of unrest was spreading across town. The two weeks after which peace and quiet were supposed to follow had passed. The fourth one was beginning, and still the German horde raged on. Blockades continued without cessation, even now when there were no longer any outsiders in the workers' quarters. The booty from these blockades consisted primarily of nonworking women and children. One evening the so-called Werkschutz, or factory police (each shop had its own police force which was housed in the workers' quarters next to the shop), ordered all workers in our factory to go to their apartments and remain indoors. The courtyards were emptied in a minute. Only the frightened faces of people timidly peering out from behind the curtains expecting a blockade gave any sign of life. An hour passed, and still everything remained quiet.

Darkness was falling, but the same quiet reigned everywhere. Only later did we learn that this had been a blockade of the commuting workers returning from work on the Aryan side. They were divided into two groups at the guardhouse. Most of them were sent to the Umschlagplatz, while the rest returned to their apartments. This took everyone by surprise. Now at last we understood that all these shops and establishments were nothing but a ruse, and that everyone was being sent away without exception; some were simply going earlier and others later. It was time to start thinking about what we could do to protect ourselves.

This was a question to which we all tried to find a satisfactory answer. First we began setting up hiding places in the apartments. We heard that during the German blockades, Ukrainian, Lithuanian, and Latvian soldiers whose main job it was to go around the apartments were mostly interested in plundering and looting. Above all else they were looking for gold watches. We had heard that during a blockade on Nalewki Street they broke down the doors of one apartment and found seven persons hiding there. Four of them were able to buy their freedom with watches. The other three, who had nothing to redeem themselves with, had to join the others waiting in the courtyard to be transported to the Umschlagplatz. During this same blockade, however, another group of Ukrainians and Latvians, after taking everything of value, killed three persons on the spot.

We began looking around our apartment to see where we might fashion at least a temporary hiding place. In our kitchen was a large old-fashioned cabinet. When we emptied out the bottom of it, two people were able to curl up inside, albeit with difficulty. Since there was an enormous number of packages, sacks, and various sorts of bundles in our apartment, my sister and I took several of the most miserable looking larger ones and wrapped them in string so that when we crouched down in the cabinet we could conceal ourselves behind them.

Over the door leading into the hallway was a large shelf holding assorted household items: pots, tubs, a wringer, and the like. It was possible for one person to lie down on this shelf and hide behind these objects. However, it required the assistance of another person, because it was only possible to get up there by a ladder which the other person would have to put back so as to cover their tracks. The most difficult question still remained: what to do with a four-month-old baby? How and where could we hide him? Unfortunately we had no answer.

At this critical period Janina, of whom I have already spoken, came to see Jadzia. Since she did piecework at home, she had a pass and could enter and leave the ghetto during the day as many times as she liked. A full-time worker in the factory was allowed to pass the guard only once in the morning and once at night. Like all of the other women workers, Janina made use of her privileges to engage in trade and smuggling. She would bring us food and buy clothing and other wares from us.

Since Jadzia was not home when she first arrived, Janina decided to wait, and she and I struck up a conversation. The subject was the block-ades and the evacuation of the Jews. Since Janina was the first Pole I had the chance to talk with during this period, I was curious to learn what she and the Polish population in general thought about the situation. I especially wanted to know where she thought they were taking everyone. When I asked this question, she looked at me with an expression of utter astonishment and replied: "You mean you don't know? All these people are being transported to Treblinka to be killed in gas chambers especially constructed for the purpose."

So they were not being taken to the East, as the Germans said, but to their death. I was unable to speak from emotion. For the rest of the day I could not think about anything else, and when my husband came home I repeated to him what Janina had told me. This was the first my husband had heard of it too. He kept saying, as everyone did in their naïvité, that no people on earth would be capable of such a barbarous act. How could they? Because they were Jews? No, that was simply not possible. My husband didn't want to believe it, but I understood right away that it was true. Who could have ever believed that the Germans were planning the complete extermination of the Jews? But the Germans were doing just that, with their customary sophistication and meticulousness, while the world remained silent. I began to fear Germans even more than before. My natural instincts were sharpened to an incredible degree by the danger hanging over us.

My every mental process, all my cunning and intelligence, were concentrated in one direction: not to give in. As never before, I wanted to live, to get out of this burrow for good and not to die in it like a rat. I wanted to stop living like a dog, in constant fear, hunted and persecuted, and to know freedom once again, to see the free world in its glory, to know the smell of the fields and meadows. When will these nightmares be over? When will this sword of Damocles at last be lifted from over our heads?

The main thing I had on my conscience was my baby, who was still very tiny. My greatest desire was at least once to hear the single word which every mother with her whole heart longs to hear from her child's mouth: Mama. Such a simple, two-syllable word, but how I longed to hear it. Such a tiny mouth, such a perfect little face, and such innocent eyes which had yet to see anything of the world. Were these eyes to be closed forever merely because of the whim of a butcher, an executioner, a human beast who had brought the world to the brink of cataclysm? No! A hundred times no! I didn't want to die, I wanted to live, to be saved! I almost went out of my mind. I begged my husband to save us and not leave us here in the utmost peril. I begged Jadzia to save us. I was so pathetic in my display of insane fear that everyone was deeply moved.

10

HIDING ON THE GROUNDS OF THE K. G. SCHULTZ FACTORY

In the meantime the Nazis continued without interruption, setting up blockades in the workers' housing, taking away the elderly, the women, and the children. We expected a blockade in our own building at any moment. My husband decided to locate me on the factory grounds until I obtained my identification papers. In this case too, Jadzia was able to come to the rescue. She knew a man who had worked for many years as a joiner in the same factory as his sons. The man enjoyed the respect of Rowiński himself, and even of Schultz. Although he already had one apartment in the workers' quarters at 76 Leszno Street, he had temporarily obtained a second one, consisting of a large kitchen and anteroom, at 78 Leszno Street. The two rooms beyond the kitchen were filled with machinery. It was in this kitchen that I and the baby were allowed to stay during the day.

Thus began the next stage in my wanderings. I would get up at four o'clock in the morning and pack diapers and food for the baby in a bag along with several pieces of bread to last me for the whole day. Then I would tear my child away from his sleep and dress him. In order to take the first opportunity to slip unnoticed through the gate before the Werkschutz arrived, I had to be at the factory gate at exactly five o'clock in the morning.

The first day I was able to get in with the help of my husband. Since the occupants of the apartment in which I was to be placed were still asleep at such an early hour, we had to wait out on the landing. I brought a bottle of warm milk with me, and I fed my poor little mite as we sat there on the stairs. Anyone seeing us sitting there on the steps would have surely wept from pity: two people gazing heart-rendingly at a tiny little creature, innocent of everything going on about him. The baby quietly sucked on his bottle while the two of us sobbed to ourselves. How miserable we were then, bound together by mutual danger, looking for some way out of this maze. The enemy was so strong, and we so helpless.

At 6:30 my husband wiped the tears from his eyes and went off to work. The minutes dragged on until finally at 7:30 they opened the door and let me into the kitchen, where I was allowed to stay until the blockades were over in the evening. The kitchen was empty except for a mattress where I put my baby. An old woman and her daughter, who had a year-and-a-half-old child, were left behind in the apartment while the others went to work. The mother and daughter had papers identifying them as factory workers, so there was a chance that they would be freed in case of a blockade. How I envied them! I was so tired and sleepy. I sat all day apathetically, praying God not to let there be a blockade. I got up only to change the baby or to fix him something to eat on the gas stove.

The factory broke for lunch at noon. The workers would stand in line for soup with their bowls and spoons in their hands. They paid fifty groszy for the meal. At the beginning of the week each worker would pay three zlotys for the entire week. Poles got one kind of soup and Jews another. My husband brought his portion of soup to share with me. It consisted of some cloudy water with a couple of pieces of potato floating in it. From time to time one might come across a piece of beet or carrot. The workers had to wait six hours to fill their empty stomachs with this stuff. Many of them took their portion of soup home, added some potatoes to it, and cooked it over again, because in its initial state it was more like a beverage than anything else.

During the lunch break I learned the latest news: where the morning blockade had taken place, where the Death Squad was headed, what people in town were saying, and so forth. Always the same subjects. We could look forward to several days of respite, since the Death Squad was supposedly heading to Otwock, a resort town near Warsaw, for new victims. Otwock had been a place of refuge for many Jews during the first days of evacuation. These were by and large the very richest, for it cost them plenty of money. However, their peace was short-lived, lasting only four weeks.[1]

Everyone thought only of himself. We eagerly seized upon the redeeming thought that we would be able to relax for a while. But the

Death Squad still had its headquarters at 103 Żelazna Street. Every morning we would look out at them with fear, trying to guess what would be the next target of their murderous activities.

After lunch, my husband returned to work. and I impatiently counted the hours until darkness. August was very hot, and the heat was having an effect on all of us. It was very difficult to sit all day long in a stifling apartment with a baby as little as mine. However, I thanked God that I at least had a place to put him and something to fix him to eat. Others didn't even have that much. They sat all day long on the stairway, their children crying for something to eat, tortured with thirst. What unhappy creatures we poor mothers were. At six o'clock my husband returned from work and took me home, where more work awaited. I had to wash the baby, clean his diapers, fix a little hot soup and get everything ready for the next day's journey.

When I arrived on the factory grounds next day, I found everyone in a state of terror. They had heard that the Death Squad was at work in the Toebbens shop on 72 Leszno Street, not more than three doors down from us. We sat there with our hearts in our throats, expecting a blockade in our own factory. The mother of the joiner and her sister and child were hidden in one of the factory cellars. A mob of people who had been staying in the anteroom now pressed into the kitchen where I was staying. The uproar, confusion, and crying children left me utterly numb and speechless. I had no idea what to do, but I was sure of one thing: I would sooner die on the spot than go out into the courtyard under any circumstances. Each moment I thought I could hear them coming, but it was a false alarm. Toward evening people came back out of the cellars. My husband was a new worker and consequently not "in" with the higher-ups, so I had no chance of belonging to the small number of lucky ones who were protected.

But I did begin asking my husband about his relationship with the other workers and whether he knew any "bigwigs." Unfortunately, my husband's position was a very lowly one. Several dozen workers were employed in the cutting department where he worked. Of these, only three were Poles, the remainder being Jews. Most of the latter were among the newly hired; only a few of them numbered among the older workers.

The director of the cutting division was Lurie. My husband was good friends with his brother because they had both belonged to the Union of Manufacturers and Commerce. Before the war Lurie had been a buyer for the Rowiński firm. After K. G. Schultz took over the factory, Lurie was removed from his post and appointed director of the cutting division. Because of this he was able to protect his family. Besides Lurie, my husband also had to curry favor with Haze, a Volks-deutsch (a Pole claiming German extraction),[2] who was head of the sewing and cutting divisions, as well as with two senior cutters, Szpilberg and Napieraj. My husband held the position of assistant cutter. The head cutter at his table was Eichel. He had escaped from the ghetto in Łódź, where he had had his own company. It was no easy matter, but he arranged to be smuggled out by the team of Kohn and Heller, infamous throughout the Warsaw ghetto as collaborators with the Nazis. They brought him to Warsaw for 9000 zlotys. They themselves were from Łódź, where they were known even before the war for their shady dealings.

I should mention that when the Warsaw evacuation began, Kohn and Heller,[3] believing that only 70,000 people were to be resettled, were most cooperative with the Germans. However, as this figure continued to rise, they went to have a talk with the Death Squad, which issued instructions every morning during briefings at the Central Head-quarters of the Jewish Police on Ogrodowa Street. During the course of this talk, or rather protest on their part, they were shot in a disgraceful manner and, evidently on the orders of the Germans, their bodies were taken away to the cemetery in a garbage truck. In this way the careers of Kohn and Heller, collaborators with the Gestapo, came to an end.

My husband soon became friends with Eichel. They were drawn together by their mutual sufferings and concern for their wives and children. My husband asked him if he would show him how to cut independently as soon as possible, because in case of a reduction in the work force, the beginners, being the more expendable, would be the first to go. Thus Eichel undertook to teach my husband. My husband was also able to win Szpilberg's favor with little difficulty, for he understood that it was a matter of life and death for me and the baby. The head director Haze, who was a decent sort despite being a Volks-deutsch, could only be won over by diligent work, although a few presents didn't hurt either.

The only person remaining was Napieraj who, even though he had no final voice in anything, could have been a definite hindrance if he had so wanted. He could only be reached through money or presents, for he was a thoroughly bad sort. Lurie, because of his brother, could not have been better disposed toward my husband. He was a very upright person and never bothered anyone in any way. In other departments, the directors made a good business out of dispensing favors for cold cash. This was the case, for example, with Pęczyna and even

Rowiński's son Sioma. (When we left Poland in 1946 we met young Rowiński at the railway station in Katowice where he, like us, was preparing to leave. Together with us, he was one of the few to survive the Holocaust.)

---

1. **Otwock massacre.** "Deportation" activities throughout suburban localities on the right side of the Vistula river, including in Otwock, took place over several days, beginning on August 18, 1942.
2. **Volksdeutsch**. Persons registered as having German ancestry in occupied countries in World War II. In Poland the Volksdeutsch were given apartments, workshops, furniture, and other belongings confiscated from persons of Polish or Jewish ethnicity. They were subject to conscription into the German army.
3. **Kohn and Heller**. Morris Kohn and Zelig Heller were part of the Thirteenth Brigade, but eventually broke with it and formed their own organization, whose demise is described here second-hand by Mrs. Schmidt.

11

JADZIA'S BROTHER'S FAMILY TAKEN

The most fortunate were those who obtained work directly from Koszutski, who was director of the entire factory. The price for obtaining work through him started at 10,000 zlotys, payable in jewelry, other valuables, or currency. The lucky man who could afford a ransom like that could work without fear of job reduction or any other calamity. In addition he was promptly assigned to an apartment, for the assignment of apartments was in the hands of the factory director.

Apartments provided another way for people to make money. By paying the right amount it was possible to get a larger apartment with a smaller number of co-tenants, and it was not necessary to wait so long. Ordinary mortals had to wait in line for several days for a room containing eight or nine other people.

Besides Koszutski 's favorites, there was also the group around K. G. Schultz himself. Foremost among these was the engineer Mazurek. These elect had for the most part been recruited from among the former owners of large factories. Such, for example, were Pęczyna, Joselson (who survived the war and now lives in New York, where he has a Necchi sewing machine outlet), Landau, Goldlust, and a whole string of others. They contributed everything they owned by way of machines, equipment, and raw materials to the factory, and for this reason they had the most privileges and occupied the better positions. Landau contributed his entire factory, located on the Aryan side at 51 Ogrodowa Street, to which every morning work groups from our factory would be taken. He himself was in charge of these groups. He had a personal pass which enabled him to move about freely on the Aryan side of town. He actually had his own personal apartment next to the factory on Ogrodowa Street, although he also had a two-room apartment with kitchen in the workers' quarters on 76 Leszno Street for himself, his wife, and his daughter. Later I was often able to observe him, for he lived across from us. He was always informed in advance by his protectors when a blockade was to be held in our area. Then he and his wife and daughter would go and stay for a few days on the Aryan side. Such was the power of the golden calf. Later on, Koszutski became known as a millionaire. I should mention that while all these factory owners contributed their property to the K. G. Schultz factory voluntarily, their aim was clear: they hoped in this way to save themselves and their families and to avoid the official confiscation of their property.

Every day workers would be missing on account of the roundups, leading to confusion and disarray in every factory department. People would come to work each day weighed down by new blows of fate. Their wives and children would have been taken while they were away. Everyone came to work worried and depressed, for they never knew whether they would still find their families or only an empty apartment when they returned home.

It was no wonder that production decreased with each passing day, and this in turn had a negative effect on all the workers. There were some days when, on account of blockades and street roundups, in some departments only three or four people would show up for work.

New changes were taking place all the time. Notices appeared on the gates of the workers' quarters at 27 and 29 Ogrodowa Street, stating that all tenants were to vacate within three days and occupy apartments in the buildings on 33, 35, and 37 Nalewki Street. Once more people had to stand in line waiting for new housing assignments, after which they would feverishly pack their belongings and start looking for carts, rickshaws, or some other means of transportation. Dawn would find the streets filled with a procession of horse-carts followed by the weary figures of men, hunched over, tired and wan, their dull eyes wearing an expression of utter hopelessness and resignation. How tragic this all was!

We heard that the apartments in our building were to be handed over for the exclusive use of the factory management, while we ordinary mortals had to move to Nalewki Street. Because of these rumors, those of us without "protection" or protectors didn't even bother to unpack, for we expected to be moving constantly from place to place.

It was our misfortune that Jadzia, on whom we had been counting so much, was in disfavor with Koszutski. His protégé, Pęczyna, had a lover whom he had situated in the same department where Jadzia was director. He wanted his lover to take over Jadzia's position, and he was impudent enough to ask Jadzia to train the girl for her own job. In the course of these dishonorable machinations he tried to make use of his influence with Koszutski, with whom he was involved in a number of shady deals and operations. Jadzia, who had been employed in that very same department for the past fifteen years, put up a rather strong resistance. She was prepared to go to Schultz himself in order to defend her job if she had to. Koszutski probably guessed as much, and for the moment the matter remained in abeyance.

During this time I continued to go with my child at five o'clock each morning to the apartment on 78 Leszno Street, because every day we heard rumors that there would be a blockade in our building. Roundups had already taken place in many small shops and even in the Big Schultz shop on Nowolipie and in the Toebbens shop on Prosta Street in the Little Ghetto as well as on Leszno in the Big Ghetto. A new section was created for our factory in the workers' quarters on 29 Ogrodowa Street, where newly hired workers were to be employed. After the tenants had moved to Nalewki Street, the buildings and grounds were cleaned up and they began to move in equipment. There was so much of it that the factory yards were literally overflowing with it all. It was said that the part of Ogrodowa Street on which our new shop was to be located was soon to be joined to the Aryan section of town. They began to sign up new workers, setting in motion a fresh flow of bribes. My husband did everything he could to get me entered on the list of workers for the new shop. I was supposed to receive my identification papers any day.

The people in our workers' quarters were setting up individual and communal hiding places. One was located in the attic of the buildings on 71 and 76 Leszno Street and in the neighboring building on 67 Nowolipie Street. Openings were knocked out in the walls so that it was possible to pass from one attic to another. That hiding place, which was reached by a ladder from our stairwell, concealed mainly women, children, and those too infirm for work.

On one of the blistering days of August, we learned that during their morning briefing the Jewish Police had received the following orders. Each one of them was to furnish six persons to the Umschlag-platz. Those unable to do so would pay with their heads. Toward this

51

end blockades were to be set up in the workers' quarters of all the shops in order to roundup all non-working persons and children.

It is difficult to imagine the kind of hell that was unleashed in the ghetto as the police began to implement this order. It was open season on people from early morning on, and even the largest of bribes was of no avail. Anyone caught was automatically lost. Thousands of victims were claimed. It was even worse than it had been with the German blockades, for the Germans didn't know about the hiding places. They knocked down all the doors and took away anyone they found by force. Sixty people were taken from the hiding place in the attic I have just mentioned. They were given away by the father of one of the policemen who had been hiding there himself the previous day. About two hundred people were taken that day from our building alone.

I returned home late that day because I was afraid of being stopped in the yard. In the apartment I found Jadzia and her mother weeping loudly. Her brother had been caught on the street with his wife and three-and-a-half-year-old daughter, the darling of the entire family. They were on their way from Nalewki to Gęsia Street to hide at some relatives' place. It was very early in the morning, and Jadzia's brother, who hadn't heard about the orders to the police, was accompanying his wife and child before going to work.

They were stopped by a policeman, to whom he offered a 10,000 zloty bribe. Normally 500 zlotys was enough for a policeman to set a person free, but now there was no question as to price; the policeman was simply glad to have caught three persons at once. He took them without delay to the Umschlagplatz, from which there was no escaping. They had on them a great amount of money, two gold watches, and a hundred-gram gold bar, all of which they offered in vain to redeem their freedom.

After several hours an officer came to check their identification papers. After showing that he belonged to the K. G. Schultz shop, Jadzia's brother was placed in a group to be set free. His wife, even though she had identification papers, was consigned to the group of the condemned because of the child. Later the group destined to return to work, including Jadzia's brother, was brutally driven off the square. At that moment something happened which Jadzia's brother would never be able to forget. His little daughter suddenly bolted and started running after her father, crying, "Daddy, kiss me one last time; do you still love me? I don't want to be killed by the Germans!"

A German officer knocked her away from her father and shoved him back into the group returning to work.

In subsequent weeks Jadzia's brother came to live with us. He would tell me over and over about being parted from his wife and about his daughter's last words. I saw him every evening weeping before going to bed, hounded by longing for his loved ones and by feelings of guilt for having left them and returned alone. The Nazis had achieved their goal: egoism held sway over morality and feelings. Everyone thought only about saving himself, and there was no longer anything of which a person was not capable.

Jadzia's brother knew not a moment's peace. Whenever he would be unpacking one of his bundles and come across a little dress or other object belonging to his daughter, he would break into a terrible sob. I understood and sympathized with him only too well. As miserable as I was, never knowing what the next day would bring, I consoled him as best I could. I tried to cheer him up by saying his wife and children were surely still alive, that they probably had been sent out into the country to work on the farms. I tried to persuade him that they had been able to buy their freedom and would be coming back some day. I didn't believe my own words even for a moment. I was certain that his wife and daughter were no longer alive. Some go earlier and others later. However, I felt that he, left all alone as he was, was in such desperate need of consolation that I did not regret my dissembling words.

12

MASSACRE IN OTWOCK

This most recent blockade made a terrifying impression on us. That same evening we heard another rumor that a complete blockade was going to be set up the following day in our building and at the factory. We began thinking about where I could go for the day so as not to be found on the factory grounds. That was August 21, and my sister was supposed to vacate her apartment on 84 Żelazna Street the next day. Since that building was not part of the workers' quarters, we knew that most of the tenants would already have moved out, so there was a chance we would be able to have one last day of peace. The following day was warm and sunny, the sky blue; how much there was to live for! We left our apartment at five o'clock in the morning, my husband walking along with us.

Leszno on the odd-numbered side was already fenced off by barbed wire. It was forbidden to live there. Groups of commuting workers were already assembled on the street by the guard house. One or another of the workers would call out our name. We looked around at them and recognized our friends; they were completely changed, pale and haggard. We exchanged a few words with each of them and went along our way.

Finally we arrived at my sister's apartment for this one last day. What a contrast there was with our own apartment. Here everything was bright and clean, and the large windows were open wide. Here there was sunshine, fresh air, and space to move about, while our apartment was cramped, stuffy, and full of bundles piled one on top of the other. It was with a great deal of pleasure that I lay my baby down on a settee near the balcony and breathed a sigh of relief. I had a whole long day to look forward to in which to rest and relax my shattered nerves. How thankful I was to Providence for such brief moments.

My sister went through the apartment from one end to the other, peering into every corner, touching every piece of furniture, stroking it as if it were a warm living object. A woman past forty, childless and unmarried, she had come to love all these things. Each thing, every object had been purchased with her own hard-earned money. It was no wonder that it was difficult for her to leave all this behind. We barely talked to each other all day long. The building was practically deserted. Some people were carrying their belongings from the apartments that were still inhabited out into the courtyard. One after another wagons would drive up and take the things away. Almost everyone was moving to Miła Street. It was relatively peaceful and quiet there compared to the noise and confusion in our building. The baby slept almost the whole day through, and I myself sat dozing. Everything good passes quickly, and this day passed too.

After work my husband came to get us and take us home. There had been no blockade that day because the Death Squad had left Warsaw for Otwock. As we later learned, there had been a general massacre there. The Jewish Police did not follow in the footsteps of their Warsaw confreres. When the Death Squad indicated to them how the population was to be evacuated, they took off their police caps and threw them at the feet of the butchers, refusing to carry out the orders. For this act they were all shot. The Jewish population was for the most part murdered on the spot. We had no more news about these events until several months later, when we chanced to hear a Polish woman recounting with horror the terrible scenes she had witnessed there.

There was unbelievable activity in the courtyard of our building. Workers were gathering before returning to the worker's quarters on Nalewki Street. In front of the food store a long line was waiting for bread, which was issued for ration cards. Business was going full swing. Pickles, tomatoes, and other vegetables were sold at makeshift stands. One could buy cigarettes, clothing and linen. Poles would come here after work in order to sell food, accepting various items in exchange. They would wear them home so as to pass through the guard station the more easily. The men would put on several shirts, two pairs of trousers, and so on. The women would wear a suit or coat over their dress and several pairs of underwear. When a German guard was on duty who looked too closely and started confiscating things, the news would spread and people would wait for a change in the guard, which took place every hour. The same kind of business would be going on at the factory, even though it was strictly forbidden. Poles caught engaging in trade could look forward to Treblinka, and Jews to the Umschlagplatz, which in the end amounted to the same thing. But no one paid any attention, and business went on as before. Various groups would get together and plunder the deserted apartments where a blockade had just occurred. They called this "going looting." They would then sell the things they had stolen.

My husband told me about a character in an adjoining department who had brought the art of looting to new levels. He had a hideous face, and all his mental faculties were concentrated in one direction—to steal and eat! He would buy the best and most expensive items and would eat all day long without stopping, until it made one sick to look at him. Everyone hated him. He would buy large quantities of food in the morning for lower prices and sell them in the evening at a good profit.

There were plenty of others like him. One day one of the workers turned to his comrades and said that someone had stolen his gold watch. When everyone said in unison that no one had touched his watch, he fell into a rage and went to the director—a German—to lodge a complaint. The director said that if the watch didn't turn up, the men would have to put together enough money to buy him a new one. There was nothing else to do. Each worker in the cutting department put in fifty zlotys for a new watch. Men had turned into beasts.

The blockades had temporarily ceased and everyone took a moment's rest. People in the house locked their doors behind them with padlocks as they went to work, leaving a note in German saying "everyone at work." My sister, the baby, and I were all that was left at home.

We moved about as quietly as possible. The windows were shaded because opposite our apartment lived the lawyer Szoszkin, commandant of our factory's Werkschutz. Being quite corpulent, he had a great deal of difficulty climbing up to and down from the fourth floor, so he would sit all day by the window and give orders to his subordinates down below. I was deathly afraid of him. Fortunately, our son was a quiet child, and when he was dry and his stomach full, he would lie for hours in his bed playing with his toes and babbling to himself. He was so delightful that my heart contracted every time I looked at him. How I cursed the fate that had visited such a cataclysm on us. I believed in my heart that what had happened up till now would have a far more

56

tragic epilogue. The worst was yet to come; this was only the calm before the storm.

The first of September arrived, my birthday and the third anniversary of the outbreak of the war. The quiet of the night was suddenly broken by the screaming of factory whistles and automobile sirens. An air raid! We were paralyzed with fear. A drowning man will clutch a straw, as the saying goes. So in our hearts, too, was rekindled just the tiniest glimmer of hope. As soon as the alarm had sounded the skies became lit up with spotlights, and the first bombs began to fall. The men took up positions on the balcony and gazed out with interest at the "Roman candles" (rockets) illuminating the city. It became bright as day. Several powerful explosions and the noise of airplanes circling overhead brought us back to reality. Once more we saw before us the specter of death. We began dressing as quickly as possible.

I wrapped my sleeping child in a feather blanket and we felt our way down the stairs in the darkness. No one said a word to anyone as we sat down on the bottom stairs in the dark, but the silence was punctuated by the increasingly loud and frequent sound of explosions. The ground rumbled beneath our feet as a thunderous noise burst upon us, knocking out all the windows on the opposite side of our building. A gigantic bloody red glare appeared in the sky. Next morning we learned that Kiercelak Square, site of the famous bazaar, had entirely gone up in flames. At the same time several bombs had fallen on the courthouse building on Leszno Street, not far from our factory. A hospital for German soldiers was located on the top two floors of this building, and a large number of them had been killed.

Slowly the noise of the airplanes died away. The candles in the sky went out, and once again it was night. All was quiet; only the glow of fires told us that it had not been a dream. The effects of this air raid were to be of great importance in determining the later course of events in our life.

Next morning Janina dropped by to see us. She was in a terrible state of fright. She told of the destruction which the Soviet air raid had caused and of the panic spreading among the population on the Aryan side. Trains and trams were full with people trying to get out of town. The price of food had sky-rocketed, and business had practically come to a standstill. People were afraid to buy anything when at any moment a bomb could wipe out everything they owned. These forecasts turned out to be justified, as the next several nights brought more alarms, air raids, and devastation. The raids had not made a particularly strong impression on us Jews. We were already condemned to death. Wasn't it better to die from a bomb than in a gas chamber? In any case, we didn't have much time to think about such matters, for several days later the Death Squad returned to Warsaw after having perpetrated its satanical acts in the ghettos of Otwock and Falenica—approximately twenty miles east of Warsaw. Once again we were overcome with terror, as long days of fearful expectation stretched out in front of us, and the blockades and transportation of fresh victims resumed. I no longer went to the factory, for by this time I had obtained identification as a worker in the company and a work permit actually stamped by the German Arbeitsamt (employment office).

13

THE TRAP SPRINGS SHUT

One day when my husband returned from work K. G. Schultz's chauffeur was waiting for him in the yard. The chauffeur wanted to buy a wall-hanging from us. He took the tapestry, said he would be back in a minute, and left. An hour passed, then two, and still my husband hadn't returned. I was not so much surprised at my husband's absence as at the silence outside in the yard. Usually business would be going full swing at this time of day, but today not a single person was to be seen, not even Jadzia's husband, who usually showed up punctually at the dinner hour.

I had little time to ponder what all this meant, since I had been doing laundry since morning, and it was time to feed the baby. Suddenly someone knocked loudly at the door. My sister in her fright opened it. In walked a policeman, asking for me. He told me to get dressed as quickly as possible, take the baby, and come with him, for my husband had so instructed. I obeyed him instantly. Because the weather that day was hot I merely put on a raincoat and wrapped the baby, who was dressed in a light batiste shirt, in a shawl. Instinctively I also took my leather handbag.

The Werkschutz by the gate stopped us and didn't want to let us in, saying that he had orders not to let anyone pass. In vain the policeman begged him as a fellow policeman to let us through. Nothing worked. Finally, seeing no other way, I tried a typical feminine guile: I began to cry, saying that I needed to be with my husband. I appealed to his fatherly instincts, for I could see that he was no longer young. Finally, after much pleading, he came over to our side and let us in. I could still hear him saying, "I just hope you won't regret it." At the time I didn't pay any attention, but later his warning rang again and again in my ears.

I got onto the factory grounds without difficulty, for my husband was waiting for me by the gate. He paid the policeman fifty zlotys for bringing me and the baby to him. I looked around the factory yard. It was full of people: in the entryways, in the yards, and on the stairs. Surprised, I asked my husband what was going on.

I learned that K. G. Schultz had issued an order in which he informed his workers that German blockades were to be set up that day in the workers' quarters on Nalewki and Leszno streets. In order to protect his workers' families and children, he advised everyone to gather at the factory, so that he would be able to defend them more effectively. He had sent a special escort of Jewish Police to accompany the workers' wives and children to the factory on Leszno Street and to see that they arrived safely.

I looked carefully around, and in the middle of the group I saw Schultz for the first time. He was of immense stature, and stood out from everyone around him. He had cold, light-blue eyes. I could read such cruelty in those eyes and such contempt for the crowd around him, that all at once, as if by divine revelation, I saw through and understood everything.

"This is a trap! It is nothing but a trick! He has tricked you all, and you were stupid enough to believe him. Now we are in his power. We have to get out of here by whatever means possible," I told my husband.

My words must have had the power of conviction, for my husband, who hasn't a bone of cunning or trickery in his body and instinctively trusts everyone, believed me without my saying a further word. We had to get out of there, but how? The Werkschutz at the gates had orders to let everyone in but not to let anyone out under pain of death. Nothing was going to work; the trap had already sprung. No one else, as it turned out, had any idea that this was a trick on the part of K. G. Schultz. On the contrary, they praised him for wanting to protect us. There was no point in standing out in the yard, so we went into the entryway where I used to sit on the third floor early in the morning and wait until I would be let into the joiner's apartment. We found it full of people, mostly women and children who expected to find shelter and safety there. I didn't want to shatter their illusions. Why not give them a few more moments of peace?

We sat down on the stairs. My husband regained his habitual faith in people and began trying to convince me that I was wrong. He said that I was hypersensitive, that my nerves were frazzled, and that was why I saw everything in dark colors. This was only going to be a personnel check. Since we both had identification and work permits, we would surely be set free. These arguments did nothing to convince me he was right, but I was so paralyzed with fear that I was unable to think clearly.

Two steps up from me sat our former neighbor and landlord, Szwejd. I looked at him as he sat there in gloomy silence with his head bent low, eating candies one after another. Next to him was one of our present neighbors, a man who worked in the same department as my husband, Ehrlich, with his wife and child. They were both concentrating so deeply on how to get out of this situation that they didn't even notice us. My husband kept trying to calm me down. As his most convincing argument, he added that as he was going through the yard, Jadzia had stopped him and asked if he knew where her husband was. If Jadzia had had any inkling of anything suspicious, he said, she would have warned us while there was still time to hide. Only later was I to learn that she actually had known then, for the factory had advance knowledge of the matter. Jadzia had gone into hiding with her husband and mother without warning us.

After a while there was some movement on the lower floors. The electrifying news reached us in a trice: Germans were in the yard! We knocked at the door of the joiner's apartment and begged him to let us in if only because of the child. They opened the door for us, and a great throng of people pressed in after us, including Schwejd and his family. A terrible uproar and dispute ensued, for the apartment owner had not wanted to let anyone in besides us. He tried to shove back the oncoming waves of people, but they were stronger than he was. Fighting broke out, and the resulting tumult and uproar attracted the attention of a policeman, who said that everyone without exception had to leave the apartment and go down to the yard. Looking through the open door, I saw how Schwejd, Ehrlich and his family, and several other persons took advantage of the policeman's distracted attention and ran upstairs. Much later I learned that they had gotten onto the roof through a trap door and made it from 78 to 76 Leszno Street and from there to 67 Nowolipie, where they climbed back down. In this way they had temporarily saved themselves.

In a few minutes the apartment became deserted except for the owner, us, and the policeman, who ordered us to go downstairs immediately. Once more I broke into tears and begged him to let us stay. He let me and the baby remain, but my husband had to go. I was left alone, because the owners of the apartment also went downstairs, leaving the keys with me. Several minutes later my husband returned and begged me not to risk death needlessly when the Germans would open the door and find me there alone in the apartment. So we both went downstairs.

In the yard stood two Germans with rubber truncheons, glowering with bloodshot eyes at the people hunched over and cowering around them. My child, tired out from the heat, was sleeping peacefully in my arms, oblivious to the fact that our lives were hanging in the balance. My legs bent underneath me when I saw those cut-throats so eager for our lives. At that moment the sister of Jadzia's husband walked past, carrying an entire loaf of bread under her arm. I remembered that we hadn't had anything to eat since morning, and asked her for a piece of bread. She declined, saying that she didn't want to cut the bread because it would dry out.

The Germans and the factory leadership were standing together at the gatehouse. One of the Germans, as it later turned out, was the renowned criminal Brandt, known for his cruelty and murder of the Jews. (He was captured after the war and imprisoned, but unfortunately managed to escape.) As he directed the action, he asked Schultz whether there were any Jews in the factory itself. Schultz replied that the only ones left there were Aryans. Then engineer Koszutski took out a list of workers and called out the names of all the bigwigs, who were let into the factory. Next the director's clique went to the entrance gate and posted a single German and the factory guards there to make sure that no one else got in.

My husband had observed what was going on in the yard from the windows of the second story. When he saw Koszutski calling out names from the list of workers, he was sure that it was only a routine identification check, as Schultz himself had said beforehand. That was why he had called me downstairs.

In the meantime the police had begun to empty out all the apartments. Sentries were placed at all the entryways. When we wanted to return to the apartment after figuring out what was happening, it was already too late. The route had been cut off.

In the factory's second courtyard, there were piles of scaffolding, and many mothers had hidden their children behind them. Without anyone looking after them, the children were crying piteously. I saw the Germans send the police over to get them out from there.

Since the second courtyard was empty, we headed for the main one, which was incredibly crowded. People pressed in on one another from all sides, the Germans were shouting, and Koszutski was trying to keep order by hitting people on the head and shoulders with a big stick. Brandt too, holding a stick in his hand like the brigand he was, was hitting anyone he could reach on the head and back. We were in the thick of the crowd, and my husband got it from Brandt on the back by trying to escape Koszutski.

All of this waiting around, full of foreboding, was trying our patience, and we began to press forward toward the exit gates. There Schultz was standing in the midst of several Germans, segregating people according to his personal whim.

"Links! Rechts!" we could hear the commands.

We were sent to the right, in other words, out into the street, where a huge throng of people was already huddled together in rows of sixes. The column of people was so long that we couldn't even see the beginning. The Jewish Police and the Ukrainians formed a barricade on one side and made certain that the command was faithfully executed. Brandt, who was in charge, told everyone in the midst of the uproar and tumult that there was no use hiding, because sooner or later everyone would be evacuated anyway.

14

MARCH TO THE UMSCHLAGPLATZ

When it came our turn, Schultz looked long enough to see that I had a child and sent me to the right. He asked my husband what section he was from and how long he had been working, and when he heard that he had only been working for a few weeks, he sent him to the right as well. Everyone going to the right was automatically beaten by the Germans, and then the Jewish Police would tell people what to do if they didn't want to get more. Anyone counting on someone's protection would shout out the name of his protector together with his own name in order to attract attention to himself. In some cases this worked, and the protector would have the man taken out of the line. In some cases it didn't work, and the shouting would only attract the attention of the Ukrainians and Germans, who would beat the person until he was quiet. We simply sat still, for we had no one to call on for help.

More and more people kept piling up in back of us. At one point Fraulein Geiger, a German woman in charge of the knitted goods department, walked past. She was engaged to Brandt, the man in charge. I remember how in my deranged state her appearance struck me like something out of a dream. Dressed in a blue taffeta dress, full of smiles and blooming with health and contentment, she presented a striking contrast to her surroundings. She seemed more like out of a film than part of our reality. It had been she who had installed little electric cutting machines in the cutting department instead of knives for fear of an uprising. Suddenly a woman sitting next to us stood up and began calling out loudly: "Fraulein Geiger, it's me!", and she gave her name. Fraulein Geiger didn't even look in her direction. The woman did attract the attention of a German, however, who told her to shut up and began beating her with a rubber truncheon. The woman was shrieking from the pain, but the German only beat her harder until she finally obeyed his command to be silent.

Suddenly we heard a command: "On your feet!" We started moving. The setting sun cast red reflections on the roofs of the houses. We walked along in silence, escorted on all sides by Germans and Ukrainians. The uneven clatter of shoes sounded against the pavement. We were being driven like animals. From time to time the heavy blows of a truncheon would ring out against someone's back. I received one blow myself. I was no longer able to carry my child, even though he weighed very little, so my husband took the precious burden from me. My sole concern was that the child not got hit by a policeman. I remember thinking that I was looking at my beloved Warsaw for the last time. The buildings which I had walked past so many times without thinking anything about it now took on symbolic meaning. I looked at the sky. The last streaks of light from the setting sun illuminated the dismal procession. The day was coming to an end. Who did not know whether we would ever see another, whether we would ever live to see the Day of Liberation which millions of unfortunate and innocently condemned people so longed for and expected. No, we would never live to see that day.

My short life passed in front of me like a moving picture show. My childhood. Trying to get an education. Trying to make a living. The trouble finding a job during the Depression. The years spent trying to put together a normal life. My mother's death. The death of my father, killed by the Germans. My happy marriage. My faithful, loving husband and friend. Our work together. Our dear little apartment, where everything had been bought with the money which we had so laboriously earned together, where every object had a special place in our hearts. This, the most beautiful period in our lives, was gone forever. And now, with two tiny daughters in the grave[1] and a three-and-a-half-month-old mite of a boy in our arms, to have everything crumble beneath our feet into nothingness. We were going to die! But why? Because we were Jews.

I looked at my dear ones walking alongside me. The little one was sleeping against the shoulders of his father. He was beautiful and pink. My true friend in fortune and misfortune was supporting me with his other arm and helping me along. I suddenly shuddered as the vision of the bloody corpse of a woman lying in front of 76 Leszno Street came to mind. On Karmelicka Street someone tried to escape from the column of the condemned, but the butchers were right on his heels, and he did not make it.

Our route led from Leszno to Karmelicka, then along Dr. Zamenhof Street to Stawki, where the Umschlagplatz was located. The same thing happened at Zamenhof: someone tried to escape from the column, but without success. In the very beginning some people had managed to leave and hide in the empty buildings. The Jewish Police looked the other way as they went, for they knew the Ukrainians only too well. It was in this way that city counselor Wolfowicz got away. He belonged to the family of Rowiński, who owned the factory, and had been on the factory grounds by accident. I must mention here that the Jewish Police during these operations was under the command of its deputy commandant, counselor Lejkin,[2] a well-known converted Jew and scoundrel. The Germans called him "Der kleine Napoleon," because he was so short. This insignificant little man always had a huge dog with him and a riding crop in his hand. Scrupulously dressed in tall knee-boots, he did whatever he could to do his German superiors' bidding.

Several people on the way to the Umschlagplatz tried to bribe the Ukrainians, who were particularly eager for gold watches. When my husband saw what was happening, he too went up to one of the Jewish policemen, but it was already too late, for we were getting close to our destination.

By the time we arrived, darkness had set in. I heard several more blows, loud shouting, and swearing in Ukrainian and German. We were driven en masse inside some building. It was pitch dark inside, and at first we couldn't get our bearings. I felt my shoes stepping into something sticky and slippery, and the awful stench of human excrement enveloped us from all sides. It seemed as though we had been driven into one large outhouse. Slowly our eyes became accustomed to the darkness. The first thing we noticed was that most of the people had gone somewhere else.

There were a few crates standing around, but there were so many people on them that it was impossible to find room. Most people had bundles and knapsacks with them, and they were using them for sitting on. I asked someone to let me sit down with the baby for ten minutes or so. Silence. I became seized with anger and started shouting in people's faces: "What's wrong with you people? Don't you have any heart? You've been sitting here for hours, and you can't find a place for me and my baby?"

Suddenly a woman who had been dozing by the wall leapt up and with a pitiful sob ran over to us and covered the arms of my son with kisses. "A baby!" she cried. "I left my own ten-year-old child at home with no one to look after him."

She let me have her place, saying that she had been there since the previous day. There were too few people to make up a shipment, so they were waiting for more. She had been taken from the factory in the same way we had. I was anxious to ask her whether the Germans, Ukrainians, and Latvians were here too, for I was afraid that at any moment the entire horde would descend on us with their customary shouting, beating, and shooting. She assured me that as soon as the cutthroats brought a load of people to the square, they would hand them over to the Jewish Police and leave. She explained that we were in the old quarters of the archives on Stawki Street, which during the war was serving as a hospital for the treatment of contagious diseases. The building next to us was a children's hospital.

When she heard that I hadn't had a bite to eat since morning, she tore off a piece of bread and offered me some. My throat and tongue were so dry that I couldn't swallow. I was dying of thirst. There was a water faucet, but nothing to hold the water in. No one wanted to loan a bottle, not trusting that people would bring it back.

While we were talking my husband was looking around for a policeman he might know who could help get us out of this inferno. Our chances were very slim, but it was still worth a try. Money was the main consideration. All we had with us was five hundred zlotys and two gold watches, one belonging to my husband and the other, with a gold band, to me. My husband had given it to me on our first anniversary. It was one of my most cherished possessions, and I never went anywhere without it. Luck was on our side, for my husband found a policeman he knew standing guard at the entrance to the building. He had lived in the building next to ours and was active in civic affairs, which was where he and my husband had met.

When he saw my husband, he was very surprised. "What, you're here, Mr. S.? Don't you worry. We'll do whatever we can to get you out."

My husband comforted me and told me to keep my spirits up. By a fortunate coincidence he had found in his pocket a small medicine bottle which he used to carry tea concentrate to work and, worth a fortune at the time, a sugar cube. Because of the bottle we were able to satisfy our thirst, and the sugar cube was our baby's meal for the night. I tore off a piece of his batiste shirt, moistened it in water and wrapped the sugar in it. The baby began to suck it greedily. There was not a single drop of milk left in my breasts.

------

1. **Two tiny daughters**. According to information provided by Marta Dutkiewicz Schmidt, Mrs. Schmidt lost two infant daughters to tuberculosis transmitted to them by their maid.
2. **Lejkin, Jakub** (1906-1942). A lawyer before the war, Lejkin was deputy commander of the Jewish Police. Known for his brutality, he played a leading role in the deportation of the Warsaw Jews to the death camp in Treblinka before being assassinated in 1942 by the Jewish Combat Organization.

15

NIGHT ON THE UMSCHLAGPLATZ

The stench and heat were unbearable. People were simply letting their excrement fall where they stood, and it smelled so horrible that we literally couldn't breathe. On the floor near the entrance lay an old woman, her face wrinkled and yellow, the last signs of life quickly fading from her eyes. People were stepping over her as if she wasn't even there. She let out such an agonized moan that it sent shivers down my spine. After a while I couldn't bear sitting there any longer and we felt our way in the dark out into the large courtyard. People were sleeping here packed tightly next to one another. It was impossible to pass by without stepping on an arm or a leg, and every time it happened it would unleash a stream of invectives and curses. I sat down on the ground and looked up at the sky. It was a beautiful night. I looked around at the dark spots that were people covering the ground, breathing heavily. Some of them were snoring. It seemed to me that I had already experienced something similar in a dream. Or maybe this here was merely a dream which would soon be over. Maybe in another minute I would wake up in a clean bed in my old apartment.

Suddenly the sound of a shot brought me back to reality. Next morning we learned what those shots, repeated several times during the night, had been about. The Umschlagplatz was surrounded by a high wall guarded by Germans and Ukrainians. Taking advantage of the dark, people would climb up onto the wall surrounding the square and try to escape. Many tried their luck, staking their life on a single card.

They had little to lose. Most of them were spotted by the German guards and shot on the spot. Very few actually made it.

I wasn't able to stay seated in the yard for very long, for I had nothing to rest my back against, so I returned to where I had come from. During my absence the old woman on the floor had passed away. I sat motionless, holding my baby in my lap. My arms and legs were very sore, but I couldn't move for fear of disturbing the baby. My heart couldn't bear the sound of his crying.

The wailing of factory sirens broke the stillness. An alarm. I began praying to God for a miracle—for bombs to knock down the walls surrounded by Germans, to reduce it all to rubble so we could get out of this living hell. Or, if we had to die, then let the bombs fall on this building and kill us without further suffering and pain. Death, yes, but not such a disgraceful death at the hands of our mortal enemies. But my prayers went unanswered. There had been no air raid, only an alarm. My husband, who was just getting over a serious attack of bronchitis, spent the night on the asphalt floor near where the Jewish Police were stationed on the outside. He was waiting for the right moment for us to make our escape, but since he didn't have any money on him, the policemen wanted nothing to do with him.

During the night my husband could probably have gotten out of the Umschlagplatz dressed as a policeman, but he didn't want to leave me and the child. They worked it in the following way. One of the policemen would lend his cap and armband (the rest of their uniform was civilian) for a thousand zlotys. For greater security he would throw in his badge for an extra five hundred zlotys. A second policeman, pretending that they were together, would smuggle the person past the German sentry. Once they were past the sentry, the policeman would put the individual up with the custodian of the house at the far end of his beat. The person would stay there until morning when he could go home, and the policeman would return to the Umschlagplatz with the cap and armband. A number of men, and supposedly also some women in men's clothing, had managed to escape in this way.

Finally this infernal night came to an end. The morning was beautiful and sunny. People got up off their bundles and stretched their bones. They looked at me with tired yellow faces, a burnt-out and hopeless expression in their eyes. Among them were sixteen- and seventeen-year-olds, clinging to the belief that they were going to work on the farms with the peasants. Whenever they would ask one of the Jewish policemen where the trains were taking them, the police would reply: "To Małkin; there they'll segregate the people. The young and

70

healthy will be sent to work somewhere, and the old people and women with children will be killed." Listening to those conversations, I asked myself: Are the police being deceived too, or is this just an act of kindness on their part, so that these young people— children really—who had never tasted anything of life would perish in ignorance and delusion? No one had even the slightest idea about the crematoria and the other satanical inventions. The day we were on the Umschlagplatz, when thousands of Jews were waiting for trains to take them to Treblinka, pretty young girls were powdering their cheeks so they would look young and fresh. Everyone believed that they were going to a camp where they would be assigned to work according to the state of their health.

My husband, who hadn't slept all night, looked terrible. He wore his face like a tragic mask. His nerves were completely frazzled. He told me that our policeman, Frogier, who had promised to help us, had gone off duty and left for home on his bicycle. My husband had sent a letter through him to Jadzia, begging her to loan us 5,000 zlotys. Frogier promised to do what he could and left, leaving us in the care of his friend. Our new protector said he would do whatever he could as soon as a "good" watch came on duty, which could be bribed. In spite of this, we were feeling very low and depressed. I was most worried about the baby.

I gave him my dry breast in the hope that he could at least get a couple of drops from it. He sucked and tugged all he could and then, frustrated, began to cry loudly and inconsolably. He was hungry and I had nothing to give him. The same thought kept rolling through my tired brain: What could I give my baby to eat so he wouldn't be hungry? I suddenly remembered there was a children's hospital in the next building. Perhaps I could get help there.

We went into the yard next to the rear part of the hospital. We noticed a number of aides bustling about, but they were deaf to our shouts. People called over to them so often that they had stopped paying any attention. I wanted one of them to take a message to Dr. Braude-Hellerowa, the head doctor.[1] She belonged to the Bund[2] and was well known for her civic and party work.

There didn't seem to be anything to do; still, the compelling thought of placing my baby in the hospital at least for a little while had taken hold of me and gave me no peace, so I stood by the exit and looked for some way. Suddenly I noticed a nurse who appeared to be coming on duty. I called out to her and asked her to take the baby, to put it in a bed for a little while and give it something to eat. She looked at my beloved baby, who looked back at her so seriously with its beautiful eyes that she took him from me, telling me to wait right there. She returned after a couple of minutes, saying that they didn't want to take him because he wasn't sick, and that my duty was to remain with my child until the end. I was thoroughly downcast, but I didn't give up. I waited in the same place until I saw another nurse. Seeing that I wasn't going to get anywhere by telling the truth, I tried lying. I told her that I wasn't the child's mother, that he belonged to another woman in my apartment who had been gone during the blockade. I had taken him because I was afraid he would be killed. I asked her to take the baby into the hospital and give it something to eat, for it hadn't had anything since the previous day. After she went off duty, she should take him back to his grandmother, who would pay her for her kindness. I gave her our address on Leszno Street and Jadzia's name. She wrote it all down and took the baby. We looked at each other with relief. The baby was taken care of for the moment.

The yard was bounded on one side by a high wall and on the other by the building we were in and the hospital. At the end was a large gate with a sign: NO ENTRY UNDER PENALTY OF DEATH. Beyond the gate were the railroad tracks where the freight trains came every evening at six o'clock to take on their wretched "load" of two hundred people per car. We looked on this place with terror. If the cars had been here yesterday evening when we arrived, we would have been loaded onto them and by now would be dead. Till his last dying breath a person keeps hoping, or deceiving himself, which amounts to the same thing.

We looked around the yard. One would have sworn that it was a camp of beggars. People who yesterday at work had looked decent and presentable now presented a deplorable sight. Their clothes were rumpled and covered with dirt and dust; their faces were unwashed and unshaven. Children with no idea of what was going on were crying for food and drink. The yard was full of smoke from fires. Some people had brought with them a pot or a pan, and there were many far-sighted people who had brought dishes with them with the idea that they would come in handy "during resettlement." They were boiling water and even kasha and potatoes. We were amazed that anyone at such a tragic moment in their lives could sit there calmly boiling soup. We realized that they didn't know what we did. I thought to myself that they had it better, for they didn't know their death was at hand.

Someone offered us a loaf of bread for sixty zlotys. We bought it even though we weren't able to swallow a bite, our mouths were so dry. We went back to our "post" in the stinking "toilet" (our name for the hall) to find out from Frogier's replacement how matters stood. He had bad news. The watch was being taken over from eight o'clock in the morning until eight o'clock at night by counselor Szmerling,[3] senior district supervisor of the Jewish Police. His very name struck fear into the hearts of his men. Frogier's friend pointed him out to us. He was sitting in the middle of the street surrounded by several policemen. He was tall, square-shouldered, about forty years old, and had a prominent belly. His sullen face wore a clearly evil expression. A close-cut dark beard covered a severe mouth. He made an utterly revolting impression on us. We asked the policeman what sort of person he was. He said that he was a converted Jew and on the Umschlagplatz lord and master. He enjoyed the confidence and trust of the Germans, because he was so zealous in carrying out their instructions. With him in charge not a single person would get out, for he sat in the middle of the street and kept his eyes on everything. Even when a German came to get someone, he had to have the proper papers or would go away empty-handed. It was our bad luck to have him on duty that day, and there seemed no question of our getting away. Later we learned that Szmerling had his price too. He would let a person go for 10,000 zlotys or more. He made a fortune that way.

We began to lose all hope. My husband asked me how I viewed our situation and I told him why bother talking about it, because it was all over now. I said bitterly that the world was full of venality and thievery and that his friend Frogier would never be back. Even if Jadzia gave him the money he would just take it and go. Why should he try to get us freed if he already had the money? I sat down on one of the crates and started crying hysterically and uncontrollably. The woman who had left her son behind joined in with me, and so did another young woman sitting on my other side. The three of us cried hopelessly, but I cried loudest of all. I was seized with an animal lust for life. I felt that I was now capable of the most desperate act in order to get out of there. I wailed that I didn't want to die a disgraceful and hideous death in the gas chambers. How could they all let themselves be led like mindless lambs to the slaughter without so much as an act or even a word of protest? The people standing around looked at me in amazement. Some of them surely thought I had gone mad.

---

1. **Braude-Hellerowa, Dr. Anna (1888-1943)**. Pediatrician and socio-polit-

ical activist of Jewish extraction, head of the Bersohn & Bauman Children's Hospital in Warsaw, located in the Jewish ghetto. Along with the sick children of the hospital, she perished in the hospital basement during the Warsaw Ghetto Uprising. Mrs. Schmidt writes that she died in Treblinka.

2. **Bund** (General Jewish Labor Bund). A Jewish socialist party in Poland that promoted the welfare of Jewish workers, sought to combat anti-Semitism, and was generally opposed to Zionism, i.e., the establishment of a Jewish homeland in the historic lands of Israel.

3. **Szmerling, Mieczysław**. A former boxer of Jewish extraction, Szmerling was district supervisor of the Jewish Police and commandant of the Umschlagplatz.

16

NEXT MORNING

The eyes of the dead woman opened wide in a glassy stare. She seemed to say: "I don't have any more earthly cares. I have it better than all of you." Whether under the influence of this gaze or for some other reason, my fit of madness left me in a second. I felt so weak and helpless, caught up in some kind of horrendous nightmare, in a trap with no exit. I was seized with a terrible wave of self-pity, for my dear ones, and for all those around me. I began praying fervently in my own words to the Lord, our only comfort and salvation. I went into a strange kind of ecstatic trance. For the first time in my life I felt that I had ceased to be a living person of flesh and blood and had become pure spirit. I prayed for a miracle, for some way out. I felt certain that if there were a God, then he surely must have heard my call. Evidently He did hear me for a miracle was about to occur.

Slowly I pulled myself together. I heard the soothing voice of my husband, and made out the comforting words he was speaking. He was stroking me on my arm and on my face, wet with tears. He said that after all I was not alone, and that everything was not yet lost.

It was nine o'clock in the morning, and the gates kept opening and shutting with a clatter as policemen appeared, loaded down with packages and knapsacks, calling out the names of those for whom they were intended. The packages, containing essential personal effects, had been sent for a certain amount of money by the families and friends of those who had been suddenly caught and sent to the Umschlagplatz.

Later a hearse drove up and carried away the corpse of the old woman and several others who had died during the night. Next some people appeared with brooms and shovels. They began to clean the whole building. Among them we recognized some of our acquaintances who had occupied important positions before the war in firms with which my husband did business. Instead of cleaning up, they leaned their brooms and shovels against the wall and started asking who wanted to send letters through them to their family or friends. People began crowding around and haggling. The price ranged from twenty to fifty zlotys per letter. The clean-up men stayed almost two hours before they finally took their brooms and shovels and left, without ever having used them for anything. They left behind the rubbish and ghastly smell, and I am certain that none of those letters ever reached its destination.

Almost the entire cutting department where my husband had worked had been taken. My husband pointed out engineer Jakubowicz to me; he had been sent to the Umschlagplatz, and his wife, a Pole, and their daughter had come along with him of their own accord. (We learned later that all three of them had been set free.) We also ran into the man with the four-year-old son in whose place I had spent several days on Ogrodowa Street. When I asked about his wife, he said that she had been sick and unable to accompany the group which K. G. Schultz had supposedly organized in order to save them. She had stayed home and thus actually been saved. Young Marek, for that was the boy's name, looked with such hungry eyes at the bread I was holding in my arm that my heart practically broke in two just looking at the poor little creature. I tore off a piece of bread and gave it to the youngster, receiving in return the thankful gaze of his father.

Suddenly we heard someone shouting. It seemed that some of the German directors from the factories had come asking for their workers to be set free. As if at the wave of a magic wand, everyone started running to get as close as possible. Hope was visible in every face. Limbs became taut, eyes full of fire. We went together with the others. Several thousand people were gathered in front of the iron gate. Through it we saw some soldiers and civilians come off the street and go over to Szmerling and show him some documents. Slowly and indifferently, he looked through them, as if it were not a matter of human lives at all. I instinctively felt that he would have preferred to send everyone under his charge to their deaths rather than part with any one of them. How intensely I loathed him at that moment!

After a long examination he returned the papers and indicated to the policeman that it was all right to call out the names on the list, almost all of which were men. People began shoving. Those with names similar to the ones being called would come forward and the police would look over their identification papers thoroughly before turning them over to Szmerling. From there they went to the waiting factory representative, who arranged them into a column of threes and marched them over to the guardhouse for further inspection, and only then were they finally let outside... "free" once again. Thousands of envious gazes followed them along their route.

Not very many were set free, several dozen at most, all of them professionals or "bigwigs" who had been taken by mistake. From our factory only Dr. Knaster and a few others were released. Most came from the Big Schultz shop on Nowolipie. We stood there for several hours, hoping in vain to hear our names called.

We were getting ready to leave when we heard such a pitiful and heart-rending whimpering that it sent chills down my spine. We looked around to see a young woman, no more than twenty years old, holding a wrapped-up blanket next to her body. It was from this bundle that the squeals were coming. We went over to her and she showed us a six-week-old baby dressed in nothing but a little shirt. She told us that when she had had to relieve herself during the night she had left the baby in the care of some people whose faces she didn't recognize because of the darkness. When she returned she found the baby undressed and his things stolen along with a large pillow. Her breasts had completely dried up and the baby hadn't eaten for more than twenty-four hours.

She was alone and didn't know what to do. I looked at the baby's little face. It was contorted into an expression of profound weariness and suffering. I started to choke; I felt that in another moment I would faint. With the greatest effort I managed to produce from my throat a voice whose sound was completely alien to me. I could see that under the circumstances it was no use trying to help the baby, but I wanted at all costs to spare the unfortunate mother from having to watch the last hours of her baby's life. I told her how I had given my own baby to the hospital and I advised her to do the same. The woman did as I said, and it must have worked, for later I saw her by herself.

After a while I noticed the presence on the square of Dr. Braude-Hellerowa. Since she had been to our apartment several times in her capacity as doctor, and we knew each other fairly well, I went up to her and told her how I had given my baby over to the hospital earlier that morning. She looked at me with a horrified expression and cried out, "Woman, what have you done? Go and get your baby while there is still time!"

I didn't even wait for her to finish before I began running. I hid so she couldn't find me, afraid that they would take my baby out of the bed where he was at least able to rest, and then my worries would begin all over again. It was only much later that I understood what this worthy doctor was trying to tell me.

Suddenly a neat and decent-looking man about fifty years old came up to us and with a pleading expression asked for some bread. We gave him a small piece and he ate it greedily, blessing and thanking us all the while. By way of explanation for his request, he said that he had been released that morning from the hospital. Since he had nowhere to go, he had tried to take his own life, once by slashing his wrists and the second time by cutting his throat. He showed us the fresh wounds. Both times he had been saved from death, but since he didn't know what to do with himself after leaving the hospital, he had come to the Umschlagplatz voluntarily. We tried to encourage him, saying that since he was a tailor, he would be sent to the provinces and would surely find work there. He thanked us warmly. We felt that at least for the time being life for him had begun to take on a different hue.

Starting at noon, new groups of people began to arrive from town for shipment. The same kind of trap had been set in the other factories. From the smaller shops almost everyone had been taken. New groups continued to arrive without interruption all through the day. As we looked at the growing throngs of people, we realized that by five o'clock there would be enough for a shipment. Then no force on earth would be able to rescue us. They told how one very rich person, after he was already in the wagon, had offered half a million zlotys for his release, but by then it was too late.

We located our policeman, who said that there was nothing to be done at the moment, and that Frogier hadn't come back yet. We were at the end of our rope. Someone told us that we could get hot tea on the second floor. After a long search we finally found the stairs. An amazing sight met us upstairs. We entered a spacious room with a number of large tables, holding for the most part people who were sleeping. On the wall were several gas outlets, and some resourceful people had put together makeshift stoves. Pots of food, water, and other things were cooking on them. We asked for a little hot water.

"Do you have a pot?" was the first question.

"No, I don't," I answered.

"Nothing's loaned here and nothing's for free," we heard, for our further edification.

I began explaining that I would drink it right there and wouldn't be taking a pot. This time I received an even briefer reply: "Nothing here's for free."

At last I understood. For two zlotys they poured a little bit of hot water into a dirty pot and added something to it that was supposed to be cocoa. Actually it was something that only gave a brownish-red tint to the water. Why they had a box of cocoa with them when they knew that the road led from here to Treblinka, I couldn't say. I swallowed a couple of mouthfuls of this abomination, but I couldn't force myself to drink any more of it. My husband, however, who had developed a very bad cough, drank it down eagerly, saying: "You haven't been in the army, so you don't know how good something can taste when there isn't anything better." We stretched out on one of the tables, where a place had suddenly been vacated, in order to rest and collect our thoughts.

Compared to the tumult downstairs, it was relatively quiet up here, but my husband was unable to sit still even for a minute. He was aware that he was losing contact with Frogier and our only chance of getting out. He had been sitting all night by a grated window facing the street and was no longer himself.

17

THE MIRACLE

I slowly dozed off. I don't know how long I lay there. I was awakened by someone at my arm. I looked around and saw it was my husband, who was very excited by something. He said that Frogier had just come on his bicycle. He had brought 3500 zlotys from Jadzia, and said that he wouldn't leave us until we were set free; if not today, then he would try to hide us until morning. He had taken another look at the watch which my husband had showed him as an incentive. Frogier said that he was mainly concerned with saving people, especially his friends, but I had the definite feeling that in the back of his mind the gold watch and its exquisitely fashioned band were the primary considerations. He had taken a real liking to that watch. Whatever he may have been thinking wasn't important. He conducted himself honorably, for he could simply have taken the money for himself and no one would have ever been the wiser.

Frogier went to look for a temporary hiding place, because soon they would be bringing up the railroad cars and loading people onto them. He ordered us to stand by the exit and wait for his return. We stood there, deaf and insensitive to the jostling and abuse people hurled at us for blocking the way. It was around three o'clock in the afternoon, and the increasing tension could be felt in the air. I gave someone our bottle (a treasure) to get water and shared our bread with several people. Our savior came at last and said that for six hundred zlotys we would be let into the hospital, but we had to be extremely careful.

We would have to go several paces along the sidewalk beneath the wall, but in such a way that counselor Szmerling, who was sitting in the middle of the street, would not notice. If we caught his attention we would have to return, and then it would be all over with us. We each had to go across alone. The main thing was to create the impression that we were out walking by ourselves. In case Szmerling should see us and find out the name of the policeman who was helping us, the policeman would have to hand in his cap on the spot, which meant he would be loaded onto the cars and sent to his death along with everyone else.

We waited until someone struck up a conversation with Szmerling, and then I, as the first, my heart in my throat and my brain reeling, stepped out in the name of God onto the pavement and tiptoed along the wall. I arrived safely, and, seconds later, so did my husband. Several policemen were standing by the gate of the hospital, guarding the entrance. Frogier asked them to let us in. He put us in a room on the ground floor and told us to wait for his return. There were several other people in the room who had gotten there in the same manner. They told us that two days ago, as the freight cars were being loaded, the Germans broke into the room and summarily shot the several dozen people hiding there. Once more a shudder went down my back. Instead of being able to relax, we remained in the utmost danger.

We looked around to see whether we could at least find a temporary hiding place. There were three other rooms in addition to ours, all of them completely empty. The grated windows looked out on the street. If someone stood on a bench and looked in from the outside, we would all be discovered, for there was no furniture of any kind to hide behind. We weren't allowed to go out into the hallway for fear the Germans might look into the building through the large glass doors.

People who had gotten there earlier had already locked themselves in the toilet. We had no other choice but to entrust ourselves to fate and try our luck. We lay down on the floor next to the radiator. For a very high price several of the women had borrowed spare nurses' aprons and caps from the hospital personnel. They put them on and, armed with rags, began straightening and cleaning up. Before long the place was swarming with these "cleaning ladies." Not being in the mood for such tricks, we stayed put.

The hands on the clock moved slowly. Suddenly several shots rang out on the street, followed by shouting. A horde of frenzied Ukrainians, Latvians, and Germans were unleashing another attack with their sticks against the bent backs of some newly arrived people being driven into the enclosure, as my husband, who couldn't resist taking a peek, was able to discern. He whispered to me that he had noticed among the crowd a new group of people from our factory who had been set free the night before by K. G. Schultz.

At the very rear of the mournful procession he had seen a man and wife whom we knew from before the war, when they had managed an elegant tourist hotel in Śródborów. We had spent the last two summers with them before the outbreak of the war. Now they walked along bent over in despair. She was wearing a robe and carrying several bundles in her arms. Evidently the blockade had caught them by surprise.

We didn't have time to think of any of the others because a deafening roar arose out of the shrieks and inhuman moans welling up from thousands of human breasts. The atmosphere among those in the room became tense with expectancy.

"The wagons! It's started!" my husband said and crouched down on the floor next to me.

Above all the infernal racket one word alone came through loud and clear and burned into our consciousness: Schnell! Each repetition of the word was accompanied by a burst of rifle or machine-gun fire. The Germans had brought the freight cars up on the tracks and had begun driving everyone on the square into them, resulting in a tremendous jam. At this point the sticks, rifles, and machine guns went into action, and the frightened and defenseless mob was driven along by beating and shouting. A second horde of Germans ran into all corners and floors of the building where we had been and shot everyone trying to hide. This went on for about two hours. All the while the butchers kept walking back and forth beneath our window, laughing loudly. We lay there motionless, holding our breath, expecting death at any moment. All we wanted was for this torment to be over. At last we heard the long mournful whistle of the engine as it pulled away from the square. I will never forget that funereal sound for as long as I live.

We came to, as if out of a deep hypnotic trance. We looked at each other, unable to believe we were still alive. The people around us seemed like phantoms. We looked at the clock: it was seven-thirty in the evening. A terrible sight met our eyes when we gazed through the window. Several dozen corpses were staining the ground of the Umschlagplatz with their innocent blood. The whole square was covered thick with the knapsacks, bundles, and pots which people had been saving so carefully and wouldn't share with anyone. A grave-like silence reigned.

Frogier appeared and told us that the German sentries guarding the exit from the Umschlagplatz had been bribed. We would be able to leave after eight o'clock, when Szmerling went off duty. I began trying to find out about my baby. I started by asking the nurse on duty at the out-patient desk. She looked at me with the same expression of horror I had seen on Dr. Braude-Hellerowa's face, and then cried out: "Oh, you poor woman! What have you done? We get a dozen or so babies like that each day and we send them off in the wagons together with the rest of the transport. Your baby has already been sent!"

It was as if I had been struck by a bolt of lightning. I cried in a hysterical voice that I had murdered my child and that I would never leave this place, because I no longer had any reason to return home. But still I had to make certain, for I was not satisfied by the assurances of the woman behind the desk. The police would not allow us onto the upper floors of the hospital, so I begged the nurses passing by on their way home to give me some kind of information. For the most part, they responded with a curt "I don't know," but one nurse, who seemed to have more sympathy than the rest, stopped in front of me long enough to say that she was absolutely certain that not a single child had been sent away that day. She asked for the name of the nurse to whom I had given the baby. I didn't know it. I was only able to describe the baby, to say that he had a mark by which he could easily be recognized. She went upstairs and brought back the dying child of the woman I had told to give her baby to the hospital. Its feeble breathing showed that the spark of life was still flowing in its frail little body, but that it had only a short time left to live. The nurse shrugged her shoulders and said that it wasn't worth the trouble taking it back upstairs. Then she left.

My husband was more successful. He remembered that the nurse had taken our baby into the building where the old public baths used to be, which had been turned into an ambulatory clinic. He sent Frogier there to have a look. Szmerling was still glued to his post, so we went out onto the square where we came upon a hearse picking up the remains of the dead. My husband went to meet Frogier. As I was following him, a man was being carried past on a stretcher, bleeding very badly, leaving huge red spots on the floor behind him. I turned my head away; I felt that I simply couldn't take any more.

Out on the sidewalk I found my husband in the process of taking our son out of Frogier's arms. Breathless, I stood there looking at him. I simply couldn't get enough of looking at him. My one and only dearest little one, alive and well, smiled back at me with the sweetest of smiles. My heart was filled with a feeling of heavenly bliss and tenderness. This smile alone was reward enough for the nightmare of the past twenty-four hours.

18

BACK IN JADZIA'S APARTMENT

At eight-thirty Szmerling finally finished his watch and deigned to move from his spot. We waited for another ten minutes and then began moving in the direction of our final obstacle—the sentry. Frogier told me to put the baby under the raincoat I was wearing. He himself escorted us on his bicycle. The exit past the sentry was about sixty paces to the right. A German and Polish policeman were on duty.

I must confess that even up to this final moment I didn't believe we would get out. I expected the German to let us past and then shoot us down. Still I went. As we neared the exit, Frogier turned to the German and said, "Hans, zwei!"—in other words, two people. Then I heard a voice whisper to me loudly in German: "To the left, several steps along the wall, then quickly to the right and up onto the sidewalk."

This was the German giving me directions, while for appearances' sake my husband went up to the Polish policeman and showed him some kind of papers. We did exactly as the German said, and only a few paces farther we were free.

It was eight forty-five. Only fifteen minutes remained for us to be on the streets. We wrapped the baby in my coat. and we took off running. I was unable to keep up the pace. My husband, who was carrying the baby, kept calling out to me: "Don't fall behind, keep up with me! Use your every last bit of strength! Just keep telling yourself that the battle is almost won!"

However, the end of our battle—complete liberation—was still very, very far away.

We ran out in the middle of the street. It was impossible to go along the sidewalk, because every so often, wherever there was a shop, it would be blockaded with fences or barbed wire. It took us five minutes to run the length of Zamenhof to the corner of Nowolipki, where Frogier said goodbye to us, promising to come by for the rest of the money. We ran along the empty streets without stopping even for a moment. The baby had fallen asleep from exhaustion in my husband's arms. The only people we met were policemen returning to their apartments. At nine o'clock we were on Leszno Street, near the workers' quarters for the Toebbens shop. Now we had to be careful not to be seen from the nearby sentry-box, for we would be shot. At last we came to the end of our road—76 Leszno Street, Of course, the gate was locked. We rang the buzzer, and after a minute the custodian opened the gate and let us in. To this day we cannot get over how he simply let us in that night.

Once inside the yard, we breathed a deep sigh of relief. We were so soaked with sweat that we could have wrung out our clothes. My sister opened the door. There was no end of hugging and kissing. Because of the late hour, everyone had given us up for lost; they had been mourning us as if we were already dead. That was a day I will always remember—Thursday, September 6, 1942.

Upon returning home, in spite of my inhuman weariness, my first thought was to take care of the baby. He was completely wet and I was afraid he would catch cold. I wiped him dry, changed him, fed him some kasha which he gulped down, and put him to sleep. As I stood above the crib and looked down at my dear one sleeping, it all seemed to me like some terrible dream. I looked around the room. By the flickering light of the kerosene lamp (the electricity was out) I made out the worried faces of Jadzia, her husband, mother, and sister, as well as the haggard face of my husband.

The initial shock of returning home had already worn off. Now we had to take stock of our present situation. According to Jadzia, momentous changes had taken place in the factory in the course of a single day. A new list of workers had been compiled from those showing up for work. It was rumored that Schultz had obtained permission to employ eight hundred Jews (previously the figure had been 2,500). Since there were still many more than eight hundred workers left even after the first blockade, a new blockade was expected on the following day. For this reason, many people didn't turn up for work but went into hiding.

The day passed full of tension and toward evening the Germans once more broke into the factory and the previous day's scene was repeated. This time the names of people were called off from a list. Anyone not present was immediately crossed off the list. Among the eight hundred persons selected by Schultz were many professionals, some of whom were already quite old. At this the Germans lodged a protest, as the result of which all of the older workers, regardless of their experience, were crossed off the list and sent to the Umschlagplatz. This was the group which my husband had seen through the window as we lay hidden in the hospital. Not a single one of those taken during this second blockade managed to escape.

Afterwards, Schultz personally signed and stamped the papers of all the remaining workers, the only ones now allowed in the factory and workers' quarters. Everyone was very surprised to hear that the custodian had not asked to see our identification papers. It was also fortunate that Szmerling, by sitting stubbornly all day long at his post, had prevented us from escaping earlier and being caught in the second blockade.

Now, however, it was necessary to marshal all our energy in order to get my husband back into the factory. We postponed worrying about the future until the following day, because we were too tired to think. After all we had lived through, we were unable to eat supper, even though we hadn't had anything to eat for two days. We just drank a little tea. It was already quite late when we finally washed ourselves thoroughly and lay down to sleep. Jadzia's sister was still crying quietly on her bed, for her fiancé, who also worked in our factory, had been taken to the Umschlagplatz that day. When she learned from us that everyone had been loaded into the freight cars as soon as they arrived, she lost all hope.

Next morning we arose very early. We decided that my husband should try to get into the factory and see what he could do from there. Jadzia's husband loaned him his papers, and he and Jadzia went to the factory together. Since the guard at the gate knew my husband, he let him in without looking at the photograph. In the factory my husband met Eichel, who was very glad to see that he was back. Eichel told him that the department had practically been wiped out, so it was likely that he would be able to find work. His co-workers advised him to go directly to Haze. When Haze arrived, my husband presented him with his proposal, and Haze promised to help. However, when noon came and still no action had been taken, my husband understood that he had gone about things the wrong way. Jadzia's husband, who was sincerely interested in our well-being, advised him to go directly to Mr. Duży, who had worked for fifteen years in the sewing room and was popular with everyone, including Schultz himself. In addition, he had been "procuring" valuable articles, jewelry, and currency for the higher-up factory officials at minimal prices. Mr. Duży smiled and said that if my husband had gotten work through him in the first place he would have avoided all his present difficulties. He vowed to take care of the matter without delay provided that my husband could come up with the requisite amount of money.

Since it was a matter of the lives of all three of us, my husband offered him 5000 zlotys on the spot, and Mr. Duży agreed. As we later found out, he gave my husband's papers directly to Jakubiak, Schultz's right-hand man, and to Wodziński. At all events, Mr. Duży cheered my husband up and assured him that he would be accepted for work. However, he advised him to remain at the factory in order to look after his affairs in person.

When Jadzia's husband returned from work he told me about everything and added that rumor had it that the factory management had made a tremendous profit from the latest tragedy, for people were willing to get work at any price. Because of the lack of workers in the cutting department, the amount accepted by Mr. Duży was comparatively modest. Others were paying as much as fifteen to twenty thousand zlotys for Schultz's signature. I saw that the entire shop operation was one big swindle, and the same was true everywhere else. The shops merely served to pull the wool over people's eyes. Their real aim was the eventual liquidation of the ghetto and all the Jews in it, but in the meantime they were stringing people along in order to extort as much money from them as possible. When the people no longer had anything to purchase their life with, then they too would be killed. After all, that's what had happened to the ones who hadn't been able to pay their ransom. They had been the first to be sent to their deaths.

Except for Jadzia and her husband, all of us in the apartment were there illegally. I knew that even if my husband should get work, the baby and I would still have to hide. Counting my sister, there were five of us there illegally against the two who were legal. That state of affairs could not last for long. We usually kept a note on the door saying that everyone was at work, and we had to keep very still, for the slightest rustle could give us away. Even though the baby had begun teething he was very quiet, as if he understood our situation. I always stayed close to him so as to comfort him immediately in case he started to cry. It was an unbelievably trying time.

19

MAKING CONTACT WITH THE "ARYAN SIDE"

The monotony of this life was broken by the frequent visits of Janina Szyderkiewiczowa. She would drop in on us several times a day in order to leave things she had bought but was unable to take past the sentries. We owed a great deal to Janina and people like her. Thanks to them we were able to sell our things and use the money to pay off our persecutors, as well as to make contact with people on the Aryan side of town.

For several weeks we had been trying to get in touch with friends who might be able to help get us out of our trap. Through Janina I sent a letter to Marysia and Stasiek Będkowski, former Polish employees of ours. They had worked for several years in our shop before the ghetto was closed off. We had done them many favors and always shown them the greatest friendship and kindness. In the letter I asked them to take our baby for a short period of time, promising to reward them handsomely for the favor. They told Janina to come back in a few days for an answer. When she did, she found the doors locked.

Next we turned to one of our customers, a very worthy and intelligent woman who, besides being one of our oldest customers, was also a close friend. I wrote her an imploring letter, begging her to come to our aid. Unfortunately, Janina was unable to get in touch with her. She had left for her daughter's in the country and wasn't going to be back for two weeks.

I knew that there was at least one woman who would not be deaf to my entreaties like everyone else. That was Jula. I had known her for a shorter period of time than the others to whom I had been turning in vain. We had met by accident a year earlier, and we had seen each other only a few times since. She had been governess and maid in the home of Fuerstenberg, our trade representative in the Poznań and Pomorze voivodeships. She had worked for fifteen years in his home, helping to raise his two sons who had come to love and respect her as their own mother. When the boys grew up, she found work in a grade school, where she was also highly thought of. Fuerstenberg visited us often and told us that Jula had done a lot for him by bringing him food packages and selling his personal belongings on the Aryan side. We had heard so much about her that I had formed an impression of her as being a very exceptional person. During the past year we had come across each other several times, but there was no special friendship or intimacy between us; I simply liked her and trusted in her integrity.

I kept hammering the idea into my head that Jula and only Jula would be able to help us. I kept repeating over and over to myself: Jula, no one but Jula! Unfortunately, we knew neither her last name nor her address, so it was necessary to find Fuerstenberg. We didn't even know whether he was still alive. He wouldn't have been living at his old address, because the Germans had evacuated all Jews from that area of town (he lived in Żoliborz). All we knew was that his son was a policeman.

An accident—or perhaps Providence—came to our assistance. The day after our return from the Umschlagplatz, Frogier's replacement dropped by for a reward for taking care of us during Frogier's absence. As soon as I saw him, an idea came into my head. I told him that we would pay him, but I asked him to do us one more favor, which was a matter of life and death. I asked him to find Fuerstenberg's son in the police housing, to give him a letter, and to wait for a reply. The policeman, who looked like a very respectable sort, swore that he would do it, and he kept his word. We learned that the parents of the young Fuerstenberg had been evacuated. We also got Jula's address, but without her last name, so I asked him to go once again and find it. I knew that another such opportunity would perhaps never present itself. My husband gave him five hundred zlotys as payment, with which he was highly satisfied.

My husband's affairs had still not been settled. Mr. Duży asked him to be patient for a little while longer. He said not to worry, because the matter would surely be taken care of. My husband continued to stay at the factory, not even coming home at night. We were afraid that the trick with Jadzia's husband's papers would not work a second time.

Fortunately, one of our former neighbors from Nowolipki Street, a painter by profession with whom my husband was on very good terms (as he was with everyone), had been renovating a number of buildings which were going to be joined to the factory. He let my husband stay there until his affairs were taken care of. The waiting around was nerve-racking, and he had to hide from Schultz and other people he didn't want to see. After living through the nightmare of the Umschlagplatz, instead of getting any rest, he had to sleep on the bare floor.

The food situation was a little better. When Jadzia went to work in the morning, she would take my husband his breakfast and a bottle of hot tea. During the day she would put on a worker's apron and bring him lunch and dinner. A number of his close friends from the factory would drop by as well, relating gossip, bringing the latest news, and trying to cheer him up. On Saturday, the office closed at noon without taking any action on his case, leaving him in a state of uncertainty until Monday. We at home did whatever we could to encourage Mr. Duży to take care of my husband. Jadzia and her husband brought him over to meet me. I already knew that he wouldn't turn down a drink.

I had in the apartment a so-called "iron reserve" of half a liter of pure grain alcohol, which I was saving for medicinal purposes. I guarded it as the apple of my eye, for at that time it was very difficult to obtain even as medicine. Nevertheless, I didn't hesitate to donate it to our cause. Over a drink I tried to stir his conscience, telling him how much we had been through, especially the baby. I knew that my words didn't make the slightest impression on him. He was, generally speaking, a good sort, but with a poorly developed sense of family and community. Even with all his acquaintances and influence, and even though he had saved many people with his own money, he hadn't done anything during the first blockade to save his own wife and son. He explained that he hadn't known about it, but I was unable to keep myself from being repelled by him. I knew that a good husband stays at his wife's side in both good fortune and bad, and doesn't abandon her at such a moment to fate. I had the example of my own husband. I remembered how he was ready to perish alongside me, even when he could have saved himself. A very small percentage of husbands were as devoted as mine. Most were like Mr. Duży. It seemed that the struggle for survival drove out all good and noble impulses in a person.

On Saturday Frogier came by for the rest of his money, which I gave him. We had already given him my watch and my husband's watch and part of the money as soon as we had gotten out of the Umschlagplatz. He also took three hundred zlotys for the nurse who had given back the baby from the hospital. In all, to save our lives it had cost us 7400 zlotys, two gold watches, and a gold watch band.

We heard at this time that some 400,000 Jews had been removed from the Warsaw ghetto and that the German blockades were now over. It was mentioned that soon the Death Squad would be leaving Warsaw for other countries like France, Holland, and so forth. We thought that our affairs would be settled and life would return to normal.

The following Monday Jadzia came back bringing the joyful news that my husband had received a card with Wodziński's signature on it saying that the gateman should let him in for work. An enormous weight was lifted from my soul. My husband would be able to return home and get some rest. I was in good spirits all the rest of the day.

After several peaceful days, early that evening we suddenly heard the characteristic whistles and several shots ring out one after the other in our courtyard. From the accompanying shouting and racket there could be no doubt: a blockade! The third one in five days.

There were three women in our apartment: my sister, Jadzia's mother, and myself with a baby. The door was padlocked on the outside, because no one had returned from work yet. It would have been no easy matter to knock down our door, because it was reinforced from top to bottom with iron bars. My sister had already successfully lived through two blockades in our apartment. Of the three of us, I was the most terrified. Still, we didn't lose our heads. We brought the ladder into the anteroom and helped Jadzia's mother get up on the mezzanine. We covered her with a wash-tub, wash-boiler, and other odds and ends. Then we put the ladder back into the bathroom. A glance at the baby assured me that he would not be any trouble. He was playing with his toes. He lay there peacefully murmuring to himself, unconscious of the danger surrounding him. I left him lying in his crib. Softly, I shut the door to his room and went with my sister to our hiding place on the lower shelf of the kitchen cabinet. After pulling up a big bundle of bedding in front of us we shut the cabinet door behind us. I felt like I was suffocating, but I didn't mind the physical discomfort. My only sensation was one of plain animal fear. My heart was beating rapidly and unevenly.

I lost all consciousness of what was happening. I would never have believed that anyone could be so afraid. My entire being was ruled at that moment by the maniacal fear that in another minute the door would be broken down and the Germans, Ukrainians, and the whole mob would burst in and throw themselves on us. It was not death I feared at that moment; I felt only fear and terror of the Germans. That feeling has remained with me to this day. Whenever I see a German on the street, even if I know that he doesn't notice me, I can't help it: the same feeling of blind fear comes over me. There was not a single coherent thought in my head.

As if by command, we suddenly heard the clatter of many feet on the stairs. Someone took hold of our door latch and tried to force the door to our apartment. Then above the noise in our ears I heard another shot, this time above our apartment. Then it was quiet again. Now in the yard I could hear the sound of many steps and numerous voices, but I was unable to make out what they were saying. I realized only one thing, that the inspection of our entry was probably over.

Then the sound of a baby crying struck my ears. From my hiding place I couldn't make out where the crying was coming from. I crawled out quietly and realized that it was my son. I proceeded into his room on all fours as quickly as possible, fearing that the Ukrainians would hear him and return. He had stuck his foot between the bars of his crib and couldn't get it out. I took my beloved child in my arms and he immediately quieted down and smiled at me. I didn't go back to the hiding place but sat down on the divan with the baby and listened. I could still hear the sound of voices. After an hour or more I heard the sound of a key turning in the lock and the voice of my husband calling out my name and telling me not to be afraid. The door opened and all the tenants of our apartment crowded inside. I looked only for the face nearest and dearest to my heart, but how changed it was. With the instinct of a loving heart I immediately understood that my husband had just been through a tragic experience.

20

MY HUSBAND'S NARROW ESCAPE

My husband had been let into the factory that morning on Wodziński's signature. His co-workers were very glad to see him back at work. Everyone congratulated him on being able to save his child. It was generally conceded that this had been the first five-month-old baby ever to return from the Umschlagplatz. Since, the cutting personnel had been severely depleted, my husband was promoted to the position of independent cutter, helped in this by Eichel.

The day at work passed peacefully. When the cutting department closed, my husband had to wait for new work papers. Since the sewing room was located next to the cutting room, he decided to wait there until Mr. Duży finished work. They stood there calmly discussing the latest events when suddenly the news arrived that Germans were in the yard. Shortly afterwards the Aryans were ordered to stop work and go home. The Jews were to go out into the yard. It is easy to imagine what my husband felt like. With no identification papers, he would be a prime candidate for the Umschlagplatz.

The danger in the present situation was all the greater in that the people taken in this blockade would be loaded directly onto the cars, as we had witnessed during our stay there. At first they wanted to hide him in the factory, but they were afraid of an intensive search and its fatal consequences, both for my husband and for everyone else. There was nothing to do but to cast fate to the winds and meet the lion in his den. On the stairs he met Wodziński, who told him that he hadn't managed to get his identification papers yet. He wasn't able to finish speaking, because a German suddenly appeared behind him.

Fearing that the German would suspect him of collusion with the workers, he began to shout at my husband to get out into the yard as quickly as possible. Of course, this didn't take place without my husband getting beaten on the back several times by the German. All of the workers were shifted from 78 Leszno Street to the courtyard of 76 Leszno. This was the movement of so many feet I had heard from my hiding place. The factory building on 78 Leszno was locked, and all rooms, cellars, and attics were thoroughly searched. This third blockade resulted in a great number of fatalities. The first victim was a four-year-old girl who was playing quietly in a little garden at the time the Germans came into the yard. A Ukrainian shot her and she fell over dead on the spot. When the workers walked into the yard they saw the ground stained with the blood from the body of that unfortunate little girl. The sight sent a shock of terror and disgust at the Germans and their Ukrainians helpers. As if spellbound their eyes continued to be fastened on the body of the little child.

Everyone was arranged into a long column of fives in the courtyard, and then they began to check identification papers. Those who weren't presently in Schultz's good graces were taken out of the line. When my husband's turn came, he ended up in the group being sent to the Umschlagplatz as he didn't have any documents. This group consisted of several dozen people. My husband immediately initiated negotiations with the policeman in charge of the group, saying that he would give him a thousand zlotys then and there if he would let him go, but there was no chance of that, for a German was standing nearby. One of the women tried to make it into one of the entryways, having made arrangements with a Polish policeman. Unfortunately, a German noticed her, ordered her to bend over and kicked her thirty or forty times in her rear end.

Jadzia and other friends and acquaintances of my husband began calling to Mr. Duży for him to do something. He turned to K. G. Schultz, who was passing by at just that moment and said to him in German: "Herr Schultz, they're taking away our best cutter!"

Schultz called over his deputy Michel, who was lame and went by the name Hopfoot. He asked in German: "Which one of you is the cutter S.?"

My husband responded. Hearing this, Wodziński and Hase, and even engineer Koszutski himself, took my husband's part. Schultz told him to return to the group of workers. My husband, overcome with emotion, broke down crying. By a strange coincidence, at that very moment our son had begun crying too. A Ukrainian standing alongside asked in his native language: "Where's that baby crying?"

At these words Eichel began coughing loudly, and the others followed and shuffled their feet, trying to drown out the noise. After checking everyone's papers, the Germans led the unlucky group of the condemned to the Umschlagplatz. The rest of the workers were allowed to return to their apartments.

Shortly after this a hearse of the "Last Rite" drove up and began picking up corpses. Among others there was the body of a paralyzed old woman. They had broken down the doors to her apartment and the poor lady had been shot in her chair. In the apartment next door a two-year-old baby had been taken.

We learned that blockades had also taken place in the worker's quarters on 33, 35, and 37 Nalewki Street. All of the workers' families had been taken and sent to the Umschlagplatz. There had been a large number of fatalities, as the Germans were killing everyone they found hiding in order to terrorize the rest. These three blockades in five days so thoroughly depressed and demoralized us that we were unable to recover and regain our equilibrium. It would have been difficult to find a normal human expression in our distraught and tormented faces.

Following this last blockade, we found a note with Jula's last name stuck to our door. Evidently, upon finding the door locked, the policeman had simply left it there. He certainly must have been a respectable person to have acted as he did. Now that I had Jula's address and full name, I asked Janina to go to her the very next day. She wasn't at home, so Janina promised to try again that coming Sunday.

By this time, in addition to our personal belongings, we had begun selling the materials which we had used in our shop. We entrusted their sale to Janina. Since we felt certain that Mrs. Hebda would want to buy them, we sent Janina to find her. Unfortunately, Mrs. Hebda was still in the country. In Mrs. Hebda's store Janina met for the second time Henryk Michalski. She offered to sell the materials to him, describing our present situation. He responded with a proposal to go into partnership with my husband. He had undertaken to find a workshop and a place for him to stay over on the Aryan side. Later we learned that this had actually been Mrs. Hebda's idea, who was trying in this way to help us. Michalski had lost his job at the post office when the ghetto had been closed, and he was unable to find any other work. He was about to be forced to go to the Germans for work, who paid so poorly that he wouldn't have been able to feed his family, which consisted of six persons. When Janina asked him about me and the baby, he said that his proposal extended only to my husband. My husband categorically refused, saying that he wasn't going to leave me and the baby in the ghetto.

21

THE GHETTO COMPLETELY SEALED OFF

Since factory personnel had been reduced to eight hundred Jews, Schultz recognized that we could now all be accommodated in the building on 76 Leszno Street, and the worker's quarters on Nalewki could be completely liquidated. The internal police received orders for us to abandon these three buildings and move to ours on 76 Leszno. In view of this state of affairs, the small handful of people remaining at work began to pack their by-now miserable belongings in order to take protection beneath the "sheltering wings" of Schultz as quickly as possible. During the day all three courtyards of our building became piled high with all sorts of furniture, bedding, dishes, and so forth. Many people set up their beds and sofas out in the yard and spent the night on them.

When we looked out from our window, it seemed too strange to be true. A single human mind simply could not take all of this in. People who up until recently had had their own apartments had been shifting from one apartment to another so often in the course of the past few weeks in order to end up living in a courtyard surrounded by an enormous pile of rubbish and horrible smelling garbage. Because of the hot weather, it was all rotting and letting off a terrible stench.

Early in the morning and after work, groups of people would go on looting expeditions to the empty houses. They returned loaded down with all sorts of objects and materials. I must confess that this looting was as repellent and despicable to us as it was natural for them. They said that after the blockades the Germans, Ukrainians, and the Jewish Police were the first to plunder the apartments.

They would take away the so-called "cream," in other words, whatever was most valuable and had the greatest resale value. It was no wonder that at a time like this people were ruled by morbid greed and desire. Temptation was everywhere, and people no longer had to reckon with public opinion or personal morals. They lived from one day to the next. Profligacy and dissolution had gained the upper hand. Drunken orgies would go on all night long. People would pay anything for food, for money was the one thing they had plenty of.

Changes continued to be introduced at the factory. Previously the Jewish workers had received a salary. My husband, for example, received seventy-five groszy (1 zloty=100 groszy) an hour. After the third blockade salaries were discontinued. From time to time workers would receive certain allowances in the form of marmalade, sugar, and artificial tea—"ersatz tea," as the Germans called it. In addition, they started going around to the apartments in order to see who was living there and where it would be possible to move new people in. This was something of a tragedy for us, because four of us were living in our place illegally. Many additional people were hired during this time in exchange for huge sums of money. Instead of the 5000 zlotys they had agreed upon, my husband had to pay Mr. Duży six. He explained that the people who had taken his side during the blockade had come around later for payment.

There were rumors that all the workers were going to receive numbers. A list was compiled of all remaining children. We thought for a long time about what to do; by this time I had a sober view of Schultz's benevolence. I asked my husband to allow me and the baby to continue to live illegally, and he respected my wishes.

The same kind of blockades that had taken place in our building had occurred in all the shops throughout the ghetto. In the Little Ghetto only the Toebbens shop on Prosta Street was left. All the other buildings had been thoroughly searched and cleaned out... It often happened that during these inspections they would come upon hiding places where people had been shot by the Germans where they lay hidden. One Polish friend of ours who lived right next to the wall on Grzybowska Street told how she had seen with her own eyes the Nazis throwing children into the sewers. In some cases they would first take the child by the feet and knock its head against the wall with such force that their brains would spill out.

Police assigned to the clean-up details told how they would open up closets and corpses would fall out of them. Many people had committed suicide, realizing that they would be killed one way or the other. They told how they found the body of one young woman in bed in one of the houses on Ceglana Street. When they touched the covers, it all came apart in their hands. Before committing suicide, she had doused everything around her with some kind of caustic liquid.

About 400,000 Jews had been exterminated in the Warsaw ghetto. The remaining 40,000 or so realized that this had been no resettlement. The Nazis had operated in such a deceitful and cunning manner that the people had been unable to prepare any defense. Now it was too late. Those of us who were left protected our own lives as best we could, believing that the war would soon be over.

It was quiet in town, and the Death Squad was getting a little rest and relaxation. The Germans provided entertainment for the aiders and abettors in their satanical deeds, arranging for them various kinds of performances—among other things, concerts in the Femina movie house on Leszno Street, performed by the Jewish Police band. Life and work in the factory returned to normal, at least superficially. My husband received new identification papers with the proper stamps and signatures.

We were on good terms with Mr. Duży, and he came to visit us often. We tried to keep him on our good side in case we should ever need him in an emergency. During the week Janina had brought some rather disquieting news. She said that the Poles were going to be completely locked out of the ghetto. Posters had been pasted on the Aryan side with the following information:

For harboring a Jew or for offering him any assistance, not only the person himself but his entire family is subject to the death penalty.

It was hardly any wonder that the Poles were afraid. For our part we sensed that there was something in the air, but it was not in our power to foresee what it was so as to forestall it. The bomb burst soon enough, however.

On a Saturday night in the first half of September, I suddenly heard movements and a voice talking with the commander of our factory's Werkschutz, Szoszkin. I woke up Jadzia and we both went down into the yard to gather information. In the yard we met many of our friends. No one knew anything definite except that the police had received orders to vacate the buildings they had been occupying on Dzielna Street and move immediately to Wołyńska Street.

The order had been given that same night at a banquet (!) given by the Death Squad in their headquarters on 103 Żelazna Street to which

Captain Lejkin had been invited. He was presently occupying the position of colonel Szeryński, chief of the Jewish Police. Szeryński had been wounded during an unsuccessful attempt on his life and was still recovering.

Jadzia and I returned to our apartment and related what we had heard. Of course, there was no question of our getting any more sleep that night. By five o'clock in the morning we managed to gather more detailed information. Janina had been correct: all contact with the Aryan side had been cut off. The guarded exit on Leszno and Żelazna streets, located right next to our factory, had been closed. By ten o'clock in the morning all those living in the workers' quarters were to leave their apartments and go to Miła Street. It was said that this was to be a total evacuation.

The news hit us like a bombshell. Jadzia and her family opened all their bags, bundles, and suitcases and started taking things out of them, and soon there was nowhere left to stand. There was so much stuff that it was difficult to understand where all of it had fitted in such a cramped apartment. Out of all of their wares they began choosing only the best and most expensive things.

They put on several shirts and dresses each. Jadzia packed an enormous knapsack for herself, as well as a large suitcase and a handbag with food. Jadzia's sister, who worked at Big Schultz's on Nowolipie, came over to our apartment because she had decided to stick together with her mother and sister. She had also packed a huge backpack for herself. Jadzia's husband packed out two large suitcases for himself and kept complaining like an old woman that he had to leave behind fifteen pieces of bed linen because he didn't have any room for it. His sister packed a suitcase full of food taken from apartments left vacant after the blockades. My sister decided to stay at home no matter what and not to go anywhere, and I had a mind for me and the baby to do the same.

I had already decided that if things got really bad I would turn on the gas and commit suicide. My husband didn't even want to hear about my staying in the apartment. He said that as long as we were together we could always find a way out, but if I stayed alone, no one would be able to look after me. We decided to go together with the rest and put ourselves in the hands of Providence. We packed a single handbag with necessary equipment for the baby: diapers, two cans of condensed milk, a kilogram of cube sugar, cream of wheat, and, what was probably most important, a loaf of bread that we still had. We packed one change of underwear each for ourselves, a towel, and a few other essentials. The biggest problem was with the clothing, because it was extremely hot that day, even though it was September. Since we did not plan on ever returning to the apartment again, we put on all of our best clothes, sweaters, and winter coats.

At nine o'clock in the morning we all gathered in the yard. For the first time I was able to gauge how many people had managed to hide. There were supposed to be only eight hundred people, but there were more than fifteen hundred of them here, including women and children. Our child was the youngest of the lot. Everyone was terribly loaded down. Even before we started moving their faces were covered with sweat and their shirts were sticking to their bodies. I remember that my attention was riveted on the shoes Jadzia's sister-in-law was wearing. They were the latest-fashion patent leather, with pointed toes and very high heels, as if she were going to a party. Against the rest of the scene they looked utterly grotesque.

We went through the gate. At that moment a detachment of helmeted German soldiers marched past, singing heartily. They didn't even look in our direction, as if we didn't exist. Our attention was caught by the sight of Mr. Duży talking with K. G. Schultz. He looked like a tourist ready for a jaunt in the countryside. He was dressed in sports clothes and had a haversack across his back. He alone was not carrying any baggage. We set out on our way along the same route we had taken a week before, in the direction of the Umschlagplatz: Leszno, Karmelicka to Zamenhof, and Miła. The only difference was that this time no one was beating us and driving us along. The heat was horrendous, or maybe it just seemed so hot because we were wearing winter clothing and carrying so much luggage. On the corner of Karmelicka and Nowolipie the gate leading into the Big Schultz shop was open wide. Inside it was empty: not a sound could be heard anywhere. On Dzielna Street we kept meeting up with hand-carts being pushed by the Jewish Police. We remembered that they too had to move today. It was good for them to feel a little of what we had been going through for the past six weeks. I must admit that I felt the same hatred and spite for the Jewish Police as I did for the Nazis; they were just too eager to carry out the orders of the invaders. On Zamenhof we ran into a scene of indescribable confusion. Long columns of people were walking along the sidewalks and pavement, all of them with bags and bundles. Once again the phrase "Jew, the eternal wanderer" passed through my mind.

22

MIŁA STREET

Our factory personnel were to occupy the building on 43 Miła Street. We arrived there to find it completely full: the yards, apartments, stairways, everywhere was full of people. Some of the workers from the Big Schultz shop were here too. On one of the first-floor balconies we spotted one of our former neighbors from Nowolipki, where we had lived before the destruction of the ghetto. At the beginning of the war he had escaped to Russia, but not being able to adapt to conditions there, he had returned. He was very glad to see us and came running to greet us. He escorted us to one of the apartments. We were very tired from our journey. Along the road to Miła Street we came across several other neighbors just as miserable and destitute as ourselves. We also met two of our closest friends. Their parents and children had already been taken away, and they themselves were completely resigned to their fate; all joy and gaiety in them had completely vanished. A great sadness and melancholy came over us to see them like this. We exchanged a few words and said goodbye... forever, for the last time. I myself was little more than an automaton. I realized that this was the end of everything.

On Miła Street we met two of my cousins. They were the only ones left of their family, and they had no baggage with them. I asked about my aunt and their wives and children. They said that they had hidden them in the attic. Apparently they had access to early notification and were able to make use of it by hiding their families. Unfortunately, very few people had access to such information. Everyone kept everything to himself and thought only about himself. Misfortune doesn't teach one anything. Egoism always takes the upper hand.

My cousins told us that this was going to be the final segregation. Whoever returned from this action would remain at work for good. (This was just another deception: the Nazis were past masters at creating one rumor after another.) The rest would gradually be removed to the Umschlagplatz. One of the cousins, who was my own age and with whom I had always been the closest of friends since early childhood, looked at me with an expression of such pity that its meaning was unmistakable: you and your little baby are surely not going to be among the ones returning. We said good-bye to each other, also as if for the last time, but they too lived through the war in spite of all the Nazis could do.

Mr. Duży assured us that he had talked to the director and that he had promised him that all the wives and children belonging to working husbands would be returning home. I knew from my own experience that any such words or promises coming from Schultz's mouth were nothing more than empty phrases. I saw that I had made a terrible mistake.

I should have stayed at home as my first impulse had dictated. It was no use blaming my husband, for he only wanted the best. His idea was simply to stand by me and the child, to preserve and protect us to the very end. Mr. Duży's reassuring words didn't make the slightest impression on me. Sitting next to me in this slovenly, stinking, louse-infested room was Eichel's wife with their four-year-old daughter. She knew as well as I did that after the segregation our husbands would be returning to the factory and we would be left here by ourselves.

There was no longer any way out of our plight, for at ten o'clock in the morning, on the corner of Gęsia and Zamenhof Streets a wooden gate had sprouted, guarded by Germans, Ukrainians, and Latvians. The same kind of gate and sentry box was also placed on the corner of Gęsia and Smocza and on the corner of Lubecki and Miła, hemming us in and surrounding us on all sides. There was no longer any question of our getting out. For the second time we were at an Umschlagplatz, the only difference being that this one was more spacious than the previous one. In either case the exit led to death.

We learned that the segregation would take place the very next day. We had a day and a night without Germans to look forward to. I noticed that some people had brought whole sacks of food with them and were cooking meals and making tea somewhere, each for his own family and close friends. If you asked someone with a kettle for a little hot water, you would always get the same gruff reply: fix it yourself! That's what people were like then. I guess it was no wonder, considering the suffering and hardship they had been through. I finally managed to make it into the kitchen and warm up a little rice paste for the baby. Fortunately I had thought to prepare a whole bottle of it at the other apartment. In the kitchen I saw a very funny sight, or it would have been funny under different circumstances. A long line of women was waiting patiently in order to cook food in a variety of pots, pans, and kettles. Each one of them was vigilantly looking after her own little pile of firewood so that no one would steal it from her. It was necessary to go to a great deal of effort and bother to get the wood, because you had to break up doors, railings, and banisters. You could hear wood being chopped on all sides, and before long there were no doors left in the entire apartment or anything else made of wood. When I returned to our place I was treated to some baked potatoes by our former neighbor. We shared them with all the people around us. I also met here the daughter of another of our neighbors. When I asked about her mother, she answered that she had been taken away, as indifferently as if she had been talking about the weather.

All day long we had been suffering from the heat and odor in our room. We sat on boxes and window-sills because, except for a table and a couple of chairs, there was no furniture of any kind. We made up a bed for the baby out of overcoats in the corner of the room. Bedbugs were swarming everywhere and didn't give the poor little thing a single moment's rest.

Every so often the Werkschutz would call out from the yard: "Everyone from the Schultz factory down to the yard!" We couldn't tell whether they meant "Big Schultz" from Nowolipie Street or "our" Schultz on Leszno, so everyone went down into the yard. After fifteen minutes or so everyone returned to their apartments, shrugging their shoulders. This went on all day long.

Around noon Jadzia's mother disappeared somewhere and didn't return for a long time. After a while we learned that she had moved to the building across from ours on 40 Miła Street. Numbers 36-42 Miła Street housed the workers from the Ursus factory, which was located on the Aryan side. All of the buildings in this complex were surrounded by a wooden fence. The gate was closed and guarded by a number of men from the Werkschutz, and no one was allowed either into or out of the buildings. Jadzia and her parents had lived in one of these buildings up until recently when, like all of us, they had had to vacate their apartment. Out of all of the former tenants only one was left, a woman who owned a grocery store. She received and distributed food for coupons to the Ursus workers. Jadzia had managed to get in touch with her and obtain permission for her mother to stay there. Of course, she couldn't simply walk through the gate and into the building. She had to go across the roof from Niska Street onto some property next to the apartment house on 40 Miła Street. She was now in the most fortunate position of any of us. We could see the results immediately in the form of a potful of hot soup, which in some mysterious fashion made its way from her to us.

We learned that Rowiński and other "worthy comrades" from his clique had in their possession a list of the eight hundred people who would receive numbers for identification and who would next day return home. People spent hours in line to see who was on the list. As could be expected, another worthy band of thieves came up with a new idea for making money. Many of those on the list hadn't come to Miła Street at all but instead had hidden themselves wherever they could, and so their places on the list were free. They were crossed off the list without any hesitation and their numbers sold for 5000 zlotys apiece. They thought up other underhanded methods as well. They denied that people were on the list when they actually were, hoping to extort another ransom from them.

This is what happened with my husband. When he asked whether he was on the list, Rowiński and his worthy comrades pretended to check and then gave a negative reply. At that my husband changed his tone and asked sharply for them to have another look. When they saw that the "victim" was too sure of himself and wasn't going to be taken in, they complied with his "request" and deigned to "notice" his name on the list.

I knew then that in all probability my husband would return to work, but what about me and the baby? We could buy another number for me, but never for the baby, so my husband looked for some other means. Mr. Duży introduced him to an important person who advised us to hide somewhere with the child for the time being; after he returned to Leszno he promised my husband that for 10,000 zlotys he would get us out of Miła Street and over to the Aryan side through a policeman friend of his. He was to come by for us and, for the same price, provide us with Aryan documents.

There didn't seem to be anything else to do. Jadzia initiated negotiations with the custodian of the apartment house where her mother was staying. It would be necessary to wait until nightfall. In the meantime numbers began to be distributed to our workers according to their place in the alphabet. It seemed to last forever, and the process was very disorderly. I sat alongside Mrs. Eichel and both of us cried heart-rendingly at the thought that tomorrow our husbands would be returning to the factory, but what would become of us? People had lain down on the floor, using their bundles for pillows, and were snoring loudly. The baby was having trouble sleeping; he kept tossing and turning, for the bedbugs and other vermin were bothering him incessantly.

Suddenly my husband came with Eichel and told me to dress the baby and come with them. I didn't pay any attention to the people sleeping on the floor, and every now and then I would hear grumbling or words of abuse from someone I had stepped on. However, none of that made any impression on me; I was walking as if in a dream. My only thought was to leave here and get to someplace else as quickly as possible. My guides led me to the street, and my husband said that in a moment the custodian in the apartment house opposite us would knock out a board in the fence and let us in.

I was to go through the opening with the baby and proceed to 40 Miła Street, where Jadzia's mother was. There I was to find someone called Saba and say that Jadzia had sent me, and she would take care of me. Then I had to be patient for two or three days, and my husband promised he would do everything in his power to get us out of there as quickly as possible. The custodian knocked out the board and let me and the baby into the apartment house. I was immediately struck by the quiet and the fresh air. After the stifling smell and indescribable confusion I had been putting up with all day long, the apartment house seemed like a wonderful oasis. The custodian, a boy around sixteen or seventeen years old, had taken over the job after his father had been evacuated. His mother, who was around forty, helped him.

In their apartment were hiding an old grandmother, the mother's sister, whose husband had also been evacuated, and the mother's other, six-year-old son. The first thing I asked was whether they ever had any German blockades here. They said that had happened only in the beginning, before the Ursus workers moved in. I was very surprised to hear that wives and children were able to live here in peace. Why were they any better than we? This was a question for which there was no answer.

23

IN THE URSUS WORKERS' QUARTERS

I asked the custodian to take me to Saba. We felt our way in the dark up to the fifth floor attic. I could not even make out the faces of Saba and the man who was also there. The women let me have their bed and went to sleep on the balcony, which they reached through a window. I have been in various situations in my life, but never before or since have I slept on such a filthy bed in such a vermin and bug-infested room. Fleas of a gigantic size jumped all over our bodies in enormous swarms. Their biting drove me crazy. Even though I was utterly exhausted I wasn't able to fall asleep. The baby kept waking up and crying.

I kept changing his position from beside the wall to the other side and back again, trying to ease his discomfort at least for a moment. At one point I dropped off to sleep and awoke with a start to find the baby nowhere to be seen. I started looking for him in the dark and finally managed to catch him as he was about to fall off the bed. I grew numb just thinking about the harm that could have come to him. I sat up for the rest of the night looking out for him.

At five o'clock in the morning the custodian's son came for me and told me to come downstairs, for my husband and Jadzia were there with a package for me. I could see my husband through a hole in the gate. He gave the custodian a package, which the custodian then gave to me. Only when he was certain that I had it in my possession did he say goodbye with a wave of his hand and the kind of glance with which one says goodbye for the last time to someone very dear. I was left by myself in this inferno, alone with a tiny baby in the hands of an evil fate. From what my husband told me later, I learned that he had spent the night in even worse circumstances than I. Since he was afraid to lie down on the floor among the vermin, he sat up all night at a table, sunk in gloomy thoughts.

Earlier Schultz had driven up in his automobile and ordered all the workers to line up in the yard in columns of fives. My husband had time to write me a few quick words, pack some essentials for the baby, put some food in a package, and deliver it to me.

It was fortunate for me that I had managed the preceding evening to get into the Ursus workers' quarters, because next day would have been too late. I tried to find out what had become of Mrs. Eichel and her daughter. During the several hours we had spent together for the first and last time in our lives I had grown to like her very much. Her brother was a policeman, and as we were walking along toward Miła Street we met him on Dzielna Street moving his things to his new apartment on Wołyńska. He promised at that time to take care of her.

With that day the "golden age" of the policemen was irretrievably past. Together with the order to change apartments, an order was issued concerning the reduction of the Jewish police force from 2000 to 500 hundred men. In other words, 1500 policemen were released; the remaining 500 were selected from the factory Werkschutz and from the upper echelons in charge of them. 1500 policemen found themselves, like the rest of us mortals, without a roof over their heads—Mrs. Eichel's brother among them. Most of these ex-policemen found some kind of job. Those who had money and good connections made it into the factories as part of the Werkschutz.

The rest were evacuated. Mrs. Eichel's brother found himself a job and kept his word to his sister. He managed to get her and the child out of the house on Miła Street and to locate her in another shop on Stawki where they had relatives occupying important positions.

Returning to the subject of our factory workers, they lined up in the yard in rows of five and began walking down Miła Street in the direction of Smocza. The workers from the Big Schultz factory on Nowolipie set off along Miła to Zamenhof, that is, in the opposite direction. It took hours to check them all, for they were allowed to have 8000 workers. On the corner of Miła and Lubecki streets our workers came upon their first wooden gate and first control station. The control was conducted by the factory Werkschutz without the assistance of the Germans. Only those who had numbers were allowed through. The rest had to turn back. The Germans, Ukrainians, and Latvians participated in the second control, on the corner of Smocza and Miła Streets.

They didn't check numbers but only counted the people so that there would be eight hundred of them and not a single person more. At first they let children through, counting them among the eight hundred workers. It didn't take Schultz long to see what was happening, and he began to throw all the children out of line, causing indescribable confusion and noise. Mothers returned to work, leaving their small children out in the streets to die. Here and there a child would slip through among the workers, but those were only isolated incidents. My husband told me how some mothers managed to carry their children— only little ones, of course— across in their knapsacks after first giving them a heavy dose of sleeping powders. Schultz caught on to that trick as well. They managed to carry them as far as the factory gates but here Schultz, who didn't want any workers to have children, because it distracted them from their work, checked everyone himself. The only children allowed inside were those belonging to protected workers whose names were already on a separate list. Later on those children received numbers themselves and were allowed to stay in the factory legally up until the final destruction of the ghetto. Children not on the list were not allowed into the factory in spite of the pleading and weeping of their unfortunate mothers. They had two choices: they could either submit voluntarily to certain death along with the children or, as happened more frequently, they could abandon the children and return to work by themselves. My husband told me of the poignant incident of a boy about ten to twelve years old who kept looking in great distress for a way to slip into the columns. He kept shifting from one row to the next, and of course no one gave him away, and somehow he managed to make it.

The sister of a certain Feinsilber family who also worked in our factory told me about another incident. A couple had three very clever and bright children: a fourteen-year-old boy and daughters of eight and three years. All three of them had been lucky enough to be in the first ranks at the control station on Miła. They managed to make it as far as the factory gate on Leszno, but no farther, because Schultz threw them out of line. Their parents, like the others, were ready to leave their children behind and go into the factory, but at this point the children began speaking up for themselves, reminding them that it was the parents' duty to be together with their children. If they didn't stay with them, they said they were going to jump out of the fourth floor windows of the apartment house next door so that their bodies would lie at the feet of their parents. Under this threat, the parents went with the children.

It seemed that the Rowiński clique had sold more numbers than they should have, for there were more than eight hundred workers with numbers. At this point Herr Goetzel appeared on the scene. He had been evacuated from Baden-Baden along with other Jews and was "working" for Schultz. He proceeded to throw everyone out of the line who didn't appeal to him, even though they had numbers and were on the list, installing in their place his own favorites from whom he had taken money beforehand. The poor souls who were thrown out didn't even have anyone to turn to for help.

After the eight hundred workers were carefully counted and checked, they moved off to the factory along Smocza Street. My husband was among the fortunate ones; it seemed that Mr. Duży's protection and influence had made the difference.

Smocza Street looked like a battleground. Where only a few weeks before the street had been throbbing with life, now a stillness hung over everything. The sidewalks and streets were littered with pots, pans, bedding, feathers, and all sorts of other objects. In the midst of all these things human bodies were lying. The sight had a demoralizing effect on my husband, who kept asking himself: What is it we are returning to, and what for? The silence was broken by the rumble of the "Last Rite" car as it headed in the direction of the cemetery, picking up corpses as it went along its way.

The police were bringing out people who had committed suicide or who had been killed by the Germans. It appeared that total blockades had taken place on Sunday in all buildings belonging to the shops. Everyone caught hiding was shot where they lay.

The long, long line of people moved slowly along the street... eight hundred pairs of feet and eight hundred tormented souls. They had ransomed themselves with everything dear to their hearts—their wives and children—and were headed themselves along the road to further torment and humiliation.

On the corner of Leszno and Zelazna Streets everyone was given the signal to stop and hand over their keys. In the meantime Schultz went over to the guardhouse and selected several policemen to take the keys and search each apartment. The Werkschutz was to help them. The people from our apartment decided not to hand over their keys, because they knew that my sister was still inside it. Let them break down the door if they want to, they thought. The apartment search lasted a long time, and everyone sat down on the street to wait. After a while they started bringing out the bodies of those killed. At one point the body of a man wearing a beautiful pair of top-boots was carried out. One of the men from the Werkschutz went up to him and removed the boots and tried to hide them under his jacket, but Schultz was quick to notice him. He took away the boots, giving the man a resounding smack on the face. Then he tore off the man's cap, which meant that he was out of the Werkschutz. Schultz called a meeting of the police, and they gave him their solemn vow that they would never, under any circumstances, allow anyone into the factory or the workers' quarters who did not have a number.

People began to be let into their apartments. At the entrance gate there was yet another control, under the direction of Herr Goetzel, well known to us as chief quartermaster, a position which he and engineer Koszutski occupied jointly. Herr Goetzel had now been appointed by Schultz to be house commissar in our building.

When they returned to our apartment, our tenants found the same mess and confusion they had left behind the day before, but not a trace of my sister. Since work would only begin the following day they began putting their things in order. After an hour had gone by my sister unexpectedly crawled out of her hiding place in the kitchen cabinet. She told how after we had left, a crushing stillness had settled over the entire building, interrupted only once by the appearance in the yard of a crazy woman, her hair all streaming down, blaspheming God in an awful voice. It seemed all the more eerie because of the silence all around. There was nothing really surprising in this incident. More than one person during this time asked God what it was we had done to deserve all this.

In the morning, she had heard noises down in the yard and the sound of shots and doors broken down in the entryways. My sister had taken to her hiding place, trembling with fear, and stayed there for several hours, but our apartment had not been searched. My husband, seeing this, began to blame himself for not leaving me and the baby in the apartment as I had asked. However, as later events were to show, Providence was at work in this instance too.

24

BEDBUGS, RATS, EXTORTION

With the departure of my husband I now had to rely on myself for everything. The custodian led me up to a hiding place in an entry that was completely uninhabited. The apartment to which I was led was located on the third floor. It looked like a rubbish heap. Wherever one stepped there were tattered clothes, broken plates, and a huge amount of junk. The smell was simply unbearable. As I later learned, the hiding place for the entire building was located in the attic above this entry, where an opening had been knocked in the wall connecting it to the attic of the building on Niska Street in which the workers' quarters for the Felix shop were located. Whenever there was a blockade in the Felix shop, all the tenants on Niska Street crawled over to the attic on Miła Street and vice versa. The apartment to which the custodian led me was used by everyone as a toilet, and this was the source of the smell.

The apartment consisted of one room and a kitchen. The room, which had two windows, was divided by a wooden wall into two parts, creating a second small room with a window; this second room was to be my hiding place. The narrow door to it was hidden by a kitchen cabinet. The compartment had the advantage that it was so indescribably messy that just looking at it was as much as most people could bear. In general it was quite a good hiding place, because it was difficult to guess that anything could be hidden behind the kitchen cabinet.

From my husband's letter I learned that he had paid three hundred zlotys to the custodian for breaking the hole in the fence and one hundred zlotys each for the three days I would be staying in the hiding place. Since my husband didn't have any more money with him, he sent me fifty gold rubles (in five coins) and his other gold watch in case I might need them to save myself. I arranged with the custodian to have him bring me every three hours a bottle of hot water, which I was going to mix with condensed milk and sugar and use to feed the baby. I promised to pay for the water separately. After unwrapping the package I discovered that there was not a crumb left of the bread; my husband, who was very kindhearted, had given it all away to the children, leaving me with nothing to eat. Soon, however, Jadzia's mother appeared, carrying a large tin box of dry noodles, a small bag of cream of wheat, and a loaf of bread which she had managed to buy for seventy-five zlotys the night before from the shop-lady she knew. She said that the Ursus workers had not gone to work the previous day. In all probability the gatehouse was going to be opened again Monday evening, and Aryans with new passes would once again be allowed to go back to work. She also told me that a segregation was going to take place later this same day on the grounds of the workers' quarters. To make matters worse, the custodian looking after us came in at that moment to tell us that we had to keep quiet so that no one in the house would find out about our presence. Besides that, he told us that an order had been issued by the Werkschutz with the following contents:

The grounds of the Ursus workers' quarters are exclusively for the use of the workers of this factory. Anyone knowing about or hiding any person not belonging to the factory will be removed from his position and turned over to the Germans authorities.

It was easy to understand that it was in the interest of the tenants of this building to have all illegal people staying there removed. There would be a re-search of all apartments, attics, and basements conducted by the Werkschutz and by the tenants themselves in order to rid the area of unwanted guests. When I asked the custodian what he wanted me to do, he answered that he would bring a friend of his over who lived on Niska Street, and he would take care of us.

After a while, during which time I took council with Jadzia's mother without coming to any conclusion, the friend showed up, a dark-eyed boy of around sixteen. He had the face, bearing, and movements of an experienced criminal and extortionist. His darting eyes took in at a glance the figure of Jadzia's mother and then alighted with interest on a new spring dress of English cotton and the excellent pair of ski boots I was wearing. Evidently the impression was favorable, for he proposed that we go through the attic over to his place on Niska

Street. He wanted twenty-five zlotys for the one-way trip, plus fifty zlotys for staying all day in their apartment. It seemed that the two boys were in business together and shared their earnings, for there were more people besides us in the building who had to pay them ransom. In fact at this very moment there was a group of six people crawling across the roof from Niska Street with their cooperation, for which they had paid ten dollars in gold. Everywhere it was time to "pay the organ grinder," as we said in the ghetto; everyone was taking bribes.

After our two youthful "protectors" had left, Jadzia's mother and I came to the conclusion that this was going to be a hard nut to crack, for we had fallen into the hands of some real "organ-grinders" who were going to threaten and terrorize us into giving them as much money as they could. However, we didn't see anything else to do, so we sat in our hiding place all day long, not daring to show ourselves to anyone.

After the day before, the baby was very restless; his entire body was covered with red spots where fleas had bitten him. Besides that, his first two teeth were coming in, which would have been a delight and joy under ordinary circumstances. Now, however, I could only look with a broken heart as he lay there on the dirty old piece of junk that had once been a sofa—the springs and stuffing sticking out of it everywhere. The vermin were now treating themselves to a second helping of his blood. The heat was simply unbearable, and the room smelled like a toilet. I was afraid to open the window for fear the baby's crying would attract someone's attention. There was hardly any space to breathe, and what air there was was swarming with flies. I sat there the whole day driving flies from the baby with a rolled up newspaper.

With darkness the shooting out on the street stopped. Jadzia's mother fixed me some noodles down in the food store and brought them up to me together with a bottle of hot cream of wheat. Then she went back to the store to get some rest, leaving me there by myself. I spread my overcoat out on the remains of the sofa and lay down beside my son. I was already beginning to fall asleep when suddenly I heard a loud scratching noise on the floor next to my handbag. The noise didn't go away, so I lit a candle which Jadzia's mother had brought and saw a rat the size of a fair-sized kitten rummaging through my things and another one just like him coming to help.

I had seen rats before in my life. Normally the sight of even a mouse running away would make me shriek in fear and dismay. Now, however, I didn't make so much as a squeak, even though I was completely numb with fear and revulsion. I pushed away the cabinet guarding the entrance to my room, grabbed the child, and ran out and down the stairs. Somehow or other I made it to the custodian's apartment. I was so overcome with fear that I couldn't even talk. The son, seeing that I had left everything upstairs, ran up to get it. He later told how he had to fight the rats off to get at my handbag. I begged the custodian to let me keep the baby there; I myself would gladly sit out in the yard for the night. She agreed to let me stay, but on the condition that I pay fifty zlotys extra for the night. Not having any other choice, I agreed. But she was even greedier than that. Without batting an eye, she asked me to give her the rest of my bread for her six-year-old little boy and two spoonfuls of condensed milk.

It hurt me most of all to give her the condensed milk, for that was all my little baby had to eat, and her six-year-old child could have eaten something else. I was dependent on her good will, and so I agreed to everything in silence. She let me put the baby at the foot of the cot where her sister was sleeping. I sat down on the floor next to him to make sure he didn't fall off and to calm him down in case he started to cry, for I was afraid that even in spite of the money the woman would get tired of our company and not let us stay the following night.

I didn't sleep all night long. Just as the previous night at Saba's, enormous fleas kept biting us mercilessly. Even the floor was covered with them, and wherever I put my hand on my body I would catch one. The baby woke up crying several times during the night. I wasn't even able to change him in the dark, because I was afraid of knocking against the feet of the sister who was asleep. It was with both relief and apprehension that I greeted the dawn, not knowing what the new day would bring.

A German and the Werkschutz appeared in the courtyard calling all the workers to the factory. It took about half an hour for everyone to assemble in columns of three and leave, led by the same German.

Through a crack in the curtain I could see that, except for a single woman, all those going to work were men. After they left, the custodian let me tidy myself up a bit, and then I had to go back to my hiding place. I had decided not to go back to Saba's because of an unpleasant incident there. During the night I spent in her apartment I had removed an inexpensive bracelet from my wrist which my husband had brought me as a souvenir from Kraków during a business trip. I forgot about it and left it underneath my pillow, and when I came back it was missing. When I asked about it, everyone said that they hadn't seen it, so I understood that they were just another gang of thieves. Besides, I had learned that they themselves were hiding illegally. They stayed all day on Niska Street, returning at night through the attic to their other apartment. They had managed to keep it due to the fact that no one among the Ursus workers had wanted such a dingy little apartment up under the roof. They lived by thieving and stealing. Such were Saba and her two accomplices, to whom Jadzia had sent me for protection. Of the two evils I chose the custodian's family, seeing that they had no need to hide from the other tenants.

I went to my hiding place in the morning, trembling with fear at the thought of running into more rats. It seemed that they only came out at night, for I didn't meet any more during the day.

That same Tuesday morning Jadzia's mother came to see me, very upset. Through a crack in the store wall she had seen Schultz's car drive up with one of the workers, Wewiorowski (a Pole), in it. He had read out the names of several women and children from a list and then, taking them on board, had headed in the direction of Smocza Street. Our names had not been on the list, and Jadzia's mother was feeling very sad and disheartened. When she saw that I didn't have any more bread, she shared with me what little was left of hers.

As my only source of encouragement, I read over and over the words of my husband's last letter in which he had written that in two or at the most three days he would get me out. Now was only the second day; I had to make it through one more day. I believed the words of my husband, and nothing else made any difference to me.

When I later gave the custodian's wife a bit of cream of wheat and some sugar to fix my baby something to eat, she brought me back a bottle of hot water with a few grains of cream of wheat in it, sweetened with saccharine. Once more I had to hold my peace, even though I was being cheated in a disgraceful manner.

The shooting continued all through this day too. The custodian's wife told me that the Germans had taken all the children they found wandering along Miła Street to a building, and shot them all there. All through Tuesday cars drove by, picking up the corpses of children and taking them to the cemetery. Mountains of corpses kept piling up in the cemetery, and the burial workers there had difficulty keeping up digging pits for all of them. They piled them one on top of the other in layers, up to dozens in a single pit. All along Miła Street the horde of Germans, Ukrainians, and Latvians raged on, unleashing their murderous instincts on their helpless victims.

The unfortunate people caught in hiding were shot on the spot, and the rest were taken in groups of several thousand to the Umschlag-platz, where they were immediately loaded into freight cars. In accordance with their by-now time-honored tradition, the Germans would open fire on the crowd with machine guns in order to expedite the loading process. The custodian's wife went on to tell how, as she swept the sidewalk that morning, she noticed on the other side of the fence the bodies of a number of newly born children. Some of them, still alive, were squealing pitifully. Abandoned by their mothers, they were dying of starvation.

This day too passed without making any particular impression on me. Like the preceding day, I spent it driving away flies and talking with Jadzia's mother. I was at least thankful that fate had provided me with a companion. We kept talking about how we were going to get out of this ghastly place. We didn't doubt for a minute that Jadzia and my husband would do everything possible to get us out.

25

MR. BRAUN

That evening the Werkschutz announced that the Ursus workers had been held up at the factory and would not be coming home that night. In the first place, it meant that we would go hungry, for we counted on their returning with food obtained on the Aryan side. Secondly, the news indicated that the factory administration had decided to hold the workers with the intention of removing their families during their absence. We all expected a blockade in our building next day. That evening the custodian's wife was nicer to me, for she allowed me to rinse out my diapers in cold water and didn't ask for any milk. The woman's sister, the baby, and I all slept together on the same cot, which enabled me to get a little rest and even to doze off for a while.

Wednesday arrived, the third day of our stay on Miła Street, the day I expected to leave this awful place. Just as the day before, Jadzia's mother came and told me that Wewiorowski had driven by in his car, taking many more women and children with him than the day before. Once more our names had not been on the list. She and I were equally angry. I began to think that maybe she hadn't heard our names when they were called, but she assured me that she had been waiting there since daybreak. She recited a few names to me, and as soon as I heard them I realized that these people were all very rich. I realized that neither Jadzia nor my husband would be able to get us out that way. My instincts were correct, for later I learned that it had cost 50,000 zlotys per head to be picked up on Miła Street by the factory automobile. We kept hoping that some kind of miracle would take place.

At seven o'clock in the morning the Werkschutz announced through a megaphone: "Attention! Attention! A blockade is expected! Everyone please hide!"

In a flash women and children began pouring out of all the entry-ways. Hunched over as they passed along the wall, they all headed for our entryway and up into the attic. Even the Werkschutz disappeared somewhere. We didn't have any more bread, but we were so upset that food was our last concern. My biggest worry was getting hot water for the baby. I had fed it that morning in the custodian's apartment, and at eight o'clock I had gotten a bottle of boiled water which I wrapped in a flannel diaper and kept under my bra between my breasts, so that it would keep warm from the heat of my body. Where was I going to get water at noon and later on?

I knew for sure that no one would leave the attic all day long to light a fire in their apartment; there wasn't any gas in the building anyway. The problem with the water worried me more than the impending blockade. Jadzia's mother and I sat there, not daring to move a muscle. Suddenly the clatter of many feet could be heard overhead, as people ran full speed across the attic above us. I was certain the ceiling was going to collapse on top of us. Soon the cupboard blocking the entrance to our hiding place was abruptly shoved aside and a huge mob of people forced their way in.

It seemed that a blockade was taking place in the Felix shop on Niska Street, and people from there were trying to hide in our building. The throng immediately began giving my overcoat and boots thoughtful glances. One of the men offered me three hundred zlotys for the overcoat. I assured him that it was not for sale, and so he offered me another deal: in exchange for the boots he would give me a can of condensed milk. When I also declined this offer, he asked if I had any currency to change. I replied politely that I had no money at all with me. I began to be a little frightened of this band from Niska, for I could see that I had run into the worst element—thieves and extortionists.

This entire conversation was followed attentively by a man of around forty, who stood out clearly from the rest of the newcomers. In spite of his relatively young age, he was almost completely gray. His face wore a kind and intelligent expression, and he was looking keenly around. I would have noticed him in any case, because he limped very badly and had to support himself with a cane. After our uninvited guests had departed, as they did after the blockade was over, this gentleman introduced himself as Wiktor Braun, Doctor of Law. He told me in a fatherly sort of way that I had to be very careful with that group of people, for they would try to steal from me any way they could. He told me that he was staying in the apartment of his brother, who worked for Ursus. He also told me what I had already figured out for myself, that my hiding place was well known to everyone. There was practically no chance that I would go unnoticed during a blockade. Besides that, the baby would give me away easily. He promised to bring me a bottle of French wine to give the baby in case I needed to make him sleep. He also promised that he would ask his friend who was hiding across the way from my apartment—likewise behind a cupboard concealing the entrance to a second room—to look after me. He would gladly do it himself, he said, but he was still recovering from a protracted joint disease. He had been bedridden for an entire year and only lately had been able to get around a little, but his legs were still stiff at the knees and walking was very difficult.

We sat there all day long, talking with each other like old friends. I felt as if we had known each other for years. Gunfire could still be heard out on the street, and I was beginning to go crazy from the continuous racket. During the day they shot people, while at night they kept up the fire just for the sake of keeping us in terror. We waited impatiently until six o'clock, which was when the workers returned from the factory, but alas! They didn't return this day either.

I hadn't had anything to eat all day except for a couple of sugar cubes. That evening Braun sent me through his sister-in-law the bottle of wine for the baby and a small piece of coarse bread for me. As I thanked her for the gifts I felt a sob spasmodically grip my throat: I appreciated so well the kindness and generosity of this gesture. Braun was the only noble and unselfish person I met, not only during my stay on Miła Street, but during the entire course of my peregrinations from one end of the ghetto to the other.

I spent the night wondering why I hadn't received any news from my husband, even though three whole days had gone by. Braun promised me that when his brother returned he would take a letter from me to my husband and give it to the gate-keeper at our factory. The gathering point for all workers going to work on the Aryan side was located on Leszno Street, right next to the K. G. Schultz factory. Unfortunately, the Ursus workers had not returned home for two days, so Braun's good intentions came to naught. I realized full well that it was very dangerous to remain in this spot any longer. I knew that the Nazis would never leave until they had shot everyone or sent them to Treblinka. I became resigned to the idea of dying without the fear and resistance I had felt before.

Next morning, thoroughly broken and exhausted both physically and mentally, I was on my way up to my hiding place when the custodian's wife appeared, asking for money. I had no other choice but to tell her that all I had was ten rubles in gold and that she could try to change it for me. She called her son and his friend from Niska Street, and they offered me four hundred zlotys. I laughed in their faces and told them that I knew that the current rate of exchange would bring eight hundred zlotys, but I would let them have it for seven hundred. The group of conniving thieves went into conference, and after a while the woman returned, bringing me an account in which she had marked such overinflated prices for boiled water and for the privilege of rinsing my diapers in cold water that there was very little change left out of the seven hundred zlotys. I was very tired of haggling and, besides, the idea of any further conversation with this woman was totally repugnant to me, so I gave her the gold without another word. She took it eagerly and put it into her already bulging purse, which she concealed beneath her blouse. I looked at her with a mixture of scorn and pity.

That same morning, Jadzia's mother had in vain looked for our factory's automobile: it had stopped coming. She came to me, sobbing like a little child. She told me that she had the feeling that today was the last day of our lives, and she insisted that we write farewell letters— she to her daughters and I to my husband—and give them to Braun so he could try to deliver them. I was so affected by her words that I too began to believe that these were the last hours of my life. We wrote our letters on a piece of heavy paper we found, I on one side and she on the other. I couldn't see what I was writing for the tears filling my eyes. In the letter I said goodbye to my husband, the dearest friend I ever had in good times or bad. My words, full of love and pain, flowed onto the paper.

I repeated over and over that my last wish and desire at the hour of my death was for him to take Michalski up on his proposal as soon as possible—not to waste any time but to leave everything and go over to the Aryan side.

My husband never had a chance to read that letter. One day he found it in the pocket of my overcoat, and when he started to read it, he burst into tears and couldn't finish it, its contents pained him so much. Jadzia's husband kept the letter as a memento, and he perished together with it in the ruins of the burning ghetto.

26

THE LAST CAN OF CONDENSED MILK

But let me return to that Thursday, so rich in events. After writing our farewell letter we handed it instead of Braun to his friend Rosenschein, who was also hiding there with his wife and nine-year-old son. They had come here across the roof from Niska Street by paying ten dollars. From what he told me I learned that he and his wife worked in the Toebbens shop on Leszno Street where they also had an apartment. He showed me his and his wife's numbers, with which they could have returned home, but they didn't want to go back without their child, so they decided either to save him or all die together.

Next day Rosenschein returned my letter, saying that he wouldn't be able to deliver it because he and his family were returning to Niska Street where they had their "hideout." He advised me, while there was still time, to do the same thing and crawl with the baby through the small opening down a ladder into the other attic on Niska Street, where he said he would give me whatever help he could. I decided to give it a try, and after crossing a number of attics I finally squeezed through a narrow opening, normally covered during blockades by an upended mattress, onto a slightly slanting roof. Then I had to crawl on my knees in order to get through an opening in the floor which led down a ladder onto another roof belonging to a building on Niska Street. A grown person would not normally have had any difficulty in making the passage, but with a child in my arms it was a difficult maneuver, and what would it be like, I thought, at a time of great danger, when everyone wanted to be first to save his own life? At such moments people changed into wild beasts and trampled one another underfoot without giving it a second thought.

I came back from the attic in a very gloomy frame of mind. I couldn't decide whether to stay here or to make the move to Niska while I still could, and I ended up staying in the old hiding place because of the child. Here at least I had somewhere to put him down and change him when I needed to, and I could get hot water to mix with my condensed milk. I lived for the baby alone and was prepared to undergo the severest hardship in order to give him anything that could make life easier for him and keep him alive. The only thought still burning in my disjointed mind was the hope that God would spare me the sight of my child's death—that he would let me be the first to die, if that was how it had to be.

We sat through this day too without anything to eat but cube sugar. Jadzia's mother became more and more restless. She couldn't stay put in one place but walked excitedly back and forth in our cramped little room, her face flushed. Finally she decided to leave me, explaining that in case of a blockade the baby might break out crying and give us away. She went across the roof to Niska Street, leaving me alone with the baby, for which I was actually quite glad.

I knew that if no one had come for us, it was because nothing could be done yet. I thought I would just stay put until they blockaded the house, and then they would either shoot me or take me away, which amounted to the same thing. I must admit that I would have preferred to die right there rather than make the final journey to Treblinka.

My sad thoughts were interrupted by the cupboard being violently shoved aside. A tall, decently dressed man about twenty years old entered my hiding place and told me sharply: "Leave this place immediately; you have no right to be in this building and endanger the work and lives of all of us by your presence."

I asked him who he was and what right he had to talk to me like that. Making his way toward the door he replied that in another minute he would bring the Werkschutz and they would explain things to me if I was so interested.

I knew that as soon as he brought the Werkschutz it would all be over, for they would simply put me outside the gates of the building into the clutches of the Germans. I tried every feminine wile at my disposal, and I am still embarrassed to think of how I let myself be taken in by this young monster. I started crying bitterly and begged him to leave me in peace if for no other reason than because of the baby, for he wouldn't want to have the death of an innocent child on his conscience. On his way out he added that a general control of all apartments was planned for later that day with the participation of a German, and that if I would give him three hundred zlotys he would give it to the German so that he wouldn't look in on me in my hiding place. I told him that I didn't have any money and he said that then there was nothing else to be done and I had to leave.

I didn't believe for a moment his story about the control with the German, but I was genuinely afraid that he would call in the Werkschutz, and I didn't see anything to do but give him my watch as a pledge until the evening. If there really was a German control, I would give him the money, but if not, he would return my watch. Finally, he left me in peace, without saying either yes or no. I was unable to calm down after he left, not because I regretted losing the watch, but because I was so upset at the sight of human depravity unleashed in the face of mortal danger.

It was with the utmost relief that I greeted the arrival of Mr. Braun, who had brought me a bottle of boiled water for the baby. The custodian's wife hadn't shown her face all day long after taking the gold from me, probably because she was afraid that I would ask for change. When Braun heard what had happened, he could hardly control his anger. He decided to stay there with me till the evening so that no one else would harass me. When I described what the boy looked like he told me that he was the son of a woman who had come here during a blockade on Niska Street and that, having picked me out as a likely victim, she must have sent her son over to "make the kill." Fortunately they lived in the same building, and Braun said he would try to get him to return my watch. Later I learned that the boy himself was living here illegally and that only his father was working.

At four o'clock in the afternoon the gate leading into our building suddenly opened and a single German burst in holding a revolver at the ready. Three shots rang out quickly one after the other. This startled the baby and he began to cry. I tried to give him some wine, but he didn't want it. He spat it out and cried all the harder. Braun, white as a sheet, asked me to calm the baby. It was easy to say, but something else again to do it. I began to understand why Jadzia's mother and all the other people ran away from me as soon as they saw the baby. My only thought was that Braun was going to perish because of me, but finally I managed to get the baby to settle down.

I heard an angry voice speaking German in the courtyard and another, quieter voice, which I recognized as being that of our custodian. Next I heard loud steps coming up the stairs and I was sure that the end was near. My eyes were riveted on the door as if hypnotized, expecting the German to come bursting in with his revolver pointed at me. Then I heard steps above in the attic, followed by the sound of steps going down the stairs, three bursts of gunfire in the courtyard, and then the alarm at the gate. Then it was quiet again, but we sat there for a long time before daring to move. The baby was asleep. I looked down at the emaciated little face, which had until recently been in full blossom but now had the color of faded ivory.

Darkness fell swiftly. Jadzia's mother came and told me what had happened. It seemed that some man had left his two children in our building and had sent a German friend of his over to pick them up. The children were hidden on Niska Street, and the custodian, when summoned, didn't know a thing about them. The German put a revolver to his head. The frightened boy took him up to the roof, but not before everyone there had scattered. The children couldn't be found, and the German promised to make a return visit the following day. He said that if the children couldn't be found by then, everyone in the building would be shot.

At six o'clock in the evening, to our great relief and joy, the Ursus workers returned loaded down with supplies. Only the workers' families got to share in the food, however, for they didn't want to sell it to anyone else. After much searching Jadzia's mother brought back a kilogram of black bread, which was impossible to swallow even though we were starved; she had paid 150 zlotys for it. That night exhaustion took the upper hand and, despite the vermin and discomforts, I slept soundly straight through until dawn.

Friday arrived, the fifth day of our stay in this building. The workers left for work in the morning. The two children being sought were located and placed in the yard in the care of the Werkschutz. We learned that there were only a few people left on Miła Street, and that blockades were going to be held in all the workers' quarters along the street, including in the building in which we were staying. At eight o'clock the Werkschutz announced that a blockade was immanent and that everyone should hide. Jadzia's mother changed her place of hiding for the day, going with the custodian's wife and a few other selected tenants into the cellar, into which the son locked them with a padlock. The others, as usual, went up into the attic.

Braun felt sick after the events of the previous day and had to remain in bed. Before locking himself into his hiding place, Rosenschein came over to ask me whether I wanted to stay there or whether I wanted him to help get me over to Niska Street. For the sake of the baby's comfort I decided to stay in my own hiding place. He pushed the cupboard in front of the door and stuffed all the crooks and crannies with rags, of which there was no lack in this junk heap, so that the camouflaged door would not be visible at first glance. I was left alone with the baby, whose first teeth had appeared just this day. The coming evening was our New Year's Eve—Rosh Hashana, the saddest and most tragic New Year's Eve in our entire lives.

The heat was very bad all day long, and the gunfire was particularly heavy. I worried about the fact that I had already opened my second can of condensed milk. I had no idea what I would do to feed the baby after that. I remembered the circumstances in which I had bought that milk in 1940, before the baby had even been conceived. A neighbor of ours had received it in a package from abroad at a time when they were already talking about closing the ghetto and about the hunger that would result. People were laying in supplies, and so I bought that can of milk, without attaching any importance to it.

Several weeks earlier, during my husband's attack of bronchitis, he had asked me to open one of the cans of milk to see if it would do anything to help his cough. I didn't open it, however, for I somehow felt an internal prohibition against it. Now this milk was saving the life of my baby, showing how sometimes even the most insignificant events can take on the greatest importance later on.

27

ROSH HASHANA, 1942

At around two o'clock in the afternoon, I suddenly heard wild shouts, shots, running, and moans. After several minutes Braun came over, barely dragging himself along on his lame legs.

From his window he had seen how a man had broken away from a group being taken to the Umschlagplatz and with a single blow of his fist had torn out a board in the fence and gotten past the gate of the neighboring building, Miła 38, also one of the buildings used by the Ursus workers. The Germans and Ukrainians had run in after him. Seeing as our executioners were right next door, Braun advised me to go with the baby to the attic and from there to Niska Street. He himself offered to stay and look after my things. I listened to the advice of this good-willed and selfless individual; the only thing I took with me was a baby bottle. Besides the ladder leading over to Niska Street stood an old man with a hideous face and a nasty expression. This turned out to be the father of Heniek—the extortion artist whom I knew so well. He wouldn't let me put a foot on the ladder until I had paid him twenty-five zlotys for "admission."

After pleading with him he finally allowed me to pass on the condition that I would pay him later that evening. I went into one of the apartments; there were so many people in this filthy stinking space that there was scarcely any air to breathe. The room was literally crawling with gigantic beetles, cockroaches, and other kinds of vermin whose names I didn't even know.

When I saw all these "suspect characters" and blackmailers gathered together, I couldn't help but ask myself why, even in the face of death, they hadn't changed their way of life. Didn't they realize that sooner or later the Nazis were going to exterminate all the Jews in the ghetto?

In the beginning, the Nazis had killed off the intelligentsia, people of education and value, such as Dr. Janusz Korczak,[1] famous the world over as a writer, psychologist, and educator. My heart contracted with sorrow at the memory of dear Dr. Korczak with his gentle gaze and sonorous voice. Before the war I often had occasion to visit the orphanage on Krochmalna Street, of which he was the organizer and director and where he was father to all those light and dark-haired boys and girls. This institution always made the impression on me of a large private home. The atmosphere of love and warmth could be felt everywhere. Even the most recalcitrant children were won over with a single look from his gentle eyes.

One day at the beginning of the evacuation, the Nazis burst into his orphanage and ordered everyone to assemble in a column and move down the street. In order to calm the children, he said to them: "We are going on a trip, children. We are all going to take a train ride and see the fields, forests, and meadows in full bloom." At the Umschlagplatz the Germans offered Dr. Korczak his freedom, but he categorically refused, saying that his place was with his children. The children together with the entire orphanage personnel perished in the gas chambers of Treblinka.

Now, as I looked at the "gangrene" that was left, I couldn't help thinking that they, like the Jewish Police, were only an embarrassment and disgrace to us. Even now, in the face of death, they were trying to prey on me by offering various kinds of "transactions." Being unable to drive off this band of thieves, I went out into the corridor.

Suddenly a cry rang out, passing through everyone like a shock: Blockade! Like a mad herd of cattle, the people dashed off. I was carried along by the crowd until I too found myself next to the ladder. But here I ran up against an obstacle in the form of Heniek's father; Heniek was already taking down the ladder. Either I pay him five hundred zlotys right now, he said, or I would be left here for the Germans. I looked around and saw that I was the only person still there. If I hadn't had the baby in my arms I would most likely have hit him. As it was, I said a few words of abuse, doing all I could to control myself, and turned away. All the doors which had previously been open were now locked. Vainly I banged on them and asked to be let in. I was left alone with the baby in an empty corridor.

Suddenly I noticed a dark recess in the farthest corner. It was very long, and I carefully moved about twenty steps into it until I came up against a door. I gave it a little push and, miraculously, it opened. I found myself in a darkened kitchen, full of straw and the most amazing assortment of rubbish. From there I entered a small room with sloping walls. I sat down on a large overturned pot and began feeding the baby the rest of the milk in the bottle, which I carried with me now at all times, warming it with my body. Two middle-aged women were sitting behind a bundle of straw, quietly murmuring prayers for the dead.

I exchanged no more than a word or two with the women, and we all fell to dozing. We sat that way for several hours. By the time we decided to leave our hiding place it was already dark in the room. The women helped me up into the attic. There I came upon my extortionist. I turned to him sharply and demanded that he return my watch, and he impudently replied that there had been a control and the German (he had in mind the one who had come for the two children) had come into our entry and he, Heniek, had personally guided him around and passed by my hiding place. For this he said I had to pay three hundred zlotys or he wouldn't return the watch. I told him to cut out the nonsense and that if he didn't give back my watch immediately I would go to the head of the Werkschutz and tell him everything; I added that I knew he was here illegally, just like me. The boy took fright and quickly changed his tune. He agreed to return the watch for only one hundred zlotys, adding that he didn't have it with him at the moment. That evening I sent the custodian's son over to get it, giving them only fifty zlotys. I wouldn't have given them anything at all, but I was afraid to carry out my threat.

When I returned from Niska Street, I found the worthy Mr. Braun waiting patiently for my return. He told me that it had been a false alarm. After I was gone, a whole band of crooks had pushed their way into my hiding place on the pretext of the blockade, so that in my absence they could steal my overcoat. Mr. Braun read them a sermon on decency, which I am sure went in one ear and out the other.

The Ursus workers once more had not returned from work, and fear came to nest once again in our hearts. I was also seriously concerned about Jadzia's mother. She had returned from the cellar with her eyes burning from fever. She complained that she felt very weak and probably had dysentery. I was very upset at the news, for during the several days we had spent together she and I had grown quite close. The only advice I could give her was not to eat and to drink only black coffee, which she was able to buy in the store. I myself had been living on nothing but cube sugar, and no longer even felt hungry.

Next day was Saturday—Rosh Hashana. Braun brought me a liter thermos full of boiled water for the baby, for which I was more grateful than I could say. Jadzia's mother brought me a little hot cream of wheat, saying that today for the first time in her life she had lighted a fire on New Year's Day. She knew that I hadn't had anything to eat for three days, even though I am not one to complain of hunger. I was touched by their kindness and concern. There were very few such people left now. I told Jadzia's mother, as if explaining something to a child, that she should go lie down in the store, for she looked very poorly. I told her about fate and about death which, once a person is chosen, will seek him out no matter where he tries to hide. She listened to my advice and went to lie down.

The Werkschutz, as every day, said that there would be a blockade and ordered everyone to hide. Soon it was quiet everywhere. Only the two children, for whom the German had not come yesterday, were sitting next to one another in the yard.

Suddenly I felt as if a great burden of sadness had been lifted from my heart. I no longer felt afraid. I am not sure whether I was becoming reconciled to my fate or whether it was because of the new year. I dozed off and the hours passed one after the other without anything happening. After some time I became aware that the shooting, which had been going on for several days without ceasing, had suddenly come to an end. Then I heard someone loudly shouting my name out in the courtyard. Curious, I went to the window. Down below I saw Jadzia's mother, purple in the face, running for all she was worth and shouting for me to come downstairs quickly, for her daughter had come for us.

I dressed myself and the baby in great haste, threw the rest of my things into my handbag, and hurried downstairs. Jadzia's younger sister who was working in the Big Schultz shop on Nowolipie was waiting for us in the street. About half an hour earlier the Germans, Ukrainians, and Latvians had left, abandoning the sentry box on Lubecki and Smocza. I listened to this news with a great deal of skepticism. Knowing the Nazis and their tricks as I did, I sensed that this was just a new one for anyone gullible enough to fall for it. Jadzia's mother didn't hesitate for a moment, but I asked a man from the Werkschutz to tell me if what she said was true. He answered that he didn't know anything about it, adding, however, that once I crossed the gate he was not going to let me back in.

That decided it for me, and I turned back. At that point Jadzia's mother, who had already gone several dozen paces down the street with her daughter, looked back and, seeing that I intended to go back, returned herself. She ripped the handbag out of my hands and shoved me out onto the street.

"Don't say anything!" she commanded, as if in a trance. "We don't have anything to lose. On the day of Rosh Hashana we should simply put ourselves in the hands of God."

Her words made such an impression on me that I stopped resisting.

---

1. **Korczak, Janusz** (1879-1942). The pen name of Henryk Goldszmit, Korczak was a Polish Jewish educator, children's author, pedagogue, and the director of an orphanage in Warsaw. When his institution was closed by the Nazis and the children were sent to Treblinka, he rejected offers to be rescued and accompanied the children to their death.

28

ESCAPE FROM MIŁA STREET

We ran down the street. The first wooden gate which the Germans had erected on the corner of Lubecki and Miła was standing open. Besides us, there wasn't a living soul on the streets. We ran out on the road because the sidewalks were blocked by piles of pans, suitcases, and blankets. Once past the sentry box we began to meet sporadic pedestrians. When they saw the four of us carrying a tiny baby in our arms they would stop us and ask where we were coming from. When we replied that we were coming from Miła Street they didn't believe us and made us repeat it: From Miła! You mean the road is clear? Along the way we met an old Jew with a long white beard—quite a rarity in those days. Looking in amazement at my son, he proclaimed in a solemn tone: If you have managed to keep that baby alive this far, then it will be saved. He made a motion above the head of the baby as if to bless it.

Jadzia's sister told us that there was no question of our returning to Leszno, because during the past six days K. G. Schultz had ordered a brick wall built around the two buildings on 76 and 78 Leszno Street, and entry was forbidden to all outsiders. The workers were in effect imprisoned and could not leave under penalty of losing their jobs, which was the same thing as death. The buildings were connected by a huge opening that had been knocked out between them. The workers went from 76 to 78 to work and then back home again through this opening. Jadzia's sister decided to put us up in her place for the time being. She had an assigned apartment on Nowolipki, and it was not as difficult to get into as ours.

Their shop had two streets designated for workers' quarters: part of the odd-numbered side of Nowolipki as far as Karmelicka and both sides of Nowolipie from Smocza to Karmelicka. On Nowolipki I noticed my cousins' brother-in-law. I called over to him and told him of my situation. He took the child from me and led me to his apartment. The Werkschutz let us into the building without any difficulty. I even had time to give my address to Jadzia's sister and mother, and soon I found myself in the arms of my dear old aunt. How changed she was from before. Until recently she had been full of life, but now she was barely able to keep to her feet. I learned that there was a disreputable band of German soldiers operating in the building who came around at night demanding money. The previous night they had come to my aunt's apartment. All of the other tenants had managed to escape through the kitchen entrance, but my aunt, paralyzed with fear, had stayed in bed. My aunt handed them a hundred zlotys, assuring them that that was all she had. They took the money and left, but my aunt still hadn't regained control of herself.

My relatives were shocked at my and the baby's appearance. I hadn't realized it myself, but when I looked more closely at the baby I saw that he had changed drastically. His face was completely colorless, and it pained me terribly to see him like that. Without milk or air, it was not going to be easy keeping him alive for much longer. In view of this, my main concern was to get out of there as quickly as possible. From that moment on my thoughts flowed in one direction only: to get to the Aryan side.

My cousins' brother-in-law came in; he was extremely agitated at the news that the Germans and their comrades-in-arms, the Ukrainians, Lithuanians, and Latvians, had returned to their stations. Miła Street was again surrounded, and a massacre was in progress. The Ursus workers' quarters—in other words, precisely where I had come from—had fallen first victim. Since there were too few for a shipment to Treblinka, everyone had been murdered on the spot. I never again met a single person from Miła or Niska Streets.

I had very much wanted to meet Mr. Braun again, in order to thank him for his kindness and generosity, but now I knew that we would never meet again in this world. Thanks to Jadzia's mother and sister, I had escaped death. Everything in life is foreordained.

Jadzia's sister brought her mother to stay with my aunt and went herself to the factory gate on 78 Leszno Street to tell my husband and Jadzia about our miraculous escape. When she returned she brought me five hundred zlotys and a photograph of myself from my husband.

He wrote that for the time being it was impossible to get me into their building because of Schultz's strict regulations. I was supposed to try to get work in the Big Schultz shop on Nowolipie, where there was a greater chance of success, for thousands of workers were still employed there, and there was no limitation on their number as there was in our factory.

I should mention that this was the last time I saw Jadzia's mother. As we learned from Jadzia's letters, she was able to hide her mother in the apartment up until the very end, that is, up until April 1943, when the remainder of the Jews perished heroically in the flames and ashes of the burning buildings, defending themselves to their last breath.

My entire family, including my aunt (my uncle had died in 1941 of spotted typhus) and my cousins, had suffered very little. They were in the fortunate position of having a hiding place in one of the apartments of the Toebbens shop where military blankets were laundered. The owner and director of this laundry was their friend from before the war, because they had been in the same business of tanning.

When blockades took place in the Big Schultz shop, my cousins were always forewarned and went with their families to the laundry, and in this way they had avoided the massacre on Miła Street. My cousins bought numbers for their wives and for the five-year-old daughter of one of them. The Big Schultz factory was more kindly disposed toward children than ours. Both cousins, one of them with his wife and five-year-old daughter, lived through the war. The older one, still married and with his daughter, lives in Israel; the younger one lives in Brazil.

After our miraculous escape from Miła Street, one of my cousins took me to my sister's apartment, where she, her husband, and eleven-year-old son were attached to the Big Schultz factory. We were able to make it to my sister's without being stopped by anyone. The way was made easier because an entire wall had been knocked down between 23 Nowolipki and 30 Nowolipie Streets.

Very little had changed in my sister's apartment, the customary confusion notwithstanding. When I walked inside, the thought occurred to me that everything I had been through had been nothing but a bad dream. Bitter reality asserted itself very quickly. Since the closing of the ghetto, my sister had been living in a deplorable situation. The store which she had been renting was located outside the ghetto, and it had been impossible to exchange it for another, as many people had done, when it had been taken over by force by Volksdeutsch.

My sister was then forced to rely on the very small and irregular earnings of her husband. If it had not been for our help they would have died of starvation long ago, along with tens of thousands of others. Now, because of the highly inflated prices (a kilogram of potatoes in their factory cost twenty zlotys as compared to ten zlotys in our factory and two zlotys on the Aryan side), they were unable to buy anything on the black market. The two of them and their eleven-year-old son, who had been lucky enough to be hired as an errand boy, lived on the food given out at the factory: three-quarters of a liter of watery soup and, from time to time, one eighth of a kilogram of bread per person.

In order to help her family, my sister did laundry at night for single men whose families had been taken away. For an entire night's washing, and a second night of ironing the same, she would get half a kilogram of millet porridge. All of this jarred terribly on my already frayed nerves. It was impossible to get work as my husband had advised, and even if I had been able to, I didn't have anyone to leave the baby with; my sister, her husband, and my nephew worked from six o'clock in the morning until six o'clock at night.

I was certain that all my privations and struggles were leading nowhere, I was just going from one trap into another. Danger lurked everywhere, and it was hardly any wonder that after so many weeks of toil I felt completely broken. Jadzia's sister stopped coming around. I had no contact with my husband at all. My sister would return at night totally exhausted and diligently start on her laundry. The eyes of this woman, barely thirty, which until recently had been so full of fire, were ringed with big red circles; she was losing her sight from malnutrition. Her husband, who before the war had weighed ninety-six kilograms, was nothing but a yellow skeleton; his only desire was to eat his fill at least one last time before he died.

For days on end I didn't get anything to eat. What good was five hundred zlotys with prices the way they were and with so many hungry mouths to feed? The condensed milk had run out, so I had to buy cream of wheat, butter, and sugar, which took most of my money.

There was one woman, Mrs. Lipowski, the daughter of the owner-director of the laundry where my cousins had their hideout, who had a large reserve, several dozen boxes, of Falier's Phosphatine, left over from before the war. When she heard that I had a baby who was in very bad condition from malnutrition, she offered to exchange some of it. When I replied that I had no food to trade but would pay anything she asked, she declined, saying that she would find a buyer who would be able to give her what she wanted. I am curious to learn whether Mrs. Lipowski was able to rescue her phosphatine from the burning ghetto and take it with her to the other world and, if so, whether she was ever able to find a suitable customer for it.

I often looked out on the street through a crack in the curtain to see what life was like in a shop which, even now, after all the blockades, still employed 8000 people. The street was swarming with people in the short section from Smocza to Karmelicka. The traffic was the same as before the evacuation, except that all the stores were closed. Here and there on the street someone would be selling bread, potatoes, or other vegetables, providing food to those who could afford it. The retail stores were open only when they received small rations of bread and other insignificant products, which could be bought for ration cards. It was possible to buy butter, ham, and other food items privately but for extremely high prices, because the food would have already passed through three or four hands by the time it reached you. This kind of food came from shops which had branches or locations on the Aryan side.

From seven o'clock in the morning, the street was deserted. Up until that time the night shift would be returning home, the day shift already being at work. The Werkschutz stood by the gate leading into the factory. From time to time trucks would drive up to take on loads of goods manufactured in the shops or old uniforms which had been reconditioned for the German soldiers. The trucks also brought raw materials and old military uniforms for reconditioning. The people working on these transports became rich, because they were able to smuggle food from the Aryan side beneath the piles of material. People were transported out of the ghetto in the same way—but only those who had someone with whom they could hide on the other side. In all fairness, it must be admitted that these drivers took great risks in doing this.

The gates of the workers' quarters were normally open from five o'clock in the morning until nine o'clock in the evening. The Werkschutz did not man the gates here as they did in our factory. Only the wooden gates leading out of the complex on Karmelicka and on the corner of Nowolipie and Smocza were guarded. Within the enclosed area, people could move about freely.

Comparing life in this shop with ours, I could see that the people in the Big Schultz shop had it much better. I noticed many mothers leading their children by the hand on the streets after work. Occasionally I would even see children being pushed in a baby carriage. In our factory, even if a mother was able to smuggle her baby in, she still had to hide it so that even her closest neighbors didn't find out about it.

Here every family had its own separate apartment, while in our factory several families lived together in two rooms, constantly having to move. When I thought about all this, I had to come to the conclusion that if at the beginning of resettlement I hadn't insisted so strongly on my husband's getting into the shop where Jadzia worked, we would have stayed at the Big Schultz shop and saved ourselves an enormous amount of suffering and pain. However, later events were to prove that my first impulse had been correct.

29

BACK AT MY SISTER'S

A young boy came to our apartment, saying that he could put me in contact with my husband by carrying a letter for me. The boy didn't make a very good impression on me, because by that time I was extremely suspicious of everybody. Since he agreed to take fifty zlotys in payment after bringing me a reply from my husband, I accepted his proposal. Before evening I had a letter in which my husband wrote for me to keep my spirits up, for he was doing everything he could so that we could be together. This news cheered me very much.

Early next morning the boy came around again, saying that I and the baby were to be ready to leave by five o'clock in the afternoon. How impatiently I waited for the hour to arrive! I simply couldn't believe that at last my fondest hopes were to be fulfilled and I would be together again with my husband. My heart was beating rapidly; I began to think that the boy would never come, but he did. I never saw my sister, her husband, or their son again. After the uprising in 1943, they were taken along with many others to the camp in Poniatowa[1] where they were shot.

My guide and I climbed aboard a rickshaw which carried a sign saying that it belonged to the Big Schultz company on Nowolipie. The rickshaws were for the use of the shops, but their owners could use them in their spare time to make money on the side. This one was run by the brother of my guide. I hid the baby as best I could under my overcoat. My guide held my handbag in his lap, which served to conceal at least partially my precious "live" cargo. The Werkschutz let us out without difficulty. I knew that along the way we had to pass two points where we would be in danger of being stopped: the headquarters of the Death Squad on the corner of Żelazna and Nowolipie and the German sentry box on Leszno and Żelazna. My lips moved soundlessly as I prayed to God for mercy.

I need not have worried, as we stopped on the sidewalk between the buildings on 76 and 78 Leszno Street without having experienced any issues. I sat in the rickshaw by myself, while the two boys disappeared somewhere. My son began to protest, twisting around and crying a little.

Finally my guide appeared and took me to 74 Leszno. This was a building belonging to the workers of the Toebbens shop. He left me there, saying that someone would come for me. I paid him and after a short while a bricklayer appeared who took me up to the top floor of a stairway. From there we climbed up a ladder onto a steep roof. At that point he took the baby from me and told me to wait. After a minute he returned, saying that the baby was already in the arms of his father. Then he told me to follow him. This was the first time in my life I had ever walked on a roof. Normally I would have been afraid of slipping and falling, but now I didn't even think about it. It seemed like nothing compared to the many dangers I had already faced. I climbed down an opening into the stairwell leading to our apartment. My husband was waiting for me. We stealthily made our way to our apartment where my sister (the one who had hidden in the kitchen cabinet during the blockade) was tearfully undressing my baby. At last we were together again.

Everything was clean and bright. What a joy it was to be able to bathe the baby for the first time in ten days and make a clean bed for him. All the way across the roof and through the hall he had behaved perfectly, not making a peep, as if he realized that his life was hanging by a thread. My husband had prepared an elegant dinner in my honor, including sardines. We would worry about tomorrow later; for the time being we all felt wonderful. I had to relate all the details of my miraculous escape. To this very day, whenever my husband and I talk about it, we simply cannot understand how it happened that for this one hour the gates were left standing open. But, as I have repeated many times, everything seemed to have been foreordained.

The factory was closed the first day after the workers returned from Miła Street. In the afternoon the Poles, after receiving new passes, were allowed back to work. The day after our workers also returned. The work didn't go well; people were depressed and weighed down by their personal cares and sorrows. Everyone had left family or friends on Miła

Street and were racking their brains trying to figure out how to get them out.

Several dozen women and children had been picked up by the factory automobile which Jadzia's mother had watched with such interest through the crack in the wall of the store. That had cost 50,000 zlotys per person, in addition to what one had to give Michel, the German who accompanied Wiewiorowski in the car. Michel took no money but accepted various items of value; Wiewiorowski and his cohorts took money easily enough. No one else was able to get out of Miła. Those who had been there told of the horrible massacre that had taken place and about the children who had been collected in one of the buildings and shot. Finally, they told of the terrible hunger everywhere. My husband, hearing all this, went around half out of his mind. He pulled every string he could think of, but no one was able to do anything. Duży had said that he had a German friend who could conduct me and the baby to the Aryan side, but nothing ever came of that.

At last my husband's friend, the well-known Zionist leader Grajek, offered to take a food package to us in the following way. Before the war Grajek had lived in an apartment on Miła Street. His wife was at this time hidden in the Ursus building with former neighbors of theirs. They arranged so that when his friend returned from work on the Aryan side, Grajek would give him a package for me and for Jadzia's mother. My husband and Jadzia packed a great deal of food, including butter, sausage, fruit, and something for the baby, and gave it to Grajek along with three hundred zlotys. Unfortunately, we never received that package. I suspect that it was opened and disposed of by one of the intermediaries.

Grajek lived through the war and is presently in Israel, where he occupies a high position in Yad Vashem, the museum dedicated to the memory of Jews murdered under Hitlerism.

My husband was overjoyed when he heard through Jadzia's sister about our escape. Someone misled him by saying that for 1000 zlotys I could be accepted for work and be given a number in the Big Schultz shop, and he had jumped at the idea. Even if I had returned together with my husband, it would have been impossible to get inside, for Schultz watched the apartments very carefully. He gave all power for enforcing his rules to Getzel who, desiring to please his superior, sniffed out all illegal persons like a bloodhound.

After receiving my long letter, my husband decided on my returning to the factory. With this in mind he went to Mr. Duży to ask for help; he promised to bribe Counselor Szoszkin so that he would let me in. Unfortunately, it turned out that I couldn't be taken in that way, because there were too many police and other people around.

My husband was going out of his mind with frustration and despair when Jadzia came to the rescue. She put him in contact with two masons whom he had also known for a long time. One of the masons went to get me; because of his occupation he was able to move freely about the factory. In this way, for seven hundred zlotys, I was home again and, what was most important, none of the police knew about it.

It turned out later that it was fortunate for me that I had not gotten into the building through the Werkschutz, because any policeman who knew where to find a "newcomer" like me and the baby would have put them back out on the street again after a couple of days, and it would have cost more money to get back in. Another matter with which Getzel was enthusiastically concerned was the housing question. Gentlemen with influence wanted to exchange their apartments for nicer ones, so Mr. Getzel would simply throw out the old tenants and give them any old place in exchange.

We, among others, fell victim to such a plot. A certain rich and influential Mrs. Goldlust took a liking to our apartment, and so Getzel did her bidding and assigned it over to her. A battle for the apartment ensued, for we were concerned that it not come out that people were hiding in our place. Jadzia went to this Mrs. Goldlust and asked her to give up her claim to our apartment and find herself another one. Because of a number of recent "purges," many apartments had been left empty. But Jadzia's request had the opposite effect. When Mrs. Goldlust saw that the apartment meant a lot to us she dug in her heels and insisted that it was precisely this apartment she wanted. Jadzia went to Getzel, but he said that because of a certain "personage" Mrs. Goldlust knew, he couldn't do anything about it, so we ended up losing the battle and having the specter of an impending move looming before us.

---

1. **Massacre in Poniatowa**. Poniatowa was a forced labor camp in Lublin voivodeship to which Jews from various ghettos had been removed. On November 3, 1943, on orders of Heinrich Himmler, some 14,000 Jews were summarily massacred and buried in mass pits which the victims had been forced to dig.

30

JULA PROMISES TO HELP

Life in this factory had become so loathsome to me that I decided to move at any price, along with my husband and baby, to the Aryan side. I wrote a letter to Jula, and Janina carried it for me. Bad luck seemed to be plaguing us, because Jula wasn't at home; however, Janina left my letter with her landlord. Next day I received an affirmative reply, stating that Jula agreed to take care of me and the baby.

As soon as we heard this wonderful piece of news, we sent word to Michalski that my husband would accept his offer and go into business with him on the Aryan side. Because Jula had agreed to help me and the baby, getting across to the Aryan side began to look more realistic. After settling the matter with our future partner, Henryk Michalski, we began sending him what remained of the raw materials from our shoe factory. The K. G. Schultz factory had a branch on the Aryan side at 51 Ogrodowa Street. Almost every day goods of one sort or another were sent by truck from our factory to there. The driver agreed—for a price— to take our packages across, mixed in with the rest of the shipments. Janina would pick them up from the driver on the Aryan side and take them in turn to Michalski. For these manipulations, we paid not only the driver, but also Janina. We were able to send most of our raw materials over to the Aryan side and thus tie the first knots with the outside.

From the day Jula agreed to take me and the baby under her protection, our spirits began to rise. In the meantime an announcement was posted in our factory with the following information: since there were several dozen fewer persons working in the factory than the eight hundred people allocated, workers were asked to sign up their children staying illegally in the factory so that they could be given numbers and the right to be there. There were still a few simpletons left who believed this and put their children on the list, but they paid dearly for their mistake.

After returning from my sister's, three days went by without any major occurrences. On the fourth day, however, which happened to be the day of our solemn holiday Yom Kippur, the Werkschutz announced that all workers were to assemble in the courtyard without delay. An enormous commotion could be heard out in the corridor; these were the "illegitimates" escaping up to the attic where a hole had just been knocked in the wall for them to pass over to 67 Nowolipie.

My sister went to the attic, where she had a hiding place beneath some boxes and rubbish lying in a dark corner. We decided that I should remain in the apartment with the baby, leaving him on the sofa and hiding myself in the kitchen cabinet. The baby cried a little then finally fell asleep. I had been sitting for quite a while in my hiding place when my husband returned, very agitated and upset. The workers had been ordered to assemble in the yard in order to exchange their paper numbers which they had received on Miła Street for metal ones.

A hunt was planned for people staying in the building illegally. Each entry was guarded by a Jewish policeman, to whom the tenants were to give the keys to their apartments. All holes leading into the attics were also under guard by the police. My husband confessed to one of the policemen whom he knew personally that he had left his baby in the apartment, and the policeman advised him to remove him immediately. We had to get out of the apartment, but it was already too late, for all the roads were blocked. Fortunately, Eichel quickly came to my husband's aid. He understood our tragic situation only too well, for he had a wife and child in another shop. There seemed nothing else to do but to try our luck in the attic by attempting to get the "Cerberus" at the entrance to let me past.

Eichel undertook this task personally. When the policeman first saw him he took him for a thief trying to rob the untended apartments, and took away his factory identification. Not rattled by this in the least, Eichel told him that he wanted to save his wife and child and would he please let us get over to Nowolipie. As luck would have it, the policeman also had a wife and child hiding in our building and agreed. Eichel came running back with the good news and urged me to hurry. I took only a baby bottle, a little cream of wheat, some sugar cubes, and some diapers.

Eichel accompanied me to the attic, where they let me past with no problem, telling me that I could either go straight or to the right. My husband had given me the name of Zaltzman and the number of their apartment, 32. These were friends of his who were presently living on 67 Nowolipie. I went straight and soon found an exit from the attic, but I couldn't get through because it was stuffed with mattresses and other pieces of furniture. I shoved as hard as I could, but they didn't budge an inch.

I didn't waste any time, but headed for the other exit, where I had more luck, for here the door leading into the stairwell was standing open. I got out of the attic, but it was no easy trick to go down the stairs without being noticed, for they were completely covered with paper, rags, kitchen utensils and broken glass. Very carefully, one step after the other, I felt my way down the stairs.

I looked carefully around so as not to fall into the hands of the building's Werkschutz. In order to get to the apartment, I had to cross the courtyard, for it was in another entry. I took courage and, keeping next to wall, cautiously made my way to my destination.

My husband, more relaxed now about our safety, went with Eichel down into the yard. All the workers were ordered to go through the hole knocked out in the wall of 76 Leszno to 78. Herr Schultz's partner Friedenstadt and the younger Rowiński stood by the opening checking numbers, while the police searched the apartments. Schultz himself was on vacation, and Herr Friedenstadt was standing in for him in his various functions. Friedenstadt was a born hangman if there ever was one; he was hated and despised by all the workers. When Schultz was around he had to remain in the background, but now he was taking advantage of his partner's absence in order to wreak all his hatred and bestiality on the workers. He threw a number of people he didn't like out of the group by taking away their paper numbers and not replacing them with metal ones. These people became prime candidates for transportation to the Umschlagplatz.

Among them were Ehrlich and his twelve-year-old daughter. Believing the announcement posted by the gate and the personal assurances of Schultz, Ehrlich had put the name of his daughter down on the list of children and didn't even try to hide her. He was greatly mistaken, however, for his daughter's name was not on the list, so she was placed in the group of people being sent away. Her father, not wanting to abandon her, joined her and his wife—in Treblinka.

More and more people were being earmarked for shipment. The police, under the command of Szoszkin, were outdoing themselves this time, ferreting out hiding places that even the Germans had missed in the course of several blockades. There were more than thirty people ready to be sent, including a baby which had been left alone in an apartment. The zealous police took it together with its carriage. The poor father, seeing it in the yard, begged the gate-keeper—an Aryan woman—to take it and hide it somewhere. The woman, taking advantage of a temporary distraction, moved the carriage slowly to the side, and she would have succeeded, for Herr Friedenstadt, whose head was turned in another direction, didn't notice her; but Szoszkin did and nullified her efforts by pushing the carriage back. He pushed the carriage himself all the way from our factory to the Umschlagplatz, because none of the policemen wanted to touch it. Herr Friedenstadt ordered all holes leading through the attic to Nowolipie to be walled up so that no one could get back from there into the factory. After receiving their numbers, the workers returned to work.

I learned about the holes in the attic being plugged up from Zaltzman, with whom I spent the day. The news hit me like a bolt out of heaven, for I was afraid that my husband would be unable to get in touch with me, and in the meantime the same thing could happen here that had taken place in our factory. In that case, there would be no saving me, for I was alone, helpless, and without money. I realized that I had managed to save my life and the baby's thus far thanks only to the efforts of my husband and, above all, to God's Providence.

The building at Nowolipie 67 where I was staying belonged to the Toebbens shop. Its inhabitants had moved there from Gęsia Street only three days earlier. Consequently, everything was in disorder. I had a feeling that in another moment there would be a blockade and everyone would be taken away. The Zaltzman family had been fortunate enough to save their two children, even though their four-year-old boy was ill with spotted typhus. Many people died from typhus due to the lack of medicine and the constant strain of moving from place to place.

When I learned that a group of people was being taken from our factory to the Umschlagplatz, I rushed to the gate as quickly as possible to see. I am unable to describe my feeling of terror and revulsion as I beheld counselor Szoszkin pushing the carriage with the little baby in it. The shamefulness of it all was too much for me. I was completely crushed by the cruelty and sadism brought to the surface during this time. All of it, which had been sleeping up till then beneath a facade of culture, morality, and good breeding, was now finding its full expression.

That evening I heard someone knocking loudly at our door. To my great joy it was my husband and Eichel who had come for us. Once more we found ourselves in the attic going through the hole in the wall, which had been opened again. Stealthily we made our way back to our apartment. It was only thanks to a strange circumstance that I was able to return home. My husband was fortunate enough to be informed that the police had opened up the hole in the wall themselves in order to bring back their wives and children whom they had hidden on Nowolipie.

So I returned home the same day I left, which was very lucky for me, because next day there was a blockade on Nowolipie where I had been staying with Zaltzman.

My sister returned from her hideout sooner than I did. Once again, we congratulated ourselves on still being alive; thus far, at least, our struggle had not been in vain. This day abounded in happenings. Later that evening Jadzia returned home, very excited. She said that an apartment control was underway with the participation of Getzel himself, and that they were at that very moment in our entry. There was no other way but for us to try and hide. My sister hid in the kitchen cabinet, while the baby and I sat in the kitchen with the light turned out. The others gathered in the main room. When Getzel came in, Jadzia started asking him about the apartment which he had assigned us; the conversation got off on another track and the original aim of the official control was lost sight of. Because of this and also, I believe, because of Jadzia, who had been working in the factory for fifteen years, he didn't look in the kitchen. He contented himself with opening the door to the bathroom under the pretext of seeing whether the water worked, and left. Through all of this, our son behaved perfectly.

We thought that now we would be able to get a little deserved rest, but it became necessary for us to change apartments without delay. Mrs. Goldlust was insistent on our leaving, for she wanted to fix the apartment up so she could have parties in it and invite people over for cards. It was difficult for me to understand the mentality of this woman. Here the Germans were dismantling the ghetto and sending large numbers of Jews away, literally to their deaths, but none of this seemed to make any impression on this woman's mind, if indeed she had one.

We were assigned to a two-room apartment with kitchen on the first floor of another entry. It was dark and gloomy, for the windows looked out onto a garbage dump in another courtyard. The garbage was rotting, for it hadn't been removed since evacuation had begun, so we had to keep the window shut at all times. That was nothing, however, in comparison to another danger. One room had a common wall with Getzel's apartment. This was very unsafe for us, for it was absolutely essential that our neighbor not find out about the baby. Besides that, there was another couple living in the apartment who were going to be sharing it with us. It turned out that they were friends of my husband from before the war, so there was no reason to be afraid of them. After enumerating the negative aspects of the apartment, I must mention one positive one. The first room had a nook in the wall measuring about one meter wide and fifty centimeters deep, and with a cupboard in front of it there was no way of guessing that there was a hiding place behind it. The nook was all the more valuable in that none of the apartments on the upper floors had one like it, so that only the people living there had any idea of its existence.

31

___

FINDING A WAY OUT OF THE
GHETTO

The matter of our going over to the Aryan side was still far off, especially since things were far from quiet over there. People were being rounded up on the streets for work in Prussia and new announcements had been posted throughout the city reminding people of the death penalty for Jews and for anyone hiding them or giving them aid. Because of this, we wanted to gain a little time to allow things to simmer down a bit. At the bottom of our hearts we were counting on a speedy conclusion to the war, resulting in the liberation of everyone.

After the blockades on Saturday, a notice appeared on the gates of our building with the following information:

Persons staying without work numbers on the factory grounds must be removed without exception. Anyone concealing illegal persons or knowing of their whereabouts must immediately inform on them to the factory administration. Failure to comply with this regulation will result in loss of work. Not only the immediate family, but every occupant in the apartment bears responsibility for harboring illegal persons.

Fear took the upper hand. My sister suffered more than anyone else. We had decided that as long as we were living in our old apartment she could stay with us, but she wasn't going to be allowed into the new apartment because Jadzia and her family wouldn't agree to it. When it came right down to it, Jadzia bore the entire responsibility for the new apartment.

At this time new posters appeared about town announcing that all remaining Jews not working in the shops could settle in the newly formed ghetto, encompassing the following four-sided area: the odd-numbered side of Nalewki from Miła to Gęsia; Gęsia to Smocza and along Smocza to Stawki; Stawki to Zamenhof; Zamenhof to Gęsia. Five hundred policemen were assigned to keep order and watch over the newly created ghetto. The city hall was moved to Zamenhof Street in the old post office building, which up until recently had been serving as the ghetto prison.

It was even noted in the announcements that the inhabitants of the new ghetto would receive food ration cards. Beyond that, the regulations were very severe; it was forbidden to engage in trade under penalty of death, and no one could be found on the streets from seven o'clock in the morning until five o'clock in the afternoon. People were allowed on the streets only from five to seven o'clock in the morning when they went to work, and from five to nine o'clock in the evening when they returned home, and even then they had to be accompanied by a policeman.

The ghetto slowly began to fill up. Many of our workers who had passes into this reduced version of the ghetto went there to buy goods which they later sold to Poles working in our factory.

We spent the last days in our old apartment in constant fear of an untimely visit by Getzel or Mrs. Goldlust. One day I had to move to Eichel's apartment, because Getzel said that he would come by during the day to check on something. I will never forget meeting two women in Eichel's apartment. One of them had had her two-year-old daughter taken from the apartment during a blockade; the other had left her twelve-year-old daughter on Miła Street and had returned to work with her husband. Both women cast envious and hateful glances in my direction as soon as they saw the five-month-old baby in my arms. The one who had left her nearly-grown daughter on Miła Street asked me whether it was worth sacrificing my life for such a little baby who didn't have any idea what was happening. I answered her straight from my heart, not realizing, for I didn't know her story yet, that I was touching her in the most sensitive spot, in a wound that had not yet healed. I said that if I were to abandon my child I would be a murderess in my own eyes, regardless of the circumstances, and I simply wouldn't be able to live with such a crime on my conscience.

Then I heard the self-accusation escape her own lips: "You must be talking about me, for I abandoned my own twelve-year-old daughter to her fate."

As she said this, her face showed such an expression of boundless grief that I could understand the torment she was going through. I felt in her words the admiration she held for me for devoting myself so blindly to the welfare of my little baby. The other mother didn't say a word about her own child. Actually, she seemed to be in a rather good mood, but perhaps she was only pretending.

That evening we began to move our furniture to our new apartment. We heaped no end of abuse and unkind remarks on the person of Mrs. Goldlust for her caprice. The men—Jadzia's husband and her brother and my husband—put in a solid night's work. My sister, the baby, and I slept that last night in the old apartment, padlocked on the outside. At the first glint of dawning my husband came for us. He wrapped the baby in a blanket so that no one would notice what was being carried and stole over to the other apartment. I followed, but my sister stayed another three days, for my husband had not yet handed over the keys to Mrs. Goldlust, saying that we still had various things in it. During these three days he tried to find a way for my sister to get over to the Aryan side.

Going over to the Aryan side by itself was no particular problem for a grown person. Each morning two groups of workers were escorted by the police leader to work at our factory branch on 51 Ogrodowa Street. By paying the group leader, it was possible to join one of these groups. After dark and after other workers had left for the ghetto, one could walk right out on the street free. It was safer if you had a Polish "guardian." My husband arranged with one of the group leaders to let my sister join his group, but she soon returned home on some trifling pretext. Obviously she didn't feel up to contending with difficulties over on the Aryan side by herself. In view of this, my husband tried to persuade her to go into the new ghetto, but she didn't want to do that either. She was afraid that with the high prices for food over there she would quickly spend everything she had and die of starvation. Eventually my husband had to give the keys to Mrs. Goldlust, for she had hired painters and was eager to begin repairing and renovating the apartment on a grand scale.

It was too bad, but the other tenants just didn't want my sister moving into the new apartment with us. The family who was already there had been hiding their fourteen-year-old daughter all this time. Before we moved in, this family, fearing that there were going to be too many illegal persons in the apartment, and seeing how severe the punishment for hiding people was becoming, voluntarily parted with their only child, sending her in the care of a policeman they knew to stay with her grandparents in the new ghetto.

After we gave up the keys, my sister entered upon a grievously painful existence in the attic. I will never forget how she went up there for the first time and evidently took fright of something, for she returned in a little while, managed only to open the door, and fell in a dead faint on the hall floor. When we brought her to her senses, she was trembling as if in a fever. We gave her a dose of hot tea, and after a little rest she had to go back into the attic.

She would come down at five o'clock in the morning to wash, extremely unwelcome in the eyes of other tenants. Then she would take some bread and a bottle of tea for the rest of the day and leave again, returning in the afternoon for a few minutes to eat a bowl of hot soup, which I prepared for everyone.

My biggest terror was knowing that Getzel was living on the other side of the wall and might hear the baby crying at any moment. I was ready to leap up at his slightest movement, for he simply couldn't be allowed to cry. When, all bathed and full, he would start playing with his toes and babbling to himself, as much as it pained me I had to stop his marvellous chatter for fear Getzel would hear and take him away. In addition, the apartment was dark and gloomy because the windows had to be shaded all day so the neighbors couldn't see in. Eternal darkness reigned except for when we turned on the electricity; the baby was experiencing daytime in the absence of sunlight.

I felt that if things went on like this for much longer I wouldn't be able to keep him alive, and all our efforts and sacrifices would have gone for naught. All of this plus the dissatisfaction of the other tenants with our presence made my life here miserable. It's true they didn't come right out and say anything, but I am sensitive by nature and could instinctively feel how they felt. All of this settled my resolve to go over to the Aryan side, and I began urging my husband to do something. However, he wanted to gain a little more time and kept putting me off.

Eventually, circumstances came to my assistance. As I already mentioned, there was a small shop on Niska Street belonging to the Felix shop which produced the same sort of goods as ours. At that time all the smaller shops were being eliminated, and the Felix shop was among those being completely dismantled. Some of the workers were taken to the Umschlagplatz, but one day a group of sixty people was escorted to our shop by the Werkschutz. They were to be employed in our factory. One can readily imagine our amazement upon seeing among these people children and nonworking women. They were to sign up for work the next day, but only thirty of them actually did; the others disappeared. Getzel and the others were mad as hornets. Getzel was resolved to employ all available means to track down the missing people, so once again we had the specter of a blockade hanging over our heads.

On the same day, my husband came back to the apartment during lunch extremely upset. He had learned that after lunch all the Jewish workers were to assemble in the courtyard. Since the intention of this gathering was still unclear, he advised me to take the baby to our hiding place behind the cabinet. There was no other choice, it seemed; time was pressing, and soon the lunch period would be over and my husband would have to return to work. I set up a little table and took a baby bottle with me and some cherry brandy to use in case I needed to make the baby sleep. My husband concealed us behind an immense oak chest and placed various sorts of packages and bundles, of which there was no lack, on all sides so as not to arouse suspicion. Then he padlocked the apartment and went back to work.

I was left shrouded in total darkness. Hot and cold chills ran through my body one after the other, and it took my every last effort not to pass out. The baby cried pitifully and kept hitting at the chest with all the strength its little arms could muster. If I had been able to push the chest away from the wall, I am sure I would have done so, for I could see that this hiding place was good only for a grown person or a child old enough to understand what was happening and who could be told to keep still. It was simply a joke trying to hide there with a baby. Everything I did served only to make him cry all the harder.

After a while my nerves were such a wreck that I began to envy those already in the other world for not being able to feel anything. After all, how long can a person endure such inhuman suffering and torture? The baby was getting hoarse from crying, and I sat there hunched over the little table, by this time not even bothering to try to calm him down. At last I was able to give him a little cherry brandy, and after a very long time, the exhausted little mite fell asleep in my arms. I sat there motionless, afraid to move lest I waken him. The clock slowly chimed the hours. My arms and legs went completely numb. It seemed that I had been sitting there for an eternity.

At last a key scraped in the lock. I was so tired and weak that I couldn't even take a step. My husband told me later that when I came out from behind the chest I was so changed in appearance that I barely looked alive. The baby, on the other hand, his mouth smeared with cherry brandy, was all smiles.

It turned out that everything had been unnecessary. It had simply been a routine control of names and signatures. All of the workers went up to one of the tables set up in advance and signed their names on one of the lists. One hundred people were assigned to each table. My husband was number 70, so he was included among the first hundred people. The real purpose of this control was to find out how many people were actually working, because so many people had escaped from the factory. The leadership wanted to drum up a little more business by selling the numbers of the absent workers for very high prices to new customers, and it was with this aim in mind that the control had been conducted.

I began to insist that we not stay a moment longer in this inferno where new tortures were devised from one day to the next in order to terrorize and torment the people. Michalski also kept urging my husband through Janina to make up his mind as quickly as possible to come over to the Aryan side. It was going to take some time to set up the workshop and, in the meantime, Michalski was living on his liquid assets. All of this combined to make us want to leave the ghetto without further delay. However, we came up against a formidable obstacle in the form of the baby. None of the Polish women working in our factory wanted to risk taking him past the sentries. Since the penalty was death, no amount of money could persuade them.

Finally, one of the women agreed to carry the baby across, but at the last minute she backed out. My husband began negotiating with the factory driver for him to take me and the baby across in one of the factory trucks, hidden beneath a shipment of goods being sent to the Aryan side, but in the end nothing came of it. At every setback my husband gathered his strength together again and redoubled his efforts to get us out.

32

MY FIRST, FAILED ATTEMPT

On one of the last days of September, my husband came home after work to inform me that in the afternoon there was to be another gathering of all Jewish workers in the yard. He was particularly upset because he had learned that this was to be a general blockade with the specific aim of uncovering all unauthorized occupants. I had no other choice but to go behind the chest again.

This time I had the benefit of experience and had become somewhat inured to the conditions in this dark cubby hole. I put myself in the hands of fate and the Lord and went. The baby protested pitifully just like before, but this time I did everything I could to make him sleep from the very beginning. I put the cherries from the brandy in the baby bottle and continuously moistened the nipple with the liquor and gave this sweet sleep-inducing drink to my little baby. I realized full well that it wasn't good for him, but it was the only means I had for quieting him in this crucial situation; I would have done anything in order to save his life. The cherry brandy took effect, and the baby fell asleep, but it was an uneasy sleep and I knew that the slightest rustle, not to mention the noise from several people forcing their way into our apartment, would waken him.

The hours dragged on. I sat there covered in cold sweat in mortal fear of someone breaking into the apartment. I could still vividly recall the picture of Szoszkin pushing the baby carriage down the street, and I knew that the hunt was on at this very moment for people like me, and especially for people with babies. It pained me most to know that I was so near salvation.

I was extremely naive then; it seemed to me that all I had to do was to go over to the Aryan side and I was free. I could hear the voices of the police in the courtyard, Szoszkin asking over and over again whether they had found anyone. There appeared to be some victims, for I could hear the voices of women crying and offering bribes. I knew that nothing would come of it.

Finally I heard the shuffle of feet and the hum of voices, and I understood that the blockade was over and once more fate had been on our side and we were saved. In another moment my husband and the other tenants returned and let us out of the hiding place. The baby looked just beautiful: his mouth was all covered with cherry brandy and his face was red as an apple. Everyone congratulated me on my escape.

Almost all illegal people had been taken away that day. Not everyone had willingly given up their keys and the police had made these apartments their first order of business. My husband had given up the keys because, as he said later, he believed in my lucky star. Thank God it didn't desert us.

That same day my husband made the acquaintance of a certain gentleman who supposedly was very well connected in the factory. He said that for 2000 zlotys he would undertake to get me and the baby across to the Aryan side. He instructed me to be ready the following morning to join a group of workers going over to work there. I was simply to take the baby in my arms and go along peaceably with the rest of the group past the sentry. After I made it past, this intermediary, whose name was Hertz, was to return to my husband for payment. After thinking it over, it didn't seem quite so simple. It wasn't enough for the group leader to accept me into the group of workers, for my baby could still be taken away from me, and even I myself could be held, for I had no metal number. It was a highly precipitous and risky gamble, but in spite of that I had to agree. One other circumstance helped me make up my mind.

After the blockade my sister, who had remained hidden in the attic, came to see me in the apartment. She was frightened at the way I looked after crawling out of my hiding place. I wasn't even able to offer her food, for I had cooked nothing that day. She bent over the baby for a long time, kissing his feet and whispering something in his ear. I think she must have felt that this was the last time she would see it, and she loved our little baby very much. After that, she left. We would never see her again.

After my sister's departure I set about doing some of the baby's laundry. It was already late in the evening; the hour was approaching eleven o'clock. Suddenly I heard the voices of several policemen looking for someone. I recalled that one of the workers in our factory, who in fact lived right next door, had escaped to the newly created ghetto, apparently feeling more secure over there. Later he had been seen returning for some of his things, so I thought that it was perhaps this "escapee" they were looking for. Then the thought flashed through my mind that perhaps this was a night-time control to look for illegal occupants. Just in case I turned the lights out and hid in the kitchen which Jadzia's sister-in-law used. I had been lying there for several minutes when an extremely powerful internal compulsion took hold of me and told me to leave that hiding place immediately. I went softly into the farthest room of the apartment in which my husband and Jadzia's family were holding a discussion. My husband let me into the hiding place and covered the baby's bed with an enormous amount of bedding, for we were afraid to wake him up by changing his location.

He hadn't even finished doing this when we heard a loud knock at the door, and it turned out that it really was a night control being conducted by our police. I shook with fear lest the baby start crying. He was so nervous and sensitive at that time that whenever anyone sneezed or even stepped loudly on the floor he would wake up crying. Fortunately, he did not wake up and betray the fact of his existence. The police did not make a very thorough search of our apartment, because one of them was close friends with one of the occupants. They only checked numbers and identification papers. They did look through the kitchen quite thoroughly, though, and even looked into the bed in which I had been hiding just a little while before. My instinct for self-preservation had once more come to the rescue and saved my life. For the rest of the night I hardly slept at all.

The following morning was to decide my fate. Either I would make it past the guards to the Aryan side or I would simply be taken straight from the sentry box to the Umschlagplatz. It seemed to me the height of folly to walk straight into the arms of my executioners. In going, I knew that I had pronounced my own death sentence, but I had to go, for it was no less dangerous to stay where I was now, with blockades happening day and night with never a moment's rest. Besides that, I had to take other people into consideration.

We received word that the night before my sister had been discovered hiding in the attic and, along with other victims, was waiting in the custodian's apartment to be taken away. All we could do for her was to send a little food without letting the police find out who had sent it.

My husband learned of her fate before leaving for the Aryan side from Ehrlich, who had managed to get himself and his daughter out of the Umschlagplatz one more time. He told how my sister, along with the others, had been taken to the Umschlagplatz rather than to the new ghetto to which the police had falsely said they were taking all illegal persons. He said that my sister had gone insane. Thus did a kind God, by taking away her mind, take pity on my poor unhappy sister who had been so terribly afraid of going to the gas chambers.

All of my sisters, and there were four of them, perished. One of them managed to make it across to the Aryan side, where she had many acquaintances among the Poles, but I never heard another word from her after that. My father had been run over by the Germans with a truck on the corner of Nalewki and Gęsia Streets as early as 1940, and so I had lost all of my closest relatives.

As I wrote this after the passing of almost a year in hiding over on the Aryan side, a shudder of terror still ran through me as I recalled the nightmare I had lived through, a nightmare which I am still in no state to fathom or understand. In the twentieth century, when culture and civilization had attained such a high level, the Germans, a highly cultured people, had embarked upon the rational extermination of millions of Jews, not to mention other nationalities, from all over Europe for no other reason than that they were Jews. And the entire world looked upon this disgraceful slaughter in silence.

After receiving news of my sister's capture, our mood that morning was gloomier than ever. My husband, as every day, punched in at work at 6:45, but instead of going to the cutting department, he returned to the yard in order to give me word before the group left so that I could join it. I bade fond farewell to the other tenants with the baby in my arms ready to go. My heart was pounding loudly and unevenly.

I felt like a condemned prisoner awaiting execution. At last my husband gave me a sign and I joined the group at the moment when it was leaving the factory courtyard. We stopped out on the street in front of the sentry box. At that moment I suddenly heard the people around me pronounce one word over and over: Frankenstein! This name, the nickname of one of the German executioners, had been known for the last two years to everyone in the ghetto, including little children. The Poles working in the ghetto were also well acquainted with him. Frankenstein used to say that he couldn't eat breakfast in the morning until he had killed someone. When he was on duty, everyone knew that someone, whether Jew or Pole, was going to get shot.

He would shoot at people walking past the guardhouse as if they were mad dogs, and then look with satisfaction at the bleeding victims lying there on the ground for as long as he stayed on duty. Only when he had left was it permitted to remove the corpses. When at first people hadn't known about this little quirk of his and had taken the bodies away, Frankenstein killed fresh ones.

This was the person, then, who was on guard that day, and I didn't doubt for a moment that I and the baby would be his first victims. The group leader approached us to check our papers and count the number of people, which had to agree with the number of passes. When he noticed me and the baby, he shouted for us to get out of line immediately. I turned back and went over to Hertz, who was standing nearby, and told him that I had been thrown out by the group leader. He talked to the group leader and told me to wait for a minute. Thanks to him and Wiewiorowski, I was able to get back into the factory yard. Next Hertz accompanied me to the door of our apartment and then ran to my husband for the keys. He returned, locked me in the apartment, and took the keys back to my husband. I was very moved by this selfless act on his part.

When I found myself back in the apartment I felt that the terror which had been crushing and tormenting me since yesterday had been lifted. I knew with utter certainty that that day, more than any time before, I had escaped death. I was overcome by a strange feeling of tranquility for the rest of the day. All I asked was that my husband not enter so rashly upon another such attempt.

33

ON THE ARYAN SIDE AT LAST

Next day, Thursday, October 1, my husband and Janina showed up suddenly in the evening and told me to dress the baby immediately. Our factory custodian's daughter had agreed to carry him across to the Aryan side. She came to the factory every day to help her father with his work. Since she had a little baby the same age as ours, she had been able to obtain a pass both for herself and the baby in and out of the ghetto.

Hurriedly, I dressed the baby. Janina was to pick him up once he was over on the Aryan side and keep him in her apartment until the following day, when I was to arrive. I prayed fervently for God to let my little baby cross safely past the gaping jaws of the enemy. When our son's rescuer returned, she told me with a happy smile that she had just walked right past and that everything had gone as planned. I handed this able woman the sum which we had agreed upon—1000 zlotys— and thanked her from the bottom of my heart. That was one day which I will remember for the rest of my life.

Our son, after two and a half months of shifting from one place to another under the constant threat of death, was now on the Aryan side. A new era began in our life of adventure. It all happened so quickly and unexpectedly that we found it hard to believe. We were so lucky that when our son was crossing over, the Germans on guard were busy inspecting workers returning from outside the ghetto. No one paid any attention to the woman walking across with a baby in her arms. Once more it seemed as if everything was going according to some higher plan. As she passed the sentry box, she simply went up to one of the Polish policemen and showed her pass. Janina was waiting for her at a proper distance on the Aryan side.

My husband had a talk with the group leader who, when he learned of our situation, agreed to take me in his group the next morning without recompense. Considering the conditions at the time, such a humanitarian gesture was quite exceptional.

I said good-bye to the other occupants of our apartment. This was to be our last meeting. As on the previous day, my husband was waiting in the yard until the work group which I was to join left. Instead of going to the factory, I was to slip out of the group one gate short and go to an apartment belonging to Janina's cousin who, by an amazing coincidence, lived in that very building. I was to wait there until dark. In order to facilitate my leaving, my husband arranged with one of the Jewish policemen for him to stop the group in front of the gate where I was to enter. As we left, I signaled to my husband with a little wave of my hand, a sign of parting for many months. We stopped out on the street along with the other work groups. After a while a German came along and checked the contents of our bags. Any money he found he kept for himself. Officially it was allowed to have only fifty zlotys on one's person, so that no large purchases could be made on the Aryan side. Of course people had their own hiding places, and carried thousands of zlotys across in their stockings and other places. They also carried all kind of goods, apparel, and linen across. When someone looked particularly suspicious, the German would ask him to step inside a little booth standing nearby, and the person would be stripped naked and thoroughly searched. If the person was a woman, she was searched by a policewoman kept there especially for that purpose. All objects found were confiscated, and frequently enough the person was beaten. I myself had nothing extra on me at all. The German who inspected us, which he actually did quite superficially, checked us off and we went through the gate.

Along the walls plainclothesmen were stationed, lying in wait for victims. They already knew that Jews were getting out of the ghetto this way. They stood there silent and watchful, peering deeply into everyone's eyes. On Ogrodowa Street I tried to walk on the side next to the wall. Fortunately we were walking on the sidewalk rather than out in the street. Three agents were standing by the gate at number 49. As had been arranged, the policeman stopped the group for a second. Taking advantage of the momentary pileup, Janina and I—for she had been following us all this time and keeping me in sight—moved out of line into the gate. I had already taken care to remove the arm-band with the star of David on it, which we had been wearing on our right arms since the Germans first encroached upon our territory. In another minute we had entered the apartment of Janina's cousin, who was at work. We found her mother at home, however. I was introduced to her as a friend of Janina's from the country. We said that I had come to do some shopping, but the stores were still closed, so I needed to wait there until they opened.

In the meantime something happened which thoroughly rattled me. Someone knocked at the door; we opened it, and in walked a gentleman who introduced himself as being from the electric company. He looked at the meter, but at the same time I could see that he was observing me. He smiled in a very friendly fashion, and a minute later very politely said goodbye and left. I had recognized him immediately, and I was sure that he recognized me as well. He had worked for the Municipal Electric Company before the war, and up until the closing of the ghetto he used to come to our apartment to check the meter.

I must admit that I was completely unnerved by this confrontation, but he was very discreet and didn't try to engage me in conversation. It was no secret that this was a very dangerous time for Jews hiding on the Aryan side. Everywhere was swarming with so-called "greasers",[1] or hustlers who would either blackmail Jews they encountered hiding on the Aryan side or simply turn them over to the Nazis for vodka and sugar. For the most part such people came from the very lowest layers of society.

Janina informed my husband that everything had gone smoothly and then went to Michalski, who in turn told Jula. Several hours later Janina returned with my son. She also brought her husband over who looked after me for the rest of the day. Jula and Michalski both came to visit me before long to congratulate me on my escape. Jula said that her cousin would come for me next day and take me and the baby to her place outside Warsaw in Wołomin. We sat around talking as if there was nothing else going on in the world around us.

Later Janina's cousin came home and helped her mother fix dinner (I never did figure out whether or not her mother understood what was happening, but if she did, she gave no indication). We ate a good and hearty meal, reminiscent of much happier times, and before we knew it, the day was over. When darkness began to fall, I said goodbye to Janina and her husband, thanking them for all they had done for us. We owed them a great deal. It was wonderful to know that even at this time, it was still possible to find honorable people here and there. We never ran across them again, even after the war. We knew, of course, that the Germans had completely razed the city of Warsaw and in particular the Old Town district where they lived.

Janina took the baby and went on ahead. Michalski took me by the arm and we too went out onto the street. Our work group had long ago returned to the ghetto, but there were still a number of agents and blue policemen standing on the street. We continued on our way, unhindered.

The streets were full of traffic, for people were returning home from work. I looked and looked and couldn't get enough of it. How is it possible, I thought: here people are, going about their everyday business, while behind the wall only a few streets away a frightful tragedy is being enacted.

We arrived at the Michalskis' apartment, and it was only here that I was finally able to breathe freely. Michalski's wife was young and very nice and made a positive impression on me. Their children were all happy and tanned, for they had just returned from the country. Happiness and light peered out of every corner, and the friendly atmosphere of their home did a great deal to assuage my frazzled nerves. I was practically in a state of shock from my return to normal life. I thought to myself that this would be my first peaceful night for the past seventy-five days, that at last I could rest secure in the belief that I would not be wakened by the familiar sound of police whistles signaling a blockade, or by the sound of rifle fire.

I felt almost happy. I also had a little carriage to put the baby in, for the Michalskis had three children and were expecting a fourth. My son seemed satisfied, for he fell right to sleep after a good meal and bath. I went to bed early, luxuriating in my momentary freedom. I had decided to do everything I could to see that my husband got out of the ghetto as quickly as possible, because I was afraid that some unforeseen circumstances might intervene and pose some unexpected danger for him. I wrote him a detailed letter, begging him to hurry and not worry about whether all of his packages had been sent; Jadzia could send them over later.

Mrs. Michalski had bought me some powder, soap, and various foodstuffs for the baby, the sort of things I couldn't even have dreamed of before. We hadn't had things like that for any price in the ghetto since the beginning of the evacuation. Michalski took my letter to Janina, who in turn passed it on to my husband.

Jula came by during the course of the day, bringing me a baptismal certificate, which was to be of great use in the near future. In the afternoon Jula's cousin came to pick me up. The train was to leave from the Eastern station in the Praga district at 4:50. After commending my husband to the care of the Michalskis, I said goodbye to them, full of gratitude, and set out on the first stage of my arduous life on the Aryan side.

I felt no fear at all. I read the announcements on the telephone poles about the death penalty for Jews and for anyone hiding them as calmly as if they didn't concern me in the least. There was a German guard house and some police standing at the point where Chłodna and Żelazna Streets ran together, directing the traffic between the so-called big and little ghettos. Chłodna Street was a main artery. Whenever it was necessary for traffic to go into the big or little ghetto, the police would stop traffic going from one ghetto into the other, for it was forbidden to pass across the main artery. As we drove past this point I looked at the soldiers and military police guarding the crossing and smiled to myself at the thought that I was a free person who had made it out of their clutches. For two years I had been living indoors in a tightly confined space. Now I looked out on the streets of Warsaw so familiar to me with a feeling of pleasure and satisfaction.

At Nowy Zjazd we met up with a long line of trucks carrying furniture. Our driver kindly informed us that they were "cleaning up" the apartments in the little ghetto. Right at the bridge we met some cars carrying some of our workers back from their jobs. At last we crossed over the bridge into the Praga district. Here we were stopped by a blue policeman who asked to see our identification papers. For a split second my heart stopped beating, but it took me only a moment to remember who I was and what I was doing, and I showed the papers which Jula had brought. That was all I had, but my companion pulled out an entire flood of documents from her handbag, including a birth certificate, a marriage certificate, a certificate showing that her husband was working in a German factory, and another certificate issued by the same company saying that she was exempt from being taken to Prussia. (The Nazis continually rounded up people on the streets and sent them to perform various sorts of work there.) The poor policeman, a venerable looking gentleman who obviously didn't understand a word of those documents, which were written in German, handed them back to us and told the driver to go ahead.

We both breathed a sigh of relief. Without further interruption we arrived at the very moment that the train, stuffed to the gills with people, pulled into the station. I hadn't ridden in a train for three years; several weeks after the Germans arrived an order was issued forbidding

Jews use of the trains. Therefore I didn't know that the number of trains allocated for civilian use had been reduced to a minimum, and this was the reason for the overcrowding. People were even sitting on the steps. I had already decided that we weren't going to be able to board when Jula suddenly arrived and packed us into a German car. An older German yielded his place to me. If you only knew, I thought to myself, who you are yielding your place to!

It was so crowded in the train that everyone was thinking only about where to put his feet. No one paid any attention to me at all. We stopped for a long time at every station. The trip to Wołomin lasted seventy-five minutes instead of the usual thirty. When we arrived the same German who had given me his place helped me get through the press of people to the exit, after which he got out and helped me alight. So here I was in Wołomin. It was a fair walk from the station to where we were staying. My new apartment was actually not in Wołomin, but in Nowa Wieś, just beyond town. Along the way we learned that the ghetto in Wołomin had been destroyed that very day. This news sent a shiver of sorrow and compassion through my body.

It was already getting dark when I arrived at my new dwelling place which was to serve as shelter for me and my baby. My husband and the other occupants of our apartment were able to breathe more freely now that I had left. Now he could prepare for going across to the Aryan side at his leisure.

---

1. "**greaser**". In Polish *szmalcownik,* from *szmalec* "lard," colloquially "dough, money." The Aryan side of Warsaw, and of Poland generally, was crawling with low-life characters willing to turn Jews over to the Nazi authorities for small rewards, or to extort Jews out of their savings. They were denounced in a radio address by General Władysław Sikorski on May 5, 1943, and in numerous articles in the underground press.

34

MY HUSBAND FOLLOWS

Life in the factory of K. G. Schultz slowly returned to normal. Since all those who had been hiding had been captured and only those possessing work permits remained, there was no longer any need for blockades or night controls. What seemed like peace settled down on the factory, but everyone knew that this period wouldn't last for long. The small remainder of Jews would be kept only for as long as they were needed to work, and after that they would be eliminated for good. Everyone realized that they had only a few weeks or months to live. It was no wonder that everyone lived in the present. People sold all their personal belongings, keeping only what was absolutely necessary. They bought only the very best things to eat for themselves, not caring about what the morrow might bring. Those who were in control and had lots of money and influence lived in grand style. They threw parties and held exquisite dinners where they played cards, drank freely, and led a thoroughly dissolute life. In short, they made life around them as pleasant as possible.

We heard the story of how an evening party arranged by the workers was held in the Hallman shop on Nowolipki, at which the world-famous cantor Gershon Sirota[1] was present. He had been cantor in the synagogue on Tłomackie Street. Just before the outbreak of war he had returned from the United States and, caught by the closing of the ghetto, he had found work in the Hallman shop. During the course of the evening's entertainment he was asked to sing something. Sirota replied that the only song he would be able to sing at the present moment (and he sang it) would be the Kadish, or prayer for the dead, for that was what the Jews left in the ghetto were. This story was told to us by Jula, who had some kind of contact with the American "Joint."[2]

Schultz slowly and systematically began removing Poles from leadership positions in the factory, replacing them with Germans. The department in which my husband worked, as well as the sewing department, acquired German women as directors. With their arrival changes began to be instituted. Among other things, the workers were forbidden to cut material with knives; instead they had to use electric cutting machines. Anyone not wanting to give up his knife was threatened with the Umschlagplatz or, if he were a Pole, with Treblinka. The number of work hours was also increased in all departments, for both Jews and Poles. People had to work from ten to fourteen hours a day. Some departments even operated on Sunday. Jadzia, for example, had to work fourteen hours a day, seven days a week.

The Jews received no payment for their work. Instead, from time to time they would be given food items in exchange for ration cards. Pots of cooked food were set up in the factory—one kind for Jews and another for Poles. Often it was my husband's turn to carry the pot along with Grajek and distribute the soup among our workers. The soup out of the pot designated for the Jews was nothing but slops. It was absolutely impossible to survive on the food distributed in the factory. In the shops where only Jews were working, the price of food sky-rocketed. People there were puffing up from the last stages of starvation.

The production director in the K. G. Schultz factory was a German named Duebler. Every day he and Schultz would make rounds of the entire factory and order everyone to work harder and harder so that production would continually rise. In the cutting department, the second in command was a Polish woman who was kindly disposed toward our workers. She would always inform them in advance about any new regulations coming from the factory briefings that all department heads attended daily. Because of her the workers were able to adapt and avoid penalties, i.e., the Umschlagplatz. When one day it was needed to determine who in the cutting department was the most productive, my husband took second place behind K. G. Schultz's countryman from Aleksandrów, Goldberg. Before the war his father had worked in a textile factory belonging to Schultz in Aleksandrów, so Schultz knew Goldberg very well. For this reason, Goldberg, wanting to curry favor with Schultz, worked diligently in order to stand out among his fellow workers.

The other workers, not wanting to be left behind, spared no effort to keep up with him. Eichel, even though he was a better cutter and had been working longer in the department than my husband, occupied third spot. All those singled out for their exemplary performance received prizes in the form of a quarter kilogram of sugar.

All trade was strictly forbidden and punishable by deportation. Every day the directors checked in to see whether someone had brought something with them to sell, confiscating anything they found. One of the German directors, Freulein Geiger, made herself particularly known to the Jewish workers. It had been her fiancé Brandt who had led the action during the German blockade. Since this was a time when the partisans were making themselves felt by blowing up trains and the like, Freulein Geiger kept saying that it was the Jews who were behind it all. This gave her an excuse to persecute her subordinates, and it was her department that had the longest work hours. She was also the first to send someone to the Umschlagplatz, as she did with a young Jewish girl whom she had caught "red-handed" selling some gloves to a Polish woman during lunch. Not only the Jewish girl was punished, but the Polish woman had her pass taken away as well, and in this way lost her job. It was forbidden now for Poles to visit Jewish apartments in order to buy and sell, but in spite of that trade flourished, and nothing the authorities could do seemed to make any difference. People simply became more circumspect.

During this time my husband decided to go to our old apartment and workshop to pick up some more goods and raw materials. Since it was forbidden to walk on the streets without a pass, it was necessary to find some other way. Thus he went through a hole into the attic of 62 Nowolipie Street and waited until a work group passed by on its way back. He joined this group and went with them to the corner of Smocza and Nowolipki Streets, in other words to the fence surrounding the Hallman shop. He made it safely to the locked gate, which was carefully guarded by the Werkschutz, and asked to see engineer Reder, a man whom my husband had met at the beginning of the evacuation. Evidently this name made an impression on the people there, for they let him inside at once. Reder had been the person who had turned to our "Housing Committee," concerning the evacuation of apartments on 57 Nowolipki for the workers in the Hallman shop. He had promised at that time that whenever my husband wanted to take things out of the factory, he would be able to help him. He kept his word and took all of my husband's packages to the food store in the same building, which was run by one of the former tenants, who also doubled as rickshaw driver for the Hallman shop. My husband deposited all of his bundles with him and, since it was already quite late, he spent the night there too.

My husband also took the opportunity to visit our old apartment in order to conjure up visions of the good old days, but he was sorely disappointed. The front door had been knocked out, probably during one of the blockades, and the apartment was in terrible condition, neglected and dirty. Everything about it was repellent; there was nothing left to remind him of our old warm and loving household. Even though the furniture was still the same, it was impossible to find even the trace of a memory there.

Even with engineer Reder's protection, my husband had to be sure not to give himself away to Herr Hirschel, shop commissar and the right-hand man of Hallman himself. Like Goetzel, he was supposedly a Jew who had fled Germany. Commissar Hirschel made sure that no one from the outside got into the factory and, whenever he caught someone, he threatened both the person caught and the person who had helped him with the Umschlagplatz.

Next morning at five o'clock my husband loaded all his packages onto the rickshaw of the grocery-store owner, who took him and the cargo to the gate of our factory. In this way he managed to rescue a little more of the materials which were to be of great use to us on the Aryan side and allowed us to create a little capital.

My husband began preparing to leave the ghetto. He would have put it off a little longer, but various things happened to speed up his departure. First among these were the rumors circulating concerning a certain "surprise" that was supposed to take place.

An article written by Dr. Goebbels, which appeared in "Das Reich",[3] had created quite a stir. He had supposedly written that beginning on January 1, 1943, all the ghettos would be liquidated. We didn't know how much truth there was in this article, because we had seen no newspapers since the beginning of the evacuation, but anything could be expected of Goebbels and, for that matter, experience showed that from the very beginning all rumors that had ever circulated in the ghetto sooner or later came true. Workers in other shops began organizing secret meetings with the aim of creating some kind of self-defense so as no longer be led to their deaths like sheep but to die fighting, and at least bring down some of the enemy in exchange for their own deaths. In our shop it was impossible to create an organization, because a large proportion of the people were unreceptive to such plans.

My husband had been in constant contact with the underground newspaper "Jutro" (Tomorrow),[4] through an intermediary known to us as "Braun," because he always wore a brown overcoat. He received the paper from a blue policeman and distributed it among the Jewish population in the ghetto. This was already in 1941 after the consolidation of the Polish underground organizations, which had been broadcasting to our organizations in the pages of "Jutro" that they were ready to send weapons into the ghetto for us to organize our own combat and defense organizations. My husband was instrumental in arranging a meeting between both sides, for he realized the importance that such cooperation would have for us in the ghetto. Negotiations went on for some time, but suddenly, for reasons which we did not know, they broke off and came to naught. Evidently unity was lacking, and where that is missing, nothing can be accomplished.

The day before my husband left the ghetto, Ehrlich and his daughter returned after a several weeks' stay at the Umschlagplatz. He said that there was nothing left there at all. The entire hospital staff, including the nurses, all the patients, and even the head physician, Dr. Braude-Hellerowa, had been sent to Treblinka. For several weeks there had been no shipment from the Umschlagplatz due to a lack of people. The small handful still remaining had received the aid of the Judenrat, who provided them with some sort of food. There they dragged out their weary lives in the same filth and stench as described earlier. There was no question of escape, but Ehrlich, being a wealthy man, managed to bribe his way out. For another amount of money he was let back into the K. G. Schultz factory.

My husband, who by this time had learned that it was best not to ignore rumors, left all of our packages in the hands of Jadzia, who promised to send them after him to the Aryan side. Early one morning, on Sunday, October 11, 1942, he bade farewell to his fellow lodgers and to his very best friends and left the ghetto in the same way I had done.

---

1. **Sirota, Gershon (1873-1943).** Sirota was one of the Europe's leading cantors, widely traveled and an early Jewish recording artist. For many years he was cantor at Warsaw's Tłomackie Street synagogue. Caught in Warsaw by the German invasion of Poland in 1939, he was locked in the ghetto and died in the Ghetto Uprising of 1943.

2. **The "Joint".** The informal name for the American Jewish Joint Distribution Committee, originally formed in 1914 to aid the impoverished Jews of Central Europe during and following World War I. Its activities lasted through the interwar period and into the years of World War II. In Warsaw its representative was Daniel Guzik.

3. **"Das Reich."** A weekly newspaper founded by Nazi propaganda minister

Joseph Goebbels in 1940. The paper contained news reports, essays on various subjects, book reviews, and editorials written by Goebbels.

4. "**Jutro**" (Tomorrow). A conspiratorial weekly newspaper published by PN (*Polska Niepodległa*, Independent Poland), a non-aligned military and civilian resistance group, at its height numbering around 20,000 members.

II

ON THE ARYAN SIDE. IN
THE OLD TINSMITH'S
SHED

35

SETTING UP SHOP

Henryk Michalski was waiting for my husband at the guardhouse gate on the corner of Żelazna and Leszno Streets. Jadzia guided him to the factory branch on the Aryan side, where Janina was standing with her husband. My husband introduced Jadzia to Michalski so that we would be able to maintain contact with her in the future.

From what my husband later told me, I learned that, just as I could not believe my own eyes, he too was dumbfounded at the sight of pedestrians moving freely about on the streets. What a surprise to see normal street traffic, trolley-cars in operation, stores open, and other such symbols of normal life. It was simply impossible to believe all this after the hell we had lived through in the ghetto, where every move-ment, every sign of life had come to a standstill. Of course, the Poles were not exactly living in clover during the German occupation either, but it is impossible to compare their situation with what we lived through. The Poles later told my husband that they could recognize the Jews circulating on the Aryan side of town by their unusually sallow complexions and by their eyes, which had the look of a hunted animal. My husband must have had exactly the look of such an animal, as his eyes darted in all directions for fear that someone was chasing him or looking at him suspiciously.

After leaving Ogrodowa Street, all four of them got on a trolley and continued on their way. During the trolley ride, my husband described how one man kept looking at him attentively, or maybe it only seemed that way to him because of his excessive sensitivity. His friends gathered around him and tried to shield him from view.

They arrived without incident at Janina's house, where they ate dinner. Michalski then took my husband with him to his apartment. From this first visit among the people who were thereafter to be his protectors, my husband had the best possible impression. Marysia, Michalski's nice blond, blue-eyed wife, received my husband very cordially. They also had a cousin of Marysia's staying with them, a Doctor of Theology, Father Edward Święcki.[1] He was a very cultured and intelligent man. Father Święcki was collaborating with the underground and was sought by the Gestapo, so he was living on false documents and under a pseudonym, as we learned later. It was for this reason that he, a priest, was wearing civilian clothing. After staying in this gracious home, my husband could feel his humor and courage returning, for he could see that he had fallen into good hands.

That evening Michalski took my husband to the place which thenceforth was to be his home and shelter. This was an old tumbledown building, practically in ruins, located at 27 Belwederska Street. In it was the tinsmith and plumbing shop belonging to Antoni Michalski, Henryk's father. The building was situated in an area which not long before the war had been built up with modern dwellings, all of which were later confiscated by the Nazis. Poles were allowed to live only in such dilapidated buildings as the one belonging to Michalski. Since he had already been renting the building for a number of years, he was allowed to stay in it and continue his work. My husband, when he observed the traffic and bustle with which this German section was throbbing, could scarcely contain himself at the sight of the comfort and plenty in which the Germans were living. From their windows came a flood of lights and the sound of radio music, which he had not heard for a long time. What a contrast this was to our poverty, not to mention the tragedy taking place at that moment in the ghetto.

After arriving at the designated spot, Michalski, after taking all due precautions, led my husband in by the back door from the courtyard side, after which he locked the door with a padlock. There was an old sofa with the springs sticking out which was to serve my husband as a bed. It was impossible to turn on the lights for fear someone might suspect his presence, so my husband lay down on the sofa in the dark and thanked God that he had at least made it out of the inferno which the Warsaw ghetto had become.

Exhausted from all that had happened that day, he was falling asleep when he heard a loud knocking at the door. My husband lay there quietly, not daring to move or breathe for fear that someone had seen him enter. The knocking grew louder and louder. After several minutes of this, my husband heard the sharp voice of a second man who came up to the first and asked gruffly what he was doing. He explained that there was no one in the building and that it was padlocked shut. After this explanation, silence ensued. The thought kept bothering my husband that here he had barely made it out of the ghetto only to meet such an early end. This was how his first night on the Aryan side passed.

Next day it turned out that some drunk had noticed Michalski and my husband entering the workshop the previous evening, and taking a liking to that place himself, with the stubbornness of a drunk had decided to get inside. Fortunately, everything ended with nothing more than a good fright and a sleepless night.

Early next morning Michalski came with his father to the workshop. His father was a small corpulent man of about fifty, with a bushy black mustache. As far as my husband was concerned, Henryk's father looked more like a Jew than a Pole, but his flawless language and accent indicated better than anything that there could be no doubt as to his origin. An official exchange of greetings was followed by mutual respect.

The older Michalski began work, and my husband, taking advantage of the fact that there were still not many people on the street because of the early hour, looked out for the first time for as long as he could remember on the "free world." He took a deep breath. At last he had freed himself from the fear, hardship, humiliation, and threats which he had borne in the K. G. Schultz factory. He ceased to cower at the sound of a police whistle.

My husband and Henryk began figuring out how to set up the shop, if only a small one—and an illegal one. Two families were to live off the production of this shop. The main challenge was to find the right kind of people to work in it, people whom one could trust. They decided to set up the little factory where the tinsmith's shop was located because, besides the shop, there were also several other rooms and a kitchen. As far as the workers were concerned, they decided to call back some of our workers from before the war, all of them Poles. Among them were Stasiek and Marysia Będkowski. They had worked for us even before they had gotten married, all the way up until the ghetto had been closed at the end of 1940. We had heard that since

175

they had been forced to quit their jobs with us, life had been going badly for them. Poles in general did not have an easy time making money. There were basically two possibilities. One could work for the Germans for nominal pay or one could smuggle and engage in the black market. We liked Marysia and Stasiek and felt quite close to them, so it was decided that Henryk would visit them as soon as possible.

Henryk found only Marysia Będkowski at home as Stasiek was being held by the German gendarmerie. Since his parents lived in Łowicz, he would go visit them from time to time in order to get food. On his last trip he had received fifteen kilograms of flour. The Germans found the flour on him, took him for a smuggler, and put him in a prison camp. Marysia did everything she could to free him but as yet with no results. Until Stasiek was freed, there was no question of her coming to work for us.

Since we still did not have all the necessary tools for work, my husband gave a list to Henryk, and he set about buying the most essential of them. It was also necessary to wait until the rest of our packages were sent from the ghetto, for in them was the material necessary for our product—fancy ladies' footwear. In brief, there were still many obstacles to be overcome.

In the meantime, my husband had the opportunity to meet the rest of Henryk's family. They consisted of a twenty-three-year-old brother, Leon, who was married and had a daughter, as well as his seventeen-year-old brother, Maniek. He also met Michalski's journeyman, Zygmunt Dobosz, who had been working there for several years already (as a matter of fact, it had been Zygmunt who had driven away the drunkard on that first night). He was a very decent sort, as we later had the opportunity to find out on more than one occasion. He was married and had three sons, of whom the oldest was seven, the middle one five, and the youngest was not yet walking. They all lived in the same building as the Michalskis, but in a different wing, on the other side of the courtyard. As everyone was carefully concealing the identity of my husband, Zygmunt did not have any idea with whom he was dealing.

The first weeks on the Aryan side were a time of relaxation, but also one of extreme hardship. Antoni Michalski's shop closed early. Since my husband had nothing else to do, he went to bed at five o'clock. By midnight he was completely slept out and did nothing but lie there nervously listening to and trembling at every sound. The Germans would walk along the street singing and talking loudly. The sound of their heavy boots on the pavement would always send a shiver of fear through him. It seemed to him that at any moment the front door would be broken down. Tiny pieces of plaster kept falling down from the ceiling onto the tin sheet on the floor, keeping him awake all night. In his weary state, the sounds seemed like grenades going off. He would wake up suddenly and his body would be covered in cold sweat. Besides that, mice were everywhere. It was a long time before he was able to recognize and become accustomed to these sounds.

This state of nervousness and perpetual fear has remained with us to the present day (I write this while still in hiding) and follows us not only when we are awake, but also in our sleep. Our nerves are taut and sharpened to the utmost. When we think about it we must conclude that even when we are set free (in the unlikely event that such a thing ever comes to pass), this state will remain with us for a long time to come, perhaps to the end of our lives.

Eventually Marysia's efforts were crowned with success, and her husband Stasiek was set free from the prison camp. Both husband and wife eagerly accepted our proposal and the opportunity of earning a steady salary. Besides themselves, there was a young son. Marysia earned money on the black market, for which she could have been sent to Germany on a work brigade. Her husband worked for the Germans on the railroad, but he received a miserable salary. It had been their deplorable situation that had prompted Stasiek to go to Łowicz in the first place. Because he was not allowed to leave his work on the railroad (such an act was viewed by the Germans to be an act of sabotage and was punished with extreme severity), he was only able to devote to our shop what time he had remaining after his work there was concluded.

Production began in our little factory. Packages containing material also began to be sent through Jadzia. However, our personal belongings had not yet arrived, and without them it was difficult to get along. My husband did not even have a change of shirts and had to wear the same underclothing for three weeks in a row. Without a towel, he wasn't even able to wash himself properly. He was too tactful to ask for anything so as not to seem a nuisance, so he suffered in silence. It never entered his partner's mind to ask whether he might need anything. Since everything in life sooner or later comes to an end, my husband's patience was rewarded, and the packages containing our personal belongings arrived. Many of them, especially the more valuable, had perished along the way. It was at this time that my husband received the first news from me through Jula. New clouds had begun to form on the horizon, bringing me much worry and concern.

1. **Święcki, Father Edward (1922-1996)**. Father Święcki eventually became parish priest in Karczew, near Otwock, in the years 1953-1984.

36

MY NEW HOME AND NEIGHBORS

Let me now return to the story of my continuing adventures. After arriving in Wołomin, we still had another two kilometers to walk to the village of Nowa Wieś. We got there in the evening, and for this reason I was not able to have a good look either at the locality or at the house in which I was to stay. The apartment consisted of a room and kitchen, and at that moment it seemed to me like a wonderful haven. However, the age of my guardian caused me some concern. I had expected that Jula would place me in the hands of a responsible woman, but my "landlady" was twenty-two years old and had been married for half a year. She seemed to me decidedly too young to bear any serious responsibility and to assure me and my child a modicum of security.

Right at the beginning I learned that her husband was working for a German company in Warsaw and came home only every other evening. She told me that she could not stand him and was thinking of getting divorced. In view of this situation, I decided not to say anything about my origins but simply to present myself as a friend of Jula's who had escaped from Warsaw for fear of the air raids. There were many people like that, especially among those who had small children for whom it was difficult at every sound of an air raid siren to go down into the basements serving as shelters. I added that my child was getting over an illness, and the doctor had advised us to take him to the country for several weeks.

On the morning following my arrival, which was Sunday, the people in our and neighboring villages enjoyed a distraction from their everyday humdrum activities. The previous day the Jews had been driven out of the Wołomin ghetto; the Death Squad had arrived from Warsaw for that very purpose. Several days before the Blue Police had been informed as to what was to take place. One of them, who was kindly disposed toward the Jews, warned them the day before, so it was no wonder that many Jews had escaped into the woods during the night. This was not as difficult to do as it would have been in Warsaw, for the Wołomin ghetto was located on the edge of the city and was only surrounded by a barbed-wire fence with one officer guarding it.

After the task of destroying and emptying the ghetto was accomplished, the rest of the population threw themselves on the empty apartments, plundering and robbing them of everything they found. This did not take place without plenty of altercations breaking out among the plunderers. Whoever was strongest took what was best. The result was such that all Sunday long people were carrying out of the buildings the most varied assortment of furniture, bedding, appliances, and many, many other things. That day was an extremely difficult one for me to bear. My heart was shredded into little pieces from the anguish I felt as I heard what was going on not far away.

Later I heard that many Jews had hidden in the Wołomin ghetto itself, in basements and even in fireplaces. All of these people, along with many escapees, had been caught by the German soldiers and shot on the spot. According to an old German custom, the condemned person had to dig his own grave and, at a given signal, he had to undress and lie down with his face to the ground, and in this position he was shot. There were many terrifying scenes which eyewitnesses related to me trembling with fear. There were even cases of people being buried while still alive.

During the first week of my stay in the country Jula had a chance to come and visit me. She was quite relieved to see that my son's health was better and that I had had a chance to rest. The morning after my husband arrived on the Aryan side, Jula went to him and told him that both I and the baby were in excellent health. My husband was especially gratified to learn that the owner of the building had a cow which was able to provide milk for our son. On the surface nothing seemed to be lacking for our happiness, if in general one can ever call people happy who have the sword of Damocles hanging over their head.

Our entire building, which consisted of several apartments, was occupied. On the bottom floor lived the building's housekeeper. She was a cripple missing one leg, but she had a prosthesis that enabled her to get around rather freely. On the other side lived Zosia's (my protectress') brother, together with his wife and child and his wife's mother and brother. This little family nest was extremely inquisitive, and its greatest activity consisting in spreading rumors. Besides that, they lived in constant strife with Zosia—the reason for which I did not yet know. On the next floor were three apartments. One was ours, another was occupied by a family who had been evacuated from Poznań, also extremely inquisitive, and the third apartment was occupied by a mother who lived alone with her son and never meddled in anyone's business. In order to hide oneself in this kind of environment, it would have been necessary to have been the hero of the novel *The Invisible Man*. In addition, there was another building located on the property of this five-acre estate, which belonged to an old bachelor, an eccentric person who was the housekeeper's brother and who was on very good terms with Zosia. He had a woman living in his building, a Mrs. Stasiowa, who was the very queen of gossipers. She seemed to be some kind of prostitute. Such was the company in which I found myself so suddenly, and in addition this was precisely at a time when Jews were the only subject of conversation.

Zosia was not very polished and had very little experience with life. Fortunately, she had absolutely no idea what danger she was subjecting herself to for taking care of a Jewish woman and child. Living in the country as she did, and not reading any newspapers, she did not know what was taking place in Warsaw and in the neighboring communities. I am certain that it didn't even enter her mind to warn me about the type of people living in these buildings. Unfortunately, she was extremely foolish, and her habits and way of life made my hiding with her an extremely unpleasant experience. She caused me a great deal of worry for which more than once I almost paid with my life. The only person I sought for advice during this period was Henryk Michalski, who had warned me that with a face like mine I should stay at home and not show myself to anyone.

The lodgers in our building were intrigued with this mysterious person who never showed her face and who never went out into the fresh air with her child. At this time people were trying to find a Jew in everyone in order to denounce them to the Nazis or extort money from them. They began to seek pretexts to come to our apartment and have a look at me. For a while I was able to remain unseen by these importunate visitors; the only person to see me was Zosia's husband, who suspected nothing. He was an honest and basically well-disposed person who believed what he was told and didn't give much thought to anything, so that when he eventually learned the truth about me after five weeks of my staying in his apartment, his eyes opened wide in amazement.

Zosia kept bragging that since she had sublet her apartment, she was able to afford meat every day. Unfortunately, talk like this had been the cause for more than one tragedy. It was the first sign people looked for.

The first other person I met, or rather whom I had to meet, was Zosia's sister in-law, Mrs. Mroziński. My guardian Zosia was engaging in illegal trade, as for that matter were most of the people during the war. Two times a week she traveled to Warsaw in order to buy various sorts of materials and luxury goods on orders she received from people in the village. She took these purchases to her native village, Ryn, an eighteen-kilometer walk from the railway station in Tłuszcz. For the money she made she would buy butter and take it to Warsaw, which was thirty kilometers from Wołomin. In this way she made money both coming and going. If she had known how to manage her affairs, she would have been able to live quite comfortably. However, I noticed in the first week of my stay with her that she was able to spend more than she could make. Money simply went through her fingers like sand, as she herself said.

During her day-long trips to Warsaw, and during her two-day long trip to the other village, I was left by myself in the apartment. Since I never took a step outside, there was not even anyone to bring me water from the well. When she left for a single day I was able to get along without anyone's help, but on her longer journeys I was forced to turn to someone and ask them to at least bring me some milk for the baby. The first time I turned to the fifteen-year-old brother of Mrs. Mroziński, Zosia's sister-in-law. Of course, she made use of the occasion, for which I am sure she had been waiting for a long time, and brought me the milk herself. In this way I was forced to establish an acquaintanceship with her. She was a twenty-four-year-old, fairly good-looking woman who would have made a good impression on me except for the expression in her yellow, cat-like eyes, in whose depths I could detect a deep reservoir of cunningness and duplicity. If anything, she was overly polite to me. She even went so far as to take it upon herself to bring me her two-year-old son's baby carriage, along with a little mattress, pillow, and a larger pillow for covering it on the top. I was inexpressibly grateful to her for that, because it was October, and the days had been growing much colder. Her true character was to appear only later.

37

I COMMIT SUICIDE

It was extremely cold in the apartment, and the baby kept coughing. My son evidently had caught cold during the trip to Wołomin, stepping out of the hot and overcrowded train into the cold October air.

I was forced to ask to see a doctor. Zosia called for him to come and then evaporated from the apartment, probably fearing some kind of unpleasant consequences arising from his visit. After checking the baby over, the doctor said that the cold was not serious. He was very pleased with the baby's physical condition and with his blooming appearance, which we had managed to preserve in spite of our continuous wanderings. There was even one comical incident. As the doctor placed the thermometer under the baby's armpit to take his temperature, my little boy took it out and threw it on the floor, and as a result I had to pay the doctor for a broken thermometer. We both had a good laugh over that.

After finishing his visit, this worthy doctor took my hand and looked me deeply in the eyes, saying: "I know who you are, and I have the greatest sympathy for you and for others like you. I help them myself whenever I can. Please listen to the advice of a man who wishes your safety. As soon and as often as you can you must change your place of residence, so that as few persons as possible know where it is, and only such people as can be trusted. Where there is no betrayal, no one will be caught. Besides that, I would advise you to give your baby to someone to take care of it for you. It will be safe and you won't draw so much attention to yourself as you do now with him."

I thanked him for his good advice and felt emboldened to ask him for a favor: a little poison for myself in case I might ever need it. The worthy doctor provided me with some along with medicine for the baby.

The advice was good, but where was I to find the kind of people I could put my trust in, and how was I to change my place of hiding, since except for Michalski and Jula I had no other friends on the Aryan side?

We knew that true understanding and sympathy could be found for the most part among the intelligentsia, but it was primarily the poorer folk who were willing to risk their lives by sheltering Jews. They did this, of course, with an eye to improving their miserable living conditions and so that they would not be subject to hard labor in Germany in armament and ammunition factories. Others with even baser motives were constantly on the lookout for ways to make easy money through blackmail and the denunciation of Jews to the Nazis. Often enough they would do this for nothing more than a bottle of vodka or a bag of sugar. There were many instances where Jews were taken over to the Aryan side with the promise of shelter, but were robbed of everything they had and turned out on the street with no further concern, or given straight into the hands of the Blue Police, who in turn would hand them over to the Nazis.

There were also such people as regarded us as enemies from the religious standpoint and who considered it a crime to offer us help. For example, even Marysia, who had a certain degree of education but who was excessively religious, had continual pangs of conscience for the help they were giving us. We owed her a great deal, but we knew that she did not offer us help out of her own impulse for kindness but because of the arguments of another person who was for her a moral authority: Father Edward Święcki. He often came to see my husband, and one time he even brought him a Gemarah—part of or a treatise on the Talmud—which he had found somewhere. He was an extremely educated and cultured person. After the war he intended to go to Jerusalem for further theological studies. Whenever the question of the Jews came up he always had the worst possible things to say about the "cultured German nation." Despite this, he did not show much sympathy for the Semitic race. He simply felt that at such a critical moment it was every Christian's duty to help those in need.

Marysia more than once confessed that she was praying to God for him not to punish her for helping us. She kept saying that after the war people would point her out on the streets for having done it. It was only in 1943, during the final stages of the destruction of the Warsaw ghetto, that General Władysław Sikorski[1] broadcast a speech over the London radio in which he called on the people to come to the aid of the Jews in any way possible. After that Marysia changed her opinion.

Life went on for me in Nowa Wieś, but with each passing day it became more difficult for me to bear. I was always being left alone. Zosia, even when she was not traveling, never stayed at home. I didn't even have ~~the~~ the most essential items. I bought a rather large supply of wood which was brought while Zosia was away by a man I didn't know. I had to let him in and pay for the wood in person, exposing myself to risk. The wood was brought by a young lad who lived not far from us. He must have said something to his mother, for she came running up not long afterwards on the pretext that Zosia had promised to give her linen to wash. The old woman began by starting in on the Jewish question. I listened in silence. After she left, the old biddy began telling stories all around the neighborhood about me and her suppositions in my regard.

However, the greatest injury was being done to me by my own protectress. During the first week of my stay with her, she behaved rather well. In the second week she began to relax the reins of her character somewhat. On days when she was not traveling, she spent a great amount of money on vodka and luxury food items.

In the evenings a numerous assortment of male friends would gather in her kitchen, drinking and singing themselves into a state of unconsciousness. The baby would keep waking up and crying loudly, which would draw curious guests into our room. These guests with their foul language were thoroughly repulsive to me. The parties lasted into the morning, and afterwards Zosia and her lover of the night, one of any number of men, would make love. Next morning the lover would leave the apartment, while she was snoring like a cow. She lost all sense of decency and ceased taking my opinion of her into account. Since my protectress's name was on everyone's lips, my presence became known throughout the neighborhood.

I realized that my continued stay in her apartment was no longer possible, and so I asked my husband to find another place for me and the baby. This was no easy matter to bring about. Jula, when she realized what was going on, made the excuse that she really hadn't known her cousin very well. For our part we knew only good things about Jula. She was a gracious woman with a good heart and a kind soul, and had the best possible intentions in our regard. If it had not been for her help, all three of us would have perished in the ghetto. Jula's true worth and character may be judged from the fact that she was working together with the director of the "Joint"—Guzik—who was providing financial aid to Jews hiding on the Aryan side, so she knew of many places where Jews were hidden. For people that had insufficient resources for renting an apartment, for paying for the minimal amount of food, or for paying off a blackmail notice, Jula was the one who would bring them help from Guzik. She was in constant contact with him and was actually his right-hand agent.

My life went on in constant fear. Zosia's betrayed husband, egged on by his brother and sister-in-law, made terrible scenes in front of his wife. These scenes would end in a fight, after which Zosia would escape from the house to one of her friends and would only return the following afternoon. It came to the point where the husband decided to take all of the furniture, for all of it belonged to him, and get a divorce. We were left sitting there in an empty apartment. Zosia foolishly decided to look for another, furnished, apartment, so she posted an announcement that she was looking for an apartment for a single person. This reached the ears of the housekeeper, who made it with some difficulty on her artificial leg up to our floor and, after excusing herself politely, stated that she had heard rumors concerning me. She asked me to render an explanation because as house-keeper she was responsible for what went on in the building. I kept to my story and I showed her my identification, saying that one's external appearance was no proof of anything. She asked me to register myself as soon as possible, because otherwise she would not be able to allow me to stay there.

After her husband filed for divorce, Zosia got drunk and told all the occupants of the building everything she knew about me and my husband. After she had sobered up, she came to me and told me that one of them had gone to report on me to the village elder, and that I might expect the arrival of the German gendarmes at any moment. She repeated this with a cold and cynical expression as if it didn't concern her at all. I knew I could expect nothing good from such a beast. Still, I asked her to take the baby to Warsaw and give it to Jula. She took the baby and a letter to my husband and left. I breathed a little more freely now. At least I would be able to perish alone, and the little one would be safe.

I spent the day in a state of nervous anticipation. I didn't touch a bite to eat. Every loud noise set my heart pounding at a rapid pace. At that moment I remembered the poison I had gotten from the doctor. I felt that I was nothing but a burden to my husband, who by himself at least had some chance of survival. After my death the Michalskis would be able to find a place for my baby. I was completely resigned—exhausted both physically and mentally, by the hopeless struggle. I preferred to die peacefully in the apartment rather than at the hands of Nazi executioners. I didn't want to dig my grave with my own hands as people had described to me, or to be buried alive. Slowly and peacefully, I poured myself a glass of water and swallowed half the contents of the vial. I sat down on the floor, leaned against the wall, and shut my eyes. I must have fallen asleep in this position. I don't know how long I sat there. Suddenly I felt a sharp pain in the lower part of my abdomen.

I leapt to my feet and ran to the bucket. I had a steady stream of diarrhea for a long time, but at least I was alive and conscious. Only later I realized that instead of poison the doctor had given me a strong diuretic.

That evening Zosia returned without the child. She told me that she had not found her aunt in Warsaw, and no one knew when she would return. She had taken the baby to the Michalskis. She also told me some cock-and-bull story about how a policeman had stopped her on the train, saying that it was a Jewish child and that he wanted to take it to the police station. She said that she had given him three hundred zlotys ransom and that he had let her go. I understood immediately that the wretch was trying to squeeze money out of me. She hadn't been on any business trips for three weeks and was living entirely on my rent. In recent days she had drunk through all her money. When I asked her what was to become of me, she replied that Henryk was going to come next morning to see what he could do. Until then, we decided that I would be locked in an empty room on the first floor, next door to Zosia's brother's.

Since Zosia's husband had stored his furniture there, I had the good luck to find myself with a sofa-bed on which I was able to sleep. Zosia's sister-in-law, Mrs. Mroziński, told the other tenants and the housekeeper that I had left for Warsaw. My nerves began to calm down, although I did miss my baby. I was also worried about having loaded the Michalskis with another burden. Mrs. Michalski was barely more than three weeks away from giving birth and had three other children of her own in the apartment already, and here was a fresh problem in the form of my seven-month-old.

1. **Sikorski, General Władysław** (1881-1943). Sikorski was prime minister of the Polish Government in Exile and commander-in-chief of the Polish Armed Forces. He perished in an airplane crash in Gibraltar in July, 1943. His speech and radio appeal to bring aid to the Warsaw ghetto uprising was aired on May 5, 1943, and was distributed by the Polish underground press as soon as the following day.

38

ZOSIA SHOWS HER TRUE COLORS

The hours dragged on in my solitude, as I sat there sunk in thought in complete darkness in the middle of the day to keep me out of the sight of inquisitive eyes. Finally, Henryk came. This was the first time I had seen him since leaving Warsaw. He came in the company of our former worker, Marysia Będkowski. We hadn't seen each other for two years, in other words, since the time she had been forced to leave work in our factory on account of the closing of the ghetto. She was amazed at the change she saw in me and said that she wouldn't have recognized me. She herself looked in blooming health. What a lucky woman, I thought. Evidently many Poles had absolutely no idea about our hopeless situation and what we had lived through and suffered.

Up until that time the feeling of envy was completely unknown to me, for before evacuation I had lived in plenty with a caring husband. Now, however, I was a woman alone, extremely unhappy, a burden and impediment to all those around me. For several months I had been hounded and persecuted at every step, knowing no peace by day or night. The sight of Marysia awakened in me so many memories of former, happier times. We were always on extremely good, even friendly, terms with all of our workers, so I hoped that with her arrival my situation would change. How happy I would be, I thought to myself, to be able to change at that moment into Marysia, to be together with my husband each day at work.

I felt the lack of my husband's care at every step. Even during the most difficult times in the ghetto I believed that there would be no obstacle, effort, or amount of money he would not have spared in order to save me and the baby. Without his close attention, I felt completely lost. How eagerly I latched on to the news that Marysia brought in such great abundance. By nature she was extremely talkative and gossiped as fast as her lips could move. She told me that our workshop had been in operation for two weeks and was going full blast. She swore that she would look after my husband's food. The biggest worry was for me and the baby, for there was no place to put us.

Everyone was trying to find an apartment for me, but thus far nothing had been found. When there seemed to be nothing else to do, she proposed to place me with her cousin, whose husband was an inveterate alcoholic. He never came home sober, and when he did come home it was only in order to threaten his wife or cause a ruckus. I made up my mind to go there, until she inadvertently mentioned that the police had their eyes on that spot from four Jewish women who had been staying there for some time, although they finally had to leave because of people continually bothering them for more money. Ever since then the police kept checking in to see whether they could find any fresh victims to squeeze a little money from.

When I asked whether her cousin would be there together with me, she answered that I would be there locked up alone with the baby, and that only Marysia would be able to bring me food. I understood that I had to do with a woman who had absolutely no idea as to the gravity of my situation and the responsibility which she was taking on. It seemed like going from the frying pan into the fire, so I declined because common sense and my instinct for life told me to do so. As it later turned out, I was right.

I knew that I had to get out of Zosia's place as soon as possible, because only now was she beginning to show her true colors. Besides the fabricated story she told about having to ransom my baby from a policeman for three hundred zlotys, there had been another incident between Zosia and Michalski's wife concerning some butter which she was supposed to bring. She asked for a price that was higher than the going rate, and when Mrs. Michalski didn't want to pay that much, Zosia said that if she wouldn't take the butter for the price she was asking, she would go straight to the German gendarmes and tell them about the child she was keeping there. After such a threat, they paid her for the butter. My husband covered the entire amount, of course. Mrs. Michalski had gotten sick and was coughing blood, so it was imperative that we do everything to see that Zosia lost all track of me, so that no such similar incidents occurred in the future.

After talking with the Mrozińskis, it was decided that I would stay in the empty room for a few days. Mrs.Mroziński brought me food. After this, the crippled housekeeper offered to take me into her apartment for the entire winter on the condition that I register, which I was prepared to do. The only hitch was Zosia. Everyone was afraid that once she found out, she would call for the police. My only hope was in her vacating the apartment and moving away as planned.

That evening I dressed, said goodbye to Zosia, went outside and walked down the road in order to put her off her guard and convince her that I really was leaving. Then I returned through an opening in the gate and went back into the empty room. In the morning I had to move into the housekeeper's apartment so that Zosia wouldn't see and so the woman who was renting the housekeeper's kitchen, who was on good terms with Zosia, wouldn't see either. When at last I managed to slip unnoticed into the housekeeper's apartment, she locked me into her spare room, where I sat motionless all day long in an armchair, not daring to make so much as a sound for fear the slightest rustle might betray my presence. In the evening I had to wait for the right moment to return to the empty room.

We kept waiting for Zosia to move out, but she showed no sign of leaving. She even began negotiating with one of the tenants in order to stay with her. To make matters worse, an incident happened which completely ruined everything. One afternoon, an automobile from the Gestapo suddenly drove up to the school building next to our apartment. The building was surrounded, and the children were locked in their classrooms. The teacher was brought out and put in the automobile. The same thing was happening throughout Wołomin and neighboring villages.

Many people from different walks of life were arrested in connection with the approaching anniversary of Poland's independence on November 11th.[1] This lasted for several hours and awakened mad panic among the population. People began to escape en masse into the woods, because no one knew exactly what was happening. Our housekeeper came hobbling on her artificial leg and told me to leave as soon as possible. Mr. Mroziński also told me to be on my way. Fortunately, his wife took pity on me and gave me a large woolen shawl. I wrapped myself tightly in it and went out to behind the barn where I squatted in a little corner and sat there until the automobile with the Gestapo had left. I understood that I could no longer stay there.

With a beating heart I returned to the Mrozińskis. I wasn't even certain they would let me in, but they did, for which I was extremely grateful. I stayed all evening long hunched over on a small table next to the stove, shaking from the cold. The Mrozińskis were just looking for a pretext to get rid of me. To my feeble request for them to loan me something to cover up with, they replied that they had nothing to give me. I could feel that a storm was brewing. At that moment, in came Marysia Będkowski carrying my baby in her arms. Behind her was Henryk Michalski. The baby was almost frozen. In the course of these few days he had changed beyond recognition. He had grown smaller and thinner, and his sad tired little eyes looked at me reproachfully.

As it turned out, the baby hadn't eaten for the last six hours. I am not able to describe what went on inside me at that moment. No one would be able to understand, but if I could have suddenly died and have my suffering cease, it would have been my greatest happiness. But death is not always at one's beck and call. I was alive and had to think about what to feed the baby. They had brought me two packages of underwear, shoes, and other things, but no one had thought about bringing even a little cream of wheat for the baby. The baby's bottle had been broken in Warsaw, and no one had bothered to get another one.

Finally we were able to come up with half a glass of milk at the Mrozińskis, which the baby drank up voraciously. Mrs. Mroziński told us that she wasn't going to allow us to spend the night with them. The landlady said the same thing. I was left out on the street with the baby, with Marysia and Henryk getting ready to go back to Warsaw. What was I supposed to do? Where was I supposed to go? Henryk, seeing my predicament, went upstairs to talk Zosia into letting me spend the night there. She agreed to keep us until Sunday, in other words for two days. Henryk and Marysia returned to Warsaw and I found myself once more in Zosia's apartment.

They didn't even explain to me why, at such a terrible moment, when I had no place to put myself, they had brought me the baby. Why were these packages necessary which, given my present situation, were completely superfluous? I didn't dare ask. Indeed I had received from them several reproaches. They said that because of the roundups taking place that day, it had been necessary to bring all of this baggage by a very circuitous route. All of this fell on my deranged mind so suddenly and unexpectedly that I was simply dumbstruck. Only one thing was clear. People had no idea how hopeless and tragic my situation was. I was a terrible bother to everyone, and no one knew how to extricate me from my dilemma.

That was the most tragic night in my entire life. Zosia slept at her neighbor's, explaining that she was afraid to sleep under the same roof with me, and that this way it would be easier for her to slip away when the police came for me.

The baby kept waking up. He was hungry, and I didn't have anything to give him. All night long I sat over him on the floor in the cold and empty apartment and cried. In vain I racked my brains trying to think of what to do and where to go. I had placed all of my trust and faith in Jula but, even though she knew what my situation was like, she didn't come, even to say a kind word and to comfort me. No one could put themselves in my place—a Jewish woman, hounded and homeless, with a little baby, both of us hovering on the very brink of destruction.

I came to the conclusion that there were two possibilities remaining —either to hand myself over to the Germans voluntarily or to commit suicide. In either case the result was death. I kept debating with myself which kind of death I preferred. Because I am a religious person, I shuddered at the thought of suicide, even though I had already tried once. On the other hand, my fear of the Germans was even greater than my fear of God. I rationalized to myself that many rabbis had committed suicide during the time of the persecution of the Jews. If I had only had a little poison I would have been able to put an end to my and the baby's sufferings that very night. I decided that, as a last resort, I could lie down on the tracks in front of a train and die that way.

---

1. **November 6 arrests**. Around 2,000 professors, teachers, journalists, lawyers, doctors, actors, and other political and cultural figures were detained by the Gestapo on this date throughout the Warsaw region in order to forestall demonstrations in commemoration of the Polish Independence Day on November 11th.

39

MRS. ZIELIŃSKI

The night seemed to last a century. At last the pale light of dawn peeked through the window. Zosia finally appeared, looking angry and gloomy and casting a hateful glance in my direction. Since I had another two hundred zlotys, I proposed that she take 150 and bring Jula from Warsaw. Zosia took me up on this idea. When she had left, I decided to try one last plan. My oldest sister had been good friends with a woman who had a private home in a small village, Sławek, near Wołomin. Her name was Mrs. Zieliński. My sister had rented a room with her for several summers in a row. When I was still a small girl attending elementary school, I had spent a few weeks at the Zielińskis' house. I remembered that time as if in a dream, and she probably wouldn't remember me at all. I decided to try my luck and go to see her.

I looked for her house, which was about one and a half kilometers away. After a long search, I finally found the place but no one was home. A neighbor informed me that Mrs. Zieliński had gone to Warsaw, and she didn't know when she would be back. I returned to the apartment without having accomplished anything.

That evening Zosia returned with the news that her aunt couldn't come, and that I should do whatever I considered necessary. That same evening the housekeeper came to me and told me that I could only stay in the apartment until the following day. She spoke politely, but I detected a clear threat in her words. Once more I spent a sleepless night—the last night of my life, I was certain of that. The baby was a little calmer and was able to sleep.

At noon Henryk came with a card to fill out for registering myself, something which was totally pointless at that point. When he learned that I had to leave that day he became very upset and tried to come to some kind of arrangement, first with the landlady and then with Mrs. Mroziński, but after having convinced himself of the futility of that idea, he was about to go back to Warsaw. I dressed myself and the baby. I thought that he would at least go to Warsaw with me in order to place me somewhere at least for the time being, but all I heard from him were the cold words, "My dear lady, I have a wife and children, and I am not free to expose myself recklessly to danger."

I asked him at least to take my things back with him, and finally, at my question as to where I was supposed to go, he told me to go to Warsaw and wait on the street. I packed several diapers and a change of underwear for the baby and dragged myself to the station.

The wind was brisk and very cold. I wrapped the baby in whatever I could and walked along the sandy road with heavy steps. I was so weak that I was barely able to support the baby's weight. When I finally reached the station, the train to Warsaw was already pulling away from the platform. The next train was not until eight o'clock. I took myself and the baby back to Zosia's, but when she saw me, Zosia shut the door in my face and told me to get out. I knocked on the Mroziński's door and asked them to let me rest with them a little and change the baby, but they showed me the door and threatened that if I didn't leave that very minute they would go to the German gendarmes. As if to lend force to their words, Mr. Mroziński put on his overcoat. Oh, you hard-hearted people: did you ever understand how much injury you did to me?

I took my precious little bundle and headed for the exit into the unknown. Zosia caught up with me, tore my handbag out of my grasp, and with her fingers, which were more like talons at this point, tore from it the police registration card which Henryk had brought, after which she disappeared and left me alone.

I walked straight ahead, without paying any attention to where I was going. All along the road I kept looking for some kind of large rock or tree stump to sit on and rest, but I couldn't find anything, so I kept walking ahead, as if in a daze. The crying of my baby brought me back to reality. The little one was tired, frozen, wet, and hungry. In the pocket of my overcoat I had a bottle, and in it was a little milk. At that very moment I was passing by a small house with a bench on the porch. I gathered up my courage and was getting ready to go up to it when a pretty girl came out of the house and looked at the child. I could see an expression of pity in her face. When I asked in a broken voice if I could rest a moment on her porch, she invited me inside. Here I was able to change the baby into dry diapers and feed him the milk which the sweet little girl was nice enough to warm up for me. When she asked where I was heading and who I was looking for, I answered that I was looking for Mrs. Zieliński's house. The girl indicated to me the direction in which I had to go, and I thanked her with tears in my eyes.

Perhaps Mrs. Zieliński had returned from Warsaw by this time and would let me find shelter with her. I soon came to her house and, with a pounding heart, asked the same woman I had seen the day before whether Mrs. Zieliński was at home. She pointed toward the depths of the entryway, where a figure was visible and said, "That's her over there."

The woman didn't ask a single question but led me into her apartment and gave me a close looking over. There were a young girl and a man in the room. Mrs. Zieliński still didn't ask any questions but told me to take off my coat and have a seat. My first request was whether there might be a little cream of wheat for the baby. The neighbor brought a little from the bottom floor, and her son went to the nearby store for me to buy a little butter and sugar. Mrs. Zieliński placed a plate of borsch and potatoes in front of me. I was overcome by a great feeling of bliss. I was so touched that it was difficult for me to control my tears. Even today, eleven months later, as I continue to write these words in hiding, I am deeply touched whenever I think about it. I will never forget how this woman stretched out a helping hand to me at such a tragic moment in my life. If it had not been for her, I and the baby would surely no longer be alive. May God bless her.

How happy I was to place my son on a bed and cover him with a feather blanket. The tired little mite fell asleep immediately. Mrs. Zieliński's daughter, the young girl who was there together with her fiancé, left. How great was my surprise to realize that Mrs. Zieliński had guessed who I was.

It was clear that she was living in very dire circumstances. She occupied a little room on the second floor of her building. She told me that her son had been working in Prussia for the past two years. She was not on good terms with her husband, who was working as a fireman in Warsaw. I remember from what my sister had told me that the husband and wife had always been at loggerheads, and that fights between them were the order of the day. The husband didn't give a penny for the maintenance of the house. The daughter was working in a German factory, earning two and a half zlotys per day. Mrs. Zieliński had already sold everything she owned in the house, and for some time everyone had been starving. For the past two weeks she had been going to Warsaw, on the suggestion of her neighbor, with meat which she sold in an open-air market in the Praga district.

I proposed to her that she go next morning to Warsaw with a letter from me to Marysia Będkowski, and that I would take care of whatever money she might lose from not selling her meat. She eagerly took me up on my proposal.

It is difficult for me to describe the sense of peace and satisfaction I felt on the bed she made up for me on the floor. At least for the next twenty-four hours, I had a roof over my head. I didn't think about tomorrow; I was only able to live in the present.

Next morning Mrs. Zieliński went on the first train to Warsaw with my letter to Marysia Będkowski. In this letter I set forth the entire drama of a poor unhappy mother begging for the last time for help. When Mrs. Zieliński returned, she told me that Michalski and Marysia would come that evening. Mrs. Zieliński told me that they were very gratified to see her in Warsaw. They had been very concerned for us and had already given us up for lost.

The rest of the day passed peacefully. Several neighbor women came to visit Mrs. Zieliński, and in such a cramped room it was difficult not to come into contact with them. However, I was completely indifferent to their conversation, being absorbed instead by one thought— whether any kind of solution could be found for us. In the evening Henryk and Marysia came and informed me that in the morning they would take the baby to Warsaw, and I was to remain for the time being at Mrs. Zieliński's, who had agreed to put me up, as long as I was without the baby.

That night I didn't get a wink of sleep thinking about my separation from the baby. At the bottom of my heart I was afraid that in another several days they would bring the baby back to me, and Mrs. Zieliński would not want to keep me any longer. I thought about the baby until I was almost sick. I was prepared to undergo the greatest possible sacrifice and privation in order to save him. I realized that a seven-month-old baby, who had been wandering from place to place for more than three and a half months, deprived of even the most basic of necessities, could not survive for long, especially now when the first November frosts had arrived and he had to endure constant traveling in stuffy overcrowded train cars without a regular diet. How many tears I shed in silence that night only the Lord knows.

At five o'clock we struggled out of bed. For the last time I fed my little son, whispering thousands of little words of endearment to him. I prayed for the Lord to take pity on my tortured soul and my poor mother's heart and allow me to see the day when I would once again be able to clasp my child to my bosom.

Since that day eleven long terrifying months have passed, so hopeless that each of them seemed like an eternity. That day has not yet arrived, but somewhere in the distance, still very far away, hovers a vision of a bright and blessed freedom.

Hoarfrost had settled on the trees. It was very cold. I dressed my little boy as warmly as I could and kissed him for the last time. It was still dark outside. Mrs. Zieliński took our friends to the station, leaving me completely alone.

40

LETTERS BACK AND FORTH

Mrs. Zieliński decided to set up a separate apartment for me across the hall where there was an empty room and kitchen. The room was virtually uninhabitable. There was a large hole in the ceiling through which the rain poured. The door out onto the balcony had rotted away. It had huge cracks in it and no panes. Cold and damp reigned. The kitchen was gigantic but hardly in better condition. Individual windows were also full of holes. When it rained, the ceiling leaked. I trembled at the thought of spending the winter in this apartment.

I must admit that Mrs. Zieliński spared no time or effort in order to make the kitchen habitable. She whitewashed the ceiling, dusted the walls, and set up a cot for me for which she had to walk three kilometers to Kobyłka. She was in her element, for she loved to be in motion and would constantly create obstacles for herself in order to stretch out her activities, so it was more than a week before she bought pipes for the kitchen stove. Finally, her preparations came to an end, and it was high time, for I was afraid that the women who came visiting would start gossiping, and that the same thing that had happened at Zosia's would be repeated here.

There was yet another reason why I wanted to move out of Mrs. Zieliński's room as quickly as possible. Her apartment was frequently visited by the police in connection with various police matters and lawsuits which she had going against her husband and, conversely, which her husband had brought against her. This man and wife were well known in the court, the police station, and even at the village

199

elder's. Whenever they were together, some kind of quarrel would break out between them, after which either Mr. or Mrs. Zieliński would go and lodge yet another complaint. There were so many of these cases that whenever a summons from the court appeared, Mrs. Zieliński had to stretch her memory in order to remember when the event had even occurred—for example, when she had caused a ruckus in the home of her husband's supposed lover by tearing out the woman's hair and breaking the windows.

During my stay with her, two such cases came before the court. The verdict was both just and uniform. Each one of the partners had to sit in jail. They appealed the case to the Warsaw court, and after this the verdict was changed to one month of prison for Mrs. Zieliński. She was heartily dissatisfied and wanted to turn to a higher court, but her neighbors advised against it. Wanting to revenge herself on her faithless husband, she wrote, or rather I wrote, because she was illiterate, a letter full of slander about him to the fire station where he was employed. It was no wonder, then, that the police continually looked in on my new guardian's apartment, seeking one or the other of the couple.

I was tortured with longing for my baby, about whom I had no news. I spent every night agonizing terribly about him. I was condemned to inactivity—I didn't go out of the house at all. I was worried about meeting someone from the Mroziński family, for I knew that they often ventured into this neighborhood in order to sell the rotgut vodka which Mr. Mroziński made and sold illegally. Besides that, this was a village where each cottage touched upon the next, and I didn't want to risk coming into contact with people who might begin gossiping. I had already had one glaring example of what human tongues were capable of, and I didn't need another.

Not far from us a farmer had begun to refine oil. On the third day the Germans came and took away everything he had made. What they couldn't take away they destroyed, and they took the poor farmer along with them to the police station in Radzymin, where he disappeared without trace. That was soon after my arrival at the Zielińskis', and I was very disturbed by it. Soon afterwards, a second incident occurred. In Zagościniec, three kilometers away, someone had denounced a forester for hiding Jews. The German gendarmes had come and shot all the Jews hiding there along with the forester and his entire family. The story spread like wildfire throughout the entire district, filling hearts with fear and terror. People were particularly terrified at the thought of collective responsibility, for if the Germans found a Jew hiding in anyone's apartment, all the inhabitants of the village were responsible with their lives. It was no wonder, then, that it was almost impossible to hide out. I prayed to God that Mrs. Zieliński would not reconsider and deprive me of the roof over my head.

I was terribly afraid of the other tenants in our building. There were two families. One lived on the first floor next to the entry. These people had escaped from Poznań, a city well known for its anti-Semitism. The woman traveled to Warsaw with Mrs. Zieliński, while the husband stayed at home and looked after the two children and worked in the garden. I was particularly afraid of him, for Mrs. Zieliński told me that he was a man without scruples or conscience. He had been thrown out of the distillery where he had worked for pilfering, and now he was nothing but a burden to his wife. He refused to take up any kind of work, explaining that he was afraid he would be rounded up and sent to Prussia. On the other side of the building lived two sisters. One was a widow, and the other was an old maid of forty years. One of them worked as a helper on the railroad, while the other worked in the garden.

Mrs. Zieliński was generally on good terms with her tenants and had no particular enemies, with the exception of her own husband. I was very careful not to run into him, which was easy to do, for he always came home by the late train in the evening and, after spending the night, went back to Warsaw when it was still dark. In general, then, my relations with the neighbors were on a much better footing than they had been at Zosia's. For the first several weeks I had an excellent excuse for staying put in the apartment. During that memorable Sunday when Zosia had behaved so disgracefully toward me and forced me to walk several kilometers, I had sprained my foot. For several days I couldn't even put my shoes on, which were tight on me to begin with. Mrs. Zieliński loaned me her own worn-out slippers.

After I had been at Mrs. Zieliński's for two weeks, Henryk visited me, bringing me money and a letter from my husband. I was not able to learn very much from the meagre information he provided about our baby, other than that he was alive and well. I deduced that work was proceeding apace and that the largest sales season was approaching. From what my husband later told me, I learned that while I was at Zosia's he had known almost nothing about my situation. Jula did not want to reveal my location in case my husband would find himself in the hands of the Gestapo, known to torture their prisoners for information. Henryk's reasoning was the same, which is why he would not supply any details about my baby's whereabouts. It was only much later that my husband learned that I was staying near Wołomin. He offered to pay Jula for everything she had done for us, but she refused. Both my husband and Henryk were greatly amazed. She was the first person who had done anything at all for us gratuitously.[1]

My husband's mind was thus put at ease about us, and he was able to devote himself to his work. It was no easy matter to organize the workshop; the workers had to be limited to a small number of trusted confidants, that is, the Będkowskis and Henryk's brothers. Since everyone was working very diligently under my husband's direction, it was not long before work was proceeding at full steam, and profits had already begun to pile up.

---

1. "She was the first person who had done anything at all for us gratuitously." This statement, while generally true of experiences both inside and outside the ghetto, is a slight misrepresentation of the facts. Mrs. Schmidt is writing under the impression of her recent experiences in Wołomin.

41

MRS. ZIELIŃSKI DISAPPOINTS

Mrs. Zieliński continued going practically every day to Warsaw with her first-floor neighbor, Mrs. Szymański. They went very early to the butcher's to buy meat, which they would take to Warsaw and sell on the black market, thus eking out a marginal existence. It was not always possible to obtain meat, because professional tradesmen and smugglers would come from Warsaw and take away most of the cow in quarters immediately after it was slaughtered. For such people as Mrs. Zieliński and her neighbor, who bought only a few kilograms at a time, , little remained. It often happened that they had to make the rounds of all of the slaughterhouses in Wołomin in order to get enough meat. Often enough they returned from their expedition with empty hands.

People, therefore, were up in our building from three o'clock in the morning. Mrs. Zieliński would prepare breakfast for herself and her daughter. This was very poor fare, consisting of soup decorated with a little tallow fat and several pieces of black bread. They ate this day in and day out. After arriving in Warsaw with the meat, she had to wait there until the market opened. By the time she sold her meat it was already late in the afternoon unless, God forbid, it had already been confiscated by the police on the train or right there at the market, which happened practically every time. Sometimes it was necessary to bribe the Blue Police or secret agents dressed in civilian clothes, who swarmed around like hyenas looking for victims to squeeze a bribe from for engaging in illicit trade. Tradesmen professionally engaged in this occupation already knew all of the agents, but newcomers like Mrs.

Zieliński often fell victim to them. Besides that, Germans would suddenly drive up in a covered truck which people called a "buda" (shack), surround the market on all sides, and take away the goods and the people. These were candidates for work camps in Prussia. In brief, it was not easy for such "greenhorns" as Mrs. Zieliński to earn a few zlotys in illicit trade. What is more, the most she ever had in capital was a hundred and fifty zlotys, with which she could buy only about five kilograms of meat.

Mrs. Zieliński would come home frozen to the bone, hungry, and upset. She would always have some terrible story to tell about what had happened to her along the way. As time went on I became so accustomed to these "tragic tales" that I felt deprived whenever she didn't have any to relate.

Mrs. Zieliński's daughter, Lilka, was a pretty seventeen-year-old girl. She was kind and eager to do me any kind of favor. I liked her very much, and it seemed to me that the feeling was mutual. Sometimes I would be puzzled at how such a pure and honest girl had fallen into such a swamp, which was what I considered her family situation to be. Lilka had a hard lot. She worked in a German metallurgical factory. The work was heavy and exhausting, lasting from seven o'clock in the morning until seven o'clock at night. She returned home frozen, exhausted, covered with tar, and saturated with the smell of machine oil, totally numb to the world and the rest of humanity. For this work she received only two and a half zlotys per day, and occasionally a pitifully small bonus in the form of marmalade, margarine, or a few eggs.

When from time to time she allowed herself to take a few days off from work, she would receive notice to appear at work immediately, or she would be crossed off the work list and receive a notice to report for a Prussian work camp. Work in Prussia was used to terrify people. Mrs. Zieliński's son had been working there for two years. In all this time he had been home on vacation only two times. Recently he had been writing letters home full of complaints and a desperate longing for home.

Lilka was visited by a boy called Stefan, who would come three kilometers from Kobyłka. He was a lad as simple and honest as she. The boy was very much in love with her, and I could also tell that Stefan liked me. When once I asked him for a book he came through a snowstorm in order to bring it to me. Reading was my sole diversion. As I read I forgot about my sad reality and found a moment's escape from my present woes. For this I was extremely grateful to Stefan.

When Mrs. Zieliński was in Warsaw and Lilka was at work, I

would sit at home alone locked up in my room, listening with a pounding heart for the sound of footsteps on the stairs. I would wait impatiently until Lilka returned from work. When she was around I at least had someone to talk to. The solitude was so oppressive that I had to force myself not to carry on conversations aloud with myself.

Mrs. Zieliński and her daughter were always careful to see that I had enough potatoes, bread, and tallow to mix with it. I didn't want to eat any better than they did, and so I lived on the same poor fare. There was another reason as well. I had no one to bring money to me, for at that time huge roundups were taking place on the train, gathering workers for Prussia. Out of fear, people wouldn't ride the trains at all. There was a time when I was so poor that I just wasn't eating at all. I tried to arrange for money to be sent from my husband through the landlady, for she was in constant contact with Marysia Będkowski, but unfortunately this turned out to be impossible for the following reason.

The preceding year the "Bank of Emission" had issued a new kind of fifty-zloty note. Since I never went out, I didn't know about it, and when I noticed that Henryk had brought a fifty-zloty note of the new type, I was certain that it was counterfeit. I showed it to Mrs. Zieliński and asked her to take it back to Marysia in order to exchange it. Mrs. Zieliński didn't say anything but took the money from me, and that evening, when she returned from Warsaw, she told me she had lost it. During Henryk's next visit I told him what had happened. Then he told me that Mrs. Zieliński, as a "merchant," knew that these bank notes were not counterfeit. When next week my husband sent me the rest of my things through Mrs. Zieliński, I didn't receive any of them. She said that the package, worth over 1000 zlotys, had been stolen from her on the train.

At that point I no longer had any delusions as to human honesty. My new landlady, and what was more, a personal acquaintance and my sister's good friend, was stealing from me on a trivial pretext. I wrote a letter to my husband full of bitterness, asking that he no longer send anything through Mrs. Zieliński.

Then I met for the first time the other tenants on the first floor—the two sisters. I was forced to come into contact with them in order to obtain coal. It was the beginning of December, and it was bitter cold in my apartment, where the windows were full of cracks and openings. I was unable to dress warmly enough, so I had to build a fire in the kitchen. It was difficult to obtain coal out in the country; one had to go to Wołomin and carry it back. I couldn't do that myself, and Mrs.

Zieliński and her daughter didn't have the time, so I was left with no choice but to freeze.

I learned from my landlady that one of the two sisters, Ewa, was working at the railway station as a cleaning woman and had coal to sell. The railway workers would give it to her willingly, as long as there were no "black Bahnschutz" men hanging around watching the tracks. (They were so called because of the black uniform the railway guards wore). The men knew that it was impossible to survive on the amount of money a cleaning woman made on the railroad. During the course of the day she would gather bucketloads of coal together, and this enabled her to survive. There were days, of course, when the black Bahnschutz men were carefully guarding the tracks, and on such days she returned from work sad and empty-handed. Woe to the railway worker who was caught by the Bahnschutz in the act. No explanation was asked for nor given. A shot in the head and the matter was settled.

It once happened that a fourteen-year-old boy was gathering pieces of coal on the track. They were just lying there, of no use to anyone. At home he had a sick mother, several younger brothers and sisters, and it was very cold in their home. Unfortunately, he didn't hear the approaching steps of the Bahnschutz until the shot rang out, and a moment later a bloody puddle spread across the black cinders of the rail-road bed. The Polish stationmaster took a look at the dead body of the child and a tear glistened in his eyes as he quietly commanded his workers to pick up the body and sprinkle the innocent blood (may it someday be avenged!) with sand. Ewa told me about this tragic incident.

Since the day I had to turn personally to Ewa about buying coal, I was no longer as cold as I had been before. She always took care to see that I had a little reserve supply and when I had no money, she would give it to me on credit. In general, both sisters showed me much sympathy and understanding, for which I was very grateful. How valuable their disinterested kindness was to me! I was accustomed to having everyone take advantage of me as much as they could.

No one understood me. My every request was looked on as some kind of caprice. Whatever I said, even the most trifling remark, was misunderstood and turned around and relayed to my husband in such a way as to discourage him and to make him want to abandon me. Jula always told my husband that she was convinced that the Michalskis' actions were all aimed toward getting rid of me. Instead of words of comfort, the only advice I received from our protector was that in a situation like mine, it was good to have a little poison around in case of need. The suggestion was only too clear. I must admit that it was only thanks to my husband's "diplomacy" and skillful behavior with respect to the entire Michalski family, both then and throughout our entire stay with them, that we were able to survive on the Aryan side.

Returning to Ewa and her sister, I recognized that they themselves did not realize how valuable their sympathy was for me during the period of my solitude and abandonment. Sometimes around dusk I allowed myself the luxury of going down to their room. Ewa would put a couple of pieces of coal on the stove, the fire would blaze merrily, and the pleasant warmth would be reflected from it throughout the room. At such times I felt happier and less abandoned. Talking with these two women was a great comfort to me, and we became quite close. Often Ewa would play cards with me or treat me to tea or hot beer. She received two bottles of beer per week from the Germans as a bonus. Sometimes she and her sister would come to my room and we would talk. Neither sister ever let on that they realized who I was. For that reason, they likewise never had any cause to fear my company. In any case, I was extremely grateful to them for all the pleasant moments they afforded me.

42

CHRISTMAS HOLIDAYS, 1942

Toward the end of November 1942 I learned from my landlady that the Warsaw ghetto had once again been surrounded by German gendarmes, and Latvian, Lithuanian, and Ukrainian detachments. During Henryk's next visit I found out that a new purge had taken place, with more than a hundred people being taken from the K. G. Schultz factory. In all, several thousand people had been taken away. The ghetto continued to be surrounded, and communication with the outside world was almost impossible.

During the time I was staying at Mrs. Zieliński's several dozen Jews from the Warsaw ghetto were working on the railway in Wołomin. They would arrive each Monday in a specially sealed freight wagon and stay all week in a one-story workshop especially constructed for the purpose. On Saturday evening they would be taken back to Warsaw. In Wołomin their supervisor was a Pole by the name of Biernacki. He had first choice of all the things they brought to sell, after which the others had their chance. So on Monday all the inhabitants of Wołomin would go to the shop in order to buy various things from the Jews. Mrs. Zieliński and Ewa went there themselves more than once. I was eager to hear news from the ghetto, and who would have known better than they what was happening there? However, I knew that it would be fool-hardy of me to visit them, so I had to satisfy myself with the sparse information provided by Mrs. Zieliński and Ewa.

One night Biernacki locked them as usual in their shed and went home for the night, taking the key with him. During the night a fire broke out. The wooden building was instantly enveloped in flames, feeding greedily on the straw on which the unfortunate men were sleeping. Some were able to jump out through the window, but all the rest perished in the flames. Those who managed to leap through the window were badly burned and injured. Next morning the local German gendarmes came and finished off all the wounded. Such was the tragic end of the Jews working in Wołomin on the railway. I wasn't able to put the event out of my mind for a long time.

The first frosts had arrived, and the earth was enveloped in a white snowy shroud. The wind whistled mournfully outside the windows. After the fire had gone out the nights were worst of all, for the temperature in the room fell to several degrees below freezing.

I slept on a worn-out cot without a mattress, covered only with a single blanket and an overcoat. I was so cold that I didn't even get undressed. Fear accompanied me day and night, never giving me a moment's peace. The nights were a terrible agony, and in the morning I would finally fall briefly and restlessly asleep. The days were monotonous and cold, and the kitchen was smoky.

The Christmas holidays had already passed. That year they fell on Friday and, together with Saturday and Sunday, they lasted three days. Two weeks before I had asked Henryk to allow me to spend the holidays with my husband. I knew that for those three days my husband would be locked in the tinsmith's shop, where he had his own workshop and hiding place. The workshop would be locked, and no one would be working there, so there was no danger that someone would see me. Henryk categorically refused. I turned to Marysia Będkowski, and through her wrote a letter to my husband beseeching him to do something. I nourished myself with the thought for an entire two weeks, but finally, on Christmas Eve, all of my dreams came tumbling down. I received a letter from Marysia in which she said that it was impossible to comply with my request because of the opposition of the Michalski family.

This was a terrible blow for me. It also made a bad impression on Mrs. Zieliński who, in order to create some semblance of cover for me, had already told her tenants that I was going to spend the holidays with my family in Warsaw. Seeing now that the entire weight of responsibility for me fell on her shoulders, and that no one wanted to make it in any easier for her, she told me that if I didn't go to Warsaw for at least a few days over the New Year's holidays, I wouldn't be able to stay with her any longer. I would say that her words were justified.

No one of my husband's protectors visited me, for there was no time. I did receive a letter from him in which he informed me that the baby had been ill but was already on the mend. Only much later did I learn that our child's life had been hanging by a thread. He had been so seriously ill that the doctor had given him up for lost.

On the first day of the holidays, my landlady invited me into her apartment for breakfast. Ewa and her sister also had me in. We even shared the Christmas wafer with one another. They shared with me whatever they had, and we exchanged mutual wishes for a better year to come. I thought in my heart that I would never live to see the end of the coming year. But life is always full of surprises. Who knew? Maybe my wishes would be granted after all.

The next evening, Mrs. Zieliński, who was in my apartment, heard the trampling of many feet on our stairs. Curious, she went out into the hall and found there a number of people from a Jewish family who were well known around Wołomin. It seemed that they had been hiding in a deserted building in Górki Mironowe on the edge of town. That old tumble-down house without windows or doors had been their only shelter, and they were living off whatever people would give them out of charity. Among them was an old man who was barely able to walk. It was clear he had not much longer to live. Mrs. Zieliński and I shared with them what little we had. Taking advantage of the darkness as best I could, I tried not to show them who I was, for I was afraid they might recognize me and needlessly give me away. After they left I thought about them for a long time. I realized that compared to them I was living in clover and ought to be thankful to God for what I had. I should believe in Him and entrust myself to His providence.

The holidays were over, and life went on as before. One day Mrs. Zieliński came on the afternoon train from Warsaw. She was extremely upset because she had learned that the previous evening the police had been looking for building number 53 and had been unable to find it. This was Mrs. Zieliński's address. She had no idea what they had been about and why they had been unable to find it, for everyone in Wołomin knew where it was. Both of us were terrified, certain that someone had given us away. Probably the police were from Warsaw, we thought, because during her trip there she visited the Będkowskis and, not finding them home, had gone over to the neighbor's to ask when she would return. The neighbor immediately began spilling out everything, giving Mrs. Zieliński's name and address and everything she knew about me. When Mrs. Zieliński tried to deny it, Marysia Będkowski's five-year-old boy, who at that moment was at the neighbor's home, seconded her, chiming in that "that woman is keeping a Jewish woman in her place." It is easy to imagine Mrs. Zieliński's fear and, at the same time, her rage upon her return. We both thought that this was the neighbor woman's way of taking out some kind of revenge on Marysia, with whom she must have had a spat. There were many such occurrences, and in most cases the victims were the Jews hiding with the Poles. We could see that Marysia was none too intelligent, but we had no idea that she would go around telling about my staying at Mrs. Zieliński's to people I didn't even know.

Mrs. Zieliński was so upset and unnerved that her mood was immediately conveyed to the other tenants in our building and ruined my situation there completely. Everyone turned against me, and no one wanted me to spend the night with them when Mrs. Zieliński asked. Fear and suspicion stole into the hearts of those who had previously been so kind to me. Outside it was cold, 22 degrees below freezing, and in combination with the wind, it was impossible to spend the night out of doors. Mrs. Zieliński's daughter had gone to work for the night at the factory, and she was the only one on my side. All night long I sat on my bed listening. Each squeak or scrape, every rustle, started my heart pounding at an insane clip.

Finally, the long night came to an end, and nothing bad had happened. Next morning Mrs. Zieliński's nerves got the better of her, and she ran to the police to find out what had happened. It turned out that the number they had been looking for was indeed 53, but more precisely 53A, in other words, a different building entirely. There was an illegal vodka distillery there, and someone had informed on them to the police. Mrs. Zieliński was very relieved, as was I, but she still insisted that I be taken to Warsaw for several weeks. I kept asking for a delay, for my husband wrote me that he was diligently trying to secure an apartment for me, and that it was only a matter of time. The tenants, seeing that everything was in order, calmed down, and I behaved with them as before, as if nothing had happened.

43

___

NEW YEAR'S, 1943. REUNION WITH MY HUSBAND

During the Christmas holidays a cold spell set in with a strong wind, and this weather lasted for two weeks. Our well froze over, and it was necessary to walk a fair piece in order to fetch water. This was very inconvenient for me, because I was not able to go by myself to a strange house for fear of giving the neighbors reason to gossip. Even though I had a fire going all day long in the kitchen, the water in my pail froze over. The doors, knocked out over and over again in the course of the Zielińskis' marital squabbles, were cracked and broken and barely hanging on their hinges. In short, wherever I turned, the cold air was coming in.

I spent all day long bent over in my overcoat, shivering from the cold. The nights were worse, for I was unable to keep a fire going. I lay in my clothing and stockings on my old worn-out cot, covered up with my blanket and overcoat. Being unable to sleep, I spent my time thinking. I didn't think about the future. I knew that my life had already come to an end, and I expected nothing more. I understood that as long as I was at Mrs. Zieliński's I wouldn't be betrayed. She wouldn't turn me out into the cold, as Zosia had done, for she was a completely different type of person. For all her faults, she had a heart and soul and sympathized with my situation.

I thought constantly about suicide. I went over the act in the greatest possible detail. I decided to go out into the fields in the night and wait patiently for death. I had heard that this was a painless way to die, and that one often even experienced pleasant visions. I remembered the well-known Andersen fairly tale "The Little Match Girl." This kind of death had the added bonus that even if I were recognized as a Jew, no one would be called to account because of it. Having made up my mind, I experienced a certain kind of relief. I kept putting off taking action until after the new year. Thinking continually about death as I did, I had time to consider the content and meaning of life. I readily admit that previously I had loved life extremely, in spite of the fact that it had not been a bed of roses but continual hard work. I loved nature, and I dreamed of a bright peaceful future working alongside my husband, bringing up our child. Now all of this had come tumbling down. The Germans had brought us to ruin and condemned us to death, for no other reason than that we were Jews.

Our life was crushed, and I myself was a cast-off. I felt alien and a burden to everyone, even to my own husband, in spite of the fact that he never gave me any reason to think so. I read in my husband's every word the despair and agony which he felt for not being able to lend any help. I knew that my death would cause him an enormous amount of sorrow. Besides that, I also felt the responsibility of a mother for its child. It was that responsibility alone that kept me from committing suicide. I waited for a miracle.

Sunken in such painful thoughts, I lived to see the New Year, 1943. Lilka went to Kobyłka to spend New Year's Eve with her fiancé. Only a year ago I myself had had my own cozy little nest, and all the neighbors were gathered in our apartment to play poker, eat pastries, and drink tea until late into the night. Now most of them were no longer alive, and I was not certain that it had not all been a dream.

On New Year's Day Stasiek Będkowski came to see me. I hadn't see him for two years, and I noticed such great changes in him that I was frightened. Somewhere along the way the old, happy Stasiek with the ever-frank expression in his eyes had disappeared. It was a completely different person that I now saw before me. His face was sunken and his vision had grown dim, from which one could conclude that he had been drinking too much. After exchanging a few words with him, I understood that here was a complete stranger. I learned from him that the apartment which my husband was counting on getting for me belonged to Marysia's half-sister. At the moment there was a subletter living in the room which was to be rented for me, to whom we were to pay 1500 zlotys. Stasiek was sounding me out discreetly in order to find out what our financial resources were. I saw through his scheme immediately. All of this bothered me a lot, and after he left I felt a great weight settle on my heart. I felt that something was in the air and I didn't know what to do about it. I wanted to write a letter to Henryk and warn him, but I did not know how to formulate my fears in such a way as to be convincing. The thought that I would be laughed at finally restrained me from imparting my thoughts to them.

The holiday of the Three Kings (Epiphany) came and went. Mrs. Zieliński kept insisting more and more firmly and frequently that I be removed from her building. Finally, seeing that her efforts were bringing no results, she set the deadline for February 1st. Seemingly she had set this date with Marysia, for her to communicate it to Henryk. I should mention that because of precautionary measures, Mrs. Zieliński knew neither Michalski's address nor that of my husband. The only person who knew my husband's whereabouts was Jula, because we trusted her more than anyone else. Mrs. Zieliński informed me that she had gone to see Marysia Będkowski, but she was not at work because of some kind of trouble with her kidneys. I didn't attach any importance to this, for anyone could get sick.

Several days later Mrs. Zieliński again visited Marysia, because with the cold weather it was impossible for her to stand out in the market with her meat, and Marysia helped her sell it among her neighbors. This time she brought me the information that I would be taken from Wołomin on or before February 1st. Marysia continued to be ill and unable to go to work, she said. I knew that she was playing for time in order to calm Mrs. Zieliński down.

The memorable day of Saturday, January 16, 1943, arrived. As usual, Mrs. Zieliński went to Warsaw. Her daughter stayed at home to clean up the apartment, because next day her engagement party was to take place. At eleven o'clock someone knocked on the door. Lilka asked who it was, and from behind the door I heard the voice of an unknown man calling out my name—Marta Piechocka, according to my present documents. That document had been procured for me by Henryk, who worked for the AK, the Polish "Home," or underground, Army. I opened the door and saw an unknown man who introduced himself to me as Janek, a friend of Jula's. He shut the door behind him and in a whisper communicated to me that I should hurry and get dressed and be ready to travel as soon as possible. He helped me get my things together and told me that he had come together with Henryk, who was waiting for us out on the road. He hadn't wanted to show his face, for he was known to Lilka, but she didn't know Janek. All of this seemed to me highly suspicious and peculiar, but I didn't ask any questions. In less than an hour I was ready to leave. I took fond farewell of Lilka and, wrapping myself in a wool shawl which had been brought for me, I set off down the road with Janek. We didn't go by regular train from Wołomin to Warsaw but on the so called "Samovar", a little commuter line, to which it was necessary to walk seven kilometers. Along the road we met Henryk, and all three of us moved briskly along. I thought to myself that Henryk was pretty smart to have thought up the entire escapade so as to leave no trace behind. It was evident that he was working in the underground and knew about such matters.

This was the only pleasant "excursion" that I had had for more than three years, that is, since the outbreak of the war. Even before the ghetto was officially closed, we would not have dreamed of going out beyond it, because when the Germans ran into a Jew they would persecute him or kill him for pleasure.

The cold spell had let up somewhat. The weather was beautiful and sunny. After passing Kobyłka, we set out across the fields and were engulfed in the fresh air. We met but few passers-by along the way. For a short time I forgot about my hard lot and the constant danger hanging over my head. I luxuriated in the sun and fresh air and breathed in deeply the revivifying scent of the pine forest. I didn't ask any questions, because I knew that Henryk didn't like that. However, when I did at one point ask about Marysia, he replied that she was no longer working for us. That seemed strange and difficult for me to understand. Finally we came to the railway, but since we still had another hour to wait, we decided to walk to the next station. We arrived there early too, but eventually, with a loud whistle and hissing, the little "Samovar" came down the tracks. No one paid any attention to me. On account of the cold there were a good many other bundled-up women. We were most concerned that the Germans would stop the train and plunder the passengers for being "smugglers," which happened frequently enough. Fortunately, our short journey passed safely, and we arrived in Warsaw without incident.

Once in Warsaw, the three of us got on a trolley. Janek got off in Praga, but Henryk and I went farther. I didn't know where we were going, because Henryk had told me on the train that there was no place to put me. Finally, we got off the trolley and took off on foot along side streets which I was not able to recognize because of the military blackout. We arrived at a small building surrounded by a garden. Henryk told me to wait while he disappeared inside. After a while the mysterious door creaked open again, and in complete darkness I walked into the building. I saw before myself the familiar face of my husband. How changed it was. He was pale, emaciated, and had dark circles under his eyes. He looked at me with the eyes of a martyr. This gaze went straight to my heart. I immediately felt that some great misfortune had occurred.

My husband took me into the apartment which connected with the workshop. Here he presented me to an older, mustachioed gentleman who turned out to be Henryk's father. I also met Henryk's youngest brother Maniek. It was rather late in the evening. The father and his sons were in a hurry to get home, for they were not supposed to be out on the streets past eight o'clock. Before that, however, my husband treated everyone to vodka and a bite to eat. The vodka warmed me up a bit. Soon the others left for home, and my husband and I were left by ourselves. Then I learned about the misfortune that had befallen him on January 7, 1943.

44

MY HUSBAND IS DENOUNCED TO THE POLICE

That day work in the little factory had been proceeding normally. No one seemed to have had any inkling of what was to take place. At three o'clock in the afternoon, my husband was busily at work when he suddenly heard steps in the kitchen next door. At first he thought that this was Henryk returning, but upon turning around to look he beheld the face of a complete stranger, and behind him were two other men. The first one cried out in a loud voice, "What's going on in here?"

Then, turning to my husband, "Aha, we have you, sir. Please show us your documents!"

My husband immediately figured out that he had been denounced. The first thought that shot through his feverish mind was, who could it have been who had informed on him? But there was no time for further thought. The first agent, a large man of great strength, began to knock my husband about with his fists, beating him mercilessly, so that before long his entire face was covered with black and blue marks. The agent kept shouting all the while for my husband to get dressed quickly and come with him. After that they searched him and took his last money and documents, as well as my letters from Wołomin. They even took the wedding ring off his finger.

The other two agents remained passive. My husband had the impression that they were watching to make sure that no one caught them by surprise. Finally, apparently deciding that it was time to bring this tragicomedy to an end, one of them told my husband that he could take care of everything with them if he wanted to. Then my husband understood that maybe everything was not yet lost, that maybe there was still a way out. In his thoughts he had already said goodbye to me and to the baby, and had given up all hope of ever seeing us again. He was most concerned that no one around him should suffer on his account, especially the Michalski family. He himself was resigned, knowing that sooner or later the same fate came to every Jew on the Aryan side.

He asked them how much they wanted. They replied 50,000 zlotys, to which my husband responded that if he had money like that there would be no need for him to sit there with other people, endangering both his life and theirs, in the first place. The elder Michalski interrupted and began to negotiate with the agents. Finally they worked out the arrangement that, in addition to what they had already taken, they would be paid another 10,000 zlotys. Mr. Michalski went out to try and find the money, while the agents stayed in the shop waiting for his return.

My husband stood at the entry to the workshop, for he knew that Henryk was due to come back at any moment, and he didn't want the agents to learn what he looked like. Whoever came knocking at the glass door of the workshop received from him the answer that "the master was not in". Among those who came knocking was Henryk himself, as my husband had foreseen, and, after understanding the warning, he withdrew, puzzled, back onto the street. In the meantime, the elder Michalski broadcast the alarm to the entire family by telephone. Shortly afterwards Henryk's wife arrived, and Henryk had time to find out from his father, whom he met on the street, what had happened. Fortunately, he had 5,000 zlotys with him, and he decided to give it to the agents with the understanding that they would get the rest the following day.

When the elder Michalski returned to the workshop, the agents accepted the offered amount of money, but they ordered my husband and Mr. Michalski to get dressed and come with them anyway. Hearing this, my husband was sure that the agents had only taken the money so as to be able to convict them of offering a bribe.

At the intersection of Belwederska and Bagatela Streets, Mr. Michalski was set free. My husband, however, was ordered to walk further. The agent who had been walking in silence alongside my husband suddenly changed his tone and began speaking to him in a friendly manner. He told my husband that among our workers was someone who had denounced him, and that in the future he should be on his guard. He said that he would have let my husband go in the workshop but he was acting in my husband's own best interest in order to fool the person who had betrayed him. He advised that the Michalskis announce to the workers that my husband had been sent back to the ghetto. He returned his wedding ring, his documents and mine, and even the letters written by me which my husband had been saving as a keepsake. Then the agents went along their way, while my husband returned to the workshop.

When my husband returned to the workshop he found the entire Michalski family gathered there. The thought passed through his mind that after these most recent incidents they would simply tell him to go on his way for fear of bearing any further responsibility for him. His fears soon vanished, for the conversation centered around the matter of who had given him into the hands of the secret agents. The consensus was that it had been Stasiek and Marysia, and there were many details to bear out this supposition. The agents had known not only the place where my husband was staying, but also that Henryk was hiding from the Gestapo. Marysia knew about this, for she had been considered worthy of everyone's trust. Marysia's brother-in-law, a metal-worker, had also been seen hanging about the workshop by Henryk.

Slowly the matter began to take on perceptible outlines. Marysia Będkowski had been living in very difficult material circumstances. As soon as the pair began to work for us, my husband began trying to improve their living conditions. After only a few weeks my husband's efforts had yielded colossal results. As Marysia herself had said, whereas previously she often wasn't able to buy her baby so much as a roll, now it had everything it needed. All would have been fine if she hadn't had a wagging tongue and "gabbed" on all sides that she was working for a Jew. The change in her situation aroused the envy of her neighbors and extended family. As the last piece of condemning evidence, on New Year's Eve she had a party for her friends and family, and once drunk she blurted out everything. Her brother-in-law was present at the party. He himself was a habitual drunk and ne'er-do-well, and had only recently been let out of a work camp for alcoholics. Having learned of this excellent occasion to make a little extra money, he had evidently made use of it. Whether or not he had acted in concert with Marysia and her husband was unclear. It was possible that her brother-in-law had been spying on her as she went to work and, in that way, learned of our whereabouts.

In order to lighten everyone's mood, my husband sent for vodka and cold cuts. Everyone's courage revived. The elder Michalski said that the agent had asked whether he was really interested in saving my husband's life, for now would be the best moment to get rid of him. Mr. Michalski replied by saying, "He's a human being, isn't he?" Hearing such an answer, they let my husband go too.

Next morning they paid the remainder of the money, which Henryk took to the address given by the agents on Ujazdowski Boulevard. Henryk recognized in the lead agent an old bribe-taker and blackmailer from the ghetto.

In order to avoid further persecution from the Będkowskis, it would be best to dismantle the factory and transfer it to another location. Next morning they set about finding a new place which, under the circumstances, was no easy matter.

Due to the denunciation of my husband, which caused us to lose all of our savings and go into debt by 10,000 zlotys to Henryk, I found myself in Warsaw to cover our tracks. By the time I arrived, the matter of the new place of work had already been settled in the following way. The journeyman Zygmunt Dobosz had been out when the agents arrived, so Henryk told him some fabricated story about how someone had informed on them for running an illegal factory. Zygmunt therefore devoted himself assiduously to finding a new location, and his efforts were soon rewarded with success.

Several buildings away and across the street from Mr. Michalski's tinshop was an unfinished building belonging to the Social Security Institute. The only person living in it was the caretaker, who was Zygmunt's acquaintance. With his co-operation, and by paying the requisite amount of money, the caretaker agreed to rent one of the unfinished rooms to us for the workshop.

Soon the unfinished room, which was located on the first floor, was changed into a workshop. Panes were put in the window, and doors, provided by the caretaker, were installed, thanks to which it was possible to lock it up tight. After a two-week interruption, once more work got under way. The absence of Stasiek and Marysia Będkowski, with whom all ties had been severed, was easily made up for by the assistance of Henryk's brother-in-law (who was an escapee from Łódź) as well as his two brothers Leon and Maniek. Even before my husband's denunciation, they had been taught a little bit about the work. Zygmunt, who had little to do at the elder Michalski's, was also able to lend a hand. In this way the entire Michalski family and Zygmunt's family too were assured of work and a steady income.

The day after the incident with the agents, Stasiek turned up at the elder Mr. Michalski's workshop in order to learn what had become of my husband. Mr. Michalski told him that he was being held at the police. He also told him about the suspicions which had fallen on his brother-in-law, who had been hanging about the workshop at the critical moment. The workshop was going to be dismantled, Stasiek was told. On the following day he came around to pick up his tools, and when he asked about my husband (who, as on the previous day, was hiding behind the other side of the door), he was told that he had been sent back to the ghetto.

That was the last we saw of Stasiek. He spread the story throughout town to all his friends that the Michalskis, wanting to get rid of my husband, had robbed him of everything he owned and then turned him over to the secret police to take care of him for good.

Having learned about everything from my husband, I was very upset. At the same time I realized that it was only due to this incident that I had been brought to Warsaw. Otherwise, I was sure that I would have been left in Wołomin for as long as it took for the German authorities or the Gestapo to catch up with me.

45

I WAKE UP SCREAMING

The Michalskis' workshop had a depressing effect on me. It was located on Belwederska Street, not far from the Belvedere Palace, formerly the residence of Marshal Józef Piłsudski.[1] The building in which the workshop was located was only one story high and in deplorable condition. In normal times it would have been good for nothing except scrap. The tracks of the Wołomin commuter train ran by the front. On the opposite side were located the buildings of the Social Security Institute. They were occupied exclusively by Germans. Only a restaurant and wine-and-vodka shop across the street belonged to a Pole, whose steady customer was old Mr. Michalski. On the left side our shanty was connected by an iron gate to an old two-story building occupied by several families, one of them being that of Zygmunt Dobosz. On the other side was a vegetable garden belonging to the Michalskis. Several yards down the road from the garden was a house occupied by a blacksmith and a certain "Volksdeutsch" (such was the designation for Poles who had claimed German citizenship; for all that they were still considered second-class German citizens). In the yard behind our old tumbledown building stood a one-family dwelling inhabited by our building's caretaker and next to that was situated the communal toilet. Behind was another vegetable garden, which stretched as far as Rakowiecka Street in Mokotów. In this way we were surrounded by vegetable gardens on several sides, which was of great importance in maintaining secrecy during our stay.

My husband's time here had been very difficult. He barely knew the Michalski family. He had to keep quiet and constantly keep his eyes open. At night he was afraid of the German patrols which frequently passed along the street, and he lived in fear that he would be seen from the Social Security Institute building. He had to keep quiet, because the room next to the one used by Michalski as a storeroom was joined to a tiny apartment occupied by a little old lady whom Zygmunt referred to as Aunt Pelasia. He also had to be on the lookout for the other tenants. It was also necessary to see that water didn't flow out of the sink into the drainpipe, for he could have easily been taken for a robber who had stolen into the workshop. In brief, he was practically afraid of his own shadow.

New worries arrived in the form of me and the child. He was unable to ask anything of Henryk, who felt absolutely no responsibility as far as me and the baby were concerned. My husband had to be extremely patient with him, and Henryk by nature was not long on words and never indicated any desire to establish a warmer relationship. His conversations always took place on a very formal level and concerned exclusively matters connected with running the workshop. To be sure, my husband noticed that Henryk behaved in the same manner with his own family as well.

My husband realized full well that he would have to put this small illegal factory on a solid footing so that it would begin bringing in the requisite profit, for the thought of this was the only thing that kept Henryk and his family going. Under the circumstances, this was an extremely difficult task, especially for a person as weary and harrassed as my husband. His sole guiding thought was, by means of the profitable financial results which the little factory was going to bring in, to persuade Henryk to eventually concern himself with me and the baby.

With the passage of the time, life in the workshop slowly settled down to some semblance of normal. The food situation was somewhat worse. For the most part he lived on dry food, although the elder Michalski had installed gas and electricity by running the lines around the meters so that it was possible to use them without limitation. Obviously this would have been considered a form of sabotage.

On that memorable night after my arrival in Warsaw, I slept for the first time in three and a half months on a bed covered with a sheet and was at last warm. I say "bed" because in comparison to my previous quarters at Zosia's and Mrs. Zieliński's, this is the best word to describe it. In actuality it was an old settee, but my husband fixed it up in such a way that I had the impression I was sleeping in a bed.

Next day was Sunday, so the workshop remained idle and locked.

We were left by ourselves, and the day passed very quickly as we told one another about the things that had happened to us since the day of our last parting. In the evening Henryk came by and informed us that his mother had agreed to keep me at her place for the time being. On the one hand, I was glad to be in Warsaw near my husband, and I hoped that our lives would somehow settle down. On the other hand, I feared moving into the new home. For a long time I lay on my "bed" thinking about it until I was finally overcome by sleep.

I dreamed that I was once more in Wołomin at Mrs. Zieliński's and that two bandits were waving revolvers and attacking me. They caught hold of me, and one of them was covering up my mouth with the palm of his hand so that I couldn't cry out while the other held me by the hands so that I was unable to defend myself. Gathering my last remaining bit of my strength, I cried out in a terrified voice. I was awakened by my own scream. With amazement I saw that I was standing up in the middle of a room and, just as in my dream, two men were holding me by the hands and covering my mouth.

I was getting ready to scream again when finally I understood what was happening. My husband's voice penetrated my consciousness, telling me to calm down. It turned out that my husband and Henryk, who that night had also decided to sleep in the workshop, had been awakened by my terrified shrieking. Both of them were too frightened to speak or move and were unable to make out what was actually happening. When they noticed that I had leapt out of bed and was trying to escape, they ran after me and tried to prevent me from shrieking again. However, they were so frightened that they were unable to say a thing.

To this day I am unable to understand what happened with me that night. Was this a delayed reaction to my several months of terrible experiences or was it the result of my having been so impressed with my husband's story? In any case, this was the first and last time that such a thing ever happened in my life. I was later to endure many difficult and terrifying days, but never again did I lose my calmness and self-control.

My screams had completely knocked Henryk off kilter. He continued to look at me out of the corner of his eyes with an expression that indicated that he thought I had lost my mind. Gradually, seeing that I was calm and in control of myself, he too calmed down. More than anything else he was afraid of the German patrols. Finally, toward morning, we all fell asleep. I spent the entire next day with my husband. That evening Henryk took me to his mother's.

1. **Piłsudski, Marshał Józef** (1867-1935). Polish military leader and Poland's most prominent statesman and political leader in the period between the two world wars.

46

AT MRS. MICHALSKI'S

My first impression upon arriving at the elder Mrs. Michalski's was very positive. Everything in the apartment was neat and clean. Being deprived during my stay in the country of even the most basic necessities, I could scarcely believe my own eyes when I found myself in this tidy apartment and realized that this was where I was to stay. I soon figured out that Mrs. Michalski was a woman who knew how to take care of herself. That night I fell asleep without fear for the first time since the beginning of the destruction of the ghetto. The feeling of peace and security that I experienced when I crossed the threshold of that apartment never left me during my stay there.

Next morning we arose early. Mrs. Michalski was hurrying off to the Trade Hall where, together with another woman, she had a stall where she sold footwear, including our own workshop products. Her son Maniek was just leaving for work. The elder Mr. Michalski had slept in his workshop. Until Mrs. Michalski returned in the afternoon, the apartment was locked shut with me in it. I had to remain as quiet as if there were no one at home. We had grown so used to employing precautionary measures that now, after the passage of a year and two months, my husband and I had almost become experts at it. None of the neighbors caught so much as a single glimpse of me, and no one had even the slightest idea that someone was staying in the apartment during the occupants' absence.

The days went by more quickly than they had in the country, for I had something to keep me busy. Cleaning, sewing, and fixing dinner took up almost my entire day. I spent the rest of my free time reading books, for there was a small library in the apartment. This was for me a period of spiritual regeneration and peace. Every day I had news from my husband, either through the elder Michalski or Maniek. I sent him milk and, to the extent I could, something warm to eat. He also had clean underwear for a change. In short, I was of the opinion that our lives had taken a definite turn for the better. How great was my joy when on Saturday evening my husband arrived together with the entire Michalski family to stay with us for all of Sunday. I felt that the change was having a positive psychological effect on him too, for this constituted a definite diversion in our monotonous existences. From the beginning of each week I only counted the days that still separated me from the next meeting with my husband.

Work in our little factory was already under way in its new location, and all technical obstacles had been successfully overcome. My husband and Henryk continued sleeping in the old workshop. Ever since my husband had been caught, Henryk slept there as the Germans were seeking him in connection with his membership in the AK.

At ten o'clock in the morning my husband left the old tinshop for the new place of work. At this time there was very little traffic on the street, so my husband was able to walk over there without attracting any attention to himself. We all breathed much more easily now, and thanked God that the storm that had visited us had passed without doing any damage and that we were all still in one piece.

Those Sundays were the most agreeable day of the whole week. Everyone came to life and we ate well. Old Mr. Michalski, without taking a single breath, was able to put away on such a day an entire goose, all the while taking swigs out of a bottle of vodka, and without ever once getting out of bed. We related to our protectors fragments of our experiences in the ghetto. We soon realized that no one understood us. Being separated from us by no more than a three-meter-high brick wall, they still had no idea about what was happening.

As far as the Poles were concerned, all the Jews in the ghetto were striking it rich. Their pockets were filled with gold, diamonds, and dollars. No one had the vaguest idea about the true state of the half-million inhabitants or that several thousand were dying of starvation and typhus each month. (One of our neighbors, who still had memories of the German occupation of Warsaw during the First World War, used to say that wherever the German sets his foot, he brings with him only hunger and typhus). The Poles couldn't imagine that the gravediggers were unable to dig graves fast enough for the bodies arriving at the cemetery, and that due to lack of space large communal graves were being dug in which as many as 1,500 bodies were buried at a single time. The former cemetery sheds on Okopowa Street were changed into storehouses for the corpses they had not managed to bury during the course of the day. The inside of these sheds, piled high with the corpses of human skeletons, left a lasting nightmarish impression on those who saw it. Sometimes the Germans would come with their cameras and take pictures.

A grave-digger who happened to live in our building told the story of how one day a certain small group of German soldiers had come to the cemetery on Okopowa Street and asked to see the grave of Dr. Ludwik Zamenhof, the originator of the Esperanto language. After looking at it and taking pictures, they saluted and went along their way.

The only one out of the entire Michalski family who had seen the poverty on the streets of the ghetto with his own eyes was Henryk, for he had visited us practically every day in order to pick up our wares. Seeing that no one was in any condition to understand our experiences, we stopped telling about them and locked them up in ourselves. But when we were by ourselves we often recalled to one another fragments of our experiences and our miraculous, simply unbelievable salvation which we owed above all to Henryk and his family.

When darkness fell on those wintry Sunday afternoons, Henryk would come for my husband and they would return together to the tinshop. In the second week my husband lived through the following experience, which shook him deeply, for he could have paid for it with his life. That Sunday my husband and Henryk, in returning to the shop from the older Michalskis', had climbed onto a trolley. They were standing on the exit platform, separated by several people, getting ready to get off. I might add that during this time the trolleys were very overcrowded. It was no mean feat to get on one, and once inside it was necessary to force one's way to the exit with one's elbows.

When the trolley stopped Henryk jumped off, but my husband, seeing that all the passengers were evidently debarking, wasn't in any particular hurry. How great his shock, then, to suddenly see the trolley start moving down the tracks again. Henryk had the tickets. My husband, seeing what was happening, began to push his way to the exit in order to leap out of the car while the trolley was in motion, but the passenger standing in front of him wouldn't let him pass. Suddenly all the passengers in the car began to stare at him and rebuke him, saying, "Where were you when the trolley was stopped?" It is easy to imagine what my husband must have gone through, finding himself the object of everyone's attention. He grew numb with fear.

One of the passengers could have been an agent of the secret police or, worse, the Gestapo. When Henryk saw that my husband hadn't managed to get off, he leapt back onto the front platform. Fate was kind this time, as the trolley had to circle all around a big square, and was forced to stop in order to let another trolley past. The passenger who had not let my husband exit while the trolley was in motion moved aside with the words, "Now you may get off."

My husband was relieved to find himself on the street next to Henryk. After that my husband either traveled by horse cart or went on foot; never again did he travel by trolley.

We had three weeks of relative quiet. In our hearts the timid hope was rekindled that perhaps we would live to see our freedom. There were already many indications of this. For some time things had not been going well for the Germans on the Russian front. At Stalingrad they suffered defeat after defeat. People stated with assurance that if they just survived until spring, the war would be over. (Of course, there had been people who said the same thing during the first year of the war in the winter of 1939-1940). In any case, we were in good spirits.

47

NEW BLACKMAILERS FROM THE BĘDKOWSKIS

One Wednesday, as I was sitting around conversing with Mrs. Michalski and Henryk's wife, Maniek ran into the apartment in a changed and terrified state. It turned out that that afternoon two German soldiers had come into the elder Michlaski's workshop and demanded the Jew who was hiding there. These Germans were fluent in Polish; they were probably Volksdeutsch. My husband was not there, because, as usual, he had gone that morning to our factory. Mr. Michalski informed them that there was no Jew there, to which the Germans replied that agents of the secret police had let him go for 5,000 zlotys. Mr. Michalski calmly replied that he didn't know anything about it, because he hadn't seen him after that and that as far as he knew he had returned to the ghetto.

The Germans carefully sifted through the contents of all the rooms, finding the materials which, for lack of space, had been left in Mr. Michalski's workshop. Among other things they found some military-grade leather, the possession of which was punishable by death, for it was forbidden for private persons to possess or trade in military goods. Fortunately, these two Germans seemed not to be aware of that, since they didn't pay any particular attention. They made a list of all the materials and promised that they would be back the next day to pick them up in a truck. Michalski responded by saying that they had no right to take away his property, for he had paid the agents out of his own pocket, and he had received the materials in exchange for hard cash. To that the Germans remarked that he had had time to sell it, but since he hadn't done so, it would be taken away from him on the following day.

At that moment Maniek walked into the shop. Dark-eyed and dark-haired like his father, the Germans were sure that here was the Jew falling into their clutches. The poor lad immediately received a powerful blow in the face. In vain did Mr. Michalski explain that this was his son. It didn't even help to show them his Kennkarte, the personal identification card issued by the Germans. The boy was forced to undress and only after making sure that he was uncircumcised did they let him go, threatening everyone with a pistol. They took down Mr. Michalski's personal residence address and, promising to be back next day for the materials, left the shop. It would be necessary to remove me from the apartment as quickly as possible, since in their search for my husband they might easily find me, which would amount to the same thing.

Mr. Michalski was staying in his workshop that night, and my husband was spending the night in the new workshop, something which was obviously connected with a good deal of risk, for the building was unfinished, hence uninhabited, and the slightest rustle could have easily attracted the attention of the caretaker. The painfully cold February weather in that unheated bare-walled brick building was also no fun for my husband. All of this, together with the overpowering feeling of being a tracked and hunted animal destined for slaughter, was not well calculated to raise his spirits.

Henryk worked all through that night in his father's workshop. He had managed to obtain some cheap leather which he stained in order to leave for the Germans. The military leather had been removed, for fear that instead of those two Germans, others might come who would turn out to be better experts than their colleagues. As for me, there was no place to put me. The only place seemed to be Henryk's apartment, but that turned out to be impossible as he was being sought by the Gestapo, and they often came around to check whether he was actually absent from home. Since it was already late, we left our fate in the hands of God and I stayed that night once more in the apartment. We lay there listening closely for the slightest sound. The smallest movement out in the yard would set our hearts pounding, and we would tremble with fear.

Next day Mrs. Michalski and her son left very early, locking me up in the apartment. I was in no condition to do anything all day long. I was visited by terrible thoughts, which I was able to dispel only by the greatest force of will. It constantly seemed to me that any minute I would hear the doors being kicked down with fists and feet, as was the custom of the German gendarmes or Gestapo. I looked helplessly around the apartment, searching for some kind of hiding place in which I might be safe. What kind of hiding place could I expect to find in a two-room apartment?

Next day the same two Germans returned to Michalski's workshop at the appointed time. My husband was actually able to see them from the window of the room where he was staying. Leon was waiting out on the street so as to see where they went. As on the previous day, the Germans began to interrogate Michalski, but he categorically declared to them that he hadn't seen my husband since the day the agents had been there and taken him away, and that the material was his personal property which he had received in exchange for the 5000 zlotys which he had paid for my husband. This explanation evidently convinced the Germans, for soon afterwards they said goodbye and left, saying they were in a hurry to get to roll-call. Once again they promised to be back next day in order to investigate the matter further.

As had been arranged, Leon walked behind them at a close distance. The Germans continually looked around to check whether anyone was following them. On Bagatela Street a man in civilian dress walked up to them who was easy to spot, for he was deformed. They carried on a lively conversation, which Leon was unable to hear. On Unia Lubelska Square one of them took off in a different direction, while the other one got on a number "o" trolley-car with the cripple. The number "o" trolleys were for the exclusive use of the Germans, so Leon lost track of them at that point.

For me, when I heard what the cripple looked like, the matter became completely clear. Marysia Będkowski had a younger brother whom I had seen several times before the war, and he had one arm all twisted around backwards. From what Marysia had told me, it appeared that he was a man without conscience or scruples. At present he was administrator of a building on Kazimierzowska Street, where he was on friendly terms with the police and agents of the Sixteenth Police Precinct, in other words, the area where Michalski's workshop and our little factory were located. He also had a number of German friends with whom he carried on various sorts of schemes and shady deals. He himself was pursued by the German authorities for registering people illegitimately in his apartment building, and in fact, when my husband proposed through Marysia to register me, not realizing what a dangerous sort he was dealing with, the rogue did not hesitate to demand a price of 6000 zlotys. Anyone else would have done the same for 750 zlotys.

Now we realized that he had initiated the chase after my husband in order to blackmail him. Whether it had been Marysia who had sent him or whether he was operating on his own account was unclear, but it was for dead certain that the matter was extremely serious, for this time we were dealing with a hardened criminal. We knew that if at first he did not succeed he would keep up the chase and continue rooting around until he found the scent again. In view of this, Michalski decided to have a drink with the Germans when they came around for their third visit and see what he could work out with them.

Mr. Michalski also went to the agents who had originally blackmailed us, thinking that it had been they who had sent the others around, but they categorically denied this, saying that it was against their principles to blackmail a person more than once. Hitting two times in the same place was just not their way, they said. They even promised to come around to the workshop the following day to have a talk with two Germans, but they never showed up.

The Michalski family, after taking council among themselves, came to the conclusion that I would have to be removed from the apartment without further delay until the matter with the Germans cleared up, for there was no telling what they intended to do. At first they wanted to put me in the same place as my husband; however, because of the caretaker who continually visited the workshop, and because of Henryk's brother-in-law, who was working for us and didn't know anything about me, the idea was abandoned.

The only place which remained seemed to be Henryk's storage-shed, which was located in the yard of the building in which he lived. Since there appeared to be nothing else to do, I opted for the shed. This was one of a whole series of sheds knocked together out of wood belonging to the tenants of the building. On one side they bordered on the street and on the other, they faced the courtyard. The shed in which I found shelter had many cracks and openings through which the cold February air poured. It was filled with a few pieces of furniture and other rubbish. Besides that, there was a fairly deep pit for keeping potatoes in for the winter. By this time there were no longer any potatoes, but the cold coming from this potato pit was so penetrating that by comparison everything else seemed a trifle. The shed had a solitary chair on which I sat down in order to spend the night. Marysia, Henryk's wife, brought me a shawl for my head and two blankets. I wrapped one of them around my legs and put the other one around my shoulders.

When the key scraped in the padlock as Marysia locked me in the shed, I was left completely by myself in total darkness. To tell the truth, I was not completely by myself, for I was soon joined by a number of mice, who let me know so well of their presence that I sat there in fear, wondering what would happen if there were also rats among them. I expected at any moment to be bitten. I wouldn't have been able to cry out or make any noise for fear of attracting the attention of the care-taker. I decided to remain still even if I should be eaten alive. However, it never came to that, because evidently there were no rats. On the other hand, the mice made fair sport of me, biting my shoes and hopping into all my pockets. I actually grabbed hold of one of them by mistake when I reached for my handkerchief. I, who was repelled at the very mention of mice, lived through that night in inexpressible anguish.

The second thing torturing me was the cold. After several hours of sitting motionless on the armchair in the damp air, I felt that all my clothing was completely soaked through. My legs were frozen and numb, hanging down lifelessly like two blocks of wood. I listened to the sounds coming from the streets, mainly to the bells of the trolleys passing down the street. As time went on gradually things quieted down, and it was dead still everywhere except for the whistling of the wind and the sounds of the mice hopping about. I was exhausted both physically and mentally and very sleepy. I had visions of a warm bed. Time and time again I would doze off only to be startled awake. I tried to remain as motionless as possible, so as not to fall out of the chair and make a noise.

This terrible night seemed to stretch into infinity, but finally it too came to an end. I could tell that it was about five o'clock by the move-ment of traffic on the street and the sounds of the first pedestrians. Soon the first glimmerings of the new day penetrated the cracks in the boards of my hideout. I thought fearfully about what would become of me. I worried how much longer I would have to sit there.

48

SEPARATE LIVES IN HIDING

Finally the key scraped in the lock, and old Mrs. Michalski appeared in the doorway. She had decided to take me into her apartment for the day so I could get some rest. Very thankful, I walked behind her at a distance. She didn't want to show herself on the street with me for fear of attracting suspicion to herself. Mrs. Michalski locked me in the apartment while she herself went to the Trade Hall. What a joy it was to be able to wash off the filth and dust. After washing I drank a cup of coffee and, with a feeling of inexpressible bliss, I lay down to sleep. But I wasn't able to fall asleep. Everything was so terrifying and uncertain. Images of the past kept visiting me with a horrifying degree of reality. Everywhere I saw our German, Ukrainian, Lithuanian, and Latvian executioners waving their revolvers at me ready to go off. How deathly afraid I was of those people. My one fervent wish and prayer to God would have been to perish in any way at all, if such was to be my lot, as long as it was not at the hands of our tormentors and persecutors.

I lay that way into the afternoon. Finally, in an effort to distract myself, I got up and began feverishly cleaning up the apartment and fixing dinner. Mrs. Michalski was late coming home, for she had stopped off to see her husband along the way. She found out that the two Germans had already come and gone. Mr. Michalski was to have offered them a drink and tried to have a talk with them, but it never got that far. Evidently completely fed up with these visits, Mr. Michalski completely lost his poise and began shouting that he knew who had sent them and wouldn't let himself be blackmailed.

He even threatened to go to the proper authorities and complain. Zygmunt who, because of a lack of work in old Mr. Michalski's shop, had changed professions and had come to work for us full time, showed up. He was purposely sent there by my husband on the pretext of doing some kind of work for him there. At the same time he was to listen to the conversation with the Germans and have a drink with them if need be. Soon after Zygmunt arrived, several other people came on various sorts of business, and the Germans, seeing that the customers had no intention of leaving the premises early, said good-bye and left, promising to be back next day on what would be their fourth visit.

In view of all this, the elder Mrs. Michalski decided to send me once more to the shed for the night. When darkness fell, I dressed without a word and went down to my prison cell. This time the place had been straightened up a little, and Henryk's wife Marysia had been able to set up in the narrow enclosure some kind of old junk which at one time had been a field cot. In addition to the blankets, I also received a cotton quilt and a caftan for putting around my shoulders.

I lay down on my bed, covered myself as best as I could, and did my best to fall asleep, in order to shorten my agony. This time I was much warmer and more comfortable. The mice didn't bother me as much this time either. I tried to cover up over my head, so that the cold could not get at me as easily. Finally exhaustion overcame me and I fell asleep. I woke up several times during the night but fell asleep again each time. Finally, I was awakened for good by the sound of traffic on the street. A new day had arrived.

The hours passed, but no one came for me. I lay there, hunched up and frozen in my bedding, thinking uneasily about what was going to happen next and why it was that no one had come. Finally, around ten o'clock in the morning, Marysia arrived. She brought me some hot coffee and bread, but told me that her mother-in-law was afraid to take me back into the apartment and that I would have to spend the day in the shed.

So I sat all through that day in my cell. The day was not as bad as the night. Children were playing in the yard, and the caretaker was cleaning up nearby. From time to time neighbor women would stop next to my shed to gossip with one another on various uninteresting topics. For me, in my monotony, their conversations were interesting enough. The day passed more or less all right, but as darkness quickly fell, I was once more enveloped by fear and doubt. What was going to happen? How long would I have to sit here?

It was already late and the caretaker had locked the gate. Slowly I readied myself to spend one more night in this miserable burrow. It was with great sorrow and bitterness at our executioners, who had been persecuting us so unjustly, that I sat down on the edge of the bed weeping bitter tears. I sat quietly crying over our broken, miserable existence and our humiliating life in exile.

It was already quite late when I heard the sound of the key, and by the light of a candle I saw Marysia. She signaled for me to come up the stairs to her place. At that moment my only thought was to get into a warm room and take off my damp clothing. My hands were so stiff and my entire body so sore that at first I wasn't even able to walk.

The two older children were already asleep, but the two younger ones, one of whom was only a few months old, were still playing. With the sight of the children my sanity and peace returned. The feeling of bitterness evaporated. A fire was lighted in the stove, and this did much to improve my spirits. I began to think that perhaps at last a gracious God had taken pity on us and would show us the proper road.

All night long, in spite of my bone weariness, I was unable to fall asleep. In the morning I arose rather early, thinking that I would have to go once more down into the shed, but young Mrs. Michalski had decided to keep me for the day in her apartment. A little later, Father Edward Święcki came to visit. I had met him only briefly during my stay at the Michalskis'. It was with a great deal of interest that I studied this man, of whom I had heard so much good spoken. After greeting me, he asked me how I was feeling and whether I hadn't caught cold sitting in the shed. This was the first and only example of instinctual sympathy which I had met during my entire stay on the Aryan side. We are still convinced today that Marysia's "impulse" to take me into her apartment had been the result of the priest's initiative.

The evening of the same day the elder Mrs. Michalski came for me and took me back to her apartment, for which I was extremely grateful. It seemed that the Germans had not been by either that day or the previous one, and had shown their faces no more in the tinshop. Whether this was because of Mr. Michalski's words, or whether they had been sent to the front, we didn't know. In any case they didn't touch any of our materials, and the whole affair ended with a good scare.

Next day was Sunday, and I learned that my husband had returned to the old workshop for the day in order to prepare materials. Because of the caretaker, he was unable to return for the night to the new workshop so he was spending the night in the first location, which I felt in my heart was an extremely rash thing for him to do.

Life went on, but I was no longer able to recover that feeling of peace and security which I had first experienced upon coming to Warsaw. I was tortured with concern for my husband and felt some kind of indefinable foreboding. My nerves continued to be stretched almost to the breaking point. I was convinced that some kind of great danger was hanging over us, but I didn't precisely know in what quarters the new blow would fall. I was continually afraid that someone was observing the Michalski family, and in that way would be led to my husband. I begged him to be careful and not to be seen too much walking from one place to the other, but this did not do much good.

After several days of quiet, discretion was thrown to the wind. Thus, for example, they would carry sawdust to light the stove from the old workshop to the new location in broad daylight, without taking into account that someone on the street could observe them. Something else was bothering me. I knew that my husband was living in extremely difficult circumstances, sleeping on a table without even getting undressed. There was no opportunity for him to wash, for there was no water in the unfinished building. There was not even a place for him to go to the bathroom. He ate no cooked food at all, and the cold weather was having a harmful effect on him.

During the day he burned sawdust in the stove, but at night the cold was painful, particularly for a person who was living on dry food and who hadn't had a bite of hot food in his mouth all day long. Another curse was the building's caretaker. First of all he was a terrible lush, and imbibed all day and all night long. People would be in his apartment drinking until the early hours of morning. Sometimes even Germans would come and take part in these drinkfests. My husband could hear exactly what was happening downstairs at the caretaker's, because in the empty building the sound of one's voice carried everywhere. Sometimes he lay there enveloped in fear that the caretaker would want to visit the workshop at night in order to see what he could steal. It was terrible to think what might have happened if my husband had dropped something on the floor when the workshop was supposed to be closed.

The situation was difficult and very tiring. The caretaker also often dropped by during the day to make sure that nothing underhanded was going on. At those times my husband went into hiding. He had a makeshift hiding place, which was a niche with shelves over it. Beneath was an empty space in which a person could sit covered up by a piece of cardboard. It was a miserable existence. The days passed, and my husband's nerves became more and more frayed. Finally, he turned to

Henryk with the request that he find some kind of place where he and I could be together and where the workshop would be separated from his own place of work. Finally, his cousin the priest promised to try to get an apartment attached to a church where he had some friends. However, it turned out that the administrator he knew had left for eight days, and so the entire matter had to wait.

49

MY HUSBAND IS ARRESTED

Barely ten days had passed since the visit of the two Germans, when suddenly someone knocked at the door of the new workshop. Since the knock was not the customary signal, my husband, thinking that it was the caretaker, took to his hiding place. Neither Henryk nor Leon were in the workshop at the time, and my husband was busy getting the accounts in order for the Saturday payroll. All day long he had been feeling very uneasy and worried. In the afternoon he had put together a package of the more valuable materials and asked Zygmunt to take them home with him.

When the door was opened, the caretaker did indeed walk in, but in the company of a blue policeman and two secret agents in the service of the Germans. As it later turned out, there was a second policeman waiting at the entry gate of the building. One of the agents asked what was going on and where the owner of the shop was. The people replied that the owner was not around, so the agents decided to stay and wait for him. The caretaker left as the agents began to sift through the contents of the room. During the course of his search one of them, by the name of Wróblewski, tore back the cardboard behind which my husband was sitting. Having the experience of the previous affair with the secret agents fresh in mind, he realized at once that this was a mock arrest, and that they were more concerned with money than with anything else. Unfortunately, there was no money left. We still owed 10,000 zlotys from the last time. Knowing the mentality of the secret agents, my husband knew that if no financial arrangement could be worked out, his life in their hands would be no better than a plaything. This was clearly the work of a person who was well acquainted with our workshop, for the other agent, whose name was Judasz, knew Marysia, Michalski's brother's name, and also the name of his son who worked for us. He even added that he knew that he had escaped from Łódź. Wróblewski, for his part, recognized Zygmunt as a metal-worker who, in the autumn of 1940, had been sent for several weeks to a work camp in Treblinka. He greeted Zygmunt as an old friend.

When Wróblewski noticed my husband hiding behind the cardboard, he asked him what he was doing there then hit him in the face by way of application of the standard method of terror. No one present except for Zygmunt reacted to that in the least. He asked him why he had to do that. My husband always remembered that with gratitude. Next, the agent called Judasz took my husband out into the stairway and told him that he knew who he was. He even read out his present name, Alexander Przybysz (Henryk and Father Święcki had managed to obtain papers for him under that name through the AK). They began to discuss price; Judasz demanded 100,000 zlotys (!) for setting my husband free. My husband replied that, as they probably already knew about the run-in with the other agents who had cleaned him out of everything, he had nothing left to give them. The most he could offer was 10,000 zlotys. He called Zygmunt to witness, who confirmed everything. Finally the agent agreed to the sum. With this, my husband found himself in a difficult situation: he didn't have the money. All the time we had been in hiding, Henryk had only given us enough money to take care of everyday expenses, keeping the rest to manage in connection with our mutual business interests. For that reason, it was necessary to put Henryk in touch with the agents, but the matter became somewhat complicated because he himself was being sought by the Germans.

Henryk then arrived from town, but already on the stairs he noticed the policeman standing outside, so he immediately withdrew to his father's shop. There he found Leon and his uncle, who had been supplying us with leather. Maniek shot straight home as soon as he was set free by the agents, going in the company of the escapee from Łódź. During the checking of identification papers, the agent noticed Maniek's name and even wanted to keep his papers, telling him that he could come around to the police station the following day to pick them up. However, my husband convinced him to return the papers to him there. My husband tried to get all the workers set free, because he knew that Mrs. Michalski's brother from Łódź had no documents and was not registered anywhere.

Henryk asked Zygmunt's wife to go call her husband on the pretext that their child was ill. Thanks to this, Henryk learned of everything and that the agents were waiting for the 10,000 zlotys they had been promised. Henryk, however, only had 3,000 zlotys on him for, as luck would have it, only the moment before he had paid his uncle several thousand zlotys for the materials.

The hour was already late, and there was no place or person to borrow the money from, so Henryk sent Zygmunt to the waiting agents and proposed that they accept 3,000 zlotys for the time being, with the understanding that they would receive the remainder on the following Thursday. If they had at least been promised payment on the following day, it is likely that they would have agreed to wait, but when they heard Thursday the agents flew into a rage, for they felt that people were trying to make a laughing stock of them. They put handcuffs on my husband and ordered him to go with them. This way, they said, his partner would have to come looking for him, and it was going to cost them a lot more to get him back. This is what my husband feared at all costs, for he wanted to avoid causing any problems for his fellow workers and the Michalski family. He began to beg the agents to let him go, saying that he would find a way to pay them the next day. The agents were unmoved by his pleading and took him in irons to the police station.

As they passed the German gendarme station, he was ordered not to speak lest one of them turn their attention to them and become interested in the matter. At the entrance to the Blue Police station, the agents once again reminded my husband to say nothing and to keep to the name on his false German documents.

50

RANSOMING MY HUSBAND

After taking my husband into the station, Wróblewski led him to a room where he filled out a report saying that he was being held as a suspicious person. While giving his personal information, my husband forgot the name of his supposed parents. Fortunately, the incident came out all right, as my husband pretended that he didn't hear the question and, while leaning forward and pretending to look for something, he caught sight of the information needed in the papers that he had deposited on the desk together with all of his personal belongings. Among these objects was a large gold Schaeffer pen, which he had received before the war as a present from our cousin in the United States. Wróblewski, catching sight of the pen, pretended that my husband was taking too long to answer his questions and slapped him across the face. As soon as everyone's attention was turned to my husband, he picked up the pen and put it in his pocket. It was only much later that my husband figured out why Wróblewski had slapped him precisely at that moment.

Next they took my husband to his cell. In one of the cells stood a young, elegantly dressed young woman. She was wearing a grey suit and high rubber Tretorn boots of the same color. Even her wide-brimmed hat was grey. She appeared to be very upset. Looking at her closely, my husband was able to notice the features of a Jewish woman, although they were not particularly strong. Since he had been warned not to betray his nationality, he walked past her indifferently. Later my husband learned that during a search in an apartment, a blue policeman had come across her and, since she had no registration papers, she was taken into custody and brought to the station. My husband still saw her behind the bars of her cell on Sunday, but early on Monday the policeman, carrying a book under one arm, took the unfortunate victim over to the German gendarme station.

There were empty cells in the block, and the policeman asked my husband whether he wished to be in a cell with others or by himself. Obviously, he chose the latter. Staying in a police station under arrest is not a pleasant experience in normal times, but that is nothing compared to the circumstances in which my husband now found himself. The tiny little cubicle covered was completely bare. One had the choice of standing or sitting down on the asphalt floor. After being led into the cell, my husband was so bent down and discouraged by the events of the day that at first he simply couldn't pull himself together. As time went on, consciousness of his situation began to return, and he began thinking about what he could do. Prospects did not look particularly bright. He realized that the agents would attempt to get whatever ransom for him they could, and that that was all they were really after. However, if they were unsuccessful, they would hand him over to the German gendarmes, which was the same as a death warrant. He was completely dependent on Henryk. On the other hand, he realized quite well that if Henryk didn't try to ransom him back, the disappointed agents would not stop with my husband but would come after Henryk and his family for revenge. The situation seemed hopeless. Nor was it known how much the agents were presently asking for. Henryk had no ready cash. To be sure, there were plenty of materials, but they couldn't be turned into cash so quickly, for the next day was Sunday.

During the night several drunkards were shown into my husband's cell. Their shouting and general behavior did nothing to sooth his crushed spirits. It was to his good fortune that they didn't recognize him as being Jewish; it was best that such a thing not even enter their mind.

The following February morning, foggy and overcast, brought no glimmer of hope. To make matters worse, one of the policemen on duty was unkindly disposed toward Jews. As soon as he saw my husband, he looked at him with a hateful expression and said, "Well, I guess we know why you're here!"

For the rest of the day he didn't let my husband out of his sight and subjected him to various sorts of abuse. He made him clean his bicycle and perform various other tasks for him. My husband simply prayed that this person wouldn't be on duty the following day, for he was sure he would be denounced by him to the German authorities. At last he finished work and left for home. Luck was with my husband, for the next day, Monday, the man didn't come to work.

Before noon the cell-keeper handed my husband a food package, which was the first sign he had not been cast to the winds. The cell-keeper changed every two hours. Some of them understood his situation and some not. Some showed my husband a certain amount of kindness, but others were openly hostile. One of them showed such hatred that he kept asking how his matter was progressing and when it would finally be possible to take him over to the German gendarme station.

Through the rest of the day my husband received no news from the outside world. His situation continued to look hopeless, and the uncertainty of his position weighed heavily on him. Early in the evening a young and kindly police officer came on duty. He allowed my husband to come out of his cell into the corridor and sit down on a bench. My husband recalls him with gratitude, for the conversation he had with him, even though it concerned nothing of particular importance, took his mind off his situation for a while.

Circumstances now began to turn in my husband's favor. A little boy turned up at that very moment, bringing lunch to one of the prisoners. My husband received permission from the young policeman to receive a visitor, and he sent a note to Zygmunt through the boy. The police station was located only a short distance from Zygmunt's home and from the elder Mr. Michalski's tinshop. As it turned out, the boy didn't find Zygmunt at home, but his wife prepared some hot coffee and decided to take it to the station herself. In the stairway she ran into her husband, who took the coffee himself and ran to the station, where the worthy policeman let him talk with my husband. Zygmunt told him that, together with the elder Michalski, he had been waiting for the agents near the steps of the police station all morning, but unfortunately they hadn't shown up. He comforted my husband by saying that they would do whatever they could to get him out, but that he had to be patient and wait until the following day, because today was Sunday and it was impossible to get anything done. He and Maniek had taken all the materials, tools, and equipment out of the new workshop back to Michalski's tinshop, so that the new workshop was now completely bare. It should be mentioned that during the negotiations with the agents, two accompanying policemen had gathered together a large pile of materials in one spot, and it later turned out that during this operation they had managed to make off with several valuable skins. Thus, there was the likelihood that they would be back the following day to appropriate the remaining materials for themselves as well.

My husband asked Zygmunt to tell the Michalskis that they must do everything in their power to get him out of this stalemate. When Henryk learned that it was possible to see my husband, he grabbed Zygmunt's coat and hat and, under the pretext that he had forgotten to say something to my husband during their conversation, rushed off to the station.

The policeman on duty, seeing a person dressed the same way as the previous person (Zygmunt and Henryk were of about the same height), didn't pay any attention to the face and let Henryk through to see my husband. Henryk could not allow his face to be seen in the police station, for the person who had turned my husband in had mentioned that there was another conspirator involved.

Henryk assured my husband that he would do everything he could and that surely it would be possible to free him. Janek had been talking with the director of the agents. (This was sure to have been over a drink, for Janek, the husband of young Marysia Michalski's sister, was a waiter and never passed up the opportunity to have a drink with someone). The director had promised to look into the matter, but for his services he was asking fifty dollars. We will have occasion to return to Janek later on, for it was through him that we practically lost our lives.

Next day Zygmunt brought my husband some food. After receiving a tip, the cell-keeper allowed him to talk to my husband, but considered it necessary to be present at their conversation. However, Zygmunt was fairly clever and was able to communicate to my husband how matters stood.

The agents were asking 30,000 zlotys. Their director, who had been unnecessarily brought into the affair by Janek (who, let us say, had only the best of intentions), lowered it to twenty, but was asking $50 for himself. This was still a substantial sum of money.

The previous day the entire Michalski family had been flying about town borrowing money from friends and from whomever else they could. Zygmunt, too, helped as best he could. He borrowed a thousand zlotys from a Volksdeutsch friend of his, leaving his best Sunday suit as a pledge. The necessary money had already been assembled. Now it was only a matter of taking care of things with the agents. As he was leaving, the cell-keeper stopped Zygmunt and asked the exact reason for my husband's being detained at the station. Zygmunt shrugged his shoulders and said,

"Oh, he's just some petty thief."

The cell-keeper had evidently heard the word "dollars" fall during the course of the conversation and, evidently connecting it with the word thief, said in amazement, "You mean a Jew was stupid enough to steal dollars?"

After Zygmunt had left, the policeman didn't give up, but went to my husband and asked him whether he really was a Jew. When my husband denied it, he said, "To tell the truth, I don't care whether you are a Turk, as long as I get something out of it."

Several hours passed, during which time my husband waited nervously and impatiently. He was worried that time was passing, and that the unfriendly policeman who had been persecuting him would return. Finally, Wróblewski entered my husband's cell and informed him that everything was arranged and that soon he would be set free. It was only necessary to sign the police report. In the report it stated that my husband had been suspected of receiving and selling stolen goods, but that for lack of evidence he was being released. My husband signed the report and was set free.

All this had cost 20,000 zlotys and fifty dollars. Before the arrest it would have been possible to settle everything for 10,000. It was with good reason that the agents had said it would cost us more if it went to the police station, for here there were many more hands amongst whom to divide up the ransom. If it had not been for malicious human tongues and the vodka which loosened them, no agent and no German would have ever discovered a Jew in hiding. If Marysia Będkowski had been smarter and had known how to hold her tongue and live more modestly, we never would have had so much trouble with the agents and wouldn't have lost so much money to blackmail and extortion artists. It was entirely due to her that the lives of the three of us had hung by a thread.

Henryk had given Zygmunt the money for the agents, thus making him the go-between so as to avoid Henryk's having direct contact with them. Henryk, as well as his entire family, had great reservations with respect to the honesty of the agents, so they advised Zygmunt to give them no money until my husband was released from the station. However, Zygmunt figured out that this was no way to do business, and that it was necessary to risk everything and give the money in advance, or nothing would get accomplished. The director of the agents was present in the office where the negotiations were taking place. When the agents stubbornly demanded 30,000 zlotys, Zygmunt winked at the director, who sent the agents out on some vague pretext. When the director was left alone with Zygmunt, he took the fifty dollars from him in secret, and when the agents returned, he told them that he had done everything possible to get the 30,000 zlotys from them, but that this person stubbornly insisted that he had no more than 20,000, so they ought to agree to that amount. The haggling thus came to a successful conclusion.

As my husband was being released, Wróblewski told him not to ask for the pen, for it was now in "his possession." When asked for its return, he merely laughed out loud. At their parting he advised my husband to clear out of that part of town altogether.

Zygmunt was waiting on Puławska Street, and on the next corner they were joined by Henryk. My husband was barely able to recognize them, for in order to disguise themselves so the agents wouldn't follow them, Henryk and Zygmunt were dressed in some kind of old rags as if they were getting ready to go to a masked ball. They circled around various little streets and alleyways for about two hours in order to cover their tracks. Finally, they came to the elder Mr. Michalski's tinshop, where the entire family, including the uncle whom I have already mentioned, were gathered. He had also loaned money in order to free my husband—he was quite a decent person. Everyone celebrated the successful conclusion with vodka and sandwiches, which put them in a good mood.

51

THE MONTH OF MARCH

When my husband was arrested, the elder Michalski telephoned immediately to his wife and told her to get rid of me. I could see on Mrs. Michalski's face an expression of great fear. She ordered me to get dressed immediately and to come with her.

I didn't ask any questions. I had a presentiment of the misfortune which I had been dreading for so long. We went to her daughter-in-law Marysia's house. Here Mrs. Michalski left me out in the yard while she went into the apartment. After a while both women came outside, and Leon arrived, but he didn't know anything about my husband's arrest since he had run away at the start of the troubles.

They locked me into the same storage shed as before. I sat down in my corner on a chair and prepared to spend another sleepless night. Gloomy thoughts descended on me like swarms of wasps. I felt that something was happening to my husband, but I was helpless to do anything about it. Slowly, I began to be filled with an immense hatred for our persecutors. I didn't doubt for a single minute that this was the further work of the Będkowskis. During the course of those long night hours spent in the cold dark shed, I began conceiving a plan of revenge. I knew that if my husband died, then I too must perish, for I had neither money to get by on nor really anything at all. The Będkowskis would have to pay for our ruined lives. It is easy to talk about revenge, but how difficult it is to actually go through with it. In the end I was sorry that such terrible thoughts kept bothering me. I kept thinking to myself that they had a little boy; I too was the mother of a baby for whom I longed very much. A feeling of great shame came over me.

Our child was sick with diphtheria, and his condition was said to be serious. At least now he was in a safe place where Father Edward Święcki had put him. At the recollection of our baby I broke down completely. I sobbed uncontrollably all night long, bidding farewell in my heart to my husband and child. The burden which I was carrying was too heavy for my frail shoulders. I prayed to God for a miracle to save my husband. I prostrated myself before Him in my misery; I practically went into a trance. Full of contrition, I begged for forgiveness.

The gray February dawn peeked through the cracks of the storage shed, and I continued to pray, indifferent to the cold which was biting into my stiffened limbs. Several hours passed without anyone coming to have a look at me. In the yard I could hear the sounds of normal life going on all around. The caretaker's wife was grumbling at her husband and straightening up the courtyard. Children were playing in the snow with sleds. It was already eleven o'clock when the key scraped in the lock and young Mrs. Michalski came in, looking pale and wan. On her face I could see the lines of worry and concern. She brought me a piece of bread and a little coffee. When I asked what was happening with my husband, she answered evasively and told me to be at ease, that everything was going to be all right. When I demanded some news about him, she answered stumblingly that he was being kept in the old tinsmith's shop. I didn't have to be much of a psychologist to understand that she was lying, but what was I to do? Marysia Michalski also brought me a warm quilted cotton vest and three blankets. She helped me set up the rickety field cot and then locked me back in the shed and left.

Some time afterward Marysia Michalski admitted to me that she had not slept that night at all, but had spent the entire night in constant fear that she would hear from my shed the same horrible cries as that night when I had just been brought from Wołomin to Warsaw. She spent the entire night straining her ears and walking back and forth to the window, peeking out. She was afraid to think about what might happen in case I awoke the caretaker or the other inhabitants of the buildings with my shrieks.

With my blankets I was now at last able to cover myself up and lie down on the bed. Exhaustion soon took the upper hand, and I fell asleep. I slept through the entire day, and when I awoke I saw that it was already getting dark. Soon after this, the elder Mrs. Michalski came, bringing me some hot soup and saying that her daughter-in-law

250

had been out visiting her friends and acquaintances since early morning, trying to find money for my husband. She told me to keep my spirits up and that someone would be by to see me next morning. We were not able to allow ourselves a longer conversation for fear that someone might be curious enough to look into our narrow little shed. The door of my little "prison" was shut once again.

This night was to be no different from the preceding one. At one point I heard the sound of heavy army boots and the voices of two men talking. The voices were coming closer and, as they did, they were joined by a third person from across the street. All three men came together right next to the shed. I heard their conversation, carried on in German. At first it concerned matters of little importance, but then I heard the third person say to the other two, "It looks like we're going to have some more work to do in the ghetto soon. April has been designated for the final eradication of the Jews in the ghetto. All the remaining Jews at work in the German shops are to be evacuated to Treblinka and Poniatów. Everyone without exception. The buildings are to be doused with gasoline and set on fire, and in this way all the Jews will be eradicated once and for all, and all that remains of the ghetto will be ashes and ruins."

I began to tremble as if in a fever. I was shaken to the depths, and for a moment I forgot about my own personal situation. I did not doubt for a moment that everything I heard was true. When I later told my husband about the conversation, he simply looked at me strangely, shook his head, and didn't say anything, and I could see from the expression on his face that he thought I had been dreaming or had a hallucination.

Finally this long night came to an end, and the new day began, gray and misty. Was it to bring final ruin to our lives, or once more a glimmer of hope? I broke out crying like a little baby. I was morally and physically broken. If any of my former friends had seen me at that moment, they would never have recognized in that miserable creature the resourceful woman so full of life I had been only a few months before.

At last Marysia came, bringing me breakfast. She told me that for this one more day I would have to stay in the shed, but that night I would be able to come out, for the matter of my husband had been successfully brought to a conclusion.

Around sunset Marysia came again. I could see that the worry had vanished from her face. We were going to her mother-in-law's. When I asked about my husband, she told me conspiratorily that everything was all right. How happy I was to cross the threshold of Mrs. Michalski's neat little apartment. I felt a purely physical delight as I washed up in the large brass bowl filled with warm water. When I had finally put my external appearance in some kind of presentable shape, I once more began asking about my husband, but no one wanted to tell me anything. In general, the entire Michalski family delighted in keeping everything a secret.

I guessed that some kind of surprise was in store for me. And indeed, it actually occurred in the form of my husband, with several days' growth of beard and so emaciated that it made my heart break, but besides that alive and well. What a joy this was. How grateful we were to old Mrs. Michalski for providing us with a roof over our heads at such a critical moment.

My husband had asked Henryk whether it wouldn't do to raise the question of the blackmail and denunciation of Jews in hiding on the pages of the underground press. Henryk promised to take up this matter and, as a matter of fact, several weeks later it was discussed for the first time in the pages of the AK's underground weekly "Informational Bulletin." We read all of the underground publications provided by Henryk. Two months later, General Władysław Sikorski, in the speech broadcast from London I have already mentioned, turned to his fellow countrymen with a sincere appeal for them to offer all possible help to Jews in hiding, who were being innocently hounded and persecuted by the Nazis. It was with a feeling of profound gratitude and with tears in our eyes that we read these first manifestations of sympathy. The result, at least for us, was that people stopped being ashamed for offering assistance to the Jews.

On the day after my husband's release, all our cares fell back upon us once again. We had enormous debts which it would be necessary to pay back in the next several days, and there was nothing to pay them with. We had no place to work and we didn't even have a place to put ourselves, for Mrs. Michalski was offering us temporary shelter only. In any case, one thing was certain: my husband could no longer live at the workshop. That was no longer necessary in any case, for the workers had already been trained to work independently. And if our persecutors were to decide to continue to hound us, they would try to pick up our tracks at the workshop.

Henryk let the news circulate that my husband had been returned to the ghetto. This news evidently made it to the ears of the Będkowskis, because several weeks later when they met Zygmunt on the street they informed him that the Michalskis had robbed my husband of everything he owned and then gotten rid of him. It was fortunate that neither the Będkowskis nor anyone else knew the location of our baby. Even we had no idea where he had been placed.

We were not able to learn too much about who had been the cause of the second denunciation, but in all likelihood it happened in the following way. Marysia Będkowski's brother, the cripple, whom Leon had seen waiting on the street for the two Germans who had plundered the elder Michalski's workshop, had a wide circle of acquaintances among the agents of the Sixteenth Police Precinct. According to information received from the two Germans he had sent—that my husband was no longer staying in the elder Michalski's workshop—he evidently had gone either to Judasz or Wróblewski and told them everything he knew about what was going on, which he had learned from his sister.

It seems the agents stumbled upon my husband almost entirely by accident. The caretaker was a sly and perfidious person who also drank a lot. In all probability it had been he who had turned the agents on to us, telling them to keep an eye out for leather, which during wartime was a priceless commodity. After renting the space, Henryk went to him and requested a door for the bathroom so that my husband would have a place to hide in case of need. The caretaker never supplied the door, but he evidently came to the conclusion that we were hiding leather in there. And so, when the agents showed up, their first question was "Where is the bathroom?" Later, when the agents stumbled upon my husband hidden behind the cardboard, they realized that they had accidentally stumbled upon the operation described to them by Marysia's brother. In this way they had been able to kill two birds with one stone.

After my husband had been released, and after the first outburst of joy and transports of happiness in which the entire Michalski family had shared together with us, and after celebrating it with a rather large quantity of vodka and delicacies purchased with our last bit of money, we were all unanimous in wanting to find a new location for our workshop. The elder Mr. Michalski came up with a brilliant idea.

It so happened that during the Soviet bombardment on September 1, 1942, several bombs had fallen on one of the buildings belonging to the apartment house complex in which the Michalskis had been living for more than thirty years. Many apartments had been completely destroyed. Others, however, were still habitable, especially those on the lower floors. The tenants had all fled, because the walls were cracked, the paint was falling off in many places, and it looked as if the remainder were going to cave in at any minute. Given our critical situation, even an apartment like this was going to be of use. Mrs. Michalski, seconding her husband's idea, proposed that we rent one. On the very next day she went to talk with the old caretaker, Jan, whom she had known since before the war. Jan promised to help by talking to the building administrator, a Volksdeutsch woman.

Since the caretaker had keys to the vacant apartments, the Michalskis were able to have a look and make a selection. They decided upon a first-floor apartment with two rooms and a vestibule, in comparatively good condition. To be sure, the ceiling was caving in at one corner and the stairway going up to the second floor was cut off, but nevertheless we decided to take over this location. The administrator was asking 2,600 zlotys for us to move in. The Michalski family began looking around for the money, and after three days the apartment was ours. It was fortunate for us that officially it was not allowed to occupy apartments in this run-down building, so that we were able to avoid the necessity of registering. We felt tremendously relieved.

I mentioned earlier that the bombardment on September 1, 1942 was to be of great significance for us. Now it is easy to see why, for thanks to it we were able to find a place to live and work, which under ordinary circumstances would have been out of the question.

There still remained the question of moving the workshop's materials and equipment. It was important to do this so that no chance observer would ever be able to trace us to our new address. Toward this end, one day all the materials were shifted from the elder Michalski's shop to young Mrs. Michalski's storage shed. Next day, at darkness, all the men in the Michalski family transferred little by little the workshop's equipment to the new location. This entire operation, including renting the space and transferring the equipment, took about a week. After this, work began anew. My husband no longer came to the shop. Old Mrs. Michalski allowed him to stay with her until we were able to find some kind of place for ourselves. My husband set up the work for all the other workers right in Mrs. Michalski's apartment, while Henryk directed the workshop downstairs in the new location.

It was the beginning of March, and the summer season was just beginning. Under normal circumstances, after the trauma we had lived through, a person wouldn't have been able to work for several weeks or more, but now, when it was necessary to pay back our debts as quickly as possible, and seeing that the Michalskis, in spite of all the trials and tribulations they had been through on our account, were not going to get rid of us, my husband quickly regained his energy and went to work with a will. He improved the old patterns, made new ones, and soon production was going full tilt.

About this same time old Mr. Michalski and Zygmunt received an assignment to work on the roof of a church located on Grzybowski Square. When he would finish his day's work on the roof with the elder Michalski, Zygmunt would come and work in our factory. Grzybowski Square had once belonged to the Jewish quarter and, along with various other streets, comprised the so-called Little Ghetto. After the latter had been "liquidated," this area had been joined to the Aryan side. The church, which during the two-year existence of the Little Ghetto had been closed, had been delivered back into the hands of the Church, and the personnel were now returning to their former apartments. Besides the rectory, which was for the exclusive use of the priests, there was a second building off the same yard in which several vacant apartments were located. One of these apartments, consisting of a room and kitchen up under the roof, had been taken by Father Edward Święcki, with the idea of giving it to us as temporary living quarters.

The apartment had only one serious drawback: it was necessary to bring water up from the yard. However, we thought we saw a way around this inconvenience. Since Michalski and Zygmunt were going to be working for several weeks on the roof of the church, they were free to make their way about the building all day long. It had been Father Święcki who had officially turned to Michalski and entrusted the repair of the apartment to him. This, of course, had been a stratagem so as to enable us both to stay locked up inside. Under the guise of making repairs, Zygmunt was to bring us food and water.

Later experience convinced us just how dangerous this kind of undertaking would have been, and how easy it would have been to be caught, but then we saw no other option. Zygmunt, good man that he was, devoted himself heart and soul to fixing up the apartment. From all the old hunks of furniture left in the apartments throughout the entryway and attic, he took whatever was best and carried it over for us. He found an old iron bed with a mattress, a commode, a table, chairs, and kitchen equipment. He even installed a little stove for cooking, since the kitchen one smoked.

For two days he worked enthusiastically, cleaning up the apartment and removing the feathers, junk, and other filth, which was all that remained after the former unfortunate occupants. He even brought our bedding from Michalski's tinshop and all our personal belongings. His enthusiasm was so great that he even bought coal for us, some wood for burning in the stove, and carried up water. The door locked with a big padlock bought especially for the purpose. A sign hung on the outside saying "Under Repair". The downstairs door was also locked with a padlock, because no one as yet lived in any of the apartments, so the entryway was completely empty. For all of the above to take place, about three weeks had passed. We had already paid back the smaller and more urgent debts and were returning to something like a state of equilibrium, although we lived in constant dread of our persecutors and any new calamity they might unexpectedly visit upon us.

Around March 10th we decided to move to the new apartment, in which everything was in readiness for our arrival. We determined that Henryk and his wife would come for us around dark and accompany us to our destination. We had even prepared a little food to take with us. All we were waiting for was the arrival of the Michalskis. Unfortunately, some kind of business in the workshop kept Henryk late and we were not able to make the move.

We made a date with him for the following day and agreed that this time nothing was going to stand in our way. The following evening at seven o'clock the Michalskis came for us. We were dressed to walk out the door when my husband asked Henryk to call his father and tell him to accompany us to the apartment. The presence of the father was to be a pretext for our coming, in case the caretaker should take undue notice of it. At first Henryk didn't want to but finally he yielded and telephoned his father. Fortunately, he was still in the restaurant opposite his workshop where he had constant use of the telephone, since he did not have one in his own shop. He advised us to wait until the following day.

"They've already stayed so long at your mother's, let them stay one more day," was his advice, which turned out to be a wonderful blessing for us.

To this very day we cannot get over how my husband suddenly had the idea of calling to the elder Mr. Michalski that night. Was it some miraculous instinct? The Lord God was surely watching over us at that moment. In any case, we listened to the elder Michalski's advice and stayed where we were.

Next afternoon both Michalskis came over, looking very disturbed. It turned out that when young Mrs. Michalski had gone to the apartment that morning with a package of food for us, she had been met by a priest with a very stern expression on his face and a lecture to read to her. The tenants who had been assigned to the apartment below ours had, by the same agreement, received all the furniture located in it. When they showed up at their apartment on that critical day, they found it empty. It seemed that this was the furniture that Zygmunt had secured for us. These tenants took their complaint to the priest, and he angrily began looking for it. All of the apartments were empty except for ours, which was locked. He called the police, who opened the apartment and found all of the missing furniture in it. The angry priest told Mrs. Michalski that as a punishment he was taking away the apartment from her cousin. It was only then that it came out into open that the Michalskis had wanted to move us in without taking care of various formalities, such as paying rent, registering in the housing office, and so forth. This was the height of frivolity on their part, and could have had fatal consequences for us. Providence alone had saved us from a new calamity.

That same day the Michalski brothers brought all our things and bedding back to Mrs. Michalski's who, as we were certain she would be, was very dissatisfied with the arrangement. As all older persons, she preferred quiet and order, and we, with our preparatory work for the workshop, were bringing in nothing but disorder and dust. We had the feeling that Mrs. Michalski would have been glad to get rid of us as soon as possible. A situation like this is not easy to bear, so we decided to rent an apartment in one of the ruined apartments in the same building where we had established the new workshop. The selection was rather large. The Michalskis settled on a single room which looked out on a blank wall. We paid 1,600 zlotys to the administrator for it. All formalities were quickly taken care of. The furnishings also caused little trouble. The Michalskis loaned us a bed, and a table was taken from the workshop. Henryk bought us a couple of chairs. Old Mrs. Michalski loaned us a few essential household items, and on March 19th, late in the evening, we stealthily moved across.

Our first sensation upon stepping into this long gloomy room with walls that were marred and scratched and had nails sticking out where pictures used to hang was simply horrible. The room was the same as our lot—sad and hopeless. Next morning upon arising, the impression was even more depressing. But it was necessary to live and get along with it somehow. We thanked God for it.

One entered our apartment from a foyer which also led to the adjacent apartment, which was completely in ruins and uninhabitable. In the foyer was a sink into which one could pour dirty water, but there was no water in the pipes. For fresh water it was necessary to go down to the basement. Every evening, Henryk or Maniek would bring us a bucket of water. We had to use that bucket for cooking, cleaning, and washing, so we had to count every drop. We used it very rationally. After washing in it, we kept the water until evening in order to wash the floor with it after work. We learned to take every kind of precaution, since now it was clear that we had little to rely on other than ourselves.

We were discreet to the point of improbability, so that none of the neighbors would be able to notice that anyone was living in our apartment. By day we didn't even go close to the window. At night I permitted myself to poke my head out into the open vent so as to inhale a few breaths of fresh air. We were left alone with each other. Sometimes Leon came by for a brief moment to pick up some missing materials. He acted as if he were coming in contact with the plague, and as soon as he had taken care of what he had come for, he was always in a hurry to get away post-haste.

In the evenings Henryk would come by and talk for an hour or so; he would tell us about the latest news and discuss the work of our little factory. My husband would make suggestions, and in this way the evenings passed rather quickly. Maniek was of great service to us. It was he who most often brought us water from the cellar, even though he himself was rather frail. He never made a sour expression when we asked him for some favor. He brought us the milk which Mrs. Michalski would buy for us, and on his own frail shoulders he would carry us coal, wood, and potatoes. He was quiet and obedient, and all the members of his household made use of him. We both liked him very much. Sometimes the elder Mrs. Michalski would come by, but after some curious neighbor peeped out of her window a couple of times to see her going into the foyer, she stopped coming to us.

Time passed slowly. We were waiting impatiently for the arrival of spring. After the final defeat of the Germans at Stalingrad in February 1943, we were in constant expectation of a great political upheaval which would bring our enemies to their knees and return to us our longed-for freedom. We waited patiently in this delusion, but unfortunately the Germans were still very firmly entrenched. In this way the month of March passed.

52

THE JEWISH GHETTO UPRISING

On April 19, 1943, a Monday, the first day of the Easter-Pesach (Passover)[1] holiday, at five o'clock in the morning the Germans began the final destruction of the Warsaw ghetto, where they soon met with armed resistance.[2] We were awakened that day by several strong detonations. Henryk told us that the entire ghetto was surrounded, hermetically sealed every twenty paces with soldiers with arms at the ready, as had occurred in the very first days of the ghetto's destruction some ten months earlier. Then people had believed that a resettlement to the "east" was to take place. Now, however, everyone realized that this was nothing other than an evacuation to death at Treblinka or Majdanek in the gas chambers.

Earlier, some eighteen to twenty thousand Jews had been "resettled" to the labor camp in Poniatowa. In order to mislead the people, the Nazis established factories there where Jews were to manufacture clothing for the German army. Those resettled Jews were taken mostly from the German shops in the Warsaw ghetto like Toebbens on Leszno Street and the "Big Schultz" shop on Nowolipie Street. They were promised by the Nazis and personally by Toebbens and Big Schultz that they would not be "touched," and that they would survive the war if they went "voluntarily" to Poniatowa. But the Nazis had other plans. One day, in order to exterminate the Jews in the forced-labor camp in Poniatowa, in an action coordinated with their planned destruction of the Warsaw ghetto, the Nazis gathered the Jews together and ordered them to run forward. They started shooting from machine guns—

massacring them all. Among them, as I mentioned earlier, were my sister and her husband along with their boy.

When on the night of April 18-19th the news spread that the walls of the ghetto were surrounded, most of the workers escaped to the ghetto created for those not employed in the shops. A dozen or so, all of them favorites of K. G. Schultz, escaped to a previously prepared hiding place on Ogrodowa Street in the factory branch on the Aryan side. The night shift in this factory, not expecting treachery, had been rounded up early that morning in a blockade by German gendarmes and taken away for shipment.

In an effort to obtain some kind of information concerning Jadzia and her husband, Henryk went to the building superintendent on 29 Ogrodowa Street, who was a Pole. Of Jadzia and her husband all trace had disappeared. The superintendent told him that from the moment the final operation had begun, he had been witness to a constant stream of satanic scenes. Several times a day searches were conducted in all apartments, cellars, and attics, and very few managed to remain hidden. All of the favorites, Mr. Duży among them, had gone through the sewers from 76 Leszno to 29 Ogrodowa Street. Their hiding place remained intact for several weeks, but finally someone gave it away and all of K. G. Schultz's favorites shared the same fate as the rest.

And so, the conversation I had heard between the two Germans unfortunately turned out to be true. Little wonder that the handful of people remaining in the ghetto were determined to make the Nazis pay dearly for their lives. In the course of those ten months the remaining people had had time to arm themselves. Henryk told us of a characteristic incident he had heard from Jadzia. It had taken place some two weeks before the final destruction of the ghetto began. Around midnight a group of men, armed to the teeth, had come around to the workers' quarters of the K. G. Schultz factory demanding money for further arms for the defense of the ghetto. Among other places, they visited Jadzia's apartment. According to Henryk, Jadzia refused to give them any money, whereupon they began waving their revolvers at the occupants and conducting a search of the apartment. They found 3,000 zlotys which they took and left. The same thing happened in other apartments. We on the Aryan side also heard tales of the terrible "robber bands" who were making armed night-time attacks on the peaceful inhabitants of the ghetto and demanding money. Hearing such news, the Poles would simply shake their heads and say, "What are the Jews coming to? It seems they don't have enough hounding and persecution from the

Nazis, so now that they have to go around murdering and oppressing their own kind."

Now, when the Germans had begun the final "liquidation" of the ghetto, it came into the open just who these "robber bands" were. Both from the underground press and from Henryk we learned that in a small four-cornered area consisting of several streets a well-organized Jewish Combat Organization[3] was operating. It even had its own radio station. According to the AK, the leader was Michał Klepfisz,[4] a reserve officer in the Polish Army who perished at the outbreak of the uprising. Later, however, it turned out that the actual leader of the uprising was Mordechaj Anielewicz.[5]

To what extent the Jewish Combat Organization was in contact with the Polish underground organizations, and how much aid the latter supplied, we are not exactly certain. Henryk was sparing in his information, for he feared that if we were to fall into the hands of the Gestapo, we might be forced to divulge everything we knew. We do know, however, that advisors were sent from the Aryan side into the ghetto as well as a certain quantity of arms. We also learned from Father Edward Święcki that the last arms shipment bought in Radom[6] had arrived too late and never made it into the ghetto.

On the Aryan side people observed the fighting with enormous interest. Several times a day either Henryk or Maniek would approach the ghetto walls in order to gather information and make their own observations in order to share them with us later. Thus, for example, Maniek saw the Germans remove a number of destroyed minitanks out of the ghetto.

The heaviest fighting was taking place on Bonifraterska Street, where the brush factories were located. On Muranowski Square the Jews raised the Jewish standard with the added words "We are fighting for your and our freedom,"[7] all the while singing the hymn "Boże coś Polskę..."[8]

After a dozen or so days of fighting, the Germans saw that the Jews would be able to defend themselves this way for several months, and that in the meanwhile they were becoming a laughing stock in the eyes of the world. They were also afraid that this might lead to an uprising on the outside, so they decided to bring the matter to a close at any cost. The general in charge of the operation was removed and leadership was handed over to SS general Stroop,[9] who carried the work through to its conclusion. He introduced artillery and the air force into the fighting. Heavy artillery fired away by day and night from the Praga district. Next the Germans cut off all water, electricity, and gas to the ghetto.

When after several weeks the insurrectionists were still defending themselves with fierce determination, the Germans embarked upon the utter annihilation of the ghetto. Incendiary bombs were dropped from airplanes, while individual fires were set on the ground, systematically burning down one building after another. Entire rows of buildings were in flames.

On the first day of the fighting, those of us Jews who were hidden on the Aryan side were still counting on some kind of outside help. As time passed, however, our hopes evaporated. We were counting on the AK or some other underground organization coming to aid the insurrectionists. Unfortunately, however, there were only sporadic individual raids carried out by small groups, and they had no influence on the general outcome.

The Jews in the ghetto fought to the last breath and perished in a sea of fire in the ruins of the crumbling buildings. The ghetto was on fire for several weeks. From the ruins the Germans dragged out the last remaining victims, and when a spark of life still burned, they shot them on the streets. Old Mr. Michalski was an eyewitness to this. He had taken on work repairing the roof on the courthouse on Leszno Street, and from the roof he was able to look beyond the wall and see the executions of a number of Jews. Several bursts of machine-gun fire put an end to their lives. After the execution a group of German soldiers threw themselves on the still warm bodies in search of money, gold and jewelry. They even took whatever good clothing and boots they could find. After their work of destruction was over, they threw the corpses onto a truck and drove off.

The building in which we were staying was located on Krochmalna Street not far from Towarowa, so we had a good view of the glow of the fires, and a good whiff of the smoke and burning. The roar of detonations and sound of gunfire tortured us day and night and drove the very thought of sleep from our minds. We lived in deathly fear of blockades. All day long we sat straining our ears to hear steps in the hall and noises in the yard to see whether we could detect the sounds of German speech. Every loud step on the stairs set us trembling, for we were certain that now they were coming after us. At night we listened to every ring of the bell at the gate.

To make matters worse, everyone around us was also enveloped in utter terror. People began to avoid us like the plague. Leon did more than anyone to spread panic. He was the primary salesman of our products, from which he made a considerable profit. When he had worked for his father in the tinsmith shop, he lived at his mother-in-law's and hadn't been able even to dream about owning his own apartment, much less furnishing it. Now, after working for us for six months, he was able to buy an apartment for himself in the same building and he had been able to renovate and furnish it. But his wife, he said, would only move in after we had left, because she was afraid. He quarreled constantly with Henryk over his not wanting to enter our apartment for anything in the world. When he would make up his mind to come by for a minute, he would make sure to tell us about the blockades and the Jews being caught in hiding by the Germans.

After he left, we were always much more terrified than before. It came to the point that after Leon's visits I would break out in hysterical weeping for the next several hours. We almost stopped eating, although there was more than enough for us to eat. The only person who did not alter his relationship toward us was Henryk, who came to visit us without showing any fear. We have to admit that if we managed to survive this most difficult period in our lives, it was due solely to him. On one occasion when Leon came to see us and regale us with his frightful stories, my husband lost his temper and told him that if he wished, we could leave for wherever our eyes led us and commit suicide. These words seemingly had some sort of effect on him, for afterwards he stopped telling his tales and calmed down a bit.

Under these circumstances the month of April passed. May arrived, bright and sunny. People around us slowly began to accustom themselves to the sight of burning and ruin. Maniek, after regaining his health, also began to visit us and bring us secret newspapers to read. He ran various errands for us. Like Henryk, he was working for the AK underground organization.

The defense of the Warsaw ghetto, which had dragged on for six weeks, rehabilitated us in the eyes of the Poles. They always held it against us that we allowed ourselves to be led like lambs to the slaughter. While my husband was still working at the K. G. Schultz factory, the Poles kept saying, "Just give the word and make the first move, and you will see that we will come to your aid." Now it was clear just how absurd these words had been. The Nazi terror was as firmly entrenched as ever, and an uprising of the Poles under these circumstances would have been suppressed in an instant and would have unnecessarily enveloped as its victims the civilian population. The Poles, despite their sincerest desires, were too weak and terrorized by the Nazis to be able to furnish us with effective support.

1. **Easter/Passover**. By coincidence, April 19, the first day of Pesach (Passover) in 1943 was also Easter Monday, Easter itself falling on the 25th of April.
2. **Warsaw Ghetto Uprising**. On April 19, 1943 the few Jews remaining in the Warsaw ghetto rose up in a desperate attempt to avoid being deported to the Treblinka death camp. Under the command of the Jewish Combat Organization, consisting of barely more than 200 members, the uprising held out for nearly a month. To end it, the Germans burned down the ghetto block by block, ending on May 16. It resulted in a total of 13,000 Jewish deaths, many from being burned alive. This was the largest revolt by Jews during World War II.
3. **Jewish Combat Organization** (*Żydowska Organizacja Bojowa*, or *ŻOB*). A World War Two Jewish resistance movement under the command of Mordechaj Anielewicz and, following Anielewicz's suicide, Marek Edelman (1919-2009). The ŻOB, numbering only in the hundreds, was the main force organizing the Warsaw Ghetto Uprising. Before that it carried out a number of assassinations, assassination attempts, and other resistance activities in the ghetto. Edelman survived the war and became a prominent cardiologist and political activist.
4. **Klepfisz, Michal** (1913-1943). Klepfisz was a chemical engineer, member of the Bund and of the Jewish Combat Organization fighting Nazi forces in Poland, for which he directed the making of explosives in the ghetto. In 1942 he escaped from a train bound for Treblinka and returned to the Warsaw ghetto. After smuggling his wife, sister, and daughter out of the ghetto (and they survived the war), he died in the Warsaw Ghetto Uprising.
5. **Anielewicz, Mordechaj** (1919-1943). Anielewicz was the 24-year-old leader of the Jewish Combat Organization and of the Jewish Ghetto Uprising of 1943. His body was never found, but he is considered to have committed suicide toward the end of the uprising. His image is engraved in Warsaw's bas-relief memorial to the uprising, next to a street named after him.
6. **Radom**. About 100 kilometers to the south of Warsaw, Radom was the site of the Łucznik (Archer) arms factory, which before the war manufactured weapons for the Polish army. It was known for its "Vis" pistol.
7. **"For your and our freedom"** (*za naszą i waszą wolność*). A motto used at various historical times by Polish insurrectionist movements, originating with the national uprising against Russia in November 1830.
8. **"Boże coś Polskę..."** (O God, who Poland [through numerous centuries hath surrounded with the brilliance of your might]). A religious and patriotic hymn dating to the early nineteenth century, praying for the restoration of Polish freedom.
9. **Stroop, General Jürgen** (1895-1952). The SS commander who took over the task of suppressing the Warsaw Ghetto Uprising and ended it by burning it to the ground. Convicted after the war in Dachau of murdering American prisoners of war, he was then extradicted to Poland, where he was tried, convicted of crimes against humanity, and executed by hanging at the Mokotów prison in Warsaw.

53

MY RIDE ACROSS TOWN IN A TRUNK

In the first days of May we concluded that we would have to change apartments, because staying in this isolated room with secret visits from our protectors was becoming increasingly dangerous both for us and for them. Seeing nothing else to do, we decided to move back to the old tinsmith's shop. Since four months had passed since the first visit of the agents and no one had seen fit to return since then, we hoped that they would leave us in peace. It remained only to obtain the permission of old Mr. Michchalski. We expected difficulties, but Henryk obtained his approval on the condition that when his workshop was open, we would have to stay in the attic. We agreed to his conditions with gratitude.

How were we going to transport ourselves from one side of town to the other? I must admit that we both felt an enormous fear at the prospect of going out onto the street. Finally, Zygmunt, who at this time was repairing various places which he had bought, heard about our problem and offered to disguise my husband as a bricklayer and accompany him to our destination. The project was worked out in detail and the day for moving was set for May 11th. There remained yet the question of my person. Henryk's wife promised to try to find a complete mourning outfit for me.

The evening before our move Zygmunt came in a rented cart with a bricklayer's implements and a ladder. He also brought a complete costume for my husband. That night he slept in the workshop. We for our part did not sleep a wink, and neither did Henryk, who was no less exited and restless than we were. I was so beside myself with worry that when I offered Henryk tea, I poured him cream of wheat instead of sugar. The three of us sat there together in our gloomy apartment, which we had nicknamed the "tomb," until three o'clock in the morning. Finally, tiptoeing quietly so as not to arouse the suspicion of the neighbors, we abandoned the room which had sheltered us for the past seven weeks. We went to the empty first-floor apartment which Henryk had bought for Jadzia and her husband, and we waited there until daybreak. Zygmunt arrived, and he and Henryk busied themselves with my husband's disguise, which made him completely unrecognizable. An old torn work suit smeared with plaster, a crumpled cap on his head, and dirty boots transformed my husband into the likeness of a bricklayer. When the cart had been loaded, I took a good look at my husband and Zygmunt and gulped in fear.

My husband's face had the sickly yellow cast of a man who has had no fresh air to breathe for ages. Henryk told me that when he had a chance to see my husband in the light of day, he too had taken fright. Zygmunt was kind by nature and always wore a smile. He was constantly in a good humor and calm. His eyes were always laughing as if he had just played a trick on someone. His manner helped give me courage. He grabbed hold of the wagon shaft in a spirited way and moved out through the gate of the building.

Zygmunt was tall in stature and had long legs, and he set such a pace that he was pulling the cart practically by himself, with my husband gaspingly tagging along behind. My husband, who was unaccustomed even to walking, could scarcely keep up. Soon his face was purple from the strain. Henryk himself was able to keep pace with them only as far as Aleje Jerozolimskie where they crossed from Krochmalna Street not far from Towarowa. He was so out of breath that he had to grab a trolley so as not to lose sight of them. On Union of Lublin Square the three of them finally came together again. They made it to the tinshop, where old Mr. Michalski had spent the night so as to be able to unlock it early in the morning. My husband was so exhausted from the trip that he was literally unable to move. His legs were sore from walking over the cobbles, and they felt like lead.

At the appointed hour, Marysia Michalski arrived. She had already been there several times before, bringing me breakfast and my mourning outfit. Unfortunately, it had been impossible to find a heavy veil. Because they also had trouble putting together mourning costumes for themselves, and because they were afraid that the neighbors might start asking which of the Michalskis had died, they abandoned the project. We began racking our brains to find some other way.

266

At one point I heard a knock at the door. I froze with fear and sat there paralyzed in the chair. The knocking grew stronger, and finally someone began kicking at it with their shoes. Behind the door were three men, whose voices I could clearly make out, but I was only able to hear isolated words and expressions which I was not in any way able to put together and make sense out of. The thought flashed through my mind that we had been betrayed again. My heart was pounding in my chest, and I could hear my pulse throbbing in my head, but my legs remained motionless. In the space of a moment I counted out my chances for and against.

Everything seemed against. I knew that Henryk and his wife had left. Leon was the only person remaining in the workshop, but it was impossible to count on him. Since I had never had anything to do with agents, I was certain that if they found no money on me, they would take me straight to the German gendarmes. I prayed fervently to a merciful God to fend this misfortune from me, to make Henryk come back. Finally the beating at the door quieted down, and I could hear steps going away. I thought to myself that this was the agents going to get the house superintendent to open the door. Then I was beset with an even greater fear, for I imagined that the agents had gone to bring the German gendarmes, and that one of them likely remained to guard the door.

Suddenly I heard the key in the lock, and Henryk and Zygmunt walked in. They were so dear to me at that moment that it seemed to me as if heaven had opened up its doors before me. Later it turned out that the supposed agents who had beaten so insistently on the door and caused me so much concern were nothing but ordinary drunks. The former tenant of this apartment had engaged in the sale of cigarettes, and it sometimes happened that people would come by, not knowing that the apartment had changed ownership.

At the moment Henryk and Zygmunt were leaving, I managed to hear only the word "trunk." It was all the same to me. I was even prepared to go out on the street and make the trip on foot just to get out of this accursed apartment and leave my fears behind.

After a short while Henryk and Zygmunt returned, bringing a large black trunk with them, which up to then had served the Michalskis for carrying things to their summer place. It had already seen a lot of use, and in the place where hinges should have been there was nothing but a gaping hole, which in the present instance would be of great use for letting in air. By drawing up my knees I was able to fit inside. As I was lying down in the trunk to see whether or not I would fit, a knocking broke out at the door. The four of us froze in our tracks (there were four of us, because Maniek had also come to see how things were shaping up). After a longish while the men decided to open the door with me remaining in the chest.

It turned out that it was the man from the electric company who had come to collect the electric bill. He was very surprised that they had taken such a long time to open the door. After he had gone, Zygmunt went to get a freight rickshaw. Henryk put a blanket and a little pillow under my head and covered me with an overcoat. In the direst of need it would be possible to last half an hour or at most an hour in it. After this, he closed the lid and nailed it shut, asking jokingly all the while how I felt there in my coffin. My last sensation before being loaded into the trunk was the sight of Maniek, whose face was completely flushed from all the excitement. For his seventeen-year-old imagination this was the sort of exploit which he had previously encountered only in adventure novels.

The rickshaw was driven out into the apartment house yard next to the entry. Henryk and Zygmunt each held one end of the trunk, and I could feel them carrying me and, finally, carefully placing me on something. Zygmunt shoved a roll of paper into the trunk next to me in order to hide my hair which, as he later told me, was clearly visible through the wide crack. In order to cover this hole, he placed in front of it a large board, used for cutting material, and piled a chair on top of all that. Finally, we set off.

At the beginning I could hear Zygmunt quarreling with the rickshaw driver over which route to take. Zygmunt wanted to go by the backstreets, whereas the driver insisted on going in a different way. Due to this, we were forced to pass by the walls of the Little Ghetto. Zygmunt later said to me, "If you wanted to have a good scare, you should have seen all the German gendarmes standing there on guard with their rifles at the ready."

When I in turn asked him whether he had been afraid, he replied that his only worry the whole way was whether one of the tires on the rickshaw might burst. It was for this reason that, instead of getting on board the rickshaw himself, he had run alongside it out in the middle of the road the entire way, holding convulsively onto the side. Next I heard the rickshaw driver asking about the contents of the trunk. "What do you have in it that weighs so much?" he asked. "It feels as if it weighs at least fifty kilos."

"The shopmaster is changing his place of work and we are transporting various sorts of implements," Zygmunt answered.

Finally, I could feel us going over cobblestones, so I knew we were near our destination. Indeed, soon afterward the rickshaw came to a stop and I could feel myself being taken off the rickshaw and carried. I heard the voice of old Mr. Michalski, opening the lid of my "coffin" and saying, "The corpse has risen."

As soon as I got up out of the trunk I felt overcome by a great feeling of happiness, and I was in such a wonderful frame of mind that I felt like leaping around and singing for joy. It was as if the war were over, and death had ceased to threaten me. All around I saw only faces near and dear. There was old Mr. Michalski, all smiles, and Henryk, who had arrived earlier by trolley, his face entirely lit up. Zygmunt was perspiring and exhausted, but happy that everything had gone so well. As usual with each successful accomplishment, we celebrated by drinking several bottles of vodka and eating a large amount of "kanapki" (tea sandwiches). Since we had had little to eat that day, the vodka soon went to our heads. With all our hearts we were happy and filled with joy.

54

BACK IN THE OLD TINSMITH'S
SHOP

.

Thus it was that on May 11, 1943, we returned to our old "haunt."

Our new shelter, or really my husband's old shelter, on Belwed-erska Street in the old, almost tumble-down building, consisted, as I have already mentioned, of four rooms, a kitchen, and two halls leading to the entrance up into the attic by a ladder. The building, which was an utter eyesore, had survived as long as it had from the ravages of war because previously it had been earmarked for demolition. The roof was full of holes and cracks, and water flowed freely from all sides into the interior. Plaster was falling off the walls and ceiling.

One room was totally unfit for use, because the ceiling threatened to cave in at any moment. It was in this "junk room" that we kept sawdust for heating the place in winter by burning it in a special stove. The only positive feature was a vegetable garden lying alongside the building. This garden was cultivated by the Michalskis, which was to our great good fortune, because no one was able to peer into the room next to it, in which we slept.

Due to the fact that the building was located in the German district, all day long we had electricity. In the other areas, inhabited by Poles, the Germans turned on the electricity for only three hours a day. In addition we also had gas, albeit illegally, for it didn't run through a meter. Old Mr. Michalski had installed a sort of stove for us, on which we were able to cook and in part heat the apartment in winter, by running a line from a pipe that was just sticking up out of ground.

Obviously we didn't use the gas during the day, for we were afraid of being controlled. On the other hand, after the shop had been locked up we burned it all through the night, being able in this way to dry out at least in part the decrepit, fungus-ridden old building. Besides this we had water and a sink, but no further plumbing, for the building was without it. The matter of the toilet was worse. This was a big problem for us, and I will tell later how we solved it. We had decided never to go outside, even to the toilet, so that none of the nearby tenants could see us. This was particularly important, because the superintendent lived directly opposite our kitchen, which was where the door out into the yard was.

We maintained the utmost in precautionary measures. After the workshop was locked up for the night, Mr. Michalski would leave by the back entrance from the kitchen into the yard, locking the door behind him with a padlock. As previously (and an entire year has passed as I write this), no one had any idea as to what was going on inside. All external appearances were excellently maintained.

Zygmunt and his wife and three children were living in the same apartment house complex. The main building, where Zygmunt and his family lived, housed about twenty families, for the most part from the laboring class. Since he was Mr. Michalski's journeyman, none of the tenants were surprised to see that he had a spare key to the workshop and came and left at all hours of the day. Everyone knew that he was working overtime. After his work for old Mr. Michalski was over, he worked as a cutter for his new employer. From the time we moved in, Zygmunt became our main protector.

On the first day, we literally had nothing to lay our heads on. We put several pieces of cardboard down on the floor and lay a little bit of material down on top of it, and covered ourselves up with our over-coats. We were able to fall asleep mainly because of the exhausting experiences we had lived through that first day, and because we were a little tipsy from the vodka. The worst problem was the mice, of which there was an entire legion.

Next morning at daybreak we leapt out of bed, because Mr. Michalski opened his workshop at seven o'clock. We were able to eat breakfast, as Henryk had left us milk and bread. We climbed up the ladder to our "proper residence" in the attic. After we were up there, we shut the lid on the hole in the ceiling, and Mr. Michalski took down the ladder and put it in the rubbish room.

Looking around at our new place, we were actually struck quite pleasantly at its appearance. It was a large attic, because it occupied the entire length of the building, and it had on each side a normal window without panes, fitted with a dense metal screen. Mr. Michalski had once used the attic for raising chickens, and had installed the grates so that they couldn't escape. Now they were of great use to us because nothing could be seen through them from the street. We even made experiments by standing near the windows and having Henryk purposely try to observe us from the street.

My husband and I sought each other's advice to see how comfortable we could make things here. After checking every inch of the attic, my husband noticed a large opening in one corner which was covered by several old pieces of sheet metal and other junk. As it turned out, this was a large hole in the ceiling above the rubbish room where part of the ceiling had fallen in from the rain constantly falling on it. My husband decided to make use of it.

We walled up and painted the original opening from the hall into the ceiling so that it was hard to recognize that it had ever been there in the first place. For ourselves we made use of the other hole by means of the ladder. This had many positive aspects to it. Above all, no one unfamiliar with the setup could ~~have~~ have suspected that there was an entrance to the attic. The rubbish room itself was completely dark, for the windows had been boarded up. No one from the outside world ever entered the place, for it was piled high with old castoff gardening tools and other stuff. Besides that, it had a pit in the floor for potatoes. Zygmunt installed for us, directly to the line which passed through the attic, an electric hot plate for cooking. In this way we were able to use the electricity without paying, and thanks to this I could cook in the attic.

That first day we looked out through the screen onto God's world. May was blossoming in full beauty. Beneath our window stood a chestnut tree covered in white flowers. Its aroma filled our lungs with delight and satisfaction. The sun shining through the holes in the screen warmed our faces. How long it had been since we had felt its life-giving rays! We closed our eyes and for a moment were able to forget the terrible poverty of our lives. On Krochmalna Street the only odors had come from the communal toilet and refuse heap, and our only view had been onto a gray, unbroken wall. After the seven nightmarish weeks spent in the "tomb," it was no wonder that the change seemed like heaven to us.

Here we were at least at a little distance from the terrible roar of the explosions, the booming of grenades, and the salvos of machine-gun fire from behind the walls of the ghetto, and we were able to breathe freely and relax for a change. We luxuriated in the quiet reigning everywhere and in the normal course of life, seemingly uninterrupted by anything from the outside. We looked out our window into the distance and could see the happy smiling faces of passers-by on the street. We envied them even the limited amount of freedom they enjoyed. To tell the truth, the Poles were also persecuted very badly by the Nazis. They were caught on the streets, in trolley-cars, and on trains and sent to forced-labor camps in Germany.

But there is no way to compare their persecution with that of the Jews. Didn't the Poles know they were at war? Didn't they realize what kind of situation we were in? Life with them seemed to be going along as if nothing had happened. Every hour the narrow-gauged "Samovar" would chug by our window with a screech and whistle, carrying passengers, while at the other end of town thousands of innocent people were perishing in a sea of flames, murdered at the command of a single tyrant and butcher named Adolf Hitler. It was difficult to believe one's own eyes and ears.

All that day we rested, feeling like people who were beginning a period of convalescence after a long illness. On the other hand, however, the specter of events in the ghetto continued to haunt us.

In the evening Mr. Michalski locked his workshop, and we were able to come downstairs. He left for home, yielding to us, as he said, the only decent place to sleep, the couch on which my husband had slept before. Two persons were barely able to fit on it, and even then, in one position only, on one side. However, after the previous sleepless night spent on the hard floor battling the mice, it seemed to us a luxurious place of rest. We went to bed early and immediately fell fast asleep.

We were aroused by a terrible explosion, followed by a second and a third. We got out of bed and quickly began putting on our clothes. Soon after these detonations, the delayed wailing of factory sirens broke the air. With a great roar, automobiles began driving past, also sounding the alarm. We ran as quickly as we could into the kitchen, where the window was unshaded, and a well-known sight greeted us. It was bright as day. Illumination bombs thrown by Soviet airplanes were burning brightly in the sky. Bombs fell one after another, their terrible whistling and explosions ripping the air. Soon the sky was crimson with the glow of burning buildings. The courtyard was seething with inde- scribable chaos and confusion. All the tenants had gathered together around the toilet, waiting their turn... impatiently. A number of women just "squatted down" in the darkest corner next to the trash pile.

Zygmunt, who performed the function of a guard, was running around in circles, completely out of his mind. He popped in to see us for a short while. We were amazed to see him so frightened, because yesterday, when he had been transporting me and my husband, death had been just as close, but he had remained calm and in control. Seemingly he had become infected with the mass hysteria of the crowd.

As for us, we received the air raid with utter tranquility. My husband took up an observation post right next to the window, while I bent down in the hall, covering my ears with my hands, because the explosions had an unnerving effect on me. The air raid lasted for two hours, from one until three o'clock in the morning. It accomplished no major harm in our area, but the downtown area suffered extensive damage. There were many fires and bombed-out buildings, and many people had been killed or wounded.

After that air raid a mass exodus began into the countryside and, taking advantage of the situation, peasants raised the price for a place to stay to fabulous heights but, driven by the fear of death, people paid anyway. Trains and the narrow-gauge railways were jam-packed. Whoever had acquaintances outside town placed their most valuable possessions with them. In a word, the capital was taut with suspense. However, as the days, and then weeks, went by, and the raids were not repeated, everything returned to normal.

Bombs had fallen on various locations, for the most part civilian; practically nothing of military importance was hit. People were thoroughly terrorized at the idea of the air raids. Various dates were set on which air raids were supposedly going to take place. For example, on June 22nd, that is, on the second anniversary of the outbreak of war with Russia, people forecast a gigantic air raid on Warsaw. However, that day passed rather peacefully.

Next morning Mr. Michalski came to the workshop in a distressed state of mind, looking as if he hadn't slept a wink. The house in which he lived on Krochmalna Street had decidedly little luck with Soviet bombs. That night, an incendiary bomb had fallen in a courtyard and started a fire. Mr. Michalski described the terrible panic he had seen. The several hundred tenants had been running around in a frenzy trying to rescue their belongings. They paid little attention to the falling bombs and the noise of airplanes all around, but began putting out the fire, which they managed to do even before the fire department arrived. The door to our room there, which we had abandoned barely the day before, had been broken down by the tenants, who had stuffed bedding and various other things inside, which they now threw out the window. I dread to think what would have happened if we had stayed in that apartment for one more day. This time too, divine Providence was looking out for us.

55

OUR LIFE IN THE ATTIC

On the third day of our stay in the old workshop, Mr. Michalski managed to come up with an old iron bed for us. Henryk bought a paper mattress, and Zygmunt's wife bought two straw mats, and in this way we set up for ourselves a relatively comfortable sleeping spot. We already had most essential kitchen implements right there in the workshop. These were things people had left to be repaired and which had not been redeemed by their owners. Zygmunt loaned us a few dishes. Considering our circumstances, this was more than we could have wished for by way of a household.

Zygmunt and my husband set up a work table in the attic. Some mangles (clothes presses) had once stood in one of the rooms downstairs, and Mr. Michalski took them apart and them up to the attic. It was from these that we made both a work table and a stand for my electric hotplate. Also, since there was no flooring in the attic, the various other pieces of the mangle were laid about so that we could freely circulate without fear of falling through down into the "lower apartments."

I even had a chair upstairs to sit on. We actually tried tanning our faces for a while, but... we were afraid that it would just "checker" them, because of the screen in the window. As time went on we installed other conveniences in our attic, and we came to love it as a reliable old friend. We even came to prefer it to staying downstairs, where the air was quite heavy from the smell of rot and mildew. For the first few days we simply lay around resting and breathing in the fresh air.

The only inhabitants of the building knowing of our presence were

Zygmunt and his wife. I freely admit that I was very much afraid of her at the time. First of all, I have no faith in the discretion of women, even though I am one myself, and in the second place, Zygmunt's person gave reasonable room for doubt, in spite of the assurances of my husband, who after all had known him longer than I had. Zygmunt liked to take to the bottle from time to time, and he would get drunk quite often. When drunk he liked to create disturbances and make scenes, but his wife for the most part kept him in line. My husband had a positive effect on him by seeing to it that he always had work to do for us and an additional income.

In spite of all that, Zygmunt sometimes just had to let loose. Whenever such a time would come, and it happened every couple of weeks, Zygmunt would drink himself into a stupor several times during the course of a week and pile up debts. Afterwards, however, he would work with enthusiasm and with the strength of two, and he was a talented, diligent, and scrupulous worker. He had a very kind disposition, just an angel of a person. Toward us he was so kind and delicate that we never met another person like him during our entire stay on the Aryan side. It was thanks to him that our living conditions were tolerable, for he saw to that, sparing neither time nor effort. He always did whatever we asked of him. Nothing was too difficult. He even carried out our trash and the discharges of our bodies, because we were afraid to use the communal toilet in the yard. Of course, in the winter we burned everything together with the sawdust in the stove.

We can confidently state that throughout our stay there (and twelve months have now passed) he was a real guardian angel for us. We both liked him very much, and we valued, treated, and respected him as he fully deserved. Even when drunk he caused us no trouble. He always remembered not to tell anyone about us, and he never mentioned us to anyone even when under the influence. Thus, my initial fears concerning him and his wife quickly evaporated. Besides that, we realized that Zygmunt was the mainstay and pinion of the entire operation. Above all, he was the intermediary between my husband and the factory. It was he who would bring packages of raw materials to us and take them away when cut by my husband.

When some new skill was required, my husband would always teach it first to Zygmunt at our place, and he would then return to the factory and pass it on to the others. None of the workers ever suspected that he hadn't known how to do it in the first place. Henryk was never particularly interested in the technical details of the work, but my husband was able to rely totally on Zygmunt.

We were never able to relax completely, for we were constantly under the impression that we were being spied on and that "they were on our trail." This is an extremely wearying feeling. From the window in our attic we were able to look beyond the garden out onto a little building occupied in front by a blacksmith and in back by a Volksdeutsch gardener. The blacksmith did most of his work shoeing horses for the Germans. Sometimes when I heard the loud shriek of a German voice my heart would freeze inside me until I looked out of the window and realized that it was only directed at a horse.

It often seemed to me that the people standing around the blacksmith's were looking at our building. I pointed them out to my husband, who knew a lot more about such matters than I did, and I would calm down only on his assurance that it was nothing. This situation lasted for many months. Only when we were finally certain that no one was spying on us or thinking about us were we able to relax.

We had a second observation point in the attic from a hole in the roof from which it was possible to see everything. Right across from us stood a long row of multi-story buildings occupied exclusively by Germans. The building directly opposite us had two entrances. On the left, evidently, lived people of some importance, because one of them in particular attracted attention to himself. Several times a day an automobile would come for him and take him away. He was assisted by two agents, and two others out on the street greeted his return and escorted him into the apartment where they would sit waiting even during his absence. He was obviously some kind of big-wig. We often peeped out through our "Judas hole" in the roof, through which we could observe everything without being observed ourselves.

We became familiar with the agents who waited for him and with the person himself, even though normally he would pass from his car to his apartment and back again with enormous speed. We were continually afraid lest someone from the underground make an attack on his life. In accordance with the collective responsibility adopted by the Nazis during that period, all the inhabitants of the surrounding buildings would have been shot.

Throughout the summer the thing that worried us the most was the specter of the blockades, which began in April after the beginning of the destruction of the ghetto. All Warsaw was seething with fear. People said that in the places where they had occurred the Nazis had taken away people's belongings, money, jewelry, and so forth. The most valuable items simply vanished from beneath people's noses. There was no place to hide, for the attics were also thoroughly searched.

Some of the blockades took place at four o'clock in the morning, while in other places they took place at night. It was said that if weapons were uncovered anywhere, all the men from the building were taken away, and none of the family ever received any word from them again. Blockades were held in different sections of town. We were not able to ascertain whether this new kind of terror was being applied in order to frighten the population, or whether it was the work of informants who had told the Germans to look for arms in given buildings.

We lived in mortal fear of what would happen to us if the entire building were surrounded by the Nazis. A thorough search of all the men would take place, including to see if they were circumcised, and all documents would be checked. Anyone whose documents were not in order would be taken away. It meant little that the door was locked with a padlock, for it would not have been difficult to knock it down. We were so watchful even in our sleep that at the slightest sound we would sit bolt upright in bed thinking that our time had come. Each morning I would get out of bed and look through a crack in the curtains to see whether there was any German on the street. Then I went to the kitchen and looked out to see if all was quiet there.

Things were hardly better during the day. In the morning when we went to the attic, we immediately began looking out both windows and through the cracks in the roof. After a short period we became familiar with the people who regularly passed by. Most noticeable among these were the German women telephone operators who lived not far from us. Each day at the same time they would walk by in their uniforms, alone or in pairs— happy, gay, and bubbling with health. We always felt very resentful at their sight.

56

MAY AND THE FIRST HALF OF
JUNE, 1943

We were expecting some kind of miracle to liberate us from this inferno, but no miracle came, and nothing happened to suggest the immanent defeat of Germany. Each day my husband would read the German papers which Henryk brought. These included *Die Allgemeine Zeitung*, *Voelkischer Beobachter*, *Die Warschauer Zeitung*, and *Das Reich*, which he would pore over all week, reading Goebbels' articles in order to decipher between the lines what the actual situation in Germany was. Unfortunately, all the papers, as well as Goebbels' articles, sung hymns of victory over military triumphs and the might of invincible Germany, not doubting for a moment that soon the entire world would be lying at its feet.

It was quiet on all fronts. The Russians were engaged in skirmishes over the Kuban bridgehead in Russia but were unable to capture it. The English and Americans were nowhere to be seen, and the Germans, puffed up with even greater pride, and praising themselves to the skies, laughed at and ridiculed their helplessness. We for our part fell into a very depressed state after reading all this news. We also assiduously studied the news from the underground press. And we waited. How terrible and hopeless our waiting was! But we were made of hard clay, and we were determined to suffer everything silently.

We put on a face in front of the people around us so that no one would guess about the worms gnawing at our insides, nor imagine what a dreadful burden we felt weighing us down. Old Mr. Michalski became very easily frightened and sensitive during this time, at even the slightest movement. My husband would soothe him by saying as if to a baby that it was nothing. He plucked up his courage by reminding him, as he himself had told it, how brave he had been at the front in 1914 and during the four years he had spent in captivity. We understood that he was just plagued by the same fear we felt. After all, he was in about as much danger as we were.

Three weeks after our arrival at the old tinshop on Belwederska Street, I had an unfortunate accident which luckily did not result in a calamity. One morning as I was going up to the attic by the ladder, being either distracted or not looking to see what I was doing, I missed the board placed between the opening and a beam, and I stepped on a weak spot where there was no flooring at all. (In 1939 following the bombing of Warsaw, the former inhabitants of our building had burned the floor of the attic for heating.) I felt one foot and then the other falling away beneath me. Desperately I tried to grab hold of something, but nothing came to hand and I tumbled back down to the rubbish room, bringing half of the ceiling with me. Mr. Michalski heard the racket and came running. The room was enveloped in a thick cloud of dust, and I lost consciousness for a moment.

When the dust had settled, I made out that I was sitting on a pile of sticks and rubble, and when I lifted my eyes to the ceiling I noted with a sinking heart that there was no longer any ceiling above me. I picked myself up and made sure that I was still in one piece. I was badly bruised and scratched, and bleeding in several places. Before I even had time to wash, I heard Mr. Michalski and Zygmunt, who fortunately had not yet gone to the shop, energetically repairing the damage I had done. After an hour the ceiling was covered with boards and one larger beam had been propped up to support it. The rubble had not been cleared away, because Mr. Michalski thought that the rubbish room could well take on an even more disreputable appearance.

After that, whenever anyone looked into the room, he had the impression that the rest of the ceiling was going to fall in. Thanks to this, the entrance to the attic was even better camouflaged than it had been before. The adventure ended up with nothing more than a few bruises and the many biting remarks of my husband. On the other hand, the rubbish room gained greatly in appearance. No one would have ever guessed that someone might be hiding in the attic.

On the whole, the second half of May and the first half of June passed peacefully. The weather was beautiful, and our living conditions were much better here than they had been on Krochmalna Street.

We always had a supply of food which we kept in a little box, which we hung from a beam to protect it from the mice.

We were at ease about our baby thanks to Father Święcki and Marysia Michalski, who visited him from time to time and brought us news. Father Święcki had placed it in the Father Boduen Institute[1] on Filtrowa Street (as we later learned, there were around forty other Jewish children being sheltered there). Father Święcki was the confessor of the nuns and mother superior under whose protection this institution functioned, and for that reason he always had access to it. Marysia, who had stated that after the war she would (supposedly) adopt our son, also had free access without arousing suspicion. Each month we sent five hundred zlotys to the mother superior. She was the only person who knew the entire truth about our baby.

Two times a month we gave Marysia those five hundred zlotys in order to buy essential items of food and clothing for our child, for the institution at this time housed over one thousand orphans, and because of the war and the lack of material means, it was in no condition to feed the children properly. Thanks to Father Święcki, we also received pictures of our baby from time to time. Of course, his appearance was far from what we would have wished, but the most important thing was that he was alive and well, and that had been the priest's doing, and his alone. Our gratitude to him has remained and will remain with us to the end of our lives. We always kept the pictures in a special hidden place, in case we ever fell into the hands of the Nazis.

My husband devoted his energy and soul to his work. We knew that we had brought the Michalskis neither gold, diamonds, nor currency, so it would be necessary to rehabilitate ourselves in their eyes in a different way. During this time we were the only ones on the Warsaw market producing fancy women's footwear.

Our small factory was well organized. Henryk would assemble from various bazaars all the materials necessary for our products, for it was not possible to obtain anything in a legal manner. For the most part we used silks and velvets which were only available in such dark colors as navy blue, brown, and so forth. We knew certain chemical secrets for restoring the dark colors to their original shades, for example light cream or white. When this was done, it was no longer difficult to dye them the necessary colors, for example pink, light blue, or coral. It was these colors which were most eagerly sought after, even during the war.

The Germans bought up our products in droves and sent it to their "Vaterland" where this sort of thing was totally unavailable, even on ration cards. I can confidently state that we were the only people during this time who were producing dress shoes made of such colorful velvets. Our prewar customer, Mrs. Jozefa Hebda, knew the secret of the origin of these beautiful shoes. Our other customers guessed that my husband was somewhere on the Aryan side engaged in business, but no one asked about it.

Since our products were simply grabbed up as soon as they were made, although we could not keep up with our orders due to a lack of raw materials, we made lots of money. The Michalski household was prospering. Marysia and the children were all well dressed and had food in abundance. The rest of the family was also living in much better circumstances than before our arrival on the Aryan side. Unfortunately, the money that we earned went to pay the debts incurred because of the blackmail. On the other hand, we had a roof over our heads, food to eat, and a safe place to stay, and we couldn't dream of anything else. We just prayed to God for him to let us live in peace.

During the so-called Green Holidays (Pentecost), the workshop was closed. The Michalskis provided us with enough food to last through the holidays, and everything looked as though it would turn out as well as possible. On the first day of the holidays, in the early evening, my husband's ears were struck by the expression "Jude", uttered in German. Next we heard several shots ring out. Through a crack in the curtains we observed what was going on out on the street.

All passers-by had their backs turned to us, and everyone was looking at a single point. Alongside our garden, separated from us by the blacksmith's and the garden belonging to the Volksdeutsch man, ran Zajączkowska Street. On this street was located a small wooden shop, where several German gendarmes were now standing. Several others were walking across the roof of this wooden shed, hollering and shooting.

As we later learned, the caretaker of this building had been hiding seven Jews in it. That day, on account of the holidays, there had been a large celebration, and a lot of vodka was drunk. At one point the drunken caretaker threw himself at one of the women and started beating her with a seltzer bottle, and a row ensued, as the result of which the woman (according to Zygmunt known throughout the district by the nickname "Stoneblind") left, threatening the caretaker.

She went to the nearby German gendarme station located on Willowa Street and gave the police the address of the Jews in hiding. The building was surrounded in a matter of minutes, and this had been the fight we had seen from the window of our room. The gendarmes were shooting blindly; one of them stood on the roof with his weapon cocked. After an hour or so, they led out four Jews with their hands above their heads. Three of them had managed to escape when the Germans had first arrived. The caretaker had also vanished, and the woman who had denounced them was held for the night at the gendarme station. Next day they let her go, and the gendarmes drove up once more and conducted another search in the building. It seemed that it was impossible to escape the legend that wherever Jews are, gold, diamonds and dollars are sure to be found too.

---

1. **Father Boduen children's hospital**. This still-existing institution in Warsaw was founded in 1732 as a home for cast-off children by French-born Father Gabriel Boudouin (1689-1768). During the war it protected more than a hundred abandoned and orphaned Jewish children both in its main facility and, especially for children with Semitic features, in its various branches outside Warsaw, in individual homes, and in monasteries and cloisters.

57

WAYS JEWS WERE DISCOVERED

Thus we were witnesses to the denunciation of Jews. This blow struck at our hearts. We were thoroughly shaken by the event and did not sleep for a number of nights afterwards. Neither one of us could take a bite to eat, we were that morally and physically depressed. Our nerves felt stretched to the breaking point, tortured by the sight of these people walking with their hands held over their heads.

This incident had a very depressing effect on everyone around us as well. In general, whenever we heard about a denunciation, we were unable to regain our equilibrium for several weeks afterwards, and there were two more such denunciations near us during that summer. One took place on Nabielak Street. The landlady had been hiding four Jewish women in her apartment for a year and a half. The apartment consisted of a room and kitchen, and supposedly a false wall had been installed and covered over with wallpaper. A cupboard stood against the wall where one entered the hiding place. These women were able to last this way for quite a while, but unfortunately their money ran out, and they had nothing more to live from nor to pay the landlady. At that point the landlady left the apartment and gave notice to the authorities through a policeman she knew. The police went straight to the apartment and took away the people they found hiding there. Later the landlady returned as if nothing had happened.

The other incident happened on Czerniakowska Street in an unfinished building similar to the one where we had had our workshop. The owner, who was a Jew, hearing that a closed ghetto was to be created into which all Jews were to be placed, decided to build a hiding place for himself. He built an apartment which on the outside was no different from any of the others, and he lived in it together with his family. There were seven of them. Food and various other items were bought by the caretaker of the building and his wife. In this way the family lived until March, 1943.

In March the caretaker's wife had a quarrel with her husband, accusing him of having a lover (another one of these miserable "lovers" who brought ruin to so many Jews). She decided to take revenge on him by going to the police station and denouncing him for hiding Jews. As a result of this treachery, they all went to their deaths, including a five-year-old child. The caretaker was also killed, but his wife continued to live there unpunished.

For us the kind of marital relations we met with on the Aryan side, even among our protectors, seemed to us abnormal. There is no lack of marital discord among our people either, but not the kind of moral depravity which we found here. For an example, I will describe an incident for which we almost paid with our lives.

One morning old Mrs. Michalski came to the workshop where we were hidden and started a row, saying that her husband was keeping a lover (I should mention that at that time they were both well past 50). The marital relations of their married sons were no better—always the question of these "lovers." With every word the quarrel became increasingly bitter. At one point we heard Mrs. Michalski shout, "I'm going to the police this minute and tell them that you're keeping Jews in here."

After that she slammed the door and left. We couldn't believe our ears. I looked at my husband and he at me. We were numb with fear. We stood next to the window and asked ourselves in our hearts: Which way is she going to go? But old Mrs. Michalski went to the left, in other words, home, for the road to the the police station was to the right. We breathed a sigh of relief, but for a long time we were unable to relax. Danger lurked everywhere, if not from strangers then from those nearest to us.

Besides this, another great plague persecuted Jews hiding on the Aryan side. These were the "greasers," or extortionists, who had unusual instincts for picking out Semitic features. There were many incidents of men being stopped on the street and dragged into a building gate for an anatomical examination. Woe to the handful of Jews who had to circulate about town for one reason or another.

It was no use for women to dye their hair and try to look like Aryan women. I will describe a characteristic incident. A blond woman was walking peacefully along Kazimierz Square, paying no attention to anything going on around her. Suddenly a band of young boys appeared on the street and began pointing their fingers at her, crying "Jew, Jew." The woman, fearing the results, started running away, but the boys ran after her shouting even louder. This went on until it finally attracted the attention of a blue policeman, who arrested the woman and took her to the Gestapo with the help of the lads.

There were many other similar events. Finally, the underground press attached to the Polish government in London began calling on the Polish people to consider what they were doing and to desist. They also began to list the names of people who had denounced and blackmailed Jews hiding on the Aryan side. The AK even issued death warrants on some of them. We were glad that finally someone was coming to our defense. Unfortunately, our joy was short-lived, for other events occurred that had a negative effect on the fate of the Jews in hiding. One of these was the Katyń massacre.[1]

At the end of 1943 the Nazis announced in the press that they had discovered the graves of 10,000 Polish officers, military prisoners who had been interned in prison camps, in the Katyń forest in Russia. The Germans accused Russia of the deed. The paper published by the Germans in Polish under the title "The New Polish Courier", popularly called "The Reptilian Press," poisoned the Poles with their anti-Bolshevik, anti-Jewish articles. They claimed that it had been Jewish Bolsheviks who had been responsible for the massacre. Each day they listed the names of the officers murdered in the Katyń forest.

We noticed among them the name of the son-in-law of Mrs. Józefa Hebda, Lieutenant Doctor Edward Gacki. We knew him from before the war; he was a young and very cultured and intelligent gentleman, with whom we had many discussions concerning one thing and another. I could well imagine what a terrible effect this news must have had on Mrs. Hebda and on her daughter, Lieutenant Gacki's wife.

Anti-Semitic propaganda in the German press had a negative effect on the Jews in hiding. If previously we had been tolerated, then after the Katyń affair we began to be hated. When diplomatic relations between the Polish government in London and Russia broke off, Poles were so hostile to us that they began to look on every Jew as a Bolshevik, and consequently an enemy of Poland.

Our protectors also changed in their behavior toward us, and they let us feel it at every step. We were extremely afraid that they would try and get rid of us in some way. However, our little factory continued to prosper and reap large profits, so for the time being the storm was held in abeyance, and we continued to lead the same life as before. We prayed to God to give us the strength to endure in this awful struggle.

At the end of June old Mr. Michalski came to us with a piece of news. He told us that in a bar on Rakowiecka Street in the Mokotów quarter he had come across two brothers by the name of Dąb. They told about an excellent opportunity which was about to present itself to all Jews in hiding. For payment they would be allowed to go abroad. All volunteers were to gather in Hotel Poland,[2] located on Długa Street. We were so exhausted and overwrought with fear and the uncertainty of every minute, constantly shifting from place to place, that it seemed to us for a moment that we had seen a flash of hope. My husband in particular became enthusiastic about this idea, but common sense took the upper hand with me. I felt this was a trap designed to catch the remainder of the Jews in hiding, and time proved me right, as those taking the bait either ended up in Auschwitz or were executed in Pawiak prison.

On July 5th the long-awaited Soviet offensive began, and we followed it with bated breath, expecting that the Soviets would be able to push forward as quickly as the Germans had done in the opposite direction. As time went on our disappointment deepened. The Germans were putting up a stubborn resistance everywhere, defending their ground every inch of the way. The Soviets were moving forward, but it was very slow going and accomplished with great loss of life.

On July 10th the Anglo-Americans began their offensive in Sicily. We turned our attention to this second front, deceiving ourselves that it would bring with it hope for our salvation, but here too we were to be disappointed. When Mussolini was removed from power in Italy on July 25th, we expected the same thing to happen in Germany. Finally, when on September 8th the Italian capitulation was officially announced, we were certain that this would not remain without repercussions in Germany.

We expected a revolution to break out any day. People thought that we would see a repetition of 1918. They kept saying, "We'll wake up one morning, and the Germans will already have gone." In short, we all believed that the war was drawing to a close.

We could hardly wait to get our hands on the German papers and the news of the underground press. The latter served to support our illusions. "We are entering the decisive phase—the moment of Germany's defeat is moving toward us with giant steps..." That is what the headlines of the articles of the underground press sounded like.

In the meantime life went on as before. One day toward the end of summer, two German deserters from the army were found and locked in irons. It all happened right next door to us. At one moment my husband noticed several gendarmes with rifles cocked passing by our yard and returning from the garden, looking carefully around them. Our hearts stopped beating. That evening Zygmunt told us that the two runaway German soldiers had hidden in the building in the middle of the vegetable garden. The woman living there had hidden them in her basement, covering them with rags and other trash. We took this as an encouraging sign, for the effects of desertion had begun to be felt on the German army, formerly known for its rigor and discipline.

We knew that the soldiers were stealing every sort of thing from their camps and selling whatever they could; this black marketeering had already reached tremendous proportions. The entire market was flooded with military and hospital bed linen, blankets and that sort of thing. All winter long we had been manufacturing warm slippers from military blankets, and not only we, but all manufacturers, were doing this. Once we bought for manufacturing purposes a shipment of banners intended to be hung from balconies. Because of the lack of normal raw materials, we were buying sheets and pillow cases, all of them originating from German military camps, using them for lining in our products.

Zygmunt's sister-in-law, who had been working in a military kitchen, decided to find some pretext for giving up her work for, as she said, it did not pay very well, and there was nothing left to steal. The soldiers were getting a miserable fare. The times when piles of bacon and crates of canned goods were lying about camp belonged to the irretrievable past.

This and other similar news served to fortify us and help keep our spirits up. We deluded ourselves into thinking that soon we would be free. From time to time the entire city would be whispering some rumor or other, for example that Hitler was seriously ill and his days were numbered. Later the rumor was that there had been an attempt on his life and he had been mortally wounded. It even reached the point where people were saying that he was no longer alive, but his clique was keeping it a deep secret for fear of causing panic among the German population. We believed these stories along with everyone else and waited impatiently for the day of liberation.

---

1. **Katyń Massacre**. "Katyń" was a series of mass executions in 1940 by the

289

Russian NKVD (security police) of around 22,000 Polish prisoners of war, in and around Katyń forest in the Soviet Union. Of that number, around 8,000 were army officers, 6,000 were police officers, and the remainder were members of the Polish intelligentsia (doctors, lawyers, priests, journalists, and others). The action was initiated by NKVD chief Lavrentij Beria and approved by Joseph Stalin. Russia denied its responsibility for the massacre until the early 1990s, while even then denying that this had been a "war crime." Many of the victims could be identified by the personal papers found on their bodies in mass graves.

2. **Hotel Poland**. In 1943, the Hotel Poland on Długa Street served as a point of internment for Jews possessing either Nansen passports (issued to displaced persons after World War I) or passports from South American countries (which were neutral in World War II, hence not subject to German laws governing the citizens of occupied countries). The latter were issued at the initiative of Swiss Jewish organizations, but most such passports could not be delivered, since the intended recipients had already died in Treblinka. Collaborators sold the undelivered passports to Jews on the Aryan side both as a money-making venture and as a ruse to get them to come out of hiding. Of some 2,500 people taking this bait, around 1,900 were sent to prisoner camps in Vittel, France, and Bergen-Belsen in Germany, but most of these were later sent to the extermination camp in Auschwitz. Some 300 internees remaining in Hotel Poland without "proper documents" were taken to Warsaw's Pawiak prison and executed.

58

MANIEK DETAINED AND RELEASED

The AK (the underground army, along with others) increased its activities. Nazi murderers and butchers who had the greatest number of crimes on their conscience, and who bore the greatest responsibility for the torture perpetrated on an innocent population, received sentences from the underground court. One by one, either in the privacy of their apartments or on the streets, they were shot. The number of beasts ushered into the other world increased. All Germans in higher positions were now afraid.[1]

We waited impatiently for the end of summer 1943, certain that the war was drawing to a close. The end of September saw a number of new blockades, taking place both day and night. They were looking for weapons, secret presses, radios, and any Jews uncovered in the process. We were living in terror. When a blockade took place not far from us on Czerniakowska Street (it was said that someone had informed on a hidden slaughter-house located there), we decided to transfer up to the attic for the night. We became completely dependent on Zygmunt who, before going home to bed, would take the ladder down after us and put it next to the other things in the rubbish room. In the morning, when Mr. Michalski brought the ladder back for us, we were able to come down to wash and take back up enough food for the whole day.

At first we slept on a bare mat. The worst of it was the mice. They hopped and squeaked all night long and wouldn't let us get a moment's rest. In vain did my husband toss pebbles into the darkness at them.

Seeing that we were not going to be able to manage with the mice this way, we brought our bed upstairs and embarked on a fairly successful battle with them with the help of traps and poison.

We slept for several months in the attic, until we were forced to move downstairs again by the cold. All summer long we had lived in fear of the night alarms. Terrorized after the air raid in May, which had done so much damage and claimed so many victims, people were deathly afraid of the alarms, so when the factory sirens sounded, the entire building came alive for several hours afterwards. Everyone came down into the yard, and their conversations would last until the alarms had been called off. In the beginning I too would awaken with a start, but later, when the alarms kept repeating themselves every other night, I became accustomed to their sound.

On the eastern front, bloody battles were taking place. The Germans were defending each little town and village. However, the Russians were inexorably marching forward, if only at a snail's pace. In spite of all their efforts, they were unable to make a greater dent in the German army and force it into a blind retreat. The Germans were being forced back, but in a neat and orderly way.

After we had observed the course of the battles for some time, we got the impression that this kind of fighting was going to last for quite a while before the Russians would be able to recapture their own land from the enemy, to say nothing of ours. My husband cut the maps of the war-fronts out of the papers and carefully saved them. Each day he would go over the maps he had collected and with a red pencil underline the towns that had been captured by the Russians. The Michalskis laughingly called this map collection "staff headquarters." When he finally saw one of the fronts liquidated (the first to go was the Kuban front), he tore the corresponding map into little pieces with great satisfaction and threw it into the fire.

We carefully followed the speeches of Churchill and President Roosevelt. Neither of them ever mentioned 1943 as being the end of the war. They spoke instead of 1944 or even 1945 as seeing the final victory over the Germans. However, we continued to delude ourselves with the belief that Germany would capitulate after the crumbling of the famous Berlin-Rome axis. After the capitulation of Italy, all the propaganda in the German press, as well as the skillfully worded articles of the world's greatest liar, Dr. Joseph Goebbels, aimed in one direction: Let's not let 1918 (the year of the Armistice in the First World War) be repeated; we're not going to yield or give up.

As I wrote this in 1943, Hitler and his clique continued to keep the

292

population in the occupied countries under control. Terror raged everywhere, gaining in extent and intensity, and absorbing increasingly greater numbers of victims as the years of the war went by. We in Warsaw felt this particularly acutely after the visit of one or another "important person." For example, in the autumn the capital was honored by the visit of General Governor Dr. Hans Frank[2] (whose seat was on the throne of the Polish Kings in Wawel Castle in Kraków), who in his many speeches gave an idyllic description of the prosperity and harmony reigning in Poland, the most peaceful country in all of Europe. We ourselves were witnesses as Poland's "benefactor" drove through the streets of the town, including ours, Belwederska. We were able to see how, half an hour before, all the corners on both sides of the streets were occupied by detachments of German gendarmes with weapons drawn. Pedestrians were forbidden to cross the street, or even to stop on the sidewalk. When all these defensive measures had been taken along the entire route, several automobiles flashed by. The ones in front and back had machine-gun barrels sticking out on either side. In the middle was Frank's car. Everything took place in a matter of seconds, like in a news reel. It was impossible to make out anything other than the automobiles rushing along and the barrels of the guns.

After the visit of the governor general, the German gendarmes, or so-called "tortoises" (the name derived from the fact that they moved so slowly) became an everyday sight. In the beginning they would walk several together, six to eight at a time, taking up the entire sidewalk and street. They would stop passers-by, for the most part men, and frisk them for hidden weapons. They would also check to see what amount of money was being carried and, if one of those stopped had a fairly large amount of money on him and could not give a satisfactory explanation, he would be arrested, and even if he were set free, the money would be confiscated.

Once Henryk was stopped. Since he had no work card, he tried another means of getting away, which turned out to be effective. He offered a bribe of five hundred zlotys and was set loose. All the Germans took bribes, even the Gestapo. My husband used to joke by saying that Hitler himself could be bought.

We observed the activity of these tortoises from our observation post in the attic. Once my husband saw one of them stop a woman pushing a baby carriage. They gave both her and the carriage a thorough going over. With time the number of those taking part in the "tortoise patrols" increased to twenty or more. Evidently they were afraid of being attacked. We also often observed how they stopped trains and took packages of food away from the travelers. People would jump out of the doors while the train was still in motion. Often, as soon as they heard the cry "buda" (a closed small covered truck, or paddy wagon, used for carrying away people in the roundups), they would throw their packages, bags, and milk jugs out of the train windows. People working for the blacksmith next to the tracks would gather the things up and return them to their rightful owners when they called for them.

In November the Nazis began applying a new form of terror which had a very demoralizing effect on the population. These were public executions held in reprisal for Germans killed by the underground organizations.[3] During the first such execution, twenty people from the Pawiak prison were killed. The executions were held several times a week in various parts of town. This went on for several months.

We ourselves were witnesses to how this awful form of terror took place, as we were able to see it from our attic. First several automobiles drove up full of gendarmes, who took up positions along the street. Pedestrian traffic came to a halt, as did all rail traffic. It was even forbidden to look out of one's window. When all of the preliminaries had been completed, and this lasted for about half an hour, a covered truck would arrive carrying the condemned. They would be escorted from the front and rear by gendarmes in trucks with rifles sticking out on both sides. The underground press said that before their execution, the condemned were administered anaesthetics in order to create a feeling of apathy among them. Their mouths were stopped up with tape, as were their eyes. My husband was only able to see one of the condemned, who was standing on the edge of the platform. He was around eighteen years old.

Several minutes later we heard the shots, and the same trucks now passed back in the opposite direction, carrying dead bodies. All that was left on the streets were streams of blood. The walls behind where the prisoners had stood were splattered with blood and pock-marked from the shower of bullets. A crowd gathered at the spot of this macabre execution. In a matter of a moment a little altar had been set up and strewn with flowers and a cross had been etched on the wall. The women would dip their scarves in the blood of the martyrs and would fall down on the street and pray for the souls of the fallen.

In spite of the executions, the acts of sabotage did not cease. Trains carrying guns and ammunition continued to be derailed, and Nazi butchers continued to be killed. It was at this time, too, that mass roundups began to be held on the streets of the town. Trolleys, horse-carts, rickshaws, and other means of transportation would be stopped.

Even pedestrians would be picked up. Passengers on trains and on the small commuter lines would be taken away. All those caught on the street would be sent by the Nazis to the old ghetto where, after the elimination of Jews, a penal camp for Poles was established.

In the first half of December the Michalskis' youngest son, Maniek, was captured in a trolley. Despair fell upon their home as soon as a woman friend who had seen the incident told his mother about it. The mother was worried sick that her boy would be shot by the Nazis. The days of Sodom and Gomorrah descended upon their household. Mr. Michalski did not open his shop at all. The entire family devoted itself to finding someone who would be able to get their boy set free. Finally, a blue policeman undertook to arrange the matter. He said that he knew many people on Litewska Street where supposedly the prisoners were first taken. Mrs. Michalski sent a food package but her son never received it, for the simple reason that he was not there.

A second package met the same fate. The policeman accepted 40,000 zlotys which he was supposed to use in order to get Maniek set free. He sat in restaurants drinking with Henryk and his father for a week, putting it off from day to day. In the end, he just took 5,000 zlotys for his efforts and was never heard from again.

In the meantime Maniek sent his mother a note through a boy who had been set free from Pawiak after spending sixty days dismantling the burned-down buildings in the ghetto. Maniek was working on Karmelicka Street, and he asked for a package of food and for his family to try to get him out.

The Michalskis went to the corner of Karmelicka and Leszno Streets, where a food store was located. This store was a "rendevous spot" where it was possible to communicate with the prisoners. Here it was that the Michalskis were able to negotiate directly with the leader of Maniek's work group about getting him released. Luck was with them this time, for after paying another 5,000 zlotys, Maniek was freed after several more days. In all this had cost 12,000 zlotys, all of which was covered by our factory.

---

1. **AK assassinations.** The AK carried out numerous assassinations, both on high-ranking Germans and on socially prominent collaborators with the Germans, for example on the Austrian-born actor Karol Juliusz "Igo" Sym (1896-1941) and the film actor Kazimierz Junosza-Stępowski (1880-1943) and his wife.
2. **Frank, Hans M.** (1900-1946). An early Nazi party member and Hitler's personal lawyer, Frank was placed in charge of the "Generalgouvernement" (the non-annexed part of Poland) with its seat in Kraków, from where he instituted a

ruthless reign of terror against both Poles and Jews. Convicted at the Nuremberg trials of war crimes and crimes against humanity, he was executed in Nuremberg.

3. **November street executions**. In fact such executions took place from the middle of October, the first being on October 16, 1943, the victims being taken from a local prison on Dzielna Street.

59

MANIEK CAUGHT WITH A CACHE
OF ARMS

Our lives during this period underwent no significant change: always the same fear, vigilance, and hypersensitivity to everything going on around us. We continued to follow with bated breath the course of all political events, but nothing was happening to make us think that the war might soon be at an end. The communiqués coming from German staff headquarters always had the same ring: "planned withdrawal from the enemy."

In the end we had to admit that we were going to have to prepare ourselves for spending the winter in the tinsmith's shop. This would be no easy matter, but since there was no other choice than death, we had to grit our teeth and gather together the strength necessary to endure. When the cold autumn days began, it was easy to see that in spite of our overcoats it was going to be impossible to survive in the attic because of the draughts. To remedy this, Zygmunt installed storm windows. He covered the cracks with paper and covered the other window with cardboard and wood. The windows of the room down-stairs where we slept were completely closed over with cardboard. Since the shutters outside were shut in any case, this gave no cause for suspicion.

It was terribly damp, so Zygmunt went after the sawdust oven we had once used in our workshop on Krochmalna Street. This oven would only burn for three hours after being lighted. When the fire went out it would be just as cold as before. We lit the fire before going to bed, but only on days when Zygmunt was working for fear that the smoke coming out of the chimney might give away our presence. On Sundays and holidays, by the time we went to bed our bedding would be thoroughly damp. We had a hot water bottle which fortunate circumstances had allowed us to preserve all this time, and we would fill it with hot water and heat our bed in this way.

Christmas was on its way. Our material situation improved considerably, and by New Year's we had paid off all debts except for the 950 zlotys we owed Father Edward Święcki. When it had been necessary to ransom my husband from the police station, it had been he who had given the lion's share: 8,000 zlotys and 50 dollars, all of which we eventually managed to repay. We owed him a tremendous debt of gratitude and respect, for he came to our aid many times.

Our warm slippers enjoyed great popularity in the marketplace, so our earnings were good. Because of this, everyone around us was content, and this had a positive effect on us as well. In our circumstances money was the only security. It was the height of satisfaction when we sold every single item in stock before the Christmas holidays. Thus the holidays, even if spent in comparative solitude, passed quietly and, all things considered, rather pleasantly for us.

On the second day of the holidays Marysia Michalski visited us, bringing with her one of her daughters, Father Święcki, and Henryk. As usual, my conversations with her cousin were very interesting. In contrast to the holidays spent the previous year at Mrs. Zieliński's, these were incomparably nicer, calmer, and more satisfying.

The time from Christmas to New Year's passed quickly. At midnight the Germans greeted the New Year by firing off shots from all manner of weapons. And so, the year 1944 had arrived.

On January 4th the Russians crossed the old border from 1939, and from that day on we began following the progress of the Russian army with increased interest. We felt that perhaps now at last, when the strongly fortified cities had been taken, the advance would be quicker. However, as time went by, we saw that we were once more to be deceived. The Germans continued to defend themselves just as strongly as before, though they kept moving backwards. Certain cities such as Tarnopol were held for several weeks, and after passing from the hands of one side into the other, they had been almost completely destroyed.

Three weeks into the new year something happened to the Michalski family which shook all of us deeply and took away our peace for a long time to come. On that day, Zygmunt came home in the evening extremely upset and distraught. He told us that at four o'clock that afternoon, when everyone was sitting and working peacefully in the workshop on Krochmalna Street, a commotion suddenly broke out in the yard and they heard the heavy steps of hob-nailed boots. Maniek went to the window and was only able to spit out the words: "It's a trap! They've got me!"

If he had acted immediately and run out the other door he might still have been able to save himself, for the stairwell was in ruins and he could have run out through one of the open doors, leaped in among the rubble, and made it into the next courtyard. However, he began putting on his sweater, sportcoat, and jacket. By the time the German gendarmes arrived, Maniek was all set to go. The gendarmes were shown the way by a man whom Maniek recognized, one of his friends from the underground. This was how he had made out so quickly that he had been betrayed.

The Germans ordered Maniek to give them the keys to the ground floor apartment. There they uncovered a package of arms hidden under a pile of sawdust. They took this but did not touch anything else. Next they began checking the identification papers of everyone present. The main person they were looking for was "Józef," the name Henryk used in the underground. They didn't find anyone named Józef, so they took only Maniek, along with the keys to the ground-floor room, and left.

Although Zygmunt took sawdust from that pile in the workshop to burn in the stove every day, he had no idea that anything was hidden underneath it. That very day, he said, he had been keeping the keys to the room on his own person but had fortunately remembered to return them to Maniek. If the keys had been found on him, and if "Józef" had been discovered, it is terrible to think what would have happened both to their families and to us. Only a year earlier all the men in the entire building would have been arrested for the discovery of the weapons, in accordance with the notion of "collective responsibility," but this time it only went as far as Maniek. We had no idea why.

In a flash the news spread to all the other tenants. There was no limit to their rage at the Michalskis. They began gossiping and whispering that now they understood why the Michalski family needed so many workplaces, for they were engaged in the manufacture of... arms! In a word, the neighbors were so outraged that old Mrs. Michalski was afraid to pass through the yard.

By a fortunate coincidence Henryk had managed to escape. If the gendarmes had only come half an hour later, they would have found all three brothers in the workshop together with their father. At the precise moment the Germans arrived, the three of them were riding a trolley on their way to work.

From that moment on the Michalski household was plunged into chaos, bewilderment, and horrible fear. No one knew whether Maniek would be able to hold up under the awful torture that was used in order to obtain information. After all, the boy was only seventeen years old, frail, and had a lung disease. We knew that the Germans possessed instruments of torture that were able to pry open the tightest-lipped mouths. The best proof of that was the person who had given Maniek away.

He had been their commandant and given them weapons to hide, and he was the only person who knew where they were kept. At first people thought that he was an agent in the service of the Germans, for Henryk had said that the man had been quite insistent about knowing the hiding place. Under pressure Henryk relented and pointed it out to him. After all, he was their commander. Later it turned out that the man, whose name in the underground was Stanisław, was an upright person. "Stanisław" worked in a photography studio and was arrested there along with the owner's daughter. Buckling under the pressure of torture by the Gestapo, he gave the names of eight other persons, including Maniek. In spite of this, "Stanisław" did his best to protect his comrades. For example, among other things, he had listed a pastry shop located on Twarda Street as being the location of underground meetings. When they brought him in a sadly beaten state to the place he had indicated, they found no one present, and the owner insisted that the shop was not his. They confronted the owner with "Stanisław," who in his state of exhaustion had fainted three times. "Stanisław" stated that this was not the owner of the shop and that he had never seen him before in his life, saving the man's life. It was supposed to be the same with Maniek. "Stanisław" brought the gendarmes at a time when he thought that they would not find any of the persons they were looking for, hoping that they would merely take the weapons and leave.

Only much later was it understood why Stanisław had first led the gendarmes to the pastry shop on Twarda Street. He wanted in this way to warn everyone that he had been arrested so that the owner would have the opportunity to inform the other members of the organization.

60

IN THE WAKE OF MANIEK'S ARREST

After going over the affair in minute detail we concluded that the cause of Maniek's downfall had been lack of attention to detail. "Stanisław" had been arrested on January 19th. The next day Maniek had gone to the photographer's to pick up a packet of illegal literature but had found the shop locked. The shop was one of the underground press's distribution points. Maniek calmly returned home without bothering to find out the reason for the store being closed. That evening both brothers had discussed the matter briefly and decided that Maniek should go next day to find out what had happened, but he did not go. Some of the members had known already on Wednesday about "Stanisław's" arrest and they were to have warned him about it. However, when they came to the ground floor room and found the padlock hanging on the door, they turned around, not knowing that there was another apartment in the same entry only one floor higher, where they could have found Maniek. Thus, circumstances had conspired against poor Maniek and resulted in this catastrophe.

It was only after the event that we learned that our former ground-floor apartment had been serving as the location for AK officer training school lectures, which were attended by both brothers. My husband never asked Henryk and Maniek about their work; we knew only as much as they told us. As time went on, we were able to deduce from various facts that Henryk occupied a very responsible position in the resistance movement. He no longer pasted posters on the walls about town or scribbled slogans such as "We'll avenge Pawiak." He often told my husband, who had also served in the army, about how to use the kind of machine gun popularly known as the "sprinkler," as well as other kinds of weapons. Once he even sought my husband's advice on whether it would be all right to keep weapons in the attic where we were staying. It never came to that, for he later changed his mind, considering us too "dangerous." He was afraid we might betray him in case of an accident.

After Maniek's arrest, fear gripped the Michalski family, for they knew that he was going to be tortured. However, Maniek gave no one away. Since they were sure that the entire family would be searched—Henryk in particular—everyone left their apartment to stay with friends and neighbors. As soon as their friends learned that the matter concerned weapons, they were received very unwillingly. Old Mr. Michalski and Leon slept with Leon's wife's relatives in Grochów. Henryk's wife Marysia was more afraid than anyone. She was sure that the German gendarmes would come in at any moment and, not finding her husband, take her hostage, as happened often enough. She put her four children in the care of her maid, who had never heard of the incident at all. Marysia herself went to sleep at her sister's—Janek's wife—who added more fuel to the fire, as she concocted the most horrible kind of theories, as if she needed to arouse any more panic in her sister than was already there. Finally she let her know that she was afraid even to have her in her apartment. Since Marysia had a priest in her family, she managed to obtain a document stating that she was separated from her husband. The only person remaining in her apartment was old Mrs. Michalski. All broken and bent down with grief at the loss of her youngest and most precious, she remained where she was.

We too remained in our place in the old tinsmith's shed, depending, as always, on the ups and downs of fate. When Zygmunt first told us what had happened, my husband decided that for the moment no one should go to work. Operations in the shop came to a standstill, for we were afraid of a second visit from the German gendarmes. A second time they might be less indulgent and take away whomever they found. We were also afraid that the shop might be under the observation of plainclothes Gestapo agents, and that they might be able to trace Henryk through the people coming in and out of the shop.

It is difficult for me to express in words what we lived through. I was utterly certain that our last hour had struck. My husband kept explaining to me that if the Germans had wanted to search any farther, they would immediately have sealed up the shop and taken down the names of those present. He kept repeating over and over again, "You'll

302

see. They won't look any further." I was possessed by a single thought, that everyone had gone into hiding and left us high and dry. My husband soon lost his equilibrium and became just as frightened as I was.

Zygmunt, who had never betrayed any fear in our presence, now only dropped by for a few minutes, and then only to bring us the necessary food. I felt that he too was living in great fear, thinking that the Gestapo were liable to come calling at any minute. Everyone kept saying that the affair was likely to drag out for a long time. Often in similar circumstances the Gestapo employed the tactic of letting a certain amount of time elapse before reappearing, so as to put people off their guard.

On the day Maniek was arrested it was cold and windy. We sat next to the gas stove and, in spite of the heat coming from it, shivered with cold. The last several months seemed like paradise to us in comparison with our present situation. Only now did we come to know what fear was really like. We were certain that every automobile that stopped on the street nearby had come for us. At the sound of German, which was by no means a rarity here, our hearts would start pounding. Periodically it would seem to me that I heard someone talking in the yard. I would leap up and run to the kitchen window and listen carefully, but everything would be quiet. When evening finally came we would lie down to rest, but we would be unable to fall asleep. Once more we would lie there, listening. Finally we would fall into a doze, ready to leap up at the slightest sound. In the morning the feeble rays of dawn would seep through the window panes and we would get up and dress wearily for a new day of agony. Of first importance was to send Zygmunt to Henryk to find out whether the Gestapo had visited anyone during the night.

It turned out that not. Henryk had taken all the finished goods out of the workshop, and Zygmunt had taken all the unfinished work to his home. After Zygmunt returned, we took council with him to decide what we should do with ourselves. We had become convinced that the tinshop was our only possible shelter. We had nothing to do but put ourselves in the hand of divine Providence and stay put. However, we did decide to eliminate everything in the attic and set up another hiding place in the tinshop. My husband had already picked out the place quite by accident.

61

OUR NEW CUBBY HOLE

In the beginning of winter an order was issued stating that electricity was to be cut off to Polish-owned shops operating in the German quarter. Since the fuse-box was located in the attic, we thought that the people coming to shut off the electricity would have to go up there, so we eliminated all traces of our presence. No one ever came. On this account, however, we were forced to sit for an entire day in a little vestibule next to a row of storage sheds belonging to the building's tenants, the door of which led out into the garden.

The entrance to this vestibule was from the room in which we slept. It looked more like a storage shed. My husband pointed out that the anteroom had no ceiling but a sloping roof. The thought occurred to him that it might be possible to put in a ceiling and make a hiding place for us there in case of need. Two or three people would be able to fit in the space between the ceiling and the roof. We now decided to put this project in motion, and who would be able to do it if not Zygmunt? After taking the measurements of the ceiling area with my husband's help, Zygmunt ordered some wood at a carpenter's.

Mr. Michalski did not open his workshop on the day following Maniek's arrest for fear the Gestapo might take him as a co-conspirator. Next morning Henryk came to spend the day as well as the night with us. He had suffered through the past two nights with some friends who had received him most timidly and reluctantly. He came to seek my husband's advice as to what he should do.

I must admit that Henryk's appearance had a very depressing effect on me. His former self-assurance had evaporated, and a feeling of depression had come to take its place. At that moment I realized that he was obsessed, with immense resignation just as we were, with the death that seemed to be awaiting him. He yielded to this idea passively and it never occurred to him to struggle against it, to defend himself, to somehow oppose it. After all he had freedom of movement and possibilities we never had. It seemed that my husband had withstood the pressure better than Henryk, even though we had already been going through this daily uncertainty for the past eighteen months, and had often stood face to face with death.

My husband matter-of-factly told Henryk to look around for a new place for the factory, someplace where he could also spend the night instead of wandering back and forth every night to a different apartment. There was no longer any question of working in the place on Krochmalna Street, for the Gestapo might appear there at any moment. In fact, the neighbors, for fear of their own skin and because of their hostility toward the Michalski family, might well put the gendarmes onto him themselves. Just because he had escaped once, there was no need to tempt fate a second time. There was also the question of his father; he should also be able to sleep with Henryk and not have to go for the night to Grochów, which was on the edge of the Praga district on the other side of the river.

In the morning old Mr. Michalski came, accompanied by Leon. When they met Henryk in the workshop, they both jumped on him immediately. A real storm broke loose, for the father put all the blame for Maniek's arrest on Henryk alone. He said that he had been foolish to put his own responsibilities on someone else's shoulders.

"We already have one victim in the family," he shouted, "now you want me to be the next one instead of you! You'd better take care of the responsibilities you already have!" (He was thinking of us). "I don't want to hear another word," he continued, "I've had it up to here with everything."

Leon, the middle son, kept egging him on, feeding the fires of his anger and outrage. We sat that day in our attic hunched over and beset by a new fear: What was going to become of us if we were left without a roof over our heads?

Henryk, acting on the advice of my husband, with the help of some friends found two rooms for the new workshop on Żurawia Street. In spite of the high rent, my husband told him to take it and carry the things over from the old workshop on Krochmalna. Above all it was important to begin work again, for work was the only thing that would help disperse the clouds of gloom that had settled everywhere. Zygmunt took care of the move.

It was imperative for us to separate Mr. Michalski from Leon, because he had a very bad effect on the old man, setting him against his brother and reminding him of what we all already knew, that Henryk was the cause of everything, and that since he had already taken one illegal affair on his shoulders, he had no right to involve himself in a second one and expose others to danger. Fortuitously, Mr. Michalski, who was extremely sensitive during this time, took offense at something Leon said, became very angry, and moved his bed into the tinsmith's shop.

Now, because of the misfortunes which had touched Mr. Michalski, as well as from the fear which now never left him alone, he lost his equilibrium, experiencing now on his own skin a little of what we had been going through for the past two years. He complained that when he spent the night at home, he knew not a moment's peace. It seemed to him that someone was constantly ringing at the gate or that a car was driving up in front of the building to pick him up. He would start at each little sound and at every heavy footstep. The despair of his wife, who sat all night crying beneath the portrait of her son, merely added to his own state of depression.

No one was better able to understand what his soul was going through, no one could have felt the tragedy of Maniek's agonies and suffering better and more profoundly than we, who had been living under the threat of death for so long. Old Mr. Michalski was so wretched and woebegone during this period that it was difficult to talk with him. Every word just seemed to aggravate him all the more.

After we had recovered from the first shock of fear (the Germans never did come back), my husband brought up with Mr. Michalski the delicate question of our continued stay in the tinsmith's shop. Mr. Michalski answered, "And where do you think you're going to go?" This single sentence served to convince us that we were not in danger of losing the roof over our heads, and that, in our present situation, was more important than anything else.

This period was extremely difficult to endure for all of us. All of Warsaw was being crushed beneath the weight of its woes and worries. Just days after Maniek's arrest, the AK assassinated a number of Germans occupying important positions, among others General Kutschera,[1] who was set to become Himmler's (head of the Nazi Schutzstaffel, or SS) son-in-law. The attack on him had supposedly been made purposely on the day of his wedding. Kutschera had organized the destruction of the Warsaw ghetto, and the AK had already made three unsuccessful attempts on his life. A real storm broke loose in the capital. On February 5th a hundred-million zloty involuntary contribution was levied on the entire population of Warsaw. Soon afterward, fifty persons were shot in public on 6 Senatorska Street, next to the rubble of a burned-down building. At 5 Leszno Street the Nazis hung a group of people from the front balconies. The corpses were left hanging there for two days. The following day they shot all prisoners in the Pawiak prison. Mass arrests were made in apartments; it came to the point that no one left his home except in dire need.

Henryk carried poison on his person to use in case of arrest, in order to spare himself the pain of torture during interrogation. Old Mr. Michalski was drinking out of despair, and that by itself was a tragedy for us, as he slept in his workshop, saying that he was just too afraid to sleep at home.

A week had passed since Maniek's arrest, and Zygmunt had installed and finished our hiding place according to my husband's instructions. He covered it over with dirty plaster in such a way that it presented a totally innocent impression. We eliminated all traces of our presence in the attic. We felt that by staying in the new hiding place we would calm Mr. Michalski's fears.

The early winter mornings would find us already on our feet. After a gulp of hot coffee and a modest breakfast, for which we usually had no appetite, we would go up to our little burrow beneath the roof. We climbed up there by a ladder which Mr. Michalski would take away once we were up and situated in the rubbish room. There was a square hole in the ceiling through which a person could just barely fit. After climbing up into our hiding place, it was closed from the inside by three boards which matched the rest of the ceiling. It was completely dark inside except for specks of light coming through cracks in the boards. It was also very uncomfortable; one could only lie down or sit up supported on one's elbow, touching at the same time the sloping roof. Zygmunt brought us several kilos of straw which we used to fill a mattress and fashion a makeshift pillow.

We had two blankets with us, as well as a hot water bottle for our feet and a thermos of hot tea. In addition, Zygmunt loaned my husband his sheepskin coat. Even so, lying down for an average of eight hours a day was pure torture. We also had to beware not to make any noise, because the anteroom was adjacent to a storage shed which was frequently visited by tenants coming to pick up coal, wood, potatoes, and other things.

For lack of anything to do we listened to the children playing in the yard, to their merry chatter and gay laughter. Sometimes the neighbor women would stand out in the yard and gossip with their friends. No one ever suspected that two miserable hounded people were lying right next to them in a little burrow beneath the roof, afraid even of the light of day.

In the afternoon, Mr. Michalski would lock up his workshop and let us out of our hiding place. Sometimes, when he had been drinking a lot, he would completely forget about the rest of creation and stay until seven o'clock or later in the evening. These were terrible times for us. Except for Sunday, we never even saw daylight. Our heads were always heavy and aching.

We lost whatever was left of our strength and health. We looked like shadows. Real day for us began after the workshop was locked up tight. My husband would begin working while I would start dinner. Sometimes my husband would have so much work to do that he wouldn't even go to bed but would stay up all night working. Then he would take a nap for several hours in our hiding place. This had its good side, because then time did not weigh so heavily on him.

The hiding place was a real torture chamber; still, it gave us a feeling of security. It always seemed strange to me, and I could never understand why, but when my husband covered the entrance and Mr. Michalski took away the ladder, I was invariably overcome by a feeling of peace, and these were the only hours during the day when I really felt safe. At the beginning, I had been tormented by gloomy thoughts. It seemed to me that this place had so much rubbish and junk lying around it that it would have been impossible to search through it properly. So when the Gestapo came either as the result of Maniek's confessions or looking for Henryk, they wouldn't bother themselves overly much thinking about it but would simply blow the whole place up sky high, with us in it. This had actually happened on other occasions.

After a while, however, when no one had come, I drove such thoughts out of my mind. Thus I came to know what the feeling of peace is really like. It is the world's most valuable feeling, and no one is able to recognize it at the time one actually possesses it. My unattainable dream for the moment was to know at least a modicum of peace and to feel that nothing was threatening us, a feeling I had not known for the past five years of the war. Was that too much to ask?

It was our good fortune that winter that year was very mild. The worst it got was seven degrees below freezing. It would have been much worse if the temperature had reached twenty degrees below or more. Then our blankets would never have been able to fend off the cold.

---

1. **Kutschera, Franz (1904-1944).** An Austrian-born high-ranking Nazi officer and SS and Police Leader (Brigadefuerer) in Warsaw. Sentenced to death by the AK (Home Army), he was assassinated in front of SS headquarters by members of a conspiratorial unit of the Boy Scouts known as the Grey Legions. In retaliation for the deaths of Kutschera and two other German officials, the Germans publically executed over four hundred prisoners, taken mainly from Pawiak prison.

62

MR. MICHALSKI'S DRINKING
PROBLEM

At this time, alongside our other miseries, the drunkenness of old Mr. Michalski caused much unpleasantness. One day, for example, Mr. Michalski forgot to take down the ladder from our entrance and put it in its hiding place. It turned out that he had spent the entire day drinking in the restaurant across the street, after locking the workshop in front. When my husband looked at his watch and saw that it was getting to be six o'clock in the evening, he decided to go downstairs and find out what was going on.

Since it was already dark, he cautiously peered out through the pane in the front door and saw some stranger coming out of the restaurant leading Mr. Michalski, who was tottering and practically falling down. The stranger took Mr. Michalski up to the shop and, after staying there with him for a while, left. Mr. Michalski used his final reserve of consciousness to remember that he had to lock the shop. However, he only managed to shut the door before falling down on the floor, passed out. Then my husband leapt out of hiding and locked up the workshop properly. After that he tried to help Mr. Michalski get up. As soon as he came to, Mr. Michalski immediately broke out in bitter tears. Then he got angry and started to break things. He kept beating on the table with a hammer and shouting. Finally, with the aid of great patience and kindness, my husband was able to get him to go to bed. His loud snoring indicated that he had fallen into a deep sleep.

Henryk and Leon came by to stay with us that evening, as if they had a presentiment that something had happened. Our talking roused

Mr. Michalski from his slumbers and then, to our great consternation, we heard him start making threats toward us. He laughed at us for wanting to become "foreigners" (he was probably thinking about the Hotel Poland incident).

"But that won't do you any good either," he said. "They'll get you anyway. I'll see to it myself."

He even threatened his older son, saying that if he got in his way he would take care of him too. Finally he threw himself on Leon and tried to hit him. Leon eventually succeeded in calming him down. It ended with us all having several rounds of vodka together and finally lying down to sleep at around two o'clock in the morning. It was with a heavy heart, for the words spoken by Mr. Michalski while drunk had given us an indication of what he was really thinking to himself when sober.

The next morning, Mr. Michalski made no mention of yesterday's threats. He acted as if nothing at all had happened. We for our part also remained silent, but there was a palpable feeling of tension between us. I began to be afraid of Mr. Michalski and his threats. My husband's arguments and explanations did nothing to help. The thorn had pierced deep into my heart.

It sometimes happened that one or two times a week he would not open the shop. On such days I was even more afraid than usual that he would report us to the gendarmes. Henryk told us that he too felt that something had gone wrong with his father under the influence of his sorrow for Maniek, and they were afraid he was losing his mind. At home he kept threatening to burn down the apartment, and his wife was living in constant fear that he might put his threats into action. He kept repeating that he had some kind of diabolical plan in store for everyone.

There was no news from Maniek, and no way to get through to the Gestapo. Since we feared that Maniek might give us away, we spent all day in our hiding place, without air or light. We spent the evenings with Mr. Michalski, who was always drunk. It wasn't every day that he was in a state like before, but he would still be "potted," as his sons called it. He was very angry and upset at the whole world, and kept saying over and over, "Everyone in the whole world is still alive, only Maniek isn't." What kind of answer could one make to that?

On this account my husband wasn't able to work, so production lagged seriously behind. He asked Henryk to take his father over to the new workshop. Henryk did what he could, but after spending one night with him, his father moved back with us. To add to our difficulties, another horrible incident occurred.

On Grojecka Street, in some vegetable gardens belonging to a Volksdeutsch couple, a bunker had been set up in a greenhouse where thirty-seven Jews had been hiding out for a year or more. One day the Gestapo drove up and, without making any kind of search, went straight to the bunker and took away all of the Jews in it as well as the Volksdeutsch, after beating him and his wife to insensibility. This news was brought to us by Mr. Michalski. Everyone had been talking about it in one of the local restaurants. This was the last drop of bitterness to fill an already overflowing cup. Mr. Michalski was overcome with a wave of panic, and he became so hypersensitive that he was just shaking with fear.

On more than one occasion we had reason to envy our fellow countrymen who had died unknowingly in the first wave at Treblinka. We understood and shared Mr. Michalski's fears, but what were we supposed to do? It was certainly true that one and a half years of terror and living in constant tension was able to undermine even the strongest of characters.

The news about the bunker turned out to be true, for the underground army's Informational Bulletin printed the story a week later. The question as to who had denounced them was never satisfactorily answered. Mr. Michalski said that it had been a plumber who had been called in to install central heating in the greenhouse, even though measures of utmost caution had been applied. Supposedly he had been brought in and taken out of the greenhouse blindfolded. Jula, when she came to visit Henryk and us, had another explanation. She said that some weapons had once been found hidden under some manure there, and that ever afterwards the gardens were kept under surveillance by the Gestapo. Besides that, too many people knew about the existence of the hiding place. In any case, the catastrophe touched us in a very painful spot.

To make matters still worse, we were now beset with yet another problem. Because of the order issued by the German authorities, in the middle of February electricity was cut off to the Poles. Not seeing what else to do, we decided to hook into the main electrical line, which ran through our attic, and run a line downstairs around the meter. We arranged for Zygmunt to buy whatever would be necessary for installing the electricity. Unfortunately, he did not show his face the following day. When he did not come around for several days we became worried, for we were sure that Zygmunt's absence was connected to Maniek's arrest, even though four weeks had already elapsed. Our fear reached even greater heights when Mr. Michalski told us that Leon had also not returned home.

We learned from Henryk that Zygmunt and Leon had left together the day before in the direction of a tavern on Grzybowska Street, famous for its fine "bimber" (home brew). As it turned out later, Zygmunt and Leon had gotten very drunk and had become involved in a row in which a German soldier, also drunk, had taken their side. Communicating by means of signs, for neither Zygmunt nor Leon knew any German, they went from there to yet another tavern and had a few more rounds, after which they lost any idea of what they were doing. As they were leaving the tavern they started bothering some boy who ran home, scared to death, and called his mother. The woman, when she saw the German and the two civilians, whom she took for Volksdeutsch, begged them to leave her boy in peace. She ended by offering them five hundred zlotys as a peace offering. At that point Zygmunt cried out "What do mean, five hundred? Fifteen hundred at least!" As if this were not bad enough, the German began firing off "salutes" into the air and attracted the attention of the neighbors, who telephoned the German gendarmes. They arrived in no time, disarmed the soldier, and took all three of them away to the station.

After twenty-four hours Zygmunt and Leon were handed over to the Polish authorities in the Office of Investigation. When we learned about the whole affair, we were extremely surprised, particularly since Leon, who feared Germans like the plague, had let himself become involved so frivolously in such a scene.

For fear of any unforeseen consequences, my husband urged Henryk to ransom them from the police as quickly as possible. It was fortunate that they had been handed over to the Polish authorities, which had probably meant the difference between life and death. The Germans would usually execute people for similar actions or for theft. Several days had passed when Leon's wife finally found someone who was able to take care of the matter for 15,000 zlotys, all of which was covered by our company, that is, by Henryk and us, as if by way of a loan. However, they never did repay the money.

After a week in jail, both drunkards regained their freedom. After Zygmunt's return, my husband read him the riot act. Zygmunt was genuinely shaken by the incident and promised not to have another drink until the war was over. At least that was what he said.

The day before Zygmunt and Leon were released, Mr. Michalski helped my husband install a line around the electric meter. Because of this, we were able to burn as much electricity as we needed, and we didn't have to limit ourselves as before.

Several peaceful days passed, and March arrived. We were glad that spring was on its way. One day we were once again sitting until late in the evening in our "burrow beneath the roof." It was already seven o'clock and the shop was still open, and Mr. Michalski still hadn't put up the ladder. We sat there apprehensively, for we understood that it was going to be another one of those "unforgettable evenings," not just a "potted" one but a thoroughly "soused" one. Finally we heard his unsteady steps beneath us and the ladder being more or less stood up. A well-known sight greeted our eyes. At that moment Zygmunt arrived and had surprisingly little trouble putting Mr. Michalski to sleep on the couch. Soon, to our immeasurable satisfaction, we heard his loud snoring.

Zygmunt had come to tell us that Mr. Michalski had got so drunk that he wasn't even able to walk and had tried to crawl on all fours across the street to the shop. However, he hadn't been able to make it quite across. Instead, he had lain down on the tracks of the Wilanów narrow-gauge railway with the evident aim of taking a snooze, but his plans were foiled by the arriving train. Several passers-by took him off the tracks and guided him to the workshop, where he still had enough sense to bar the door with an iron rod and tumble down into the storeroom. Zygmunt's wife, who was concerned about us, peeped through the panes in the door and saw him lying on the floor passed out. He evidently had lain like that for several hours before coming to somewhat and remembering our existence.

That evening Henryk came to spend the night with us. After sleeping for several hours, Mr. Michalski woke up and began uttering threats. He kept repeating that no matter what we did, we would still end up as "goat-skin" (fine-leather—the only "good use" for human skin), and that we shouldn't delude ourselves into thinking that we would live to see the end of the war; in fact he himself would see to it that we didn't.

My husband lost his temper, and when Mr. Michalski once more began bullying him, he could not hold back any longer and began shouting, "You only know how to persecute and torture a person! If it's really so hard for you, we can leave right this instant and go wherever our legs carry us!"

He unburdened himself of all the sorrow and bitterness which had been welling up inside him all this time. Mr. Michalski remembered these words, for some time later he brought up the subject in a conversation and tried to justify himself. My husband intended to ask him why he continually made threats at us, but the subject was so slippery and sensitive that he decided to wait for another occasion. However, Mr. Michalski carefully avoided further conversation with him, as if he were ashamed of his outbursts. Maybe his conscience was bothering him.

63

NEWS OF MANIEK'S EXECUTION

Why am I writing about all these incidents? ...In order to emphasize how foolhardy people were during this time—not only those around us, but absolutely everyone. On the one hand they hid Jews, while on the other hand they were turning them in to the Nazis. The main causes for the latter were: drunkenness, jealous wives and, worst of all, pointless gossip. All of them played into the hands of the Nazis. Under the influence of anger and momentary thoughtlessness, a steady stream of betrayed wives and faithless lovers carried their denunciations to the Nazis.

Because of alcohol and unnecessary disclosures in bars and taverns, which were always full of agents, thousands of Poles and Jews paid with their lives for the thoughtlessness of others. They worked with the underground organizations, but without bothering to maintain the proper security, as if it were all really a joke. We must admit that they were great patriots though, and we blessed them for it from the bottom of our hearts. Our own protector was no drunk, but he could be extremely careless. He knew very little about conspiracy, but he was a true patriot.

Our only moral support was Father Edward Święcki. Since the Michalski family was deeply religious, whatever Father Święcki said was law for them. More than once in difficult circumstances we would have been left high and dry if it had not been for their fear of the priest, whom we have to thank to a large extent for our own lives and for that of our child.

March 19th was the name-day for Józef. According to Polish tradition, all men named Józef celebrate their name-day on that date. Because my husband had the same name, and since we had been living on the Aryan side for some time now, it had become the custom for people to celebrate his name-day.

He and I had a talk and decided to hold a small party that day for the Michalski family in order to smoothe things over with them if possible over a few drinks of vodka. This was not a very wise move on our part, for it might have attracted the attention of the neighbors, who were sure to be intrigued by the fact that so many people had assembled in the workshop on a Sunday. However, we decided for once to throw caution to the winds, and we prepared an excellent dinner, at least excellent for the fifth year of the war. Most importantly, we prepared a large amount of liquor, also against our better judgement. Even our gloomy little room with its cracked walls took on a festive appearance. The previous evening Zygmunt and my husband had scrubbed the floor, and I had washed the curtains. Instead of a tablecloth we covered the table with a sheet, one from the German barracks purchased at the bazaar which I had washed as well.

The entire Michalski family, including Marysia's sister and her husband, Janek, as well as Zygmunt turned out in full, bringing flowers and sweets. As a precaution against gossiping neighbors, Mr. Michalski arrived early and opened the front door. He let the guests in one at a time without attracting anyone's attention. The vodka put everyone in a festive mood. Zygmunt immediately became drunk. The guests were merry and gay. Henryk's wife Marysia brought my husband a little basket of white lilac tied up with a red ribbon and handed it to him on behalf of her children. This was a very kind gesture and touched us deeply. At the same time it reminded us of our own child, who in two weeks would be having his second birthday (for we Jews celebrate birthdays). Almost a year and a half had passed since we had last seen him. I tried to imagine what he looked like now, and sadness descended upon my heart. I forgot for a moment about my guests and the name-day and was carried away in my thoughts to those peaceful, happy days before the war.

I was aroused from my reverie by Mr. Michalski's voice, which announced that it was getting dark and that people should be heading home. Everyone left by the front door and the shop was closed. Once more we were left by ourselves, sunk in depression, wondering when we too would be able to walk freely out onto the street without fear of attracting attention.

The month of March passed with no major changes. In the beginning of April, the Michalskis were informed that Maniek, together with a group of more than twenty other people, had been executed on Senatorska Street. Mrs. Michalski was so overcome by despair that she no longer went to trade at the bazaar but sat at home crying for days on end. Mr. Michalski didn't open his shop for several days. He didn't come home either, so no one knew where he was. Except for Zygmunt, who dropped by in the evening for a while, no one came to see us. Maniek's death touched us very deeply too.

I remembered a certain conversation I had had with him the preceding year when I was staying in their apartment. It was winter, and we were sitting in the kitchen reading aloud an article from the underground press sent over by Henryk. The article described the German rout and defeat at Stalingrad. It told of the terrible battles which had taken place, the awful starvation in the besieged town and, finally, the rout of the German army and the defeat of the famous general Paulus. The news put me in very good spirits. Finally, after so many years of triumph, the Germans were beginning to withdraw. A ray of hope now shone in my weary heart. Almost without my realizing it, my lips started saying, "Maniek, what do you think? Do you think we will live through the war?"

Maniek replied unhesitatingly, "I will for sure, but I don't know about you."

After Maniek's death, the words of this poor quiet boy returned to me vividly. He was so polite, obedient, and had done so much to make our lives easier. We were very sorry for him. He died the death of a true patriot. I kept thinking to myself how they must have tortured him to get the names of other members of the underground. But Maniek betrayed no one, and died a hero's death.

We wanted to express our sympathy and condolences to the Michalskis. I kept thinking over the words I would say, full of warmth and feeling, but everything fell apart the day Mr. Michalski first came back after the news of Maniek's death. His deep black eyes fell on me and seemed to cry, "My child is dead and you are still living, and I am the one who is helping you to live."

But his tight lips remained shut. I could see that it was all he could do to keep from falling on me right then and there. All the words I had intended to say about Maniek died on my lips, and I left the room without saying a word. I decided to remain quietly in the shadows and keep out of sight.

Several days later we covered up our hiding place in the anteroom with boards and moved back to the attic. In the evening, after the shop was locked for the night and Mr. Michalski had left, we came downstairs to sleep.

Whenever Mr. Michalski would drink himself into a stupor in some bar he would return to the workshop to sleep. At such times I would shake with fear and stay awake the whole night, listening to his snoring. In the morning, after a sleepless night, I felt like I had been taken down from the cross. My nerves would be completely frazzled. I would sob for hours on end over our sad lot, that we were nothing but a burden and a bother to everyone and were completely helpless to do anything about it.

Of the Michalskis, no one besides Henryk came to see us. He would drop by from time to time to ask my husband about some matter connected with running our little factory. Zygmunt would buy necessities and satisfy our modest needs. He too had changed a lot. The carefree smile which had always played on his lips disappeared. He had become sadder and, it seemed, suddenly much older and more mature. Although he was thirty-five years old, he had always seemed to me rather like a big boy.

64

PREPARING FOR THE UPRISING

Spring arrived in all its glory. We would spend hours looking out of our grated window at the people strolling along the street, and at the trees covered with green buds. After a long winter, nature was coming alive. In the house next door, a nanny goat had given birth to two kids which would jump around playfully and get between their mother's legs. We would look out at them completely enthralled as they did various tricks. They gave us moments of comfort, but we envied them their freedom.

On Sundays afternoon, we looked out on the people returning from their trips to the country as they disembarked from the Wilanów narrow-gauge railway. They were sunburned and happy. Some of them carried bouquets of wildflowers in their arms, and their children would run alongside chattering merrily. Didn't these people realize there was a war going on?

Through our window in the attic we also observed troops of German soldiers as they marched past on the street. They were all young; some of them looked like children. They were well dressed and clean, and they would sing merry songs as they marched along. They looked completely invincible to us.

The month of May brought no changes. I had grown much thinner, for I had lost all interest in food. My body was nothing but skin and bones. Henryk had brought me one of my summer dresses from before the war, which he had found in one of the packages we had sent out of the ghetto. I tried it on, and it hung on me like on a hanger. It reached almost to my ankles. My husband looked on, scarcely able to believe his

320

eyes, then slowly turned to the wall, stifling a sob. After that, I decided not to try on any more clothes.

Compared to me, my husband always lived with a spark of hope in his heart. He read the German newspapers with the greatest of interest, trying to read between the lines on the basis of words dropped here and there in various articles about problems and shortages in Germany. In his recent articles, Dr. Joseph Goebels, the propaganda minister, had been calling on the German population to "improvise." I could see that my husband was firmly convinced that the defeat of Germany was at hand.

Finally, the long-awaited day of June 6, 1944, arrived: D-Day. At last the Allies had landed in Normandy. This invasion kindled enormous hopes and expectations in us and in all the Jews in hiding, so weary of this endless waiting. The first to bring us this important news was Mr. Michalski. He hit the workshop that morning like a bomb. For the first time since Maniek' s death his doleful face brightened with a smile. As soon as he had related this sensational news, it seemed to us as if the miserable tinsmith's shop was filled with sunlight. We felt gay and light-hearted. There was no end to our questions, but Mr. Michalski knew very little as yet.

Obviously it was necessary to celebrate such an important event. My husband ordered food and vodka to be brought from the restaurant across the street, and we treated Mr. Michalski generously. That evening Henryk and Zygmunt dropped by in an excellent mood and once more we celebrated and toasted the news of the day. There was yet another piece of news which lifted our spirits and gave us enormous satisfaction. The underground press carried reports about enormous allied bombing raids carried out on German cities. Now the German population would have a taste of what we had known so well and paid so dearly for these past few years.

We continued to observe the movements of the fronts. The fighting was fast and furious. The Germans were retreating before the advance of the superior allied forces, but at a snail's pace. Each war must last as long as it needs to, and no war lasts longer that it has to. In any event, the Russian front was slowly approaching Warsaw.

In the first days of July our street began to come alive. The inhabitants of the buildings across from our shed began packing their belongings feverishly. The first to go were the "bigwigs," Germans occupying important positions. They took their priceless stolen pictures off the walls and packed their carpets, silver, and other things. We had an excellent observation point through the cracks in our attic. We would sit there for hours on end watching the first signs of the Germans' reversal. The apartments slowly emptied. Bright lights no longer poured out of them onto the street at night; no longer could one hear the lively sounds of radio music. Along the streets plodded a continuous caravan of peasant wagons loaded with booty. Behind the wagons walked cattle. These were the Volksdeutsch returning to their "Heimatland." Our one major disappointment during this time was news about the unsuccessful attempt on Hitler's life on July 20, 1944.[1]Unfortunately, our sufferings were not soon to be over. We would first have to drink the bitter cup to the dregs.

Warsaw was preparing itself for an uprising against Germany. No one knew when it would begin. The underground press stated that the exact date was to be determined by General Bór-Komorowski. We took all our raw materials from our new workshop on Zurawia Street and brought them to where we were on Belwederska. They were worth around 350,000 zlotys and were the fruit of our and Henryk's mutual work during the time spent on the Aryan side—about two years by this time. Zygmunt hid all our goods in a big pit which he dug in the bottom of his storage shed. He worked by night so as not to attract the notice of his neighbors. He covered the pit with old pieces of sheet metal, of which there was no lack in our shop. In another spot in the rubbish room we buried all our diaries along with the papers printed by the underground press which we had collected during our stay. On Henryk's advice we bought a substantial amount of food in anticipation of the uprising, for no one knew how long it was supposed to last. It was already possible to hear the sounds of Russian artillery approaching Warsaw. It could be heard most clearly during the night when all in the city was quiet. This was a time of feverish excitement. We impatiently awaited the longed-for call to revolt, not anticipating how much more we would have to endure. Our gehenna was far from over.

The days were hot. The sun shone brightly, but the German telephone girls could no longer be seen walking along the street with smiling faces. There were no more Sunday excursionists either. This is the calm before the storm, I told my husband. I could feel the tension rising in the air.

On July 31st Henryk came to us in the evening. This time we talked not about business as we usually did, but about the uprising which was to take place. He told us that the Russians were already very near, on the other side of the Vistula. Soon the day of liberation for everyone would come, and our waiting would be over. He talked with us for a little longer and then said goodbye warmly, promising to come by and see us the next day. That day was Tuesday, August 1st. We arose very early in the morning, in expectation of the older Mr. Michalski's arrival, but Mr. Michalski did not come. We looked furtively out of the window many times, hoping to see Zygmunt, but he was not around either. Henryk, who had promised to drop by, also did not show up. We began to be worried, but we saw nothing else to do but be patient.

At noon we heard the whine of factory sirens. We listened carefully, thinking that a Soviet air raid would follow. However, this was not the normal alarm sounding the approach of an air raid, but rather the signal calling one off. We waited for a fairly long time in order to see what would happen, but nothing disturbed the quiet. Traffic on the street proceeded as normal. We concluded that this must have been some signal worked out by the Germans. From time to time the stillness was interrupted by the noise of Soviet artillery. We had the impression that the front was very close. The day was sunny, but we felt very heavy at heart, abandoned by everyone and facing the great unknown. A fine rain began to fall.

---

1. **Attempt on Hitler's life.** On July 20, 1944 Captain Claus von Stauffenberg led an unsuccessful attempt on Adolf Hitler's life at the so-called Wolfsschanze (wolf's lair) in East Prussia, from which Hitler was directing his campaign against Russia. Escaping to Berlin, where he was captured along with two other conspirators, Von Stauffenberg was executed by firing squad.

III

THE WARSAW UPRISING OF 1944. EVACUATION AND LIBERATION

65

THE UPRISING BREAKS OUT

In the late afternoon the first shots fell. In the beginning the shots were sporadic; later we heard machine-gun fire. We looked out of the window and saw somebody shooting from a rifle on the corner of Podchorąży Street. It seemed that the uprising had begun. We didn't know whether to be glad or to think that our final hour had come.

From the direction of Spacerowa and Zajączkowska Streets came the sound of machine-gun fire mixed with the far-off detonations of Soviet cannon. From what Zygmunt later told us, we learned that it was precisely in the direction of Spacerowa Street in Mokotów that the Germans had set up bunkers before the outbreak of the uprising, from which they had excellent range and field position across the vegetable gardens down onto Belwederska Street. Passers-by trying to get home fell first victims to the German shells. The white flags they held high in their hands were of no aid. There were many casualties that day. Toward evening, when the action had calmed down, orderlies from the Red Cross came and took the bodies away on litters.

Next morning Zygmunt finally showed up in our workshop. He told us that during the night insurgents had taken up positions in our garden but had withdrawn toward morning. My husband was very sorry that he had not known about it, because we might have been able to join them. We begged Zygmunt to keep us up to date on what was happening. We peered out of the cracks in our window all day long. Profiting from the sad experience of former days, people didn't poke their heads out of doors at all. The sounds of the nearby Soviet artillery died down completely. It turned out that after the uprising had begun the Soviets had pulled back thirty kilometers to Wołomin. The insurgents had been left to their own devices.

The Germans fired unceasingly from their bunkers. When we went into the attic in the evening to take up a more convenient observation point, we saw smoke and the glare of fires far away on the horizon. We continued to maintain all manner of security precautions, just as before. In the afternoon we positioned a large sack of sawdust so that we could climb up into the hiding place in case of need.

One day we noticed a group of German soldiers stopping by the blacksmith's house. Some of them went inside while others remained outside and began to approach our building. We dashed into the anteroom as quickly as we could and shut the door behind us. I stood on the sack of sawdust and my husband shoved from below and helped me get up. Next he came up in the same way. He covered the opening with boards and we lay there, listening carefully. Our hearts were pounding like hammers.

Suddenly we heard the sounds of German and the voice of a woman accompanying them. She was speaking Polish, but because of the noise in our ears and our pounding hearts, we were unable to make out her words. We heard the door to the anteroom being opened, and later the door out into the garden. The Germans looked outside and, not seeing anything suspicious, shut the door and left. We continued to sit there for a long time afterwards, not daring to come out. Finally Zygmunt came and told us that we could come down.

He said that he and his wife had died a thousand deaths when they saw the Germans in the yard. We assumed that they had been looking for members of the uprising, for they even inspected the storage sheds. When they learned from the neighbors that the Dobosz family had the key to the tinshop, they told them to open it. Zygmunt lost his nerve. He was sure that we would not be able to hide in time and that the Germans would find us and shoot us on the spot. Zygmunt's wife, knowing her husband's ways, gathered up her courage, picked up the key to the tinshop, and accompanied the Germans. Zygmunt told us that as his wife inserted the key in the lock she was busy making the sign of the cross to herself. We lived in constant fear of being disturbed for almost three weeks.

In the meantime we put together some makeshift white flags from some old towels. We made two large bags in the form of knapsacks out of some sheets, and packed them with food— sugar, flour, kasha, and rusks which I had dried from white bread. All of this lay in readiness to be picked up at a moment's notice.

August that year was exceptionally warm, and we felt its effects in this stifling little tinsmith's shop which never had a chance to air out. One morning, we noticed a high barricade which had evidently been created during the night from various sorts of furniture on Belwederska Street, near the corner of Grotgier Street. I asked my husband whether it would be possible for the insurrectionists to be behind that barricade, so close to us. We stood near the window and watched everything closely, but no movement could be seen. Suddenly we saw the barricade become covered in a curtain of smoke, and everything around it became enveloped in a thick, impenetrable haze. After a while the haze began to thin out and a terrible sight met our eyes: the barricade was on fire. Red flames quickly took control of the pile of furniture and mattresses, and a dense black column of smoke wafted up into the sky. After a couple of hours, all that remained was a pile of black ashes.

In the afternoon there was a commotion out on our street. German soldiers appeared on the corner of Belwederska and Podchorąży. The officers stationed their soldiers at intervals, while they themselves withdrew to Podchorąży Street. They began calling to the inhabitants of the surrounding buildings to abandon their apartments. The Germans were burning down the buildings one after another. Soon afterwards groups of people appeared on the street carrying bundles on their shoulders and white flags in their hands. The Germans directed them toward Grotgier Street—in the direction of the insurrectionists.

My husband took in the situation at a glance and said, "If we don't make use of this opportunity, we may never have another one."

There was no time to lose. Because of the danger we were in, we decided to leave separately. We thought that in case of an accident perhaps at least one of us would be saved. Because the day was very hot, I was wearing a light summer dress and sandals. I hurriedly put on a raincoat, and my husband helped me pick up the knapsack with food. I took hold of the white flag we had in readiness and, for the first time since coming to hide in the tinshop, I stepped out onto the street. I quickly joined one of the groups passing by. At every ten paces or so stood a German with arms at the ready. We soon passed the ashes of the barricade. Here we had to be careful, for the asphalt underneath was hot and soft. Some pieces of wood were still on fire. I tried to walk in the footsteps of those who had gone in front.

As soon as my husband saw that I had mingled with the crowd, he opened the front door of the tinshop and, holding a white flag, left the building. He started running to catch up with the group of people leaving in the distance. A German soldier standing on the sidewalk keeping order called out to him, "Laufen Sie nicht, laufen Sie nicht, es droht Ihnen gar nichts." (Don't run, don't run, you're not in any danger).

You'd sing a different tune if you knew who I was, my husband thought to himself.

My husband joined me, and soon afterwards Zygmunt and his two older boys turned up. Zygmunt was pushing a baby carriage loaded down with various articles. When I asked about his wife, he said that since she was in her eighth month of pregnancy she was in no condition to make the trip, and neither was their two-year-old son. Zygmunt, as it later turned out, was one of the last to be directed toward Grotgier Street. When the German officers returned from Podchorąży Street, they ordered the following groups to head in the direction of Ujazdowski Boulevard and from there toward Gestapo headquarters, which was located on Szucha Boulevard. Fortune was once more on our side.

Since we now found ourselves on the side of the insurrectionists, we finally felt happy and free. We breathed deeply, and smiles appeared on our faces for the first time in recent years. We could see the first insurrectionists up on some balconies. They wore blue and white armbands on their left sleeves and were carrying small automatic rifles. They were sunburned, and their faces shone with enthusiasm and self-assurance. As we looked at them we were overcome with a feeling of happiness and security such as we had not known for many long years.

We continued walking, not really knowing where we were headed. After a while we came to a parting in the road. Straight ahead led toward Wilanów, while left took us toward Sadyba Oficerska (officers' housing) in Czerniaków, a garden-town suburb. Someone said that that area of town had been occupied by the insurgents the preceding night, so we decided to take the road to Sadyba Oficerska. The sun was beginning to set, and the air grew a little cooler.

In Sadyba Oficerska Zygmunt met a friend of his who at that moment was serving as the commander of an antiaircraft squadron. With his help we were assigned to a deserted villa not far from the Wilanów highway. The inhabitants of this section had escaped downtown before the uprising, while from downtown people had come running to the outskirts, looking like they were escaping Sodom and Gomorrah. This two-story villa was surrounded by a vegetable garden from which we derived incomparable benefit in the form of as many fresh vegetables as we could eat.

Since the time when the Germans had first occupied Warsaw, in other words, since the autumn of 1939, we had had no glimpse of green fields, wildflowers, or other wonders of nature's creation. I stood for the rest of the day in the open door of this villa drawing the fresh air into my lungs and looking at each little leaf as if I had never seen one before. From afar I could hear shooting, but I was not thinking of anything further away than the present moment. Jurek, a nice eight-year-old blond child, similar to his father, and the younger Waldek, a thin, dark seven year-old, both sons of Zygmunt, asked me, "Where's our mama?" Their voices took me away from my contemplation. I comforted them and assured them that their mother would soon be there together with their little brother.

The following day my husband went to the local AK headquarters to sign up. He filled out all forms according to our Aryan documents, but also gave our real names. He was received very warmly. The commandant in charge asked my husband whether we needed any help by way of money. My husband said no, and thanked him sincerely. Instead, he asked for protection for us both. To this the commandant replied, "You are now within the borders of the Polish Republic, and you are in no danger. Whoever is with us will be with you too."

Finally, after two years of persecution and hardship, we could breathe a little more freely. From time to time German patrols came close to our villa, for it was located not far from the Wilanów highway, but in general there was little going on. Sometimes at night we could hear artillery fire.

We had plenty to eat. The garden in the rear of the house provided us with fresh vegetables and potatoes. It is true that there was no fat in our diet, but we were more than satisfied with everything. Zygmunt was a great help to me in managing this makeshift household. Once he even stumbled on a stray hen, from which we made some wonderful-tasting chicken soup.

Now the Russian front moved forward again, and battles began taking shape not far from Warsaw. Since the German army had no desire to wage war on a "second front," they decided to destroy the uprising at all costs. All hell broke loose around us.

Our days of so-called rest and relaxation were drawing to an end. Every day German bombers appeared over our little settlement, throwing both incendiary and demolition bombs, setting fires and sowing death and destruction. Our short-lived joy went up in smoke, and we were brought back to grim reality. The war was still on. The enemy was lurking not far away, bringing death along with him. Whenever the raids were finished, shooting from heavy artillery would begin. The Germans could just not leave us in peace. The villa which in the beginning had seemed like a garden in heaven now shook like a leaf with every explosion. However, during these difficult days spent at Sadyba Oficerska I felt no fear, for a person can eventually get used to anything. On the contrary, I kept thinking that it would be better to die from an artillery shell or bomb dropped from an airplane than from a bullet aimed directly at me by a German.

Far away on the horizon we could see the contours of the Red Cross hospital. A large white flag with a red cross was waving in the breeze. One day the Germans made a special attack on that hospital, even though it contained a number of wounded German soldiers who had been taken prisoner by the insurgents. Their airplanes kept circling, unloading a steady stream of destruction from above. The hospital was turned into one great glowing mass of smoke and conflagration. We looked on this terrible sight in horror.

Toward evening we noticed a group of people heading in the direction of our settlement. An orderly from the Red Cross was supporting a young woman who was limping badly, barely able to move her legs. They came to our villa and asked for help and shelter. We let them have the apartment on the first floor. They were husband and wife, Roman and Wanda. They were very dear and peaceful people. He was a medical orderly and had been working in the Red Cross hospital. From them we learned about its complete destruction, during which almost all the sick and wounded had perished.

During the next several days the German bombardments became increasingly severe. Not far from us in the Sadyba Oficerska district were the forts in which the main strength of the uprising was concentrated. These forts were bombarded twice daily. It seemed certain to us that we would never make it out alive, for death was on every side.

We felt that the end was near. The insurrectionists defended themselves with might and main, but the superiority of the enemy was too great. The critical day of September 1st—my birthday—arrived. After days of fierce fighting the insurgents were forced to abandon their forts and withdraw toward Mokotów. We too were forced to leave the dear little house which had been our shelter.

66

ROUNDED UP BY THE GERMANS

On September 1st German airplanes circled above Sadyba Oficerska from early morning, unloading their heavy cargo of bombs. From the Wilanów highway the firing from small tanks began, and the whistle of shells could be heard in the air. We decided to take our packs with what food we had left and get out. Zygmunt loaded his handcart and we were merely waiting for a break in the action to leave toward the center of the settlement in order to get away from the highway. Wanda and Roman stayed behind, for she was unable to walk. We said good-bye to them warmly and left. Zygmunt went in front, pushing the baby carriage. Next there was my husband, followed by me and, finally, Waldek and Jurek. There was no cessation in the firing. Shots continued whistling overhead.

We met many wounded along the way. The head and hands of one of them were a bluish-gray color; they looked as if they were covered in lead. I don't know how long we walked along the road, for we had lost all track of time. We did not even have a very good idea of where we were. At last we came to a burned-out building surrounded by trees and a garden. We could hear the voices of people inside, so we decided to seek shelter there too. We entered and sat down on the floor, exhausted and out of breath from the forced march. The room was full of men, women, and children. They said that under pressure the insurgents had been forced to evacuate Sadyba Oficerska and were withdrawing through the gardens in this area in the direction of Mokotów. They also said that the Germans, when they came, were going to shoot all of the men. Everyone was in a dreadful panic. My husband and Zygmunt looked at each other and in a flash saw what they had to do: join the AK insurgents and retreat together with them. Zygmunt turned to his sons and, indicating me, said, "This is your aunt Marta" (according to my falsified AK documents my name was Marta Piechocka). "She is your mother's sister. You are to go with her and do whatever she tells you."

Then he told me "I know that I am leaving my children in good hands, and that I can rely on you."

We said goodbye to one another warmly, each one of us surely doubting in their hearts that we would ever see each other again.

The men left, and I stood there for a long time looking after them. Airplanes continued circling overhead. The whistling of shells mingled with the rumble of the airplanes, and I was left alone with the two boys whom Zygmunt had left in my care. We sat down on the floor, and I sat there listening more or less in a daze to the conversations of the other people in the room. I couldn't tell what they were talking about. My thoughts kept flying to where my husband and Zygmunt must be, passing under the fire of artillery and aircraft through the vegetable gardens to Mokotów. I had no great confidence that they would make it through alive and well.

I don't know how long I had sat there, mulling over various gloomy thoughts in my deranged mind, when suddenly I heard the sound of German voices, always sure to send a shock of fear through me. The room filled with a horde of Ukrainians holding their rifles ready to fire. Two of them ran up to me, pressed the muzzle of the rifles to my body and demanded my watch and money. I had several hundred zlotys which my husband had left with me and I didn't hesitate to give it to them. Pointing at Zygmunt's carriage, I said in a choking voice, "Take whatever you want."

The horde of Ukrainians cleaned out everyone in a similar fashion and then, poking along with the snub end of their rifles, pointed for us to leave. I was blinded by the light outside. Holding the boys by their hands, I walked in the indicated direction and joined a group of people. I left the packages of food and the carriage in the bombed-out building. What good were they to me now, I thought, in the face of the unknown.

We had no idea what the Germans would do with us. We stood there for a fairly long time, the crowd growing larger and larger. The sky was covered with leaden-gray clouds and a light rain was falling, but no one paid any attention to it. People were all possessed by fear and panic. Suddenly a command rang out: "Forward." We started moving. The Ukrainians were driving us in the direction of the burning forts. As we moved closer, a terrible sight met our eyes. The forts were entirely enveloped in flames and a stifling smoke from which it was impossible to avoid coughing. One place was still free of fire, and it was through this opening that the Ukrainians began driving people inside.

"They are going to burn us alive," I heard people saying around me.

These words caused blind panic among the people, but there was no way out, for every dozen or so paces walked a Ukrainian soldier with his rifle at the ready, so we had to go. We found ourselves in something like an island, surrounded on all sides by flames. The thought flashed through my addled mind: What had been the good of struggling to save my life for these past two years? Wouldn't it have been better to die in the ghetto along with my own kind? Now I was Marta Piechocka and playing the role of a Catholic who was about to be burned alive.

I was very tired and reacted numbly to everything that was happening. Waldek, Jurek, and I sat down on the ground. People around us were cursing, the women were lamenting, children were wailing; it looked like Sodom and Gomorrah all over again. Maybe two hours passed before the flames slowly began to die down. A fresh wind blew in and cleaned up the air. Then some Germans arrived and everyone was seized again with panic. They had brought some large cardboard boxes with them, which they slowly unpacked, taking out some smaller square boxes containing artificial honey and distributing them to the people.

Everyone pressed forward and stretched out their hands greedily. The young girls I had heard a while before cursing and swearing at the Germans now threw themselves on their necks and, wonder of wonders, began speaking German and ingratiating themselves, to see whether they could wangle a second box of honey. Waldek and Jurek started running over there too, and it was no wonder, for we hadn't eaten since morning. I didn't move. After a while a slightly older German soldier came over to me and said, "Why are you sitting here so sadly instead of going over to get your box of honey?"

"I'm not hungry," I answered in Polish.

Then he took two pairs of stockings out of his pocket, undoubtedly stolen somewhere, along with a box of honey, and gave them to me. I thanked him, but in my heart I prayed to God that this "noble gesture" of his would not attract the attention of anyone undesirable. However, everyone was occupied with himself, and no one paid any attention to anything other than satisfying their hunger with the honey offered so graciously by the Germans. I too slowly began feeding myself, but I immediately became very thirsty, and water was nowhere to be seen. At least I managed to regain a little of my strength, and my wearisome and gloomy thoughts left me alone for a while.

The sun was already setting when the Germans began arranging us into columns of sixes. In the front were women and children, then the men. When we were finally arranged, the Germans gave the signal and we began moving forward toward the highway. Along the way the Germans combined other groups with ours, and our number continued to increase, almost to infinity, it seemed to me.

Darkness had fallen, and we were given ten minutes' rest. We fell down on the ground and I immediately fell asleep. It was with great regret that I heard a voice shouting at us to get moving once again. We walked that way through the entire night like soldiers: fifty minutes of marching and ten minutes of rest. It was chilly and the ground was damp, but exhaustion took the upper hand and I slept soundly through every rest period. At one point we passed by a cemetery, and I could see that under the cover of night people were escaping from the columns and disappearing behind the gravestones. Many people managed to get away. The Germans accompanying us seemed not to pay much attention to it.

Jurek understood what was happening and asked me whether I thought it would be worthwhile. After a moment's thought, I replied that I didn't see what sense that would make, for there was nothing to be seen all around us, and we had no food or money. It was better to go along with the crowd, which by this time consisted of several thousand people.

The sun was already high in the sky, and we kept walking forward. Finally, hungry, thirsty, exhausted, and dirty, we arrived at a train station on which we read the sign Warsaw West. Because of the fighting, it had been necessary to walk around Warsaw in order to arrive at our destination. My first thought was to find a water faucet and extinguish my thirst, but unfortunately the place with water was already surrounded by thousands of people. I had to give up the idea, for I was afraid that Zygmunt's boys would get lost in the crowd.

67

THE DETENTION CAMP IN PRUSZKÓW

After a while we heard the command: "Everyone into the wagons."

In a flash people began moving forward like wild animals. There was an indescribable crush.

I grabbed tightly hold of the two boys, and the crowd pushed us along. I didn't even understand how we managed to find ourselves in a cattle wagon. It was so packed that it was difficult even to breathe. The question flashed through my weary mind: Are they taking us to concentration camps, the same as my fellow countrymen from the Umschlagplatz?

Luckily, this ghastly journey did not last long. The train came to a stop and I was able to read the name of the station: Pruszków. Once more we were arranged into columns and ordered to march forward.

We did not have far to walk. We came to an enormous hall surrounded by barbed wire, located right next to the station. We went inside, where there were already a large number of people. I looked the place over and concluded that this must have been the local railyards and shops which the Germans had converted into a temporary camp. I asked a woman standing next to me where she was from. She said she was from the Old Town district, popularly called Old Market, in Warsaw. There had been terrible fighting in her district all through the previous day, she said, and the AK had had Old Town under their control for a certain period of time. The fate of those people was identical to ours. They had been bombarded without cessation by the Germans until finally the insurgents had been forced to capitulate.

It was said that 40,000 people were in the temporary camp in Pruszków. Some kind person allowed me to squeeze onto a wooden plank bed nearby, where I sat down to give my weary feet some rest. I began dozing. Waldek and Jurek had run off somewhere, but I was not worried about them, for I was sure they would find me.

After a while I noticed them in the company of a young woman. She came up to me and told me that she was Zygmunt's younger sister Henka Trochim. She looked me over carefully and then, as if remembering something, said, "Oh, I know who you are!"

I thought to myself, Well, it seems that Zygmunt hadn't kept us a secret after all.

I looked back cautiously at the young woman. She was more or less my age and completely unlike Zygmunt in appearance. She had a cunning expression and shifty eyes which at that moment were firmly planted on my face. She said that since she was the real aunt of Zygmunt's children she would take over from me. I could see that I would have to be careful with this woman, for she looked capable of doing harm.

When I asked her whether she was there alone, she said that she was with her husband and three-year-old child. I proposed that I join their family and that we all travel together to where the Germans were sending us. She took me to her husband, and after a short discussion we came to an agreement. I promised them that once we were free, in return for their protection I would give them part of the goods from our factory that Zygmunt had buried. The Trochims had a little food with them, and they offered me and the boys a piece of coarse bread each and a little water.

Henka disappeared somewhere for a while, and when she returned she was carrying two new pairs of stockings in her hands. She said that while she had been wandering about the camp she overheard a man asking his neighbors whether or not they were going to be bathed. Henka immediately went up to the man and said, "You're afraid of a bath because you're a Jew."

The frightened man gave her the two pairs of stockings, and she laughed, quite satisfied with herself, while her husband added, "My wife can spot a Jew two kilometers away."

I've really fallen into some delightful company, I thought to myself.

Henka was very resourceful, and she immediately began trying to find out what the Germans were intending to do with us. One of the railway officials, a Pole, informed her that this was only a transitional camp, in order to segregate people for work. The young, healthy, and unmarried would be sent to German work camps. Women with children would be sent into the countryside to work with the peasants. We decided that we should try to get out of the camp as quickly as possible.

Darkness was falling. I decided that it would be safer to have a look around the camp under the cover of night. This was the Umschlagplatz in a slightly improved version. Just as there, people had lighted fires on bricks and were boiling water in tin cans. The more provident of them had brought pots and pans. Dirt and filth were everywhere. I had already noticed that lice in great quantities were crawling all over the people, without anyone paying any notice.

As I walked around, I began to reconsider my situation. I had my identification papers with me, a so-called Kennkarte, which told of a Catholic by the name Marta Piechocka. Henryk had brought the card to me in Wołomin, when I had been living with Mrs. Zieliński almost two years earlier. He had brought some blue India ink with him, and instructed me on how to place my thumbprint on the card and sign it. However, I had made a mistake in not holding my thumb the right way. Later, when I had the opportunity to look at other people's Kennkarten, I understood that mine would immediately attract the attention of anyone checking my papers.

During the day I had heard people in the camp saying that their documents had burned up, or that they had not had time to take them down into the cellars (air-raid shelters) with them during the bombardments. I concluded that it would be better to get rid of my Kennkarte rather than have a falsified one that would immediately attract attention. I tore it into little bits and pieces and scattered them at various places along the railway tracks. Much more at ease now, I returned to my supposed family and fell asleep on the ground.

I was awakened by a commotion in the camp. Henka was not around, for she had gone on a reconnaissance mission. When she returned, she told us that women with children, as well as men who had been separated from their wives during the uprising and who had their children with them, would be sent away on the first transport. After a brief council, we decided that Henka's husband would take their three-year-old son, Henka would take Jurek, and I would take Waldek. That way the Germans would not be able to separate us, and we would be able to travel together.

We began pushing forward to the exit so as to make it aboard the first transport. Finally, after great effort, pushed and shoved by the surrounding people, we forced our way close to the exit. We stood there so long that our legs began aching from lack of movement, but we endured until at last the Germans gave the command to board the train. We went through the same experience as the day before, and I soon found myself together with Waldek in a cattle car. The rest of our "family" by a fortunate turn of events had made it into the same wagon. The train was a long one, and the wagons were not as stuffed as they had been the day before.

We sat down on the floor, out of breath and pouring down with sweat, and tried to rest. Henka, who had been circulating about the camp all through the night, told me that many people, mostly men, had escaped. We concluded that the further away from Warsaw we were, the better it would be for us. We would wait out in the country until the Russians came and set us free. Everyone in the wagon was sure that after so many years of suffering and hardship, the Germans would finally capitulate within the next several weeks and we would be free at last.

As the train drew farther away, the mood of everyone around us improved. I sat quietly in the corner of the wagon with my eyes shut and didn't take part in the general conversation. I was mindful of Henryk's warnings, for he had cautioned me to do as little talking as possible when I was around Poles.

"Your Polish is perfect," he told me, "but your accent gives you away."

I pretended to sleep and didn't say a single word along the entire journey, which lasted several hours.

The train finally came to a grinding halt. We were let out of the cramped and stifling cattle cars and read the sign on the railway station: Opoczno. I thought to myself that this was probably very close to Tomaszów Mazowiecki, where a well-known factory had existed before the war. No Germans were to be seen. I was feeling very weak, for I hadn't eaten for several days, and my head was spinning. I felt everything going black in front of me and, for the first time in my life, I fainted.

As I later found out, Henka was able to profit from this, for she began calling out that her sister-in-law had passed out and that she had to have some place where she could be placed to rest. In the meantime the first horse-carts began to arrive from the village of Janków,[1] about fifteen kilometers from Opoczno. I was placed on a peasant wagon strewn with straw. My entire "family" was there together with me, along with two other persons. There were five wagons in all, with eight people in each, making a total of forty evacuees from Warsaw assigned to the village of Janków.

340

The surrounding countryside was beautiful. The fresh wind acted on me like balsam, as I was finally able to rid myself of the vision of the uniformed Germans of whom I was so deathly afraid. As if guessing my thoughts, Henka asked the driver whether there were any Germans stationed in Janków. He answered that they saw the Germans only once a month, and even then, not in their village. At the beginning of each month each farmer had to provide quantities of butter, cheese, milk, chickens, and grain for the German army. The collection point was in Opoczno.

"The peasants out in the country are doing very badly," the driver said. "The Germans squeeze from us almost everything we produce, and there isn't enough left over for us. Now to top it all off they have quartered forty evacuees on us whom we'll have to feed when we don't even have enough to feed ourselves."

---

1. **Janków,** a small village contemporarily known as Psary, is located about ten kilometers to the west south-west of Opoczno.

68

WORKING ON THE FARM IN JANKÓW

By the time we got to Janków it was completely dark. We were taken to the village elder's house, where all the farmers in the village had assembled. Their faces were downcast and sour, obviously not kindly disposed toward us. The elder began writing down our names and other information. When my turn came, he asked me whether I was married. I answered that my husband had left along with the insurgents together with my brother-in-law, who had entrusted to me the care of his two sons.

I and the boys were assigned to a childless older farming couple. They were a very grumpy and miserly pair. I was pointed in the direction of their house and we set off. I greeted them with the standard formula used by peasants in the country: "Jesus Christ be praised," and they answered, "For ever and ever, Amen." I told them in a muffled voice that we were tired and hungry, for we had had nothing to eat for three days.

A cheerful fire was blazing in the stove, and it was nice and warm in the room. The woman placed a large bowl of soup before us and gave us three spoons. We crossed ourselves and the boys threw themselves at the food and began to gulp it down greedily. I had only eaten a few spoonfuls when the bowl was empty. We were all still hungry, but we had to be satisfied with what we got.

The man, seeing that we were literally toppling over from exhaustion, brought in some straw from the barn, placed it on the ground, and allowed us to lie down on it. I kneeled down in front of their picture of

342

the Virgin Mary. I didn't know any prayers, but I resolved to learn one as soon as possible. I knew that the peasants in the country were very pious, and I had heard that if some woman were suspected of being a Jew the first thing they would do would be to make her say prayers and pass an examination in the catechism, of which I had not even the most elementary knowledge. I resolved that first evening that I would make up for my lack of knowledge in this area in the quickest possible way.

Henka and her husband had more luck. They were assigned to some farmers who were a little better off and more generous than ours. This was an older couple who had married children living in neighboring villages. They had an old grandmother living with them who served as the local midwife. The peasants called her "Granny," and the whole family was well thought of around the village. The Trochims were even given two of the beds in their house and so were able to sleep in human fashion. Henka was very clever and "refined" and, on the excuse that she had to look after her baby, was able to get out of working in the fields altogether. Her husband, lazy by nature, also provided little assistance to their hosts.

My life in the village of Janków began early next morning when it was still completely dark outside. The couple lighted a little oil lamp and pointed to a pile of potatoes that needed peeling. That's for our newly-born piglets, she told me. She meant that she boiled the peelings for the pigs. I sat myself down on a little stool, tired, sleepy, and hungry and, as willingly as possible, set to work. The woman kept asking me to work faster, because as soon as the sun was up, I would have to go into the fields to dig potatoes. The boys were set to other tasks. Seven-year-old Waldek had to feed the geese, and eight-year-old Jurek the cows. I had no idea how they were to manage, for they were born and raised in a big city and had never been out in the country before.

For breakfast we were given dry, meatless potatoes and some home-made borshch made from rye flour, called zalewajka—potato soup. During our stay in this peasant household we ate this zalewajka three times a day. When the sun came up, I went together with the couple into the field. I was given a hoe to dig potatoes. For a person who had never done anything of the sort before, this was very strenuous work. I stood there bent over until noon, patiently digging potatoes and throwing them into a large basket. When noon came, there was a break. I tried to stand upright, but I was simply unable to. My legs, arms, and back were completely stiff. I fell down on the ground, completely exhausted. The woman brought me a little cold borshch and a piece of coarse bread, but in spite of my hunger I wasn't able to swallow a bite. I only managed a little water which was brought to me in a clay pitcher.

Then, I was shown three more long rows of potatoes to dig up before sundown. I gritted my teeth and set about my task as quickly as I could. After that day of difficult and wearisome work, I was barely able to drag myself back to the cottage. Once back, I found a pile of potatoes waiting for me to peel for dinner, but my only thought was when I would finally be able to lie down on the straw and rest for a while.

Waldek and Jurek fared better than I. They were allowed to feed the geese and cattle alongside one another. They built a fire, dug up a few potatoes, and baked them. They found them delicious; so the boys, at least, seemed content.

Almost through the entire month of September, six days a week, I worked strenuously out in the fields digging potatoes. Each night it seemed to me that I would never be able to get up the following morning, but I always did, and I always worked just as hard as the day before. The worst thing was the hunger which I felt tearing my insides apart.

Besides that, I was worried about my husband. I had a good understanding of what they had probably run up against, and I couldn't help asking myself whether Zygmunt and my husband had managed to escape with their lives through the gardens from Czerniaków to Mokotów, when the air was alive with low-flying airplanes. I also kept worrying about what had become of the orphanage where our son was kept. Was our son still alive, or had the Germans bombed the orphanage too? What would have become of the children? These and similar questions kept me awake through the night. News from the rest of the world never made it to Janków.

During the first week of my stay in Janków I learned to say a prayer fluently and from memory. I carefully read through an entire prayer book. I prayed every day, conspicuously beating my breast. In brief, my behavior aroused no suspicions.

I kept clear of the other evacuees as best I could. I really had no opportunity to come into contact with them anyway. Most of them had a little money, and they would frequently travel to Opoczno and buy food and even engage in whatever little trade they could. They were not dependent on their hosts and didn't have to work in the fields. All of that was far outside my possibilities, for Opoczno was full of Germans. I was also afraid that someone might recognize me and point me out as a Jew.

I did make rather good friends with two young girls who had been evacuated from Warsaw's Old Town. The younger was nineteen years old. She was nice and good-looking, and her name was Jadźka. Her sister, Irka, several years older, was a short, thin blonde. These two girls showed me much sympathy and understanding. They had been assigned to the richest farm-owners in the village, by the name of Baran. The Barans were young and had three small children. Jadźka and Irka took care of them when their parents were at work in the fields, and they also cooked meals for the entire family. From time to time Irka would give me half of her bread and would also steal me a little soup. These two girls were my one consolation, and they helped keep my spirits up.

I kept as far away from Henka as I could. It had not taken long to see through her base, cunning, and greedy nature, in complete opposition to her brother Zygmunt. Her character was similar to that of my first "protectress" Zosia. On the excuse of work and tiredness I endeavored to avoid seeing her and her husband.

Sundays were for me days of blessed relaxation and joy. The nearest church was located five kilometers from Janków. The road there led through a forest and, since I am very fond of nature, I walked those five kilometers without the slightest hesitation. I learned to walk barefoot, and my feet ceased being sensitive to the little pebbles I would encounter along the road. My dress, the same summer outfit in which I had left the old workshop on Belwederska Street in August, was by this time in a most sorry state. I took great care to save my sandals and usually went about barefoot, peasant fashion. It was with considerable misgivings that I thought about the coming rains and wet days of the rapidly approaching autumn.

When I went into a church for the first time in my life, it was with a throbbing heart. I looked carefully to see what the others were doing and imitated them. As I kneeled in church I asked God to let me see my husband alive and well at least one more time in my life, and that I be able to cuddle my little child and press him to my breast. After prayers the priest usually delivered a sermon which, in general, had little interest for me. I sat there sunk in my own gloomy thoughts, while people around me probably thought that I was paying close attention to the sermon which the priest was delivering from the pulpit.

For the most part the evacuees from Warsaw did not go to church, and I was just as glad that no one was around to point a finger at me. I would return from church on these days with a great crowd of young boys and girls from our village. The return walk was the pleasantest moment of the day, and I longed for it during the rest of the week. On the way home we sang various songs, stopping for a while to rest in the forest and lying down on the green moss. At such times I felt completely at peace with the world and was able to forget all my cares and worries.

After returning to the cottage, Waldek and Jurek would always greet me with the words, "Auntie, we're hungry!" The poor boys were always hungry, and I was not able to do much about it. I always gave them some of my potatoes and zalewajka, but that did little to help.

I began wondering what I could do. I recalled that when I had been in Wołomin with Mrs. Zieliński, the two women living in her building who had shown me so much kindness had also shown me how to tell fortunes with cards. They told me the meaning of each card and what was associated with their combinations. I made up the rest out of my own imagination and ability to spin yarns. Since God has favored me with a good memory, during my spare time I decided to try my luck at fortune-telling.

69

MURDEROUS PARTISANS

About two weeks had passed since my arrival in Janków. One Saturday after work in the field was over, I went visiting to Henka. She was not at home when I arrived, but her hosts received me warmly. By a strange coincidence there was a pack of cards lying on the table. I turned to the old grandmother and asked her whether she would like me to tell her fortune. She eagerly agreed, and I began to deal out her cards. Almost all of them were black. They meant death, personal troubles, and problems with the authorities. But I had to say what the cards told me: "Granny, I am sorry to have to say this, but you must beware of everything in the next couple of days, for nothing good will come of it, though it will all eventually pass."

I returned home and didn't think any more about it, but on the following Monday as I was returning from the field Henka's landlady came running up to me, all red in the face and out of breath. She embraced me with tears in her eyes and told me that I had saved her mother. As it turned out, that Sunday evening she was sent for from a neighboring village in order to assist at a childbirth. The old woman left immediately, for it was the woman's first child, and the birth was not going well; the woman had begun hemorrhaging.

The old woman, mindful of my words, ordered the people to harness the wagon immediately and take the woman to the hospital in Opoczno. The child was born dead, but they managed to save the mother's life. The old woman was detained by the police but then let go the following day. By a miraculous coincidence, my prophecy had been fulfilled. I laughed to myself at the idea that anyone could attach such importance to fortune-telling from cards. My fame immediately spread throughout the village, which was hardly to my liking, for I had been trying to remain in the shadows and not attract any attention to myself. Next day the old woman came over to us and, as a sign of her gratitude, brought me a loaf of freshly baked bread.

What a joy that loaf of bread was for us. The boys were simply jumping up and down in their excitement. I divided the bread into three parts and we "dug in" with great enthusiasm. That evening was probably the first time we lay down to sleep without being hungry.

Ever after this incident our lives were changed. The peasants began inviting me to their cottages and asking me to tell their fortunes. I never took any money from them. Instead, they would give me bread which I always shared with the boys. Once I even received a bar of tallow soap, with which I was able to wash out the boys' and my things. Waldek and Jurek behaved very dearly toward me. They were polite in every way and always minded. I taught them to pray, something which they had not known how to do before.

The month of September passed, and with it the digging of potatoes. I spent the last days of this month engaged in work that was, if anything, even harder. The old woman harnessed their horse to the plow and had me walking behind it, picking up the remaining potatoes and tossing them into a large basket which I carried in my hand. Slowly the basket became filled, getting heavier and heavier all the time. This work was really beyond my ability. I was frail and underfed, and my body was nothing but skin and bones. However, I kept telling myself that man was harder than iron, and I endured this too.

After finishing the work in the fields, the old couple went to the village elder and said that they had kept me and the boys for a whole month and were unable to feed us any longer. As a result, Jurek was assigned to some more prosperous farmers, while Waldek and I were given to a poor widow with two children. Our new landlady was a virtuous woman with a kind heart, but she was living in direst poverty. She had only three morgs (similar to acres) of land and neither a cow nor a horse. I simply felt unable to take a bite of the food she offered me. She had almost no work to give me. Her little piece of land was sown with rutabagas, so she had me sitting in the field from morning to night peeling rutabagas, which she sold or exchanged for food with other village farmers, who used the rutabagas as fodder for their cattle.

One night in the first days of October some people knocked at night at the home of the Barans. They turned out to be partisans from the nearby forests and were asking for food. The Barans gave them a little but asked them to come the following night, promising that they would bake some bread for them. These night-time visits were repeated several times weekly, always at night. The richer farmers would provide them with food. No one ever came to our hut, because we were so poor. I was intrigued by these nightly visits of the "boys from the forest," as the peasants in the village called them. However, not knowing to which underground organization they belonged, I remained very cautious.

On the first Sunday of October I learned in church that the uprising in Warsaw had gone under. The final capitulation had taken place on October 2nd. A number of evacuees from Warsaw, including Jadźka, decided to leave the village and head in the direction of the city.

About two weeks passed and we had no news from them. Irka, who was not only Jadźka's sister but her dearest friend, began to worry. She came to ask my advice and urged me to come along with her and go toward Warsaw. However, I was hesitant to agree to the idea because of incidents that had taken place, changing my situation. Mrs. Baran had a brother who was a priest in a village about seven kilometers away. One day she paid a visit to him and, upon returning, she told that she had learned from her brother that some partisans belonging to a radical right-wing and anti-Semitic underground organization (the NSZ, or National Armed Forces) had shot three Jews, two men and a woman, in the village of Rudniki, located about two kilometers from ours.

These Jews had gone to the priest in Rudniki and, under the pretext of taking confession, revealed that they were Jews and asked for his help. The priest gave them into the hands of the NSZ, who shot them in the forest. Both the Barans and Mrs. Baran's brother the priest condemned the other priest's contemptible deed. People in our and the surrounding villages talked about nothing else. Wherever you went the subject was on the agenda. The knowledge that the enemy was located so close to me, and not at all in the form of Germans, but rather Polish partisans, completely destroyed my sense of security and well-being. I felt the ground crumbling beneath my feet, and I understood that I would not be able to stay in the village any longer.

70

IN THE RUINS OF WARSAW

Winter was drawing closer, and my sandals were already completely worn out. I had neither shoes, clothing, nor any money, and I didn't know what to do. The only object that I still possessed was my gold wedding ring. I attached great importance to it and considered it my good luck charm. However, I saw nothing else to do, and began looking around for a buyer. Many people were willing, and I finally found a woman who offered me eight hundred zlotys for it. The transaction was accomplished, and with a heavy heart I separated with my last treasure.

The Trochims and I began asking ourselves what we should do next. As soon as Henka learned that I had money (there were no secrets in the village), she became sweet as sugar, and told me that she was ready to do anything for me, even go to Warsaw. Since I had no personal identification papers, having torn up the German Kennkarte and thrown it on the railway tracks in Pruszków, I decided to go to the village of Końskie, about forty kilometers away, where a German office was located that issued passes to people heading toward Warsaw in search of their families. There was a great risk involved, but I staked everything on a single card.

Kindhearted Irka loaned me a short jacket of hers and gave me a piece of bread for the road. The village elder pointed out the direction in which I was to head, and I set off into the unknown.

I had gone about three kilometers down the road when a German truck pulled up alongside me. The German soldier sitting behind the wheel leaned out of the window and asked me in German where I was heading. I answered in Polish, telling him the goal of my journey, and he told me to get in, for he would take me twelve kilometers of the way, for that was the direction he was headed too. I was very grateful to be able to save time and get to my destination all the more quickly.

That part of the road was traveled without any obstacle, and the soldier gave me several pieces of dried bread for my further journey and began asking along the way who was headed toward Końskie. He finally found a farmer going that way who was willing to take me another eight kilometers.

We drove into a fairly large village, and I went to the village elder and asked for a place to spend the night. He gave me a quite large bowl of delicious soup and a piece of bread. The elder began asking me the reason for my trip. When he learned where I was going and why, he advised me to get a couple of photographs made, for they would be necessary for the document I was seeking.

That night for the first time in six weeks, I slept on a bed covered with a quilt. I regained courage and began to feel surer of myself.

Next day I put my external appearance in as good order as possible and went to the local photographer. For twenty-five zlotys he made me several photographs. The village elder found a farmer headed for Końskie and the trip passed very pleasantly, and late in the afternoon we arrived at our destination.

I headed straightway to the police station. I felt quite calm and confident. Several military men were sitting behind a desk. When they asked whether I spoke German, I replied that I understood a little, but did not know how to speak. They brought in an officer who spoke fluent Polish. He evidently was from Poznań, where the people spoke German too. I encountered no obstacle in obtaining a document with my photograph attached, stating my identity and covered with all sorts of stamps, among which was a swastika. I also received a pass allowing me to travel in the vicinity of Warsaw in order to search for my missing family.

As soon as I found myself in the possession of these valuable documents, a new life began for me. I was practically happy. I made the return trip to Janków in the same way, over three days. Upon my return, Henka informed me that she had ordered in Opoczno a dozen or so kilograms of various sorts of sausage, for which I, of course, was to pay. The idea was to sell the sausage at much higher price in the vicinity of Warsaw and divide the profits.

351

I didn't even have the right to put my fingers on any of these meats. After I gave her the money, the avaricious woman took it home with her, and I never set eyes on the sausages or the money again.

I went to the village elder and showed him the documents which the Germans had issued to me. I entrusted Waldek and Jurek to his care, promising that as soon as I found their parents I would immediately return for them. He assigned Waldek to some rather prosperous farmers in the area and we began preparing for our trip. I bought some wooden-soled leather shoes. Since they were too large for me, I wrapped my feet in pieces of linen, so-called "onuce," or footcloths. Irka joined our party, and on October 20th we set out on our way. Autumn that year was sunny and beautiful. We walked in the direction of Nowe Miasto, about fifty kilometers from Janków. The trip took us four days. We stopped along the way in the neighboring villages where we were provided with food and lodging. The peasants in the villages had grown used to travelers such as we.

On the morning of the fifth day we made it to Nowe Miasto, where we waited three hours for the train to Piaseczno. With great difficulty we pushed our way into the overcrowded wagon, where Irka and I found a spot on the floor next to the window, while Henka began walking around the train to see if she could find anyone she knew. Evidently she did, for she was gone for a very long time. Finally, she turned up, red in the face and terribly angry. Without warning she jumped on me and began insulting me in the worst way possible, shouting as loud as she could that because of me and my husband her brother had died. It seemed that some friend of hers had recognized Zygmunt's corpse lying out in the street, the location of which she mentioned. Several paces away from him lay the body of another man, shorter in stature than Zygmunt. It was easy to suppose that this had been my husband, for they were always together.

Henka continued shouting, but by this time I was no longer paying any attention, for I was sunk deep into despair. The train dragged slowly along the tracks. I decided that without fail I would go to the spot which the woman had indicated and find out for myself whether by some fantastic coincidence those really were the remains of Zygmunt and my husband. I knew from previous experience that the bodies of many people who had died during the uprising still lay about unburied.

After a number of stops and false alarms from people worried that the Germans would take away the goods they were smuggling, the train finally made it to Piaseczno. I was tired, apathetic, and resigned to my fate. I went to the village elder and asked for a place to stay. He told us that the town was already overflowing with evacuees from Warsaw. The best he could do was to find us a place in a barn on some hay. Since there was nothing else to do, the barn seemed like a good enough place to take a rest. At least it was a roof over our heads. The elder's wife fed us some hot soup and bread which reinvigorated us, and we went to our accommodation.

I told Irka about my plan of going to Warsaw and checking the remains of the two men. The virtuous girl declared her readiness to accompany me and now, with my mind at rest, I buried myself in the fragrant straw and fell fast asleep.

Next day we began to gather information about how best to get to Warsaw. It appeared that my beautiful native town no longer existed. The Germans had turned it into ashes and rubble. It was said that 250,000 people had died there during the uprising. Afterwards, entrance to Warsaw was forbidden under penalty of death. People paid this little heed, however. They would gather together into groups of looters and plunder the buildings and ruins, taking away whatever they could find that was still usable. The surrounding towns where the escapees from Warsaw had for the most part gathered were full of sundry things for sale. Irka said that if we might be able to find some pillows and quilts to cover ourselves up with during the winter, it would be our greatest possible good fortune.

That same day we decided to go in the direction of Warsaw, after arranging with the Trochims for them to leave word with the village elder as to where they could be found. Piaseczno is located not far from Warsaw; besides, labor and hardship strengthen man beyond the strength of iron. In our case, we were young and healthy, so Irka and I took off on foot. Along the way we joined other people headed in the same direction. We had gone several kilometers down the road when suddenly, as if out of nowhere, a group of German soldiers appeared and surrounded us. We were sure that they would order us to return. Instead, they pointed us to a large field in which carrots were growing; they ordered us to tear them out with our hands and put them in piles. There was nothing else to do but follow their orders, and we worked for a rather long time.

The Germans guarded us carefully, so it was impossible to escape. Finally, I had an idea. I nodded my head at Irka for her to follow me. We went up to the Germans and, making signs, explained that we wanted to go to some bushes that were located at some distance in order to take care of our natural needs. They agreed, and we headed over in that direction. As it turned out, what we had taken for bushes was actually a small forest. We soon became lost in it and quickly began heading in the opposite direction from the soldiers. No one followed us, and finally we were free again.

We left the forest and began looking around to see if we could determine which direction we should be heading. In the distance we spotted a group of people. We joined them, and all together we marched briskly along in the direction of Warsaw. Without any interference we came to a place where a large sign was posted in German: "Warning! Entrance Beyond this Point Prohibited under Penalty of Death!"

Paying no heed, we walked ahead. In the distance we could already see the outlines of the town. The short October day was drawing to a close. We hastened our steps, for it was time to start worrying about where we were going to spend the night. As we entered one of the suburbs of the ruined town, I was at first unable to recognize where we were. We did not worry overly long about where to go, but quickly entered a burned-out one-story building. Inside we found a room we could use. The window still had its panes in place, and the door could be shut, even though the lock had been torn off. All together we were four women and five men. For fear of unexpected intrusions during the night, the men barricaded the door with boards. One of the people came up with a candle and matches. We also found a few pillows, mattresses, and so forth. We lay down on the floor on our improvised bedding and, exhausted from our long march, we fell fast asleep.

I awoke to a pale foggy morning and began to inquire which road Irka and I should take. It turned out that two of the people who had slept with us that night, a married couple, were headed for the same street. They had lived there before the uprising and wanted to see whether anything of their old apartment and belongings was still worth saving. There wasn't a living soul anywhere. All of the buildings had burned down. As far as the eyes could see there was nothing but ashes and ruin.

We walked down the middle of the road, looking with very sad hearts at this picture of destruction. So this was what had become of our beautiful Warsaw, which up until recently had been bustling with life and activity. Uneasily we looked around for fear a German would come jumping out from behind the corner of a building, but there wasn't anyone.

After a long march we finally arrived at our destination. Our friends went along their own way, leaving Irka and me alone. Slowly we began looking for the exact place described by Henka. This was on the outskirts of town. My heart was beating like a hammer, and my eyes were covered in a fog. The noise pounding in my ears told me that I was close to fainting. Suddenly I heard Irka's shout: "Come here quickly! I've found them!"

I moved as if shot from a catapult. Several steps down the road lay two bodies, almost completely disintegrated. Along the entire way I had been reminding myself, and repeating over and over: *That memorable day we parted Zygmunt had been wearing a navy-blue checkered suit and my husband had been dressed in gray. Zygmunt had several teeth missing on the right side of his upper jaw, while my husband had all his teeth in perfect condition.*

I went up to the longer of the two skeletons and bent over it to look at the teeth. The upper jaw had all its teeth, and so did the lower. Besides that there were three metal crowns. I glanced at what remained of the clothing: the color was gray, and could never have been navy-blue. Now that I was somewhat at ease, I went up to the second skeleton, and looked at the teeth. There were two teeth missing in the lower jaw. The teeth in the upper jaw were jagged and in very bad condition. The clothing had been green.

I breathed a deep sigh of relief, as a huge burden had fallen from my heart. I was overcome by a feeling of incomparable joy and bliss. I heard everything within me singing out: My husband and Zygmunt were still alive! Irka guessed my thoughts, tugged on my sleeve and said, "Let's get out of here, Marta."

I quickly came back down to earth and we walked forward, getting as far away from this terrible spot as we could.

Along the way, in one of the bombed-out buildings, Irka found a feather comforter and two pillows in good condition. Loaded down with this, but nevertheless happy and gay, I walked down the road as if wings had suddenly sprouted from my shoulders. Along the way we met several groups of people headed toward Warsaw who pointed out the direction of Piaseczno to us, to which we returned without any difficulty. The village elder told us that Henka had found her elder sister Regina and he pointed out a building not far away where they were all staying. I told them of my adventures, and Zygmunt's older sister Regina embraced me warmly and said, "You are a very brave and resourceful woman and deserve our greatest respect. You must stay here with us until you find your husband."

Henka continually circulated about town in search of friends from Warsaw.

People during this period were wandering like restless spirits from town to town in search of their missing families. We were all dirty and louse-infested, for we had no extra clothing or undergarments to change into. All a person could hope for was a little bit of hot soup to warm one's weary bones.

71

REUNITING ZYGMUNT'S WIFE WITH JUREK AND WALDEK

After returning from the ruins of Warsaw, the feeling of happiness did not leave me for a moment. I no longer doubted that sooner or later I would stumble on the trace of my husband. Irka and I slept that night on straw. For the first time in many weeks we had pillows beneath our heads, and we felt very cozy beneath the feather comforter. Kind-hearted Regina had fixed us some hot soup and given each of us a large piece of bread. On the outside she bore no resemblance at all to her brother; she was short and dark-haired. However, they had one thing in common: their warm and open hearts. Beneath Regina's sheltering wings I felt safe and secure.

Next afternoon, Henka brought some woman, their former neighbor, who had only just arrived in Piaseczno. She told them that Zygmunt's wife Sabina was staying with their youngest son in the town from which she had come. Sabina had told the woman that she had heard from Zygmunt and knew where he was staying. It turned out that by traveling along the railroad tracks from early morning until sunset I could make it to this town, and so I decided to go there by myself the very next day. I left Irka in the care of Regina. I didn't sleep a wink all night; my heart was racing madly, and all sorts of thoughts passed through my head, not all of them happy.

The woman had mentioned Zygmunt, but nothing about anyone accompanying him. I began to doubt whether my husband was still alive. I waited impatiently for the dawn. Everyone except Regina was still asleep. She had risen together with me and had lighted a fire in the kitchen, giving me a little bundle of food for the journey, along with a glass of warm milk. She loaned me her woolen shawl to wrap myself in. Then she embraced me warmly and said goodbye, making the sign of the cross over me.

I walked steadily the whole day long, stopping only for short rests and to eat from the food which Regina had given me. The day was foggy and windy. It was the beginning of November, and winter was drawing close. I wrapped myself tightly in the shawl and kept going. It was dark by the time I arrived at my destination. The village elder pointed out to me the house in which Sabina and her baby were living. I had seen her only two times during our stay in Mr. Michalski's shop. For fear of attracting the neighbors' attention he had strictly forbidden her ever coming into the shop during his absence.

It was with a trembling heart that I entered the apartment—and at first I didn't recognize her. She was a thin woman, small in stature, with brown hair, a dusky complexion, and sad, black eyes. At first glance, I thought, she looked more like a Jew than I did. Sabina recognized me immediately. She looked at me and called out in a sharp voice: "Where are my children?"

I began relating to her the threads of our adventures since leaving the workshop on Belwederska Street. When I came to the point where I had left Waldek and Jurek in the country in the care of the Janków village elder, not wanting to expose them to the rigors of a journey into the unknown, especially since they had no warm clothing, she softened a little and told me about her own adventures.

After Zygmunt had left with the boys, she had remained with the youngest child at home until the arrival of the Germans. When she saw them beginning to set fire to the buildings, she came out and surrendered to them. She was taken along with other people, almost all of whom were women or children, along Szucha Boulevard to the Gestapo building. There they were kept until the following day. Next morning they were divided up. Because Sabina was in her eighth month of pregnancy, she was sent along with her youngest child to Częstochowa. Toward the end of September she had given birth to a little girl in one of the hospitals there. Since she was unable to look after the baby given her present circumstances, one of the nuns in the hospital took the baby and promised to keep it in the convent until such a time as the parents would be able to look after it.

When she had gathered enough strength, she took her little son Janusz and headed toward Warsaw in search of Zygmunt. With the help of some neighbors, relatives, and friends, she had been able to come across his trail. Zygmunt had visited her for the first time a week ago, she said. He told her that my husband was still alive and that he had been in contact with Henryk before the fall of the uprising. After the capitulation of the AK, they had headed in the direction of Grodzisk, where supposedly Henryk's wife Marysia was staying with the children.

I was greatly encouraged at this news. When I asked her where Zygmunt was presently staying, she said that he was somewhere around Warsaw. He went into the town every day to gather various sorts of things which he found in the half burnt-out buildings. Since Zygmunt had been able to provide his wife and child with warm clothing and shoes, a little money, and even a carriage for little Janusz, we decided that next morning we would head to Piaseczno, where we would leave Janusz in the care of Regina, while we went to Janków to pick up Waldek and Jurek. Sabina informed the village elder and left Regina's address with him in case Zygmunt should return.

Early next morning we put Janusz in the carriage, packed a few of Sabina's belongings, and set off on our journey. The weather was pleasant, and the journey passed much more quickly in the company of Sabina.

Regina was very glad to see her sister-in-law and the baby. After talking things over, we decided to rest for a day in Piaseczno before leaving for Janków. Irka decided to accompany us and to stay with the Barans until the arrival of the Soviets.

And so, two days later (we rested one day more), in the early morning the three of us set off down the road. We took the shortest route. Since Sabina had a little money, we were able to travel most of the way in horsecarts, paying peasants to drive us. I was being eaten up with impatience, as I wanted to fulfil my obligation to Zygmunt and Sabina as soon as possible by giving Waldek and Jurek to their mother, and head without delay to Grodzisk to find my husband.

On the third day we arrived in Janków. Waldek and Jurek burst out crying from joy as they ran into their mother's arms and began asking about their father and little brother. Waldek told us that after I had left Janków, a rumor began circulating that Waldek and Jurek were not brothers and that Waldek was the son of a Jew. As a matter of fact he looked Jewish, for he had a dark complexion and dark eyes and hair, just like his mother. The peasants began grumbling that they didn't want to feed a little Jew, and to make matters worse, Waldek was unable to learn his prayers by heart in spite of my best efforts. It resulted in several of the older farmers taking Waldek to the village elder in order to check whether the boy was circumcized or not. When it turned out that he was not, the peasants relented and allowed him to stay in the village until our return. As soon as Sabina learned about this incident, she became terribly angry and began threatening that they hadn't heard the last of the matter, but I begged her to calm down on account of me.

Irka returned to the Barans, where I also stayed for the night. Sabina decided to stay in Janków for several more days in order to rest after her journey and to find her boys some shoes. I for my part bought some wooden-soled shoes with the last of my money, for after my peregrinations my other ones were very far gone. I bade a very fond farewell to all the inhabitants of the village and to the village elder, thanking him for everything. It was with a great deal of emotion that I parted with Irka.

This was the last time we were to see each other. After the Russians entered Warsaw after the final defeat of the Germans, she left the village, as the Barans later told me, and she was never heard from again. After we had been set free the Barans visited us at our invitation, and learned for the first time that we were Jews.

72

MY HUSBAND LOCATED

I headed in the direction of Grodzisk to find my husband. The road from Janków to Grodzisk was rarely traveled by people evacuated from Warsaw and this was the longest journey I had ever attempted by myself on foot. In Janków they pointed out to me the way to the next village, located about eight kilometers away. It led along the edge of a forest and across fields.

The day was cloudy and a light rain was falling. After walking for two hours I became very stiff and sore and thoroughly soaked, but there was no building along the road in which I could take shelter and rest for a while. From time to time I would go partway into the forest and sit down on the wet moss and allow myself to be overcome with gloomy thoughts, such as:

What will happen if I don't find my husband in Grodzisk? Maybe he is also wandering from place to place just as I am. Where would I be able to go without money? Who could I go to for help? Who knew when the Russians would decide to begin the offensive and bring an end to our misery?

By force of will I would slowly rise to my feet and walk steadily onward.

The road became more and more slippery. Often when I took a step my wooden sole would sink so deeply into the soft ground that I would have to take my foot out of it and pull the shoe out with my hands. That journey was the most wearisome and difficult one I had ever made. When toward evening I finally dragged myself into a tiny little village, I knocked at the door of the first cottage I came to and asked if I could spend the night in the barn or stable. It was all the same to me where I stayed as long as it was beneath a roof and out of the rain.

It was warm in the hut, and the entire family was sitting down to their evening meal. I must have looked simply frightful, for the woman of the house let me inside without saying a word. She told me to go into the next room, where she poured some warm water into a large basin for me to wash myself off. She also gave me some dry clothes to change into. Next she indicated a place next to the table and I was given a large bowl of boiling soup, a mug of hot milk, and a piece of bread. I ate slowly and, as I did, big tears rolled down my cheeks and plopped into my soup.

When I had finished eating, my hosts asked me where I was from and where I was going all alone like that. I briefly described the events in my life since leaving Czerniaków up until the present moment. That night I slept on a bed covered with a warm feather comforter, and I prayed to God not to let the dawn come for another month at least, for I felt so wonderfully warm and comfortable. Next morning I awoke to find it was raining cats and dogs. I asked the woman if I could stay until it stopped raining, and she agreed. By the third day the weather had improved somewhat, and a local peasant was located who would be able to take me to another village eleven kilometers away.

While on the road I learned that there was a narrow-gauge railway that ran from a certain spot to Podkowa Leśna, which was fairly close to Grodzisk. Fortunately I still had thirty zlotys, which Irka had given me for my journey. The road I traveled to the railway was wearisome and long. When finally I found myself in the overcrowded railway car, I breathed a sigh of enormous relief.

I was sitting there in the car wrapped up in my own private thoughts about the past, when suddenly I noticed some kind of commotion. People were throwing packages out of the windows and then leaping out after them. It was said that Germans were waiting for the train in Podkowa Leśna in order to confiscate smuggled goods. In addition, roundups for work in Prussia had been taking place all day long. Soon the train was almost entirely empty, but I remained seated where I was. It was all the same to me what they did with me and where they sent me, and if they did kill me, then so much the better. I just wasn't able to put up a fight any longer. Tired, hungry, dirty, and louse-infested, my clothing in tatters, I was at the limits of my endurance.

The train arrived at its destination. I looked cautiously out of the windows, but I didn't see any Germans. Everything seemed as normal. Evidently the smugglers had been given a false alarm.

It was already afternoon by the time I left Podkowa Leśna and continued on my way. I dragged myself slowly along, shaking from the cold. Soaked to the skin, I arrived in Grodzisk with little difficulty. I went first to the market square, knowing that in any small town that would be the place to spot friends.

The market square in Grodzisk was no different from any other ones I had seen. Makeshift stalls were set up, selling all sorts of things, for the most part food and used clothing. I began looking carefully around in search of a familiar face. Suddenly, sitting next to one of the stalls under an umbrella (for it was still raining), I noticed Wanda and Roman, the couple to whom we had offered shelter during the bombardment of the hospital in Sadyba Oficerska. I headed in their direction, certain that the next few seconds would decide my fate.

Wanda noticed me at once, and an expression of immense pity showed itself on her face. Her first words were: "Your husband is staying not far from here. We'll take you there at once."

I felt my legs folding beneath me. My long and weary journey had been crowned with success. Roman walked ahead, showing the way. We came to a small building facing the market. In the front was a small store selling wickerware. Roman went inside, telling me to wait. In a moment he reappeared, followed by my husband. He stood there looking at me as if he couldn't believe his own eyes. I realized that he surely had no idea what a tremendously long journey I had made to see him and how much difficulty, toil, and effort it had cost me. After saying hello, the first words he said were, "It's good you came today, because if you had come tomorrow you probably wouldn't have found me."

I was so tired at that moment that I did not bother trying to compre-hend the meaning of those words.

The owner of the wicker store, an elderly single woman, lived in a large room in the back. She rented the room to escapees from Warsaw, including my husband. My husband took me inside, introduced me to his landlady, and asked if I could be allowed to live with him, to which she agreed. There was warm water, soap, and a towel, and finally I was able to put my external appearance into some kind of order. I drank a glass of hot tea with sugar, and ate my fill of bread and butter, after which I felt like a completely new person.

Next day my husband took me to the market and bought me a used winter coat in very good condition, a used dress, and a few underthings.

Since my feet were swelled and blistered in many places from the long march and the uncomfortable shoes, my husband gave me a spare pair of his. Of course they were too big for me, but for the moment they felt wonderful on my tired sore feet. Little by little we began telling each other our adventures since the time we had parted.

73

MY HUSBAND'S STORY

"After leaving the bombed-out villa in Sadyba Oficerska in Czerniaków," my husband began telling me, "Zygmunt and I started in the direction of Mokotów across a section of vegetable gardens. We followed in the tracks of the retreating insurgents, but at a certain distance, for they were under a constant barrage of fire from airplanes overhead. All day long they circled in search of a target. Two of them in particular were active. They would circle very low and strafe anything moving with machine-gun fire.

"For this reason the march to Mokotów stretched out considerably. Every few minutes we had to duck down between the rows of vegetables or potatoes. Only toward evening, when it began to get darker, did the airplanes finally disappear over the horizon. Zygmunt and I then came out from the cover of the gardens and went into Mokotów, where the insurgents were centered. In one of the buildings we entered, an anti-aircraft commander assigned us to a spot on some straw in one of the rooms, together with some other evacuees.

"After several minutes, the commander called everyone together for the burial of one of the men who had been killed on duty not far away. He was buried in the garden in the back of the building. Softly enough so as not to attract any attention, the men sang "Boże coś Polskę." It was a depressing ceremony, after which it was necessary to return to the present, and the continuing struggle for life and death.

"After a while Zygmunt and I lay down on the straw to get some rest after a long day and arduous journey. Despite my exhaustion, I was unable to fall asleep for worry about you. I imagined that if the Germans came to Sadyba Oficerska, someone wanting to "get in good" with them (and there were many such people) would point you out as a Jew, and then it would be all over.

"My conscience especially bothered me for leaving you alone, for two heads are always better than one. On the other hand, common sense told me that it was safer for us to separate and each to go off on our own, for then the chances that at least one of us would survive would be all the greater. We had to do this if only for the sake of our two-and-a-half-year-old son. If we both perished, then what kind of future would our son have? In a Catholic institution he would certainly be christened, but even so he would always be pointed out as a Jew.

"The first day after my arrival in Mokotów passed rather peacefully compared to what we had been living through in Sadyba Oficerska. Fighting occurred only sporadically. The only thing really bothering us were the airplanes, commonly referred to as "the four," which without any interference flew not only over Mokotów, but all over Warsaw. The insistent bombing of "the four" lasted until the Russians once more began moving toward Warsaw and arriving in the Praga district east of the Vistula river. Then the Russian antiaircraft artillery opened up on the German airplanes and drove them away, and the population of Warsaw was able to breathe more freely.

"The so-called "moo-cows"[1] also did considerable damage. These were rockets which were released one after another, a dozen or more at a time. The noise and roar made by them reminded people of the sound of a herd of lowing cattle. Other machines causing damage were the so-called tigers—small miniature tanks filled with explosives and directed by remote control. They did tremendous damage, both to people and to buildings. The AK counterattacked with Molotov cocktails and grenades of their own fabrication. Even young teenage boys took part in the action.

"During the entire period of the Warsaw uprising, neither the Allies nor the Russians came to the help of the insurrection. Every once in a while, before the final capitulation, a Russian airplane would appear during the night on the horizon, sounding something like a child's rattle. Then the rebels would unfold large white sheets to signal their location. These little airplanes dropped small arms and machine guns, so-called "pepeshes," medicine, and rusks of black bread, hard as rock. This they called "bringing aid to the uprising." However, they provided greater help to the partisans of the AL (Armia Ludowa), that is, the communist-led People's Army.

"One day everyone was caught unawares by the sound of a large number of airplanes. As they drew nearer, the men counted around twenty of them, and they could make out American insignia on the wings.[2] My first thought upon seeing them was '"The Invasion!"—the invasion for which we had been longing. I immediately began regretting that we had not stuck together at such an important moment for which we had been waiting so long, so that we could be freed together.

"My joy was unfortunately short-lived and followed by even greater disappointment. It turned out that this had not been the invasion we had been expecting, and the parachutes which had at first been dropped turned out to be boxes, oblong boxes in various colors. The colors designated their contents: one was for weapons, another for medicine and so forth. Unfortunately, the majority of these boxes fell into the hands of the enemy.

"'The biggest problem we had was with food. It was impossible to purchase it for money, but the problem had to be solved one way or another. And so, when the action would quiet down for a while, we would go on foraging expeditions into the gardens. Often enough the Germans would notice us and begin firing, and we could hear the shells whistling over our heads. We would fall down on our stomachs and try to crawl up close to the tall apartment buildings which served as protection from the enemy.

"After several such incidents, Zygmunt and I decided to go dig potatoes at night. They were growing in the fields located between the German positions and those of the AK. We dug the potatoes with our hands in the darkness and put them into bags. Zygmunt, who was tall, strong, and well-built, was always able to dig up the most. He could easily lift a bag weighing 50 kilograms or more onto his back and walk with it.

"Luck was not always with us, however. One night the Germans spotted us and began firing. We both grabbed as many as we had been able to gather and started running. Not one of us left our potatoes behind, for they were a real treasure at that time. They could also be traded for bread, vodka, and even cigarettes. Cigarettes were worth a real fortune. For lack of them people tried smoking the leaves of the chestnuts growing along the streets. One day Zygmunt made a surprise for us by preparing an excellent dinner (excellent for the time, at least) with an extremely tasty piece of meat. There was plenty of vodka to go around too. Zygmunt also invited an officer from the PAL (Polska Armia Ludowa, the Polish People's Army, organized by the Polish Socialist Workers' Party)[3] to the feast.

"After we had finished eating, Zygmunt asked us whether we recognized the taste of the meat which we had eaten. None of us did, so Zygmunt told us: it was dog meat. This news made absolutely no impression on us, except that we all laughed out loud. We were all a little bit tipsy anyway, and the lieutenant in particular had had a lot to drink.

"Our conversation touched upon current events, and we even latched onto the question of the Jews—their persecution and suffering. At one point the lieutenant turned his bloodshot eyes on me and said, "I hate Jews with all my heart, and if I didn't feel bad about wasting a bullet, I'd shoot you right here and now." Of course, not all officers in the PAL were such bloodthirsty anti-Semites as this man. In general, they treated me in a perfectly civil manner and on the same level as the others. One of them even warned me that for my own good I ought not to reveal my nationality.

"Since the staff headquarters of the PAL was located in the building in which Zygmunt and I were staying, we were able to listen in on radio broadcasts. For the most part we listened to the transmissions coming in every afternoon from Lublin. Lublin had been captured by the Russians before the outbreak of the Warsaw uprising, and a provisional Polish government[4] had been installed there, obviously with the backing of the Soviets. The Polish government rebroadcast news from the rest of the world, and because of this we heard about the Allied invasion in France—about its successes and about the hurdles which it still faced.

"One day on a radio broadcast for the combined New Year's and Rosh Hashana holiday, the president of the United States, Franklin Roosevelt, sent his wishes for a happy new year to the Jews of the world. At that one of the officers standing around called out, "What's the point of saying that? No one cares about that"— and he turned off the radio. I felt at that moment as if someone had hit me on the head with a hammer.

"It must be mentioned that many Jews, after the uprising had forced them out of hiding, volunteered for the AK and fought against the Germans. Many of them died on the field of battle, but many of them perished as well at the hands of such anti-Semitic groups as the NSZ and others.

"Zygmunt and I also went out during the night to help dig trenches. I worked hard and tried to be as much help as I could. One night the Germans spotted us and began firing. A grenade fragment hit me in the right cheek near my eye, but the wound was not serious, I was given an inoculation against lockjaw, and the wound mended quickly.

---

1. **"moo-cows".** The so-called "bellowing cows" (*ryczące krowy*) were actually not rocket launchers, as the author's husband says, but incendiary mine throwers, and the "tigers" were not miniature remote-control explosive "tanks," which were called "goliaths." The "tigers" were full-size heavily armored tanks.
2. **American airplanes.** In an operation known as "Frantic," on September 18, 1944, after gaining Soviet air clearance, 107 four-engine American airplanes flying in from the northwest dropped a large amount of food and ammunition intended for the Polish insurgents, but by that time the territory on which they dropped their load had already been captured by the Germans.
3. **Polish People's Army** (*Polska Armia Ludowa*, PAL). A fairly small partisan group with a leftist ideology, but independent of the Soviet-supported People's Army (*Armia Ludowa*, AL) operating around Warsaw and several other cities. The PAL also maintained its independence from the Home Army (*Armia Krajowa*, AK) but fought alongside it in the Warsaw Uprising.
4. **The Polish Provisional Government** was not created in Lublin until December 31, 1944. Mrs. Schmidt apparently has in mind its predecessor, the Polish Committee for National Liberation.

74

ESCAPE THROUGH THE SEWERS

"Days passed monotonously one after another. Then, after a temporary lull and period of sporadic fighting, the end for the insurgents drew near.

"After occupying Praga, the Russians began fighting to capture Warsaw. The Germans did not want to have two fronts going at the same time so bloody battles ensued, with the AK losing one position after another. The Germains tried to draw the knot tighter and tighter around the partisans fighting in the suburbs, and communication with the downtown area became increasingly difficult. The only remaining means of communication from one part of the city to the other was through the sewers. Messengers for this purpose were mostly chosen from among young girls. This was an extremely arduous task, for it was necessary to walk for hours and hours to get from the middle of town to the outlying positions. With each passing day the situation of the uprising in Mokotów became more difficult, until finally the leaders decided to abandon their positions and join the main forces which were still holding out in the downtown quarter.

"As a Jew, I found myself in a hopeless situation. I had heard from many people that during the uprising the Germans were killing any man they got hold of. After talking things over, Zygmunt and I decided to follow the retreating AK through the sewers to the center of town. However, there was one difficulty, in that it was not allowed to evacuate civilians through the sewers.

"One of the officers from the PAL with whom I was friendly took my situation into consideration and promised to let us join his detachment. The evacuation through the sewers was in full swing. We waited all day for our chance, until finally toward evening our turn came.

"In the meantime the Germans were giving us no rest, and continually shot at us from tanks returning from the Russian front. We were forced to take up hiding in a nearby factory, but it wasn't any safer there than it had been outside. Grenades were tossed into the factory, and several people were killed or wounded. Finally, towards evening, after a long and wearisome wait, the signal was given for us to approach the sewer opening. We descended slowly one after the other, holding on to the sturdy iron ladder embedded in the sewer wall. The group to which we had been assigned consisted of about 2,000 soldiers, all of them lightly wounded. After leaving the ladder we found ourselves in a small sewer tunnel, along which we had to crawl for about a hundred meters before reaching the main tunnel, where it was possible to stand up straight. The inside of the sewer reminded me of an egg. The sides were far enough apart so that one could touch either side with one's arms outstretched. Lower down, however, the walls narrowed and it was necessary to walk holding one's legs crooked. So we goose-stepped like this one after the other in the darkness.

"We had been ordered to keep quiet so as not to betray our presence, for the Germans knew that the insurrectionists were being evacuated through the sewers. We were also forbidden to smoke or use flashlights or candles. At first everyone behaved in exemplary fashion. We all walked along in silence, the only sound being the splash of water beneath our feet. The water reached as high as our knees. Fortunately it had not been raining recently, so the water level was comparatively low. Also, water pipes were inoperative during this time, for the Germans had cut off water to the Warsaw population.

"Before descending into the sewer I had accidentally overheard a conversation between the officer under whose care I was (I constantly kept him in sight) and another PAL officer. The latter advised the former to keep a close lookout for a small opening leading to a smaller tunnel eventually leading to the outside. He warned him that before the uprising the Germans had placed various kinds of obstacles and booby traps in the sewers so as to make communication as difficult for the AK as possible.

"After a brief march, we began encountering these obstacles, first in the form of a barbed wire barricade. It took quite a while before we managed to pass by this and continue on our way. As we marched ahead, we continued to come upon other such barricades. We lost a lot of time getting rid of them, but we patiently kept moving ahead in the hope that soon we would come to the end of our journey and arrive at the sewer opening that was our destination.

"Soon we came to another kind of blockade: a high brick wall whose purpose was to raise the level of the water. At this point the water came up to our necks. We had to crawl over this wall to pass to the other side. Several of the wounded were unable to do this by themselves. Two partisans stood nearby with lighted candles, helping them over. This was no easy task. The wounded kept moaning from the pain, complaining and talking loudly. Confusion broke out, and discipline broke down. Several men decided to turn back.

"In spite of the mounting difficulties, Zygmunt and I decided to forge ahead. We had to wait a long time before it was our turn to climb over the wall. In the meantime the people who had returned were forced to rejoin us, for the Germans were already in control of the exit. We later learned that about a hundred and fifty persons whom the Germans had dragged out of the sewer had been shot on the spot.

"After passing the wall, the water level returned to normal, that is, up to our knees, and we continued marching steadily forward. Our clothing stuck to our skin. We were sure we had gotten lost, for we were unable to find the opening leading out. We lost all track of time and didn't know whether it was day or night. We had neither food to eat nor water to drink.

"I happened to put my hand in my pocket and found some sugar cubes in it. Since working in the Karl George Schultz factory, I had grown accustomed to carrying sugar with me in case of an emergency. I shared the cubes with Zygmunt and we felt stronger. We were reminded of the pre-war advertising slogan well known throughout Poland: "Sugar invigorates!" As we continued walking lethargically ahead, we heard a large explosion, followed by a shock wave which knocked all us over into the water. With difficulty we picked ourselves up again and began moving forward. We could hear moans and cries for help echoing against the walls of the tunnel.

"We heard someone calling out: "Colonel Leon is wounded and needs help!" The further we went along, the louder the desperate cries for help became. When we finally came to the spot where the cries were coming from we could see that a large number of people had been killed and wounded. Those who were unable to stand up on their own legs slipped down into the water and drowned. Some people were trying to lift themselves back up, but they were too weak. They were completely helpless.

"New waves of people kept pressing us forward and we were forced to move on. As we later learned, this was but another of the many satanical devices set up by the Germans. They had hung grenades under the manholes of the sewers and it was impossible to spot them because of the darkness. As people moved past, someone would knock his head against them, and they would fall down and explode, wounding or killing anyone in the area.

"Tired, hungry, and thirsty, we had to stop from time to time and rest against the walls of the sewer. However, it seemed that even resting was dangerous, for people would drift off to sleep and fall down into the water and drown. We were all faint from lack of air, and we began to lose touch with reality. I began hallucinating. I imagined I was walking through a forest, and that the ground was covered with tree stumps which I had to jump over. I even called out to Zygmunt: "Watch your step! Look out for the trees!" Zygmunt answered in amazement that he didn't see any trees. But it turned out that there was something there: the people who had drowned.

"As we continued marching forward we suddenly saw as if in a smog a small flashing light ahead of us. Someone remarked aloud: "There's a tank coming toward us." We were all seized with terror. Suddenly the blinking light stopped close to us. The supposed tank turned out to be a man with a flashlight who had been sent out on reconnaissance to see if he could find the entrance into the little tunnel. Zygmunt started laughing out loud, saying "We all must have gone crazy! What would a tank be doing in a sewer?"

"People began quarreling among themselves and fights would start over the most insignificant trifles. Once two such "addled" soldiers, no one knew why, suddenly started fighting viciously, stark-naked but for the helmets on their heads.

"After this hopeless march forward, there came a moment when all of us were resigned and ready to hand ourselves over to the Germans if only to put an end to our torture and suffering. But no one could find the manhole leading outside. Not seeing anything else to do, we dragged our weary legs through the water.

"Suddenly we heard a woman's voice ring out in the distance: "Come back! Come back!" The sound of her voice echoed in the tunnel like thunder. We came to a stop and turned our heads around and noticed a little blinking light far off in the distance. We began moving in the direction of the little light. When we finally reached it we noticed a girl holding a candle in her hand.

"First she told us to lean against the wall and rest for a minute. We were all so tired that she didn't have to repeat it twice. To each of us she handed out a sugar cube, which she was carrying in a bag slung over her shoulder. It turned out that she had been sent out specifically to find us and point out the right path which we had passed up and so had gone astray. She told us that she was the daughter of a colonel who lived on Ujazdowski Boulevard, and that the proper exit from the sewer which we were looking for was located there.

"In principle, a straight-line journey from Mokotów to Ujazdowski Boulevard was comparatively short. Unfortunately, it had been necessary to travel a long and circuitous route by way of Czerniaków, for many of the intervening streets were now occupied by the Germans. If we had continued going in the direction in which we were headed, she said, we would have drowned and never seen the light of day, for it led to the Vistula river, where the opening was barred, and the water only got deeper and deeper.

"It was hard for us to believe that we had been so lucky, and that we would be able to get out of this subterranean tomb. As to how many people perished in the sewers, I would not be able to say. No one would be able to answer that question. But they hadn't forgotten about us! We were very grateful, and those of who made it through alive will never forget that anonymous messenger who came to our aid and rescued us at the risk of her own life.

"After a short rest, and much lifted in spirit by this wonderful girl, we continued our march. It was still a long way before we finally saw the light of day. The girl walked in front, because she was well acquainted with the sewers, having been through them more than once. Because Zygmunt and I had been walking in the front of the group, now that we had turned around we were two of the last. We thus had to keep a careful lookout for those who had given up in weariness and rested for a moment against the walls, lest they fall asleep, sink down into the water, and drown. This cost us much effort, as we had to push and shove them along by force and shouting.

"Finally, barely able to drag our weary limbs along, we came to a tall wall. I was so tired that I thought I saw a big wardrobe case in front of me, and I said to Zygmunt: "How do you think we are going to make it past that wardrobe?" To this he replied: "That's no wardrobe; it's a wall with a ladder of iron bars built in to it, the same kind we used to climb into the sewers in the first place. We have to climb up this ladder in order to get into the little sewer, where we will find the way out." I was so weary by this time that I was no longer able to lift my legs to the first rung on the ladder. If it hadn't been for Zygmunt's help, who walked behind me and pushed me ahead, watching out for me every step of the way, I am sure that I would never have made it past this final hurdle.

"At last, after an enormous effort, we made it into the little sewer and, crawling on our knees, we continued forward. The messenger girl kept pointing the way, holding a burning candle in her hand.

"We crawled in this manner for several hundred meters until at last we came to another wall containing another ladder, similar to the others. Just as before, Zygmunt helped me climb the ladder. My head stuck out of the manhole, and a current of fresh air hit me, which I eagerly sucked into my lungs. I felt two strong arms grip me and pull me up. When at last I found myself on the outside, my tortured brain was still unable to comprehend: Was it really possible that I was still alive and had escaped from that horrible tomb? Everyone must have been asking themselves the same question.

"I looked around and saw that I was in a large garden, or really a park. Everything around me looked white: the trees, earth, and so forth. I asked one of the partisans who helped me out of the sewer whether it had snowed that day. He replied that I had probably clean lost my senses; what would snow be doing falling in September? Later it turned out that all of us were half blind. We were taken to an infirmary where we lay for several days until we regained our sight. In the hospital they explained to us that our temporary blindness had been caused by carbide which the Germans had thrown into the sewers. In addition, our footsteps had stirred up other harmful chemical agents that had accumulated on the bottom of the sewers over the course of many years.

75

MY HUSBAND'S STORY CONCLUDED: FROM WARSAW TO GRODZISK

"We were almost starving in the hospital. Our only food was a wheat soup from grain that had been milled by hand in a coffee mill. All during this time there were rumors that the AK was negotiating with the Germans concerning a ceasefire.

"After staying for several days in the improvised hospital, I regained my vision and was able to leave. I decided to go to one of our customers from before the war, Mrs. Jozefa Hebda, who lived on 77 Marsza-lkowska Street.

"It was an easy journey from Ujazdowki Boulevard to Marsza-lkowska, because the insurgents had knocked out holes from one building to the next, and they had dug tunnels under the streets. Mrs. Hebda received me very warmly. First of all she gave me some water to wash in, which was a real treasure at this time; the provident Mrs. Hebda had kept a reserve supply of water in her bathtub and in various kinds of kitchen containers. Since after my adventures in the sewers all my clothing and underwear were in rags, Mrs. Hebda offered me one of her husband's suits. He was slightly taller and thicker than I was, but I was quite satisfied and inexpressibly gratified for what I received.

"She told me about her son-in-law, the doctor of medicine and officer in the regular Polish Army who had perished in the Katyń forest massacre in Russia where he was a prisoner of war. We had known him quite well before the war.

"Mrs. Hebda had no trouble putting me in touch with Henryk, who had been by to see her several times during the uprising, for he was staying not far away in the building where our little factory had been.

"The rumors concerning the ceasefire turned out to be well founded. On October 2, 1944 the insurgents capitulated. The Germans took the insurgents captive, along with their commander, General Bór-Komorowski. The population received two weeks' notice to evacuate Warsaw. Henryk and I decided to leave with no further delay. We were joined by his brother-in-law, Janek. On the day before the capitulation, Henryk advised me to go to AK headquarters and ask for a document under my assumed name, Aleksander Przybysz, since my documents had been burned. I did as he advised, and the Germans honored all documents issued by the AK.

"We said goodbye to Zygmunt, who was going in search of his wife. The three of us left Warsaw in the direction of Pruszków, as the Germans had instructed. It was late in the afternoon, and throngs of people were headed in that direction. On both sides of the sidewalk stood Germans armed with rifles, maintaining order. At one point along the way Henryk pointed out to me the place in which all this time our son had been staying. This was the Father Boduen orphanage[1] on Filtrowa Street. Since the outbreak of the uprising, we had had no information concerning him. I looked through the iron fence into the yard, but I saw no signs of life.

"The farther we drew away from the city, the fewer Germans there were escorting us. As darkness overtook us, a strong rain began to fall. We took advantage by separating ourselves from the others and going off on a side road, putting as much distance as possible between us and them. Soaked to the skin and bone-weary, we knocked at the first peasant cottage we came to, and we were allowed to spend the night. Next morning we bought a number of farming implements from the owner of the cottage and went along our way, pretending to be workers.

"We walked this way from village to village. At one point we ran into a Wehrmacht patrol who checked our documents. They took us for workers and allowed us to proceed. Later we were stopped and sent to the local German gendarme headquarters. After checking my documents, the Germans let me go, but Henryk and Janek, despite their having authentic "Kennkarten," were detained. I went about half a kilometer down the road and stopped to wait for them. After a while, they too came along. I had a good laugh at the Germans setting me free, while holding them up.

"We continued walking along back roads in the direction of Grodzisk, where Henryk's wife and children were supposed to be staying, along with Father Święcki. We stopped for the night in the villages, carefully avoiding German patrols.

"One evening, as I was staying in a peasant's hut (Henryk and Janek were staying in a different place), I met a young man about twenty years of age from Warsaw. He told me that the Germans had caught him and sent him to work in Majdanek, where his job had been to pile the corpses of Jews on a grate and push them into the ovens for burning. Unable to endure this grizzly work, he had escaped. Because of the uprising he had been unable to get to Warsaw, and so at present he was wandering about the surrounding towns. His stories thoroughly depressed me, and it was good that because of the weak light of the oil lamp in the room, no one could see my face. I quickly went to bed, covering my head with the blanket.

"On the following day we arrived in Grodzisk. We first went to the market square where we expected to meet some of our friends from Warsaw. Fortune was with me, for behind one of the stalls I noticed Roman and Wanda. They were selling homemade snacks. I told them I was in search of a place to stay. Wanda immediately took me to a wickerware store located across the way. She introduced me to the woman shop-owner and asked if she could rent me a corner somewhere. The woman agreed, but only on condition that I register with the police. The document which the AK had given me was honored everywhere, and everything went smoothly in the registry office, where I received a registration slip and, by the same token, a roof over my head.

"I began looking around for some way to earn some money, for after all I had to live somehow. Wanda and Roman advised me to do what they were doing and sell things in the marketplace. Several days of observation persuaded me that cigarettes and bread were in the greatest demand. I learned that very early in the morning smugglers would come to town from Radom, where a tobacco factory was located. I got up at daybreak and went to the marketplace, where there were already a goodly number of people with same idea, and I bought cigarettes from the smugglers at wholesale prices. During the day I sold them by the pack on the square where I found a special place. I tried not to look anyone in the eyes for fear that some ill-meaning person or "greaser" would recognize me as a Jew and denounce me.

"Even here in Grodzisk the Germans gave us no peace. They would organize raids by surrounding the marketplace and seize people for work digging trenches. Usually we would receive warning about this the day before. On such days I would leave my quarters in the morning and wander through the neighboring villages and return to

Grodzisk only late in the afternoon. As time went on the situation in Grodzisk became increasingly dangerous. Among other things, there was Henryk's brother-in-law, Janek. He was a waiter by trade and liked to drink. In Grodzisk he had met a friend of his, an undercover agent from Warsaw, and once while drinking Janek blurted out what he knew about me.

"Janek, whose wife was Marysia Michalski's sister, told Henryk about it, and Henryk told me, and once more I felt danger hanging over my head. When Father Święcki learned about what had happened he advised me to go over to the Russian side. Henryk, who during the entire period of the German occupation was living under an assumed name, was in constant fear that someone would denounce him for belonging to the AK, and eagerly seized on the idea and wanted to accompany me. Everything was quiet on the front, and the end of the war was still not in sight.

"We knew that the Russians had established a bridgehead a dozen kilometers or so to the east of Warsaw and were holding on valiantly. It was said that with the help of the right kind of guide it was possible to go over to the Russian side there. Through Henryk's various acquaintances, a guide was recommended to him by the name of Włodek. In all probability he was Ukrainian. For taking us over to the Russian side he was asking fifty dollars a head which, when translated into Polish money, came to quite a sum. Not seeing anything else to do, we agreed to his terms, and the approximate date of departure was set.

---

1. **Father Boduen children's hospital.** This still-existing institution in Warsaw was founded in 1732 as a home for cast-off children by French-born Father Gabriel Boudouin (1689-1768). During the war it protected more than a hundred abandoned and orphaned Jewish children both in its main facility and, especially for children with Semitic features, in its various branches outside Warsaw, in individual homes, and in monasteries and cloisters.

76

OUT OF GRODZISK

"In the meantime, on one cold and rainy winter's day, with intermittent snow flurries (on such days I did not do business but stayed inside) Roman suddenly came to me and told me that someone was waiting for me outside. Walking through the corridor I spotted my wife. What an unexpected surprise this was! I stood there rooted to the spot, unable to believe my own eyes. I had had no news about her since we had parted ways in Sadyba Oficerska. It was a real miracle. She was alive and well, and standing out on the sidewalk only a few steps away. After our initial greetings, and after the initial joy of seeing her alive had passed, I could see that my wife presented a most heart-breaking sight. She was pale, wan, emaciated, and in rags. In spite of the cold she was dressed in a light summer raincoat with wooden clogs on her feet. She was soaked to the skin and looked simply miserable.

"I thanked Roman and took her into the apartment. At last, after such a long time of separation, we were together once again. The first thing I told her was that she was lucky, because I was preparing to leave for the Russian side. We told each other what we had been through since last seeing each other, and I also told her of the danger I was presently in because of Janek, and that the date Henryk and I had set for going over to the Russian side was to have been tomorrow. Because of my wife's pitiful state I could see that she would have to rest and that I would need to find some warm winter clothing for her."

[Mrs. Schmidt's Narrative, Resumed]

Now I will pick up my story where I left off.

The evening of that same day Henryk came to see my husband. His face burst out in a broad smile at the unexpected sight of me. I was pleasantly surprised, for that was the first time I had ever seen him smile since I had gone over to the Aryan side. When he had come to pick up our products in the ghetto he had always worn a grumpy expression. That was his nature.

I had been a constant weight around his neck, which he would have been just as glad to get rid of, and he always made that perfectly clear. I was always quiet in his presence and tried to keep in the shadows. That evening, however, he came up to me with a smile on his face and said,

"Since you've returned alive, I am beginning to believe that everything will turn out all right, and that you will live to see the end of the war."

"God grant it," I replied.

My husband and Henryk began a lively discussion of their plans to cross over to the Soviet side. Henryk was full of trust and enthusiasm. In general he loved any kind of adventure, and this was for him another one, and a fascinating one to boot. My own view of the undertaking was extremely skeptical.

"Could I have a look at this guide Włodek?" I asked.

"I'll send him around tomorrow," Henryk promised, for it would be necessary to make arrangements concerning the addition of another person to the party.

Włodek came by next day. He was about twenty-eight years old. His face could have been called pretty if it had not been for the expression in his eyes. They were impertinent, audacious and unscrupulous. I was certain that he was Ukrainian, because of his accent and his way of saying certain things in Polish. The thought flashed through my mind: *This Satan in human form will lead us to extermination. As soon as we are close to the Soviet zone, after taking the hundred and fifty dollars he'll denounce us to the Germans.* I told him in brief about the suffering, torture, and terrible experiences we had endured. I also told him that as far as I was concerned, the idea of our ever getting to the Russian side seemed doubtful. If he had any doubt whatsoever about the venture, then he should leave us in peace and we should forget about the whole thing. After sitting some time in silence, Włodek got up from his chair and said that he would have to think the whole thing over again before giving a final answer.

Since my husband still had a large supply of cigarettes, we decided that each of us would stand by ourselves in the market selling them, so as to get rid of them all the quicker. Several days passed peacefully as we were thus engaged. Sales were good, and if it were not for our immediate enemies, we would easily be able to make it this way to the end of the war. Unfortunately, there were no indications of an early conclusion to the war, and our insides were being eaten out from fear. We were constantly under the impression that we were being observed. After all, the devil never sleeps.

One afternoon while standing out on the market square, I noticed a man walk up to my husband and engage him in conversation. I immediately became uneasy. My husband pointed me out to him and he came over with rapid strides. He said that he was Janek, Henryk's brother-in-law, and that I had probably heard about him. He said that he only wanted to say hello to me. I replied politely, and after a minute he left. I didn't like anything about this incident, and that evening I said to my husband that there was something suspicious about it. My husband told me to settle down, that it was impossible living like this.

After another week had passed, a second guide came around to us on Włodek's recommendation. He was also Ukrainian. He told us that Włodek would be unable to escort us to the Russian side, but that he would undertake to do it, since he knew certain places and had already taken many people across. This guide made a somewhat better impression on me, because he was well past forty years old. My suspicions had not disappeared, but I no longer had the courage to openly oppose the venture, especially in front of Henryk. We decided that the guide would come to get us the following evening.

At the appointed hour, Henryk came to our place. He was carrying a white knapsack on his shoulders, stuffed completely full. When I commented that the white color of his bag would be easily noticed, he laughed heartily and said, "You see nothing but danger everywhere you look."

The guide turned up on time. Of course, he demanded payment in advance. Henryk gave him three fifty-dollar bills, and we set out on our way, boarding the electric train running through the city. At the first station, in Milanówek, the guide told us to get off and follow him. He brought us to a tiny villa and ordered us to wait, saying that he would be right back. We sat down on the steps and waited. The guide did not return. Henryk and my husband took a look around the villa and located a second exit. Then we understood that our guide had deceived us. He had taken our money and run out on us through the other exit.

Because of the late hour we had to run back to the station so as not to miss the last train. We got into the very last wagon, and it was very late by the time we got back to Grodzisk. Henryk ran home, but we stayed out on the street, not knowing what to do, for we were sure that those thugs, Wlodek and his friend, would set the police on us. Let's go to Wanda's, I told my husband.

When we got to Roman and Wanda's place they didn't ask us about anything but let us stay the night. They were living in a tiny little room not far from the basket store. The room was dark and gloomy, and its window faced a wall, but at least it was a place for the night. Being evacuees from Warsaw, they were quite satisfied with this little room. Wanda's sister, a twelve-year-old girl, was living with them, and she gave us her bed, herself sleeping on a mattress on the floor.

The following day Wanda and Roman turned to us with the proposition that we stay in their home for two weeks, because they had certain things to take care of in Kraków, and they were afraid to leave Wanda's sister there all alone. We were practically struck dumb by this proposal; it fell on us like a blessing from God. Of course we agreed, and Wanda and Roman began seeing about obtaining railway passes. My husband went to the market in order to find out any news. He returned pale and upset. He said that German gendarmes had twice come to our former quarters looking for us. Once again we had escaped death by a hair's breadth.

We decided not to show our faces in town for the entire two weeks. Wanda's sister bought us whatever we needed from the market. She was a polite and quiet little girl, and we came to like her very much.

December had arrived, and it snowed almost every day. It was impossible to buy coal in Grodzisk, so we burned wood in the kitchen. The wood was damp, and the tiny room was always full of smoke. In spite of this we felt happy. No one, not even Henryk, knew where we were staying. We rested both physically and mentally and gathered our strength for the battle that lay ahead. We had decided that after Wanda and Roman returned we would move to Milanówek, about four kilometers from Grodzisk. We left early one morning on foot by back roads to scout out Miłanówek. In a place off the beaten track, in a large but almost completely tumble-down wooden building by the name of "Zakopane" we noticed a small notice on a little card that a room was for rent. The landlady of the apartment, a young but clearly disease-ravaged woman, gave us a thoughtful looking over and, after considering it for a rather long time, agreed to rent us a bed for a certain amount of money. We gave her a deposit and, now in a much better frame of mind, returned by the same back roads to Grodzisk.

After two weeks, Wanda and Roman came back from Kraków. They were very grateful to us for looking after the sister, and we were even more grateful for being able to stay there. We packed our miserable belongings and left for our new place. Our landlady, a quiet and quite decent woman, was sick with tuberculosis. She spat blood and was sleeping in the same bed with her four-year-old daughter. I was certain that the woman knew who we were, but poverty forced her into pretending that she didn't know anything.

77

SMUGGLING SUGAR IN
MILANÓWEK

Difficult days were once more ahead of us. We were unable to stay in
the apartment during the day and, besides that, we had to look around
for something to do to earn a living, since our savings from selling cigarettes were dwindling by the day.

Our landlady told us that a dozen or so kilometers away was the
Józefów sugar refinery, where they illegally sold a certain amount of
sugar to smugglers, who would then take it to Piaseczno and sell it on
the market at a good profit. The idea appealed to us and early next day
we set out on our way. During this time it was customary to ride on
peasant wagons, because the trains were not running regularly.
Whoever had a horse and wagon was automatically ensured of a good
living.

Since the collection point was the market square, and we were
afraid of showing our faces there, out of consideration for our personal
safety we went on foot. We arrived in Józefów at daybreak. We were
told that in order to buy a fifty-kilogram bag of sugar we had to stand in
line at the sugar refinery from five o'clock in the morning. Along with
some other smugglers we spent the night in some building, and next
morning, while it was still dark, we took our place as one of the first in
line at the refinery. The previous day we had bought two clean white
bags so as to be able to share the weight on two backs.

At six o'clock the gates of the refinery opened, and we managed to
buy our sugar without any difficulty. We divided it on the spot, so that
my husband carried thirty kilos and I carried twenty. The drivers, who

were already waiting for passengers, took us and our baggage back to Milanówek. As a rule there were seven to eight people to a wagon. Sometimes we would meet up with "faces" similar to ours, but we pretended that we didn't see anything.

Next day, after looking around carefully in all directions, we went to the station to catch the train to Piaseczno. Actually the train went only as far as Okęcie (Warsaw's airport), and it was necessary to ride from Okęcie to Piaseczno by horsecart. At the market in Piaseczno we sold our sugar and, with the money we made, we bought butter, sausage, and bread for our own use. Up until Christmastime we went three times a week to Jozefów for sugar and another three times to Piaseczno. Sunday was our day of rest. Our landlady was fond of us, for we gave her small amounts of sugar, butter, and bread, which were a real treasure for her.

Since we knew the address of the house in which Henryk and his family were staying, my husband decided to go and see him. Henryk was very glad to see my husband. He had been certain that the Germans must have found us and put an end to us. Once more he reminded my husband that he must be on his guard for, as we have said, his brother-in law Janek had blabbed to the agent about us. Henryk told Janek that if so much as a hair on our heads was harmed, they would both answer for it, and Janek knew that Henryk's threats were no joke, for he belonged to the AK. Janek was well aware of the death sentences that were still being carried out by the AK on traitors.

This news depressed us. I was reminded of the scene in the market when Janek first went up to my husband and then to me. I understood that the agent must have been nearby. They also discussed the question of the money which Włodek had tricked them out of. Father Święcki advised Henryk and my husband to go to Włodek for the hundred and fifty dollars which he had stolen. Włodek lived some four kilometers from Grodzisk in a small village with his father-in-law, who was the village elder there. When they went there next day he promised to return the money, but he did not keep his word. With Henryk's influence the death sentence was passed on Włodek by the AK leadership. However, when the executors of the sentence came for him, he was no longer staying there, and so the scoundrel escaped his just deserts.

The Christmas holidays arrived. Henryk and his wife invited us over for Christmas Eve. This was the first time we had ever spent Christmas Eve in a Catholic home. We were very grateful to them for the pleasant evening we spent in their company and with their children. We could not stop thinking about our son. Who knew where he was now or whether he was still alive. Father Święcki, who was also present that evening, told us that the children from the Father Boduen orphanage had been evacuated during the uprising. They had been sent in various directions. Some of them had found shelter in a silk factory in Milanówek. After the holidays my husband and I walked by this factory several times in the hope of seeing our child at least from a distance. Unfortunately, the factory was surrounded by a high wall, and it was impossible to see anything.

Henryk's wife Marysia had been the last to see our son, at the end of July. She said that all the children in the orphanage were very hungry. One day she brought our baby a roll with butter and some sausage. Since she saw that his hands were dirty, she took back the roll in order to wash them first. The baby, afraid that the roll was being taken away from him, threw himself on the floor in a terrible tantrum. Marysia understood then how terribly hungry he was. This story upset us very much, but we were helpless to do anything about it. All night long I lay on the bed at the Michalskis' (we had stayed there because it was past curfew) and cried quietly so as not to waken anyone.

During dinner the conversation primarily concerned us. My husband said that in Milanówek he had met one of the PAL officers with whom he had been acquainted in Mokotów. He had asked him to try to put him in touch with the partisans in the forest. The officer listened to him seriously without saying a word, and finally left him there and went away. Father Święcki and Henryk once again warned us to go carefully with the partisans. If we happened into the hands of the NSZ, we were as good as lost, for they shot any Jew on sight.

Next day the woman with whom we had been staying told us that she would be unable to keep us any longer, but that since she liked us very much, she had found a place for us with her brother, who lived about six kilometers out of Milanówek. This was just as well with us, for Milanówek was still very close to Grodzisk, and we were afraid that the agents would find our tracks and come looking for us.

Our landlady's brother received us very cordially. It appeared that his sister had been saying good things about us. We were given a bed in a large, bright, and clean room which our hosts shared with us.

The house in which we were now staying was located on the edge of a forest. Winter that year was beautiful. Dry snow fell almost every day. The ground froze and everything around was a glistening white. The air was clean and pleasant. Winter has its own beauty and charm, and in any case I always felt more at ease surrounded by nature. In short, we were pleased with the change in our housing arrangements.

In order to keep up appearances in front of our rural hosts, I kneeled every morning and evening in front of the Virgin Mary and pretended to say my prayers. I advised my husband to do the same. Since my husband knew no prayers, I advised him to count from one to a hundred and then to cross himself and rise. He did as I said, and our new hosts had absolutely no idea who we were.

78

ARRESTED IN PIASECZNO

After the Christmas holidays and New Year's, we continued traveling for sugar to the refinery in Jozefów and from there to Piaseczno. Sales were brisk, but sometimes there were raids and roundups in the market-place in Piaseczno for work in the trenches. Together with other smugglers, we would hide in one of the apartments near the marketplace.

The life which we were now leading was extremely fatiguing. The never-ending journeys by horsecart, the bitter cold, carrying the heavy bags of sugar on our backs—all of this undermined our health and strength. We saw nothing else to do, however, so we had to keep walking the same road in order to live. New Year's 1945 did not make a very big impression on us. This was the sixth year of the war, and no one knew how much longer the Germans would be able to hold out. It seemed to us that this long, terrible war would never come to an end. Every pair of eyes that rested on us for more than a moment made us afraid that we had been discovered.

One day, this was January 10, 1945, as I was returning with a heavy bag of sugar over my shoulders, I slipped and fell over back-wards. I managed to rise to my feet again only with the greatest diffi-culty and with my husband's help. A terrible pain shot through my back in the area of my tailbone. I barely managed to drag myself back home. Each step of the way was nothing but agony. I lay in bed for a while, but the pain did not cease. I was worried that next morning, which was Thursday, I would be in no shape to make the trip to Piaseczno. My husband comforted me, saying that I could stay in bed for a few days and wait until it passed. But how could I stay in bed when the entire home consisted of one room, in which our landlady spent practically the entire day, and where neighbors were constantly dropping by? It was always noisy and full of activity, for the people we were staying with had two children. I lay all day in bed, and toward evening I began to feel a little better.

I got up and began putting one foot in front of the other. The more I walked around the easier it became, and so I said to my husband, "Tomorrow is Friday, and it is a big market day in Piaseczno. We simply have to go there."

My husband asked me to wait until I felt a little better. He used one argument after another, but I was unmoved. Finally, seeing that there was no way to persuade me, he gave in.

In everyone's life there are moments of tremendous importance. Sometimes one's human instinct leads to good and sometimes not. However, it is too strong for anyone to be able to control it. That thing happened with me that memorable Friday. Some internal compulsion, as if it were Satan whispering in my ear, kept telling me: Go! Something was driving me on. I was determined to overcome my pain and make the trip to Piaseczno.

We arrived in Piaseczno in the afternoon. The day was crisp and sunny. We decided to spend the night there and return home on Saturday. We bought some butter, sausage, and bread at the market and took it to the apartment where we normally spent the night with the other smugglers. Next we took up our bags of sugar and went to the marketplace. We found an excellent spot in the very center of the square, and we set our bags down and waited for some customers to turn up. After a moment two men came up to us, one of them young, the other well past forty, and asked the price of sugar. Suddenly the older man said, "We are police agents. Please pick up your bags quickly and come with us."

There was nothing else to do. The younger agent walked in front, with us in the middle and the older man closing the formation in the rear. As we were crossing the street, we caught sight of Janek, Henryk's brother-in-law. As soon as his eyes met those of my husband's, he turned his head. We understood that this had been his doing.

The agents walked for a long time. The buildings of Piaseczno began to thin out, and we soon found ourselves outside town. They took us into some sort of villa. The younger one disappeared somewhere for a while, leaving the older one to guard us. He had an intelligent face with a shrewd and cunning expression in his eyes. We sat down in some chairs which the agents indicated to us, and a long period of silence ensued. The agent was first to speak. He had a strong Russian accent; he must have come from around Wilno. First he told us what our real names were, and then our assumed ones. He knew almost everything about us. Janek had done a good job. The only good thing was that he didn't seem to know about our child. Evidently Janek had not mentioned it, and it was clear why not: his cousin Father Święcki would have gotten mixed up in the affair.

At one point we heard the sound of heavy artillery far off in the distance. I thought to myself how wonderful it would be if one of the shells fell on the villa, destroying it and everything in it, killing us all, including these hideous agents. That way we would at least have a decent death, if such was to be our fate. While still at the market we had heard the far-away explosions but had not paid any particular attention to them. After all, Piaseczno was fairly close to the Vistula, and the Russians were on the other side of the river.

At the sound of this artillery action the agent smiled derisively and said, "Aha! So the Russians are beginning their offensive again. But they won't do any better this time than the last!"

At one point the agent said that if we gave him all our money he would let us go free. Hope was rekindled in my heart. I had fifty dollars sewn into the jacket I was wearing. This was the last money we possessed. When my husband had met Henryk at Mrs. Hebda's, he had given my husband a hundred and fifty dollars which he owed him after all the accounts were settled. Włodek had tricked us out of a hundred of them, and my husband had given me the remainder. I had been keeping this treasure for a dark hour. Without hesitation I unsewed this last fifty dollars and gave it to the agent, along with the money in Polish zlotys which we had with us.

The agent shook his head and said that that was not enough. I told him that we still had some butter, sausage, and bread in the apartment, and we would give that to him too. After a long period of silence, the agent called in the younger man and ordered me to go with him to pick up the things we had left. The agent didn't say a single word to me the whole way.

I thought to myself that even if had I been able to escape I wouldn't have taken advantage of it and left my husband there to fend for himself. We had already spent the last eight years together through good and bad. We were not only man and wife, but the truest of friends and comrades. My husband was all that I possessed in life, my sole support at the most difficult times of our mutual struggle for survival. We would perish together, and surely in those final moments of life things would be better for us. In the bottom of my heart I still had a tiny ray of hope. Maybe the agent would keep his word. Twice already my husband had ransomed himself from such agents and gotten out of their clutches.

It was beginning to get dark when we arrived back at the villa. I found my husband in the same room as before. I gave the agent the packages we had brought and we waited for him to set us free. He told my husband to take off the overcoat he was wearing, which was in fairly good condition. In exchange he gave him an old worn-out jacket. He left us there in the room without saying a further word.

79

IMPRISONMENT

Suddenly we heard the sound of a key in the lock. The doors opened and all we could see were flashlights pointed in our direction. "Heraus!" Our hearts came to a stop. These were Germans from the field police. They signaled to us to walk in front of them. Everything is lost, I thought to myself. Our struggle has been for nothing. The sly and unscrupulous agent had cleaned us out of everything we had and then handed us over to the Germans.

We walked in front, with the Germans at a little distance behind, holding their weapons on us. I was certain that suddenly out of the darkness shots would ring out, and our dead bodies would crumple down in the little beech forest through which we were passing. I began talking aloud to myself in Polish. I spoke of the tortures and suffering we had endured over the past several years, about the perfidity and insolence of the agents through whom we now found ourselves in the hands of the Germans, our deadliest enemy, a miserable nation of murders.

"God's revenge will come some day to you too," I said to them. "You'll pay for all your crimes. Your end is approaching with giant steps."

The Germans walked along in silence behind us. Finally we came to a building with a sign saying "Feldgendarmerie". The doors opened and one of the gendarmes who had been walking behind us said in perfect Polish with a Poznań accent,

"Won't you please step inside?"

I could only think to myself with satisfaction: So, at least you listened to me and heard everything I was saying.

We were escorted to an empty cell. Some straw was lying in a corner, and we sat down on it in silence. After a while the jailer came along, bringing some bread and a cup of steaming hot coffee. All day long we had had nothing to eat, but only my husband had a drink of the coffee. I was unable to take even a sip. My throat was closed tight and I couldn't manage a single swallow. We returned the bread untouched.

The jailer took a look at our tragic faces and said, "Now there's no reason to get so terribly upset; everything's going to be all right."

He obviously didn't know why we were being held.

After the jailer left we lay down on the straw, our hearts filled with despair. All words were superfluous. I had only one desire: for them to finish with us as quickly as possible and not stretch out our agony any longer than necessary. I remembered that on this very same day my mother had died. What an irony of fate! I also thought to myself that I was the last remaining member of my family, and that now no one at all would be left.

When it began to grow light, the doors of our cell opened and the jailer entered, accompanied by a gendarme, and ordered us out. The gendarme escorted us to the railway station, where a locomotive and a car had been brought in especially for us. There was no one besides us and the gendarme in the entire car. Along the way one other passenger got on board. He looked like some kind of a "big fish." He was thick and fat as a pig and wore a dark uniform. He must have been going hunting, for the train stopped somewhere in the middle of the forest and let him out.

I do not know how long we rode, but the sun was shining when the train came to a stop. The sign on the station said Grojec. We began walking. It was a beautiful sunny winter's day. I looked up into the sky and couldn't take my eyes off it for a long time. I kept thinking that these were the last days of my young life. I did not doubt for a minute that the gendarme, according to the custom of the blood-thirsty German beasts, would take us to an out-of-the way spot, order us to dig our own graves, and then let go with his automatic weapon.

The road stretched out into the distance, and we left the railway station far behind. Finally the gendarme took us to a gray building on which a sign was posted saying "Prison." The gates closed behind us and we were led to the first floor and locked in a cell. This was a tiny little cage, almost completely dark. In one of the corners there was a wooden bench, and on it was a straw-filled mattress. In another corner was a small table and two chairs. We had never had any previous experience with prisons, or even with the court. We were peaceful citizens who had always walked the straight and narrow.

"Why are they going through all this rigmarole?" I asked my husband. "What do they think we are going to do? What do they want from us?"

"I don't know," my husband replied, "but we'll probably find out soon enough."

The jailer, wearing a military uniform, brought us a little watery soup and a piece of bread. My husband ate his, but I wasn't able to touch a bite. That evening I didn't touch any food either. I had decided not to eat. As long as they have us, I thought, I would rather die of starvation. I tried to think how long that might take. How long could it take for the mind to become clouded over and sink into oblivion?

"Just be patient," I kept saying to myself, "and surely you'll get there soon enough."

It was already rather late when the jailer opened the door of our cell and motioned for my husband to follow him. My first thought was that they were probably going to beat and torture him, eventually killing him. I cried bitterly. Streams of tears rolled down my cheeks, and I sat there sobbing that way for several hours. My husband did not return, and I had not the slightest hope that he ever would. I strained my ears to try to catch the sounds of his moans or of shots, but there was no interruption to the silence all around. After two or maybe three hours I heard the key scrape in the lock, and I sat down on the bed. The thought flashed through my mind like lightning: *They've come for me.* The door opened, and my husband appeared in the door with a lighted cigarette in his hand. He was smiling faintly.

"What happened to you? Where have you been for so long?" I asked him.

The jailer had taken him to the prison office where an officer of the German gendarmes was waiting. He indicated a chair and asked him politely to have a seat. First he asked him what language he preferred to speak in, German or Polish. He said that he was from Poznań. My husband said Polish. The next question he asked was where we had managed to hide for so long. My husband answered that he had many friends in Warsaw who had helped him. He did not give any names, but even if he had it wouldn't have mattered, for Warsaw was in ruins and without inhabitants. No one knew where anyone was.

The officer knew our real names and what our occupation had been before the war. Clearly this had been Janek's work. There was not even any point in denying anything. Next the officer asked him whether he knew any people who belonged to the AK, and where their present headquarters might be located, where their radio station was, and so forth. He asked a large number of questions on that subject. My husband responded in the negative, and his answers were recorded in the protocol. Upon the conclusion of the interrogation, the officer offered my husband a cigarette, and the conversation switched to other subjects, primarily the suffering borne by the Jews during the German occupation.

After a while the officer said, "This is one more link in the chain of the suffering of the Jewish people."

My husband told me that during the course of the several hours of interrogation, he had not once had the slightest impression that he was being held prisoner. On the contrary, they had conversed like two friends who had met on neutral territory.

Eventually the officer told my husband, "Don't you worry, sir. I'll send over a package of food and cigarettes tomorrow."

After listening to the end of this tale, I said to my husband, "Don't be taken in by him. Germans know how to be sweet as sugar when they want to pull wool over someone's eyes and get a confession out of him. The officer probably thinks he has caught a "big fish" who will be able to inform on people in the AK, and that's the only reason we are still alive. One way or the other, they've got us, and that's all there is to it."

80

LIBERATION

Next day was Sunday, the third day of our confinement. I continued not to take any food. My overwrought nerves kept me in a state of constant agitation. I was sensitive to every little sound and movement. My mind worked clearly; the cloud of darkness for which I had been waiting so patiently did not arrive. In the afternoon the jailer told us to pick up our things and come with him. Now they're taking us to our deaths, I thought. But the jailer led us to another wing of the prison and gave us another cell in which there was a coal stove. All day long my husband waited to see whether the package promised by the officer would arrive. It never did.

The fourth day of our detainment arrived, Monday. I continued not to consume anything except for a little coffee. All other food was abhorrent to me: always some kind of watery soup in which a few pieces of beet or cabbage would be swimming. When I was standing next to the stove I accidentally burned a hole in my only dress. My husband saw it and said, "Why aren't you more careful? What do you look like in that dress now?"

I laughed bitterly and said, "They'll take me in the other world just as well in this one as in any other."

At four o'clock, the jailer appeared and took us downstairs to the ground floor. Here he separated us. First he took my husband to a cell for men, and then me to one for women. In the cell I found a number of other young women, all of them obviously Polish. The stove had been

397

lighted and a merry fire was burning. It was all merriment and gaiety here, it seemed.

"What's your name?" they all asked.

"Marta," I replied.

"Don't be so gloomy; smile a little. This is the last day of our stay in prison. They're going to let us all out tomorrow."

You, maybe, but not me, I thought to myself.

"It seems the Germans are withdrawing," they said.

One of the women offered me a glass of vodka, and I drank it straight down. The hot liquid warmed my empty stomach and set my head spinning. Another woman gave me a large piece of bread and some sausage.

"Eat something, Marta," she said. "My mother sent me a package from home. You've got to keep up your strength, because you could just as easily croak from the slops they give you in this prison."

I ate heartily and had another glass of vodka. The food and drink did put me in a better frame of mind. Under the influence of the alcohol, I even began to believe that what I heard might actually come to pass, that it wasn't only a dream. One of the girls handed me a needle and thread, saying,

"You've got a hole in your stocking; sew it up, because what are you going to look like tomorrow when you get out?"

Another girl sewed up the hole in the back of my dress which I had burned on the stove.

It turned out that a Blue Police station was located on the ground floor of this part of the prison. People were mostly being held there for smuggling, while the upstairs was for military prisoners or for people like us. I racked my brains trying to figure out why the Germans had handed us over to the Blue Police. The answer, however, was not long in coming.

More or less the same goings on were taking place in the cell for men where my husband had been led. In it were smugglers and a blue policeman, who was also being held for smuggling. At first my husband did not know how they would act in his presence. He became sad and depressed, but his fellow inmates began trying to lift his spirits. They gave him vodka, bread, and sausage. No one asked him what he was being held for. Once the blue policeman turned to him and said,

"Don't worry! I found a "grapevine" note folded up in the potatoes I got from my mother. She says that the Germans are folding up camp and evacuating."

My husband told him that ever since the war began, there had been one hoax after another, and this was probably just another one.

In the evening we heard some terrible explosions, the sounds of grenades, artillery fire, and the noise of various kinds of handweapons and automatic rifles. All hell broke loose. The red glow of fires flared through the grated windows of our cells. We all bent down in the corner, for that seemed the safest thing to do. The girls began saying prayers. Once a shell struck the prison building and a tremendous explosion shook the entire edifice. Next day we learned that the shell had completely demolished the cell in which my husband and I had been staying the day before. Even now, our luck was holding.

In the men's cell, the shooting caused general panic. The smugglers hid beneath the bed, while my husband and the policeman took shelter underneath the table. Everyone thought that an uprising had broken out in Grojec.

"As if one uprising wasn't enough," they cried. "Warsaw wasn't enough, so now they had to start another one here."

As it later turned out, the Russians had begun their January offensive on January 12th, moving westward toward Berlin, the same day that the agent who had caught us had laughed so derisively.

The shooting lasted for about three hours, then everything quieted down and not a further sound was heard. The girls in our cell all sighed with relief.

As soon as the shooting stopped, my husband once more was overcome with sadness. Up until then he had still hoped that maybe something would happen to set us free, but now that everything was silent, his hopes went up in smoke.

At midnight we heard the sound of tanks driving past. The earth shook beneath their weight. One after another, in an unending stream they kept driving by until almost three o'clock. Early in the morning, a sergeant of the Blue Police came by: "Hey, boys! You're free! The Russians have taken the town!"

"If that's the case, then let us go," said my husband.

"No," replied the sergeant. "We have to wait until the commandant arrives together with the mayor, and they will let you out." Then he brought the same news to our cell.

The girls ran out of patience and began protesting vociferously, asking to be set free. When that didn't help, they flew into a terrible rage. They began beating the door with their shoes and crying, "Open up! Let us out!"

The jailer came and asked us to be a little more patient. We asked him to at least let us out into the corridor. We promised to behave calmly. The jailer agreed and opened the door. The first thing I did was to go up to my husband's cell, open the "Judas hole" and shout: We're free! I was seized with my joy. We're free! We're free! I kept shouting in ecstasy. We ran up and down the corridor out of our minds, hugging and kissing one another with joy.

Finally, the commandant of the Blue Police arrived together with the local mayor. The door was opened from the corridor into the court-yard, and next was the prison gate, which opened onto the main street of the town. I walked over to the other side of the street and waited for my husband. I looked around and could scarcely believe my eyes. As far as the eye could see there was nothing but ashes, ruins, and broken German artillery pieces and tanks. The road was littered with tele-phone poles, broken street lights, the bodies of German soldiers, and dead horses. The stores were all destroyed.

In the meantime, the men were also let out of their cells. The sergeant of the Blue Police put his hand on my husband's shoulder and said,

"Do you know that the Germans left you in our hands with orders to shoot you?"

"Thank you very much for leaving us alive," my husband told him. But in his heart he thought,

"You wouldn't have had the nerve to shoot us, knowing that the Russians were already on the edge of town."

Continuing to hold onto my husband's shoulder, the sergeant asked him whether he could get him some bread or anything else he might need. My husband was so dumbstruck at his suddenly regained freedom that he declined. Later he was sorry, for all day long we found nothing else to eat.

At last my husband came out of the prison gate onto the street. We looked at each other in disbelief and then fell into each other arms with a cry, literally out of our minds with happiness. After five years of wandering and a daily struggle for our lives, in the end we had endured. With death lurking on all sides at every moment, we had won!

We stood there for a while, looking at the devastation spread out before us. The streets were full of noise and activity. An expression of joy and contentment could be seen in the faces of the passers-by. At last they had rid themselves of their enemies. People everywhere were hugging and kissing, especially those who had just been released from prison.

We now had the rest of our lives ahead of us.

EPILOGUE

After the liberation, we made it to Żyrardów, about forty kilometers from Warsaw, which had been so damaged that it was impossible to live in. In Żyrardów we found a roof over our heads in the home of my two cousins who had survived the war in a bunker they had had specially constructed by a Polish friend of theirs in Milanówek. Their house and tannery had fortunately survived the ravages of war. The wife and daughter of one of them were also saved. At present they are living in Israel. My cousins were a much-needed support for us in the difficult post-war period and shared with us every piece of bread.

After a brief rest, my husband went to Warsaw, where he got in touch with Henryk Michalski. When he learned about our most recent adventures, and when he heard that we had seen his brother-in-law Janek when the agents arrested us in Piaseczno, he was beside himself with rage. He asked whether we wanted to seek revenge, but my husband told him that we Jews are not a vengeful people, and that God would mete out vengeance to our enemies. And so we parted ways with Henryk Michalski. We never again met anyone from the Michalski family. Henryk moved to former German lands in the west, the so-called "Recovered Territories."[1] His parents and his brother and his family remained in Dąbrowa Górnicza, where they had been evacuated by the Germans during the uprising.

While in Warsaw, my husband also met Zygmunt. It seemed that the tinsmith's place on Belwederska Street which had served as our place of hiding had been totally destroyed. The materials which

Zygmunt had so carefully buried in the bottom of the storage shed had all been lost in the flames. All he found was the heel of one of my boots. On the other hand, all of our notes had been saved. My husband had had the foresight to bury them separately in the workshop's "rubbish room." Zygmunt, who was the first to arrive after Warsaw's liberation, unburied them and gave them to my husband.

As soon as we got set up in Żyrardów, we initiated a search for our son. According to the information we had received from Father Święcki, the children from the orphanage had been evacuated to a silk factory in Milanówek. It was here that my husband went first. We had a photograph of our child taken before the uprising. We had buried it together with our notes. In Milanówek the mother superior informed my husband that our child had been evacuated to Kowaniec, two kilometers out of Nowy Targ, not far from Zakopane. In March 1945 he set out on his way. After a long and very difficult journey by freight train (no other means of long-distance locomotion was available during this period), my husband finally made it there. His legs were crumbling beneath him as he entered the door of the orphanage, for he was by no means certain that our child had been able to survive all the rigors and starvation.

My husband showed the superior the photograph with the assumed name of our boy: Rysio Węczyński. He said that he was the child's father and that he had come to retrieve him. He was taken to a big room containing a large number of children. Our son was standing up in his bed and my husband said that he recognized him as soon as he saw him. He was shown a number of other Jewish children (there were around forty of them) who had found shelter in this orphanage.

On March 13th my husband brought our son to Żyrardów. The child was weak, anemic, and terribly thin, but for all that, alive and well. He had spent two years and four months in the Father Boduen orphanage. At the time we retrieved him he was not quite three years old.

In the autumn of 1945 we moved to Kraków, intending to establish ourselves there permanently. However, after pogroms in Kraków and Kielce,[2] where around fifty Jews perished who, as we, had miraculously survived the war, we understood that Poland was no longer any place for Jews. We decided to emigrate. There were also other reasons for our choice. It frequently happened that Polish partisans fighting against the Soviets would stop trains. Any Jew they found would be cast out of the train, whether it was moving or not. Unfortunately, incidents like this occurred with increasing frequency. Since once in Kraków we had returned to our former profession, my husband was obliged to travel by train in order to sell our wares in various towns. He was thus constantly exposed to danger, and even now we knew no peace.

In the beginning of November 1946, legally, with passports and with no regrets, we left Poland forever, in the company of our two sons. The youngest had been born in Żyrardów shortly after the war.

After a year's stay in Paris, France, we arrived in Caracas, Venezuela, where we lived for fifteen years. After waiting the required amount of time (because of the immigration quota) for a visa, we finally arrived in the blessed land of our dreams, the United States of America. At present we are already American citizens, and are leading a quiet and peaceful life. We are proud to have provided a university education for our two sons.

To all those who, whether directly or indirectly, contributed to our salvations, and especially to the Michalski family, Zygmunt Dobosz, and Father Edward Święcki, we extend our sincerest thanks and appreciation.

- Leokadia Schmidt

---

1. **The "Recovered Territories."** After Poland, by the decision of the Big Three, "ceded" to the Soviet Union its former immense territories in the east at the Yalta conference of 1945, the country was "compensated" by being given German territory in the west and north (East Prussia), land which became known self-justifyingly as the "Recovered Territories", since much of it had, at one historical period or another, been under Polish rule.

2. **Kielce pogrom.** The deadliest of several pogroms against Jews in Poland immediately after the war occurred in Kielce on July 4, 1946. Reacting to a preposterously fabricated story about a Polish boy having been kidnapped by Jews for ritual purposes, a mob of local militia and citizens shot, stabbed, or beat to death forty-two Jews and wounded an equal number of others, among them women and children. Twelve people were put on trial and nine were executed in connection with the incident, which nevertheless irreparably damaged Poland in the eyes of the world and persuaded a large part of the surviving Polish Jewish community to emigrate. The referred-to events in Kraków mostly occurred in June, 1945.

AFTERWORD BY ARTHUR SCHMIDT

My father, the late Marian Schmidt, frequently shared with me his parents' memories from the war and the Holocaust and, judging from what he told me, the fate of our family was even more dramatic than is described in his mother's (my grandmother's) journal. My father was born toward the end of the war in Żyrardów, in a wooden house next to a tannery owned by some of my grandmother's cousins. Marian was the second son, and fourth child, of Joseph and Leokadia Knobelman Schmidt. Their two daughters died in infancy before the war, and their first son, Kazimierz, was saved from the Holocaust, as is described in these pages.

In her memoir my grandmother Leokadia fails to note that during the entire period of August 1944 to April 1945, she was pregnant with my father, making her situation during this period all the more drastic. When my grandparents left their hideout in the attic of the tinsmith's shed on Belwederska Street and decided to part ways for their mutual safety, neither of them knew about my grandmother's pregnancy. In November 1944, they managed to find each other again in Grodzisk. When they were both captured in Piaseczno in January and imprisoned in the death cell in Grojec, my grandmother would have been in her sixth month of pregnancy. They avoided execution by nothing short of a miracle, and so it is also by a miracle that my father, Marian Schmidt, came into the world on April 21, 1945. He was named in memory of Marian (Maniek) Michalski, who had been caught and executed by the Gestapo for stockpiling weapons.

My father Marian Schmidt (known in the United States as Mark Schmidt) died on March 7, 2018 in Kraków, Poland, leaving behind a wife, the Polish actress Marta Dutkiewicz-Schmidt, and me, his only child. Marian was a well-known photographer and the author of many albums, books, and articles. He founded the Warsaw School of Photography and Graphic Design, where he taught for many years and was considered to be a distinguished pedagogue. After my father's death I am continuing his work at the school he built.

Marian's older brother by three years, Kazimierz Schmidt (known in the United States as Kenneth Schmidt) lives in retirement in Cherry Hill, New Jersey after a career as a computer programmer and IT specialist—among other companies—with the Kraft Corporation and Amtrak, together with his wife Shelley Friedman Schmidt, a retired mathematics teacher. Both Kenneth and Marian obtained degrees in mathematics from the University of California in Berkeley. Kenneth and Shelley have four children and sixteen grandchildren.

My grandparents, whom I never met, died in Phoenix, Arizona— Joseph in 1975 and Leokadia in 1980. They are buried next to each other in the Beth El Cemetery in Phoenix, Arizona.

- Arthur Schmidt

PHOTOS

Leokadia Schmidt, ca.1936. Photograph taken for an
identity card.

Joseph Schmidt, from a 1936 Warsaw residency
card.

Father Edward Święcki (1922-1996), in his
apartment in Karczew, where he was parish priest
in the years 1953-83. Doctor of theology and a
member of the underground resistance during
World War II, Father Święcki was instrumental in
placing the Schmidts' son Kazimierz in the Father
Boduen children's home in Warsaw and for looking
after both him and the Schmidt family on the
"Aryan side" of Warsaw during the Nazi
occupation. More than anyone else, he deserves
credit for the Schmidts surviving the Holocaust.
Photograph by Marian Schmidt, 1991.

Schmidt family, Kraków, 1946, before emigrating from
Poland.

Leokadia Schmidt. Photograph for a temporary
identity card issued on 25 February 1946 in Kraków.

Schmidt family, Caracas. Venezuela, 1952.

Dry-goods store which Joseph Schmidt
established in Caracas.

Leokadia and Joseph Schmidt, Oakland, California,
31 August 1964.

Schmidt family, Oakland, California, ca. 1964.

Joseph and Leokadia Schmidt gravestones,
Phoenix, Arizona.